Vanderbilt Divinity School

Education, Contest, and Change

VANDERBILT DIVINITY SCHOOL

Education, Contest, and Change

EDITED BY

Dale A. Johnson

VANDERBILT UNIVERSITY PRESS

Nashville

Library of Congress Cataloging-in-Publication Data

Vanderbilt Divinity School : education, contest, and change / edited by
Dale A. Johnson.
    p. cm.
Includes bibliographical references and index.
ISBN 0-8265-1386-7 (alk. paper)
1. Vanderbilt University. Divinity School—History. I. Johnson, Dale A.,
1936–
BV4070.V36   2001
230'.071'176855—dc21   2001004171

Contents

Illustrations

Preface

The Divinity School has been part of Vanderbilt University since its inception; the year 2000 marked its 125th year. It is one of the nation's few university-based, interdenominational institutions for the preparation of ministers, and the only one in the South. As the first book-length history of the Divinity School, this volume is an important addition to the history of theological education in America.[1] It developed as a multiauthored study, in which a range of topics and viewpoints helps to give a more complete picture of the school's context and history than a more straightforward narrative could do.

The chapters explore the school's history in terms of three primary themes, which can be seen as sequential but overlapping. The first is the various ways in which the school has engaged with the region, most particularly with elements of southern culture. Present from the opening of the University, with its connections to the hopes of the New South, this engagement took on special significance in the mid–twentieth century around the issue of race. A second theme is the transition from being an institution of the church to one that was independent and interdenominational, with a liberal Protestant orientation (chiefly identified by its ecumenical perspective and its approach to the critical study of the Bible). While this shift occurred rather abruptly, even with a dispute that had to be settled in court, its implications developed much more slowly. The third is the development, since the nineteenth century, of the modern research university. This has been a prominent part of the Divinity School's identity for much of the twentieth century, especially the second half of the century with the development of its graduate programs. Each of these themes has given rise to tensions and conflicts over the course of the school's existence as the Biblical Department (1875–1914), the School of Religion (1915–56), and the Divinity School (since 1956). In its years as the Divinity School an additional theme has gradually taken shape, in keeping with emerging national and international issues and religious and cultural developments: its sense of ecumenism has broadened, and its commitments to social justice have deepened. This has clearly influenced the approach to theological questions explored here as well as the shape of the school's educational programs. Across more than two centuries, theological education in America has taken a variety of institutional forms, making the interdenominational university divinity school only a small part of a much larger picture. Yet, while the Divinity School's own history of engagement with the themes noted above is distinctive and has shaped a general institutional ethos, it is in a broader sense a case study of many larger national developments in theological education.

The faculty group that initially discussed the possibility of a history of the school included Ed Farley, Jack Fitzmier, Joe Hough, Gene TeSelle, and myself. When Dean Hough asked me to supervise the project, I consulted a number of persons connected with Vanderbilt about topics for chapters and about potential authors; to them and to all those who took on writing assignments, I am especially grateful. The staffs of the Divinity Library and of the Vanderbilt University Special Collections gave generously of their time and expertise to assist research and respond to questions. John Compton was a very helpful adviser as well as participant in the Lawson affair conversation; the school is indebted to him and to the others who agreed to come for that weekend session to recall and record. Special thanks go to Dean Hough, Acting Dean Jack Forstman, and Dean James Hudnut-Beumler for support and encouragement along the way. The Louisville Institute provided a small grant to initiate the project. Two church history graduate students provided considerable assistance as the volume took shape: Scott Seay contributed an acute editorial eye in the revision process, and Michael Stephens was present from the beginning of the work and has been a thoughtful conversation partner, careful reader, and dedicated colleague through it all.

In the past decade or two there has been a growing scholarly interest in theological education as a subject for investigation, including its conceptualities, varying forms, changes over the past generation, and prospects for the future. We hope that this volume will interest not only persons involved in the work of theological education and those connected with Vanderbilt itself, but also those who are interested in the role of religion in culture, both historically and in the present.

Vanderbilt Divinity School

Education, Contest, and Change

PART I
Contexts

To borrow a word from a real estate expression, location is the key to institutional identity. For an educational institution, location is partly geographical, but it involves a number of other dimensions as well. The chapters in Part I explore the university and the nation as contexts for theological education and as ways of locating Vanderbilt Divinity School. Joseph C. Hough, Jr., takes his theme from the school's most visible current location and pursues issues in the historical relationship between divinity schools and modern universities, showing that the role of divinity schools in this context has been considerably contested. He traces this contest to debates in Germany at the end of the eighteenth century over whether theology was an appropriate subject matter for the university. Similar issues were raised in the United States by the mid–nineteenth century, he notes, but the development of independent denominational seminaries on the one hand, and the emergence of the secular state university on the other, made for a distinctive American situation: it raised in even more vigorous ways the question of the validity of theology as an academic discipline within the university. Hough introduces a number of recent perspectives on the question as he puts forth his own argument that a divinity school is important to a university because of the way it contributes to the university's general aims, the most important of which he sees as that of promoting the common good of the society.

Glenn T. Miller applies each of the three primary contexts noted previously within the framework of developments in theological education in America. Thus, he puts the school's beginnings in the context of other Methodist ventures in higher education, as well as comparative developments concerning the tension between critical scholarship and academic freedom; he shows how the school's main lecture series can be seen in relation to the general interest of the school's dean and faculty to participate in wider national and international theological discussions;

I

he considers developments in education for ministry within the framework of national conversations, giving illustrations of places where Vanderbilt led other schools as well as those where it lagged; and he calls attention to the national implications of the Lawson case in 1960, in which the school was the location for an engagement with southern culture over the issue of race. These subjects all warrant further discussion and are taken up in greater detail in succeeding chapters.

Theological Studies in the Context of the University

Joseph C. Hough, Jr.

I N THE LATE 1980S, ROBERT LYNN, THEOLOGICAL EDUCATOR AND vice president for religion at the Lilly Endowment, launched a major project on the university-related divinity schools in the United States. The purpose of the study was to assess the current state of university-related divinity schools, to identify their problems, and to recommend future action. Included in this study were sixteen institutions that met the following criteria:

1. They participate in the ethos of a major university or university setting.
2. They offer graduate doctoral programs that prepare potential faculty of theological schools.
3. They engage in critical research according to standards practiced in the modern university.
4. They exercise leadership within the community of theological schools.

Led by James Waits, dean of Candler School of Theology at Emory University, the project consisted of commissioned books and papers and several major consultations.[1]

The final report was, on the whole, very positive about the status of university divinity schools and their contributions to the churches and to their universities, but it acknowledged some very serious challenges that have not been resolved. One of these challenges is the persisting question about the role of the divinity school within the university.

> Despite its apparent acceptance by other university faculty and officials, the divinity school will be increasingly pressed to justify its place within the overall purpose of the university. To do so, it must be attentive not only to its participation in university affairs: it will be expected to offer intellectual leadership as well. Its reputation for productive faculty scholarship and publication, rigorous admissions standards and the quality of its teaching will be important measures of its acceptance. The initiatives of the divinity school in behalf of interdisciplinary and interprofessional studies will demonstrate a larger citizenship and intellectual participation within the university.[2]

In this chapter I offer a brief historical rehearsal of the changing status of theological faculties in the university, with a particular focus on the factors leading to the development of departments of religion and divinity schools in the universities of the United States. I conclude with arguments in support of university divinity schools and the teaching of theology in the modern American university. Finally, I discuss the relationship of Vanderbilt Divinity School to its own university, with a particular focus on the past decade.

Theology and the University in Historical Perspective

Professors of theology have been citizens of the university since the rise of the great medieval institutions of higher learning.[3] The universities themselves were understood theologically as one of the great "pillars" of medieval society, and university instruction was always seen to be in the service of Christian piety. In large measure, the vocation of the teacher in the university was hardly distinguishable from the vocation of ministry in general. The professors had a distinctive responsibility for learning, but all were clerics and their primary loyalty was to the church. Theology was the highest pinnacle of university study, and even those who studied for the other learned professions were schooled in theology as well.

The Reformation did little to challenge this essential idea of the university. In fact, at Geneva, Calvin included university teachers within the orders of the ministry, and the university was clearly an instrument for fashioning the social order in the image of Christ.[4] At first, Protestants cooperated with the humanists in a struggle to displace Catholic domination of the universities, but this cooperation was transitory and enmity soon appeared. Confessional interests increasingly dominated the thinking of the Protestant reformers regarding the university, leading Erasmus at one point to declare that "knowledge perished wherever Lutheranism became dominant." The dispute grew increasingly rank, and by the end of the sixteenth century Protestantism had swept the humanists out of Protestant-dominated universities.[5]

Not until the end of the seventeenth century, with the establishment of the University of Halle in Germany, was the place of theology in the university seriously challenged. Under the leadership of Christian Wolff, philosophy replaced theology at the center of the university. Wolff championed the pursuit of truth based on reason alone. Morality and law, he argued, were no longer to be grounded theologically but would be based on rational knowledge of the human person and society. Moreover, rational knowledge was to be advanced by research. Knowledge was no longer seen as the wisdom of the past that was simply to be transmitted to students, nor was it the function of the university to preserve and secure ancient truths against challenge. Rather, the new university instruction was to be based on the assumption that truth was to be discovered.[6] The university professor was to be free of any regulations by state or church that would limit research leading to discovery, and he also would, of necessity, be free to encourage students to follow a similar path.

Theology was effectively dethroned and cast out of the universities, at least for a while. A resurgence occurred in the late eighteenth century when Frederick William II launched a campaign to restore the primacy of confessional theology and to silence criticism of orthodox confessional tenets. Obviously, this was a serious threat to the freedom of university faculties to do research.

By the end of the century, the freedom of the university faculty had become sufficiently compromised to prompt Immanuel Kant to compose a strong defense of the freedom to teach and learn. In this treatise, *Der Streit der Fakultäten* (1798), Kant was primarily concerned with responding to ecclesiastical criticisms of his own work and the limitations that ecclesiastical leaders were attempting to impose on the freedom of the faculty of philosophy. In the course of his argument, he also discussed the education of professionals in the university. Kant reasoned that it was in the ruler's interest to have medical faculty in the university in order to ensure a steady supply of well-trained doctors who would promote the health of the citizens. Similar arguments were advanced in support of a faculty of law to combat radical ideas and ensure legal rationality. His argument for a faculty of theology in the university rested on the ruler's interest in preventing heresy, fanaticism, and religious anarchy—all of which could disrupt public order.

Kant argued that the only way the ruler could insure the highest standards in the professional faculties was to place them in the university, a context in which their teaching and writing would be subject to the rational criticism of the philosophy faculty. Conversely, the philosophy faculty could not do its work of rational criticism in service of the state unless it was free to be critical of the teachings of any of the professional faculties. Concerning a faculty of theology, Kant argued that the theology that dominated the life of the churches could be important for keeping order in the state. That would be possible only if there were a community of theological scholars dedicated to the highest ideals of critical thinking. In other words, the university cannot fulfill its proper end—the promotion of the good of the state—unless it has a theological faculty. As with the other professions, Kant did not deny the right of the ruler to limit the scope of the teaching of the professions. He simply insisted that the limitations should be imposed on the basis of rational criticism if the aim of the ruler is to preserve order for the good of the state. Thus, Kant's argument for a theological faculty in the university had the same foundation as his argument for faculties of law, medicine, and civil service. The presence of all these faculties served the aims of the university as it, in turn, served the interests of the society as a whole.

It is important to note that Kant did not argue, as Friedrich Schleiermacher would a few years later, that a university-based theology should be a "scientific" theology. While there is no doubt that Kant thought that religion based on reason was superior to confessional religion, he acknowledged the right of the biblical faculty to teach the tenets of the Bible in a confessional manner. But he argued forcefully that the confessional manner must be subject to the critical appraisal insured by the faculty of philosophy, and that the philosophy faculty must be at the heart of the university.

In the early nineteenth century, the discussion of the place of the theological faculty in the university focused on the founding of the University of Berlin. The issue here, once again, was whether there was a place in a modern scientific university for the study of theology. The related argument over just what should be taught in a university faculty of theology was addressed as well. The chief disputants in the debate were Johann Fichte and Friedrich Schleiermacher.

Fichte did not think that theology as such belonged in the new university because it was not a positive science, that is, it had no identifiable and unified subject matter of its own. He argued that historical theology and philological studies in theology could easily be assigned to other faculty. Since dogmatics could not yield scientific knowledge, it had no place in a scientific university.[7] Schleiermacher countered that theology was in fact a positive science because it represented a "body of scientific elements which [had] a connectedness of their own." This connectedness resided first in the essential relation of all the elements of theological studies to a determinate faith, a mode of God-consciousness.

Schleiermacher went on to say that the sciences cannot merely be speculative; they must be practical. Therefore, theology is a science to the degree that it provides guidance for the church in the broadest sense possible. But theological studies are not for everyone. The unity of theological studies lies in the fact that each of its elements is necessary for the preparation of those who will lead the church.[8] In other words, theological science is in complete harmony with the purpose of the university—namely, to produce educated leadership for one of the major professions essential to the life of the state. Schleiermacher thus indirectly answered Fichte by changing the terms of the discussion.[9] The "scientific" character of theological studies as a whole resides in its reference to the possibility of advancing a particular kind of knowledge—that is, knowledge concerning the character of God-consciousness represented in Christian faith. This is also secured by the test of practicality. It is knowledge of faith that is directed toward the practical manifestation of that God-consciousness in the institutional life of the church.[10]

The disagreement at Berlin involved two separate but related issues. First, there was the question of whether theological studies, necessary for the preparation of church leaders, would be included in the university at all. In other words, the future of the program in theological studies, including all matters of science as well as those affecting the life and governance of the church, was at stake. Second, there was the question of the appropriateness of including dogmatic theology as such in university theological studies. Could any dogmatic studies be scientific? Schleiermacher had to answer both questions at once. If studies of determinate faiths did not include dogmatics, Fichte could win the argument, and theological studies could be dispersed among other related sciences. But this would mean that in the new university, no specific attention would be paid to the matters affecting the guidance and governance of the church. Thus, even if there were room in other faculties of the university for historical, philosophical, and philological studies focused on Christianity, theological studies as a coherent subject matter would have no practical base in the university.

In the immediate setting of the controversy, Schleiermacher was successful,[11] but two problems were created that are at the center of the discussion of the place of theology in the university today. First, although his argument focused specifically on the needs of leadership for the church, it was close to Kant's, who claimed that it was in the interest of the state to insist that the university include faculties of medicine, law, and theology to assure control over the quality and even the content of training for the leaders of key social institutions. Schleiermacher, too, argued for a faculty of theology on the basis of the university's interest in providing cultured leaders for the major institutions of the state. That political argument, however, tended to subordinate the more substantive argument for the scientific nature of theological studies as a unified approach to knowledge of a certain kind.[12] A second problem was Schleiermacher's assertion that professors responsible for theological studies must have standing in another of the scientific faculties in the university in order to be considered for teaching theological subjects. By implication, this conceded much that had been won. Although the place of theological studies in the university had been secured, the status of theological faculty was derivative, and that cast doubt on the status of theology as a scientific subject appropriate for university study.

Theology in the American Universities

Only in the mid–nineteenth century did the issues that came into focus during the founding of the University of Berlin begin to bedevil America's private colleges and universities. By then, German theology and scholarship were influencing nearly all American theological faculties.[13] As more and more theological students returned from Germany to teach in American colleges, universities, and theological seminaries, the teaching of religion in these institutions changed radically. At Harvard, especially, fascination with "scientific" theology gave a historical cast to all theological studies by the end of the nineteenth century. Although specific reference to "scientific" theology faded along the way, the dominance of the historical method made it difficult to sustain strong interest in and support for systematic theology, the descendant of the old dogmatics. Even though President Charles Eliot at Harvard gave a ringing endorsement to theological studies in the university in 1879, he meant theological studies in the historical mode.[14] This was true not only at schools like Harvard, but also in the small denominational colleges as well.

The growing hegemony of scientific theological studies exacerbated the doctrinal disputes that had created turmoil in the colleges early in the nineteenth century. That turmoil led in 1808 to the establishment of Andover Theological Seminary, the first such institution in the United States that was separate from a university. According to George H. Williams, the founding of Andover set in motion "a disastrous pattern in American higher education," namely, the separation of theological studies and other studies for the professions from the center of the university.[15] Harvard responded by establishing the first university divinity school in America in 1811; Yale's was founded in 1822. Following the example of the Congregational churches at Andover, other denominational groups moved to establish freestanding theological seminaries as well, such as Princeton Theological Seminary, founded in 1812. These developments cannot be understood merely as the fragmentation of theological education as a result of theological differences. They were also a reflection of concerns within the university about the appropriateness of theological studies as subject matter. Moreover, as Roland Bainton has argued, the formation of divinity schools and seminaries must also be seen as part of the dawn of professional schools in America.[16]

However one sees the separation of the seminaries from the universities, the establishment of church-related theological seminaries outside the university surely reflected the legitimate concern of church leaders about the capacity of the university to give due attention to those matters that, in Schleiermacher's terms, affected the guidance and governance of the churches. If, from their perspective, the scholarship of the universities was out of touch with the practical needs of the churches and the faculty disdainful of orthodox beliefs and practices, the churches clearly had a problem with locating the educational programs for ministers in the universities. Thus, by mid-century, a distinctly American pattern had emerged: most theological education would take place in denominational seminaries apart from the universities, but theological education of a similar sort would also take place in university divinity schools.

Another peculiarly American phenomenon was the state university, in which the teaching of theology was for all practical purposes prohibited. Although early state universities were often controlled informally by specific denominational groups, Thomas Jefferson's proposals for the College of William & Mary abolished the professorships in theology. When the University of Virginia opened in 1818, it had no theological faculty, nor was there any provision for religious activities on campus. All religious studies were relegated to "Schools on the Confines," that is, in sectarian institutions outside the curriculum and off the campus of the university, which would at least allow those students to take courses in the sciences at the university. Still, for Jefferson, those parts of religion that were held in common by the various sects, such as morality and the proofs for the existence of God, were permissible in the university curriculum.[17] That pattern was adopted in other state-supported institutions, essentially for many of the same reasons.

Henry Tappan's proposal for the University of Michigan is a good example. In Tappan's view, there was no place for a faculty of theology in a "true" university. Given his professed admiration for the German universities, Tappan was aware that this would seem odd. He explained the omission this way:

> It will be remarked that we have omitted a Faculty of Theology in the constitution of this University. As each denomination of Christians has its peculiar Theological views and interests, it would be impossible to unite them harmoniously in one Faculty. It is most expedient, therefore, to leave this branch to the Theological Institutions already es-

tablished by the several denominations. But still a connection of an unobjectionable character might be formed between Theological Institutions, especially those existing in this city, and the University, productive of very rich benefits.[18]

Tappan further suggested the possibility of cross-registration of students and inter-institutional accreditation of work toward degrees as means for creating a cooperative relationship between the state university and private, sectarian theological schools.

Tappan's exclusion of theological study from the university was not based on any question about its academic respectability. Nor was his objection due to any bias against religion as such. He was an ordained minister committed to the maintenance of a strong Christian ethos in the university. He was even committed to the support of compulsory religious practices for the students.[19] His opposition, like Jefferson's, was based on his direct experience of the contentiousness and competitiveness among the various denominations. He could see no end to that problem and concluded that in a community of largely Christian denominational pluralism, under the constitutional provisions for separation of church and state, it was simply impossible to have theological instruction in public institutions.[20]

Another American phenomenon was the development of departments of religious studies that were separate, at least organizationally, from the divinity schools. By 1890, Yale had an official chair of English Bible in the university faculty; William Rainey Harper was its first occupant. Harper believed that the study of the Bible must be in strict accord with the latest critical scientific scholarship.[21] In 1893 Harper sent one of his students, J. L. Willett, to the University of Michigan to teach English Bible. Soon thereafter, Michigan became the first state university to establish a chair in the English study of the Bible. Other state institutions followed suit, including Georgia, Texas, Missouri, Illinois, and Virginia. Instruction in the Bible usually began where both Jefferson and Tappan had defined its place—at the periphery of the campus—often as a project of a pastor in the "university church." Universities gradually incorporated these courses into their curricula, first granting academic credit for courses and then faculty status to the instructors.

In the major private universities with divinity schools, there was little to distinguish the research methodology and content of Bible and church history classes in departments of religion from those in divinity schools. Even the teaching of systematic theology in the divinity school was often hardly distinguishable from philosophy of religion in the department of religion.[22] In fact, the faculties of church history, Bible, and theology in the divinity schools often constituted the major portion of the faculty in religion as well.

By the 1930s, however, the validity of systematic theology as an academic discipline was being openly questioned. This time the problem was not just sectarian strife, but also the perceived lack of academic integrity of theological studies. In 1930 Abraham Flexner, author of a highly influential report on medical education, wrote a very critical book in which he decried the presence of divinity schools in the American university. Because of their commitment to presuppositions not subject to scientific verification and because of their inevitable denominational biases, said Flexner, they were an anomaly in a university dedicated to disinterested, objective research.[23] Six years later, Robert Hutchins, president of the University of Chicago, declared that theology as a subject area had compromised itself to such an extent that it could no longer provide the central organizing principle of the university. Hutchins argued that the divinity school, succumbing to the pressures of "vocationalism," had become "a feeble imitator" of the other professional schools.[24] Because Hutchins thought that the university should be clearly separate from all vocational and utilitarian education, he doubted whether such a divinity school really belonged in the university. At about the same time, James B. Conant of Harvard University was openly arguing that theology was a divisive rather than a unifying principle in the university.[25]

William Adams Brown of Union Theological Seminary in New York offered a vigorous counterattack, arguing that the study of a more scientific theology should occupy a central place in the university.[26] He actually won a concession from Hutchins that there was a place in the university for a critical theology, but Hutchins never altered his judgment that theology was no longer capable of serving as a unifying force in the university. As late as 1954, George H. Williams pleaded the case at Harvard for the centrality of theology in the university. The withdrawal of theology, he argued, would seriously weaken the constitution of the university and place in jeopardy its connection with its past. He contended that the time was ripe for the revival of interest in the "larger dimension of life," a subject that could be addressed adequately in the university only by theology. Furthermore, he believed that the "integrity of the University, the conservation of its universality, its refusal to accommodate itself to mere expediency," might finally depend upon "courageous churchmen who will come to the defense of their fellow-citizens in the University in the pursuit of that truth whereby we may all remain free."[27] But there is no evidence that Williams's views were taken with any seriousness at Harvard outside of the divinity school.

Despite the stature of their critics, however, the major divinity schools

appear to have survived the attack very well. In 1976, George Lindbeck of Yale
Divinity School published the results of a study that focused on seven university
divinity schools (Chicago, Harvard, Vanderbilt, Yale, Union Theological Seminary in New York, the Graduate Theological Union, and the Theology Department of the University of Notre Dame). At the time, this list included four
of the top five theological schools in the country; the seven schools educated
most of the Ph.D. students in religious studies, and many theological school
faculty members had received their graduate degrees there. Thus, their influence on the teaching of religion in America's institutions of higher learning was
considerable; and even though they enrolled less than a tenth of all seminary and
divinity school students, their graduates were often found in positions of great
influence in the churches.

In spite of his positive assessment of the status of the independent divinity
schools, Lindbeck was not altogether sanguine about their future prospects.
While their positions seemed strong, he saw signs of trouble ahead:

> The future of these schools as a group is more uncertain than one would
> expect given their prominence within theological education. The lay
> philanthropy from which they once benefited has diminished and, in a
> time of contracting resources, churches are tempted to regard them as
> competitive with their own seminaries *while universities might see them as
> dispensable anachronisms.* Whether, or in what sense, they can or should
> continue their traditional task of training for religious ministries within
> organized religion is a debated question, and what the alternatives are
> is unclear.[28]

The report contained a rich analysis of the changes in the religious landscape.
The membership and financial resources of mainline religious denominations
had declined, promoting within the denominations a preoccupation with the
survival of their own institutions. Lindbeck was convinced that the impact of
these trends on the university divinity schools could be quite serious. With
a greater focus on denominational identity, there was less interest in persons
whose theological education reflected a broad ecumenical commitment. Many
of the great ecumenical organizations that were prime placement opportunities
for graduates of the university divinity schools were losing support as well, as
they faced retrenchment. In sum, the prospects for the independent university
divinity schools to recruit persons headed for ministry in progressive Protestant
churches were not very promising. More pertinent to my interests, Lindbeck
also pointed to the low status of theological studies in those secular universities
where theology was still taught, indicating that it was often difficult for the

theological faculties to explain and defend what they were doing in a university context.

Vanderbilt Divinity School and the Continuing Conversation

Three years after Lindbeck's study, Vanderbilt's Edward Farley wrote an essay that provoked the most wide-ranging discussion of theological education since the early nineteenth century. Farley argued that the ideas about theological education inherited from the eighteenth century had created a pattern emphasizing specific fields of study (e.g., biblical and historical) that thus lacked theological coherence. What was required was a rethinking of theological education with respect to its aims and purposes, and these aims and purposes had to be understood theologically.[29] Dean Sallie McFague convened a national discussion of Farley's paper, and the Vanderbilt faculty launched a three-year study that produced a new curriculum for the school's basic theological degree. It was organized around the concept of "the minister as theologian," with the expressed aim to develop in students the capacity to think theologically. This was precisely the sort of reform that Lindbeck had suggested for the university divinity schools, and Vanderbilt led the way, moving in new directions in its Master of Divinity and Master of Theological Studies programs.

Farley expanded his reflections into *Theologia: The Fragmentation and Unity of Theological Education* (1983), which became the most important book on theological education published in the United States since the turn of the century. It was read and discussed by hundreds of faculty members, deans, and presidents of Protestant and Catholic theological schools; the Association of Theological Schools in the United States and Canada sponsored regional discussions that included responses to Farley and contributions that developed some of his suggestions for reform. As a result of the widespread interest generated by these discussions, the Executive Committee of the Association of Theological Schools, with the encouragement of Robert Lynn of the Lilly Endowment, launched a ten-year conversation on the future of theological education in the United States and Canada. The "Basic Issues Research Project" involved regular summer convocations on various topics related to theological education, such as educating ministers in a pluralistic world, global theological education, and theological education as formation. More than fifty books and articles related to this initiative have been published, and it is safe to say that these discussions have spurred a host of new experiments and several new conceptions of theological education.[30]

In light of these developments, or perhaps because of them, Lindbeck's dire prediction of the early decline of the leadership position of the university divinity schools was a bit premature. Although the leadership of this latest round of creative discussions has been widely shared, the university divinity school faculties made a major contribution to the success of the Basic Issues Research Project. In a very real sense, Farley launched the project with his own colleagues, and several of them remained active participants throughout the decade of international conversations.

The Divinity School's Contributions to the Aims of the University

Is the university the proper home for a theological school whose primary mission is the education of leaders for religious institutions? With Kant, I believe that the presence of a divinity school is important to the university in its effort to achieve its goal of serving the common good.[31] Thomas Jefferson at Virginia, Daniel Coit Gilman at Johns Hopkins, Andrew Dickson White at Cornell, Charles William Eliot at Harvard, Woodrow Wilson at Princeton, and James B. Angell at Michigan, all influential leaders in the conceptualization of the modern American university, clearly believed that a major purpose of the universities was to serve the common good by educating persons committed to public service to lead the major institutions of the society. In every case, these modern university leaders believed that the responsibility of the universities to the society was to educate competent professional and institutional leaders capable of guiding the society in making just decisions about urgent moral, social, and political issues. This commitment remains one of the most clearly articulated aims of universities today.

Because the churches continue to be important social institutions in America, the divinity schools can make a significant contribution to the effort of a university to achieve its own aims by enhancing the quality of leadership in religious institutions. It is important to note that this variation of the arguments by Kant and Schleiermacher does not imply that only a university with a divinity school can achieve its aim of serving the common good. Rather, it is to assert that a divinity school faculty can and does make important *additional* contributions to the life and purpose of its university. It is, therefore, not only appropriate but desirable that there be university divinity schools for the good of the universities themselves.

The university's aim of educating leaders for the common good can be served only if the institutions receiving those leaders will actually be served well; in the case of the divinity schools, the church is the primary receiving institution. Therefore, the education of leaders in university divinity schools must be important for developing certain kinds of leadership for the churches. Here, Kant's warning about the dangers of fanaticism and divisive sectarianism was prophetic.

Our world is the scene of dangerous, self-righteous separatism among religious groups bent on uprooting contrary religious beliefs and imposing their own beliefs on others by force or by law. Moreover, the constituency for a global religious vision among Christian groups in the United States is diminishing. There has been a sharp decline in the influence and size of the traditionally ecumenical denominations, and many historically ecumenical denominations are torn from within by strident sectarian factions. As a result, the focus in the various councils and boards of theological education in the several ecumenical denominations has shifted from ecumenical cooperation and planning to matters of institutional survival. In this situation, it is important for the churches and for theological education generally that at least some of their leaders be educated in strongly ecumenical settings. Leaders who are educated ecumenically can help the churches overcome their divisiveness. They can help faithful religious communities engage in the kind of spiritual reflection that will yield a more global religious vision of peace and justice in the world, one that goes beyond the confines of their particular religious traditions.

The university divinity schools can and do provide settings for precisely this sort of global reflection. Again, the force of the argument is not that the university divinity schools are the only locations for theological education of this sort. It is rather the more modest arguments that they are less subject to ecclesiastical pressures and that, on the whole, they are much more ecumenical in outlook and practice than the denominational seminaries. They are, therefore, important for the future of ecumenically-minded churches and for the leadership of major social institutions. Because they are providing critically important leadership for the churches, they are, at the same time, making a genuine contribution to the common good of the whole society.

The status of divinity school faculty members in the university is not grounded in their membership in some other discipline, as Schleiermacher had argued that it must be. Rather, they are important university faculty because they are members of the faculty of the divinity school, a school that itself is important for the university in the pursuit of its aims.

Even if we accept that a divinity school, as a location for educating ministers, belongs in the university alongside other professional schools, there remains the other question raised in the discussions at Berlin and by the critics of theological studies within the American university: Does theological thinking have anything to offer to the intellectual life of a modern secular research university? Even if a theological faculty is at home in the institutional setting of a divinity school, are its members really fully contributing citizens of the university?

I noted earlier that William Adams Brown won a concession from Robert Hutchins in the 1930s that theology of a certain kind belonged in the university.

According to Brown, dogmatic theology had no place in a research university, but a genuinely ecumenical theology, not wedded to any set of dogmas, not only had a legitimate place in the university but was important to its intellectual life. Later, George H. Williams argued that theology was important to the life of the university because it represented the university's legitimate interest in the "larger questions of life." More recent commentators such as Gordon Kaufman, Schubert Ogden, H. Richard Niebuhr, and Edward Farley have offered perspectives on the role of critical theology in the life of the university.

Kaufman argues that theology provides the university with a discipline devoted to the criticism of belief, not just Christian beliefs, but any "faith commitment" that represents the fundamental belief systems of groups of persons. He therefore envisions a faculty of theology explicitly devoted to faith criticism that would be composed of representatives from a variety of faiths, themselves believers, but who function as internal critics of their own belief systems. Continuing dialogue with other theological critics representing belief systems from other religions and secular faith communities would enhance their critical capacity. Kaufman argues that a faculty of theology of this sort represents a necessary intellectual enterprise present nowhere else in the university.[32]

Focusing more on the role of the Christian theologian in the university, Ogden also views theology as a critical discipline because the study of theology must conform in every way to the scholarly canons of the modern university. Like Kaufman, he notes that since the Enlightenment the role of the scholar has been transformed from mastering and transferring a received tradition of truth to discovering the truth by careful investigation, criticism, and rational argument. Theology located in a university context cannot thus be circumscribed by any official formulation of dogma, nor can it be subject to the limitations of ecclesiastical interests. In the university, the theological professor is free to learn, teach, and publish whatever his or her critical research produces. The only requirement is that one's theological formulations, like the formulations of other citizens of the university, be subject to critical appraisal and the rational criteria for validation or invalidation. In so doing, the Christian theologian makes a contribution to the intellectual life of the university by advancing criticism of a body of literature that constitutes a major segment of the intellectual history of the West. It also subjects to criticism a global network of intellectual discourse that makes claims about the way in which our understanding of the world is formed and transformed. The theological work done in this context may still be of service to the church, Ogden adds, but the service will be indirect. That is, it does not assist the church directly by bearing witness to its faith. It serves the church by continually subjecting the claims of Christian witness to the scrutiny of historical and rational inquiry to determine whether or not those claims are true. It may or may not support particular claims, but this process will surely sharpen and strengthen those claims found to meet the critical test of rational validation.[33]

In Niebuhr's view, the constant reference to God the absolute, the "one beyond the many," constantly relativizes any claims to the possession of knowledge that is final and absolute by any scholar in the university, any representative of the state, or any theologian in the church. But this critical theology not only has the function of relativizing all knowledge; Niebuhr insists that it serves the university in a positive way as well. For one thing, the relativizing effect of radical theological thinking invites freedom for new voices and facilitates mutual correction and creative conflict. It can also be the basis for the university's resistance to domination by church or state. In addition, the radically monotheistic posture of theological discourse points beyond the disunity and fragmentation of life toward a shared loyalty to the good of the whole. In this sense, theological thinking at its best serves as a reminder to the parts of the university of their obligation for the whole of knowledge, as well as the university's obligation for the common good of the human community.[34]

Farley calls this two-sided contribution to the life of the university a "third critical principle," one that is as important to knowledge in its own way as the critical principles of the Enlightenment. The Enlightenment, he says, grasped the relativity of knowledge and the necessity for the university to be free from dogmatism. It also understood the necessity for completing and correcting paradigms of knowing. It did not, however, understand fully the dialectical character of human striving, that all of our efforts at correction are themselves subject to corruption. Thinking grounded in the Christian mythos provides an understanding of the depth, reality, and persistence of human corruption in a way not comprehended by the other critical principles of the Enlightenment.[35] Thus, radical theological thinking invites a kind of modesty about truth claims that is important for the promotion of intellectual discourse across the entire university.

This is not the end of the matter, for the promise of redemption, Farley contends, is also at the heart of the Christian mythos. Recognition of the corruptibility of knowledge is always set in the context of new possibilities of knowing. This undergirds a positive commitment to the human quest for truth while avoiding the temptation to see that quest as capable of perfecting knowledge. This, in turn, might create a tendency in university discourse to anticipate new paradigms of knowledge; theological thinking might provide a mirror of redemptive possibilities in the pursuit of knowledge that is scarcely present elsewhere in the fragmented life of the modern university.[36] This in itself would advance the pursuit of knowledge in the university.

The assumption behind all these arguments is that the primary base of the university theologian will be the divinity school, but a strong case can be made that the presence of theological thinking is also important in departments of religious studies. As I indicated earlier, Schleiermacher believed that "dogmatic theology," or, as we say today, "constructive theology," belonged in the university because any study of the history of religion that ignored the history of religious thought and belief was simply not complete. A religion, after all, is a historical "determinate faith." Therefore, the "scientific" study of religion must include constructive theology because one cannot comprehend historical faith apart from an examination of the practice of theological reflection. In the modern American university, one might argue that in addition to such important areas as the history of religion and the sociology of religion, theological studies are a necessary part of religious studies because the nature of religion cannot be fully understood apart from some clear understanding of religious belief systems. They are important because they arise in response to religious experience and constitute the subject matter from which religious communities form their shared identity. In a pluralistic religious world, of course, this sort of study must include theological thinking in its broadest sense, namely the study of the belief systems of a variety of the world's great religions.

In sum, the integrity of university-based religious studies requires the inclusion of theological studies in the university. Of course, any such argument rests on the assumption that religious studies constitutes an appropriate and coherent field of inquiry in the modern university. The ghost of Fichte is ever present to remind us that it is conceivable that the history of religion properly belongs to history, the sociology of religion to sociology, the philosophy of religion to philosophy, and so on. Thus it could be conceded that the study of religion is important in the university without conceding the need for a separate department of religious studies.[37] That is not a matter I have argued here because at present the status of religious studies in both public and private universities seems secure.[38]

Theological faculties are rightfully citizens of the university. Not only does the presence of a university divinity school assist the university in the pursuit of its aims, theological thinking makes a significant contribution to the intellectual life and discourse of the university.

Vanderbilt Divinity School and Vanderbilt University

The history of the Vanderbilt Divinity School, like that of divinity schools in other universities, has its own unique character. This is quite evident in the other chapters in this book. For example, the Methodist church that founded

Vanderbilt had in mind aims similar to those of the Puritan founders of Harvard. Although the university would be open to persons representing a variety of pursuits, the southern Methodists, like Harvard's founders, were primarily interested in providing higher education for those persons who would lead the churches. That program was the beginning of a long history of cooperation within the University between persons interested in ministerial education and those interested in graduate education in religious studies. Today, members of the Divinity School faculty teach more than 80 percent of all courses offered by the Graduate Department of Religion. As late as 1993, the Council on Research ranked the Graduate Department of Religion seventh among all similar graduate programs in the country, and that was the highest ranking of any major graduate program in the University.

Partly as a result of this peculiar history, the Divinity School has never suffered from the "embarrassment" to which Lindbeck referred in his 1976 study of university divinity schools. Quite the contrary, Vanderbilt's Divinity School has been a leader in research and scholarship in its university, and that leadership has been acknowledged on many occasions. For example, the Divinity School faculty is the most published faculty in the university on a per capita basis. In addition, Divinity School faculty members have been named winners of every major university award available to them—for excellence in teaching, scholarship, and leadership; for distinctive contributions to the understanding of contemporary social problems; and for extraordinary contributions in the councils and governance of the University.

Since 1974 the Divinity School and the Law School have offered a joint degree program, and graduates of that program have made distinguished records in both institutions. In 1997, as a result of an initiative by the Divinity School, the University launched the Cal Turner Program in Moral Leadership for the Professions. This joint program, funded by an initial $4 million grant from Cal Turner, Jr., and including the Divinity School, the Law School, the Medical School, and the Owen Graduate School of Management, has brought distinguished lecturers to the University, sponsored forums for business executives and the general public, and established chairs in moral leadership in both the Law School and the Owen Graduate School of Management. Another major initiative launched by the Divinity School involving participation by faculty in other schools in the University has been the E. Rhodes and Leona B. Carpenter Program in Religion, Gender, and Sexuality. These are but institutional examples of the Divinity School's initiatives toward other faculties within the University that demonstrate the important role that the Divinity School continues to play in the University's intellectual life.

I have argued that the presence of a divinity school in a university is important not only because of the scholarship and citizenship of its faculty but because of the contribution it can make to the realization of the university's general aims. In the immediate environs of Vanderbilt University, few would question the importance of the churches as social institutions crucial for promoting the common good of the society. There is ample evidence also that the Divinity School is providing education for the kind of ecumenical religious leadership for churches and church-related organizations that will serve the common good. In 1993, the faculty adopted a long-range plan that included the expansion of the school's ecumenical character. The plan called for the establishment of chairs in Jewish studies and Catholic studies before the end of the decade. Since then, the Mary Jane Werthan Chair in Jewish Studies and the Edward A. Malloy Chair in Catholic Studies have been established. These chairs will help to ensure the continuing ecumenical emphasis of the Divinity School.

In addition, the Divinity School has taken steps to increase its cooperation with its major Protestant church constituencies. In 1985, the Kelly Miller Smith Institute on Black Church Studies was established to promote educational opportunities for leaders in the black churches. With initial foundation grants and the appointment of a permanent director, the programs of the Institute became national in scope. A successful endowment campaign has enabled the Institute to become a permanent part of the Divinity School's efforts to serve a major constituency by helping to develop strong lay and clergy leadership for predominantly black churches, especially those located in Nashville and its surrounding region.

Since the 1940s, the Divinity School has enjoyed a strong affiliation with the Disciples Divinity House, an entity of the Christian Church (Disciples of Christ). The House was established to further the theological education of Disciples of Christ ministers by providing scholarships and reasonably priced housing. Over the years, Vanderbilt has educated a significant number of persons in its divinity and graduate programs who are now giving important leadership in Disciples of Christ institutions.

Another major effort on the part of the Divinity School to increase its contribution to the development of leadership for its constituent churches was the establishment of the Cal Turner Chancellor's Chair in Wesleyan Studies in 1997. The chair was established as one element in a partnership with local conferences of the United Methodist Church. The other element was a new Office of Pastoral Formation to be developed under the direction of Bishop Kenneth Carder and his successors for ministers in congregations of both the Tennessee and the Memphis Conferences. Both elements of the partnership were partially funded by gifts of more than $2 million from Cal Turner, Jr., with support for the chair itself significantly augmented by funds allocated by the

Chancellor's office at Vanderbilt. The terms of the partnership call for mutual cooperation in the development of ministerial leadership for United Methodist churches.

This partnership is especially significant for the history of Vanderbilt Divinity School. Although Vanderbilt was founded as a Methodist university, that relationship was severed in 1914. Despite that rupture, Methodists have continued to be the largest denominational group among Divinity School students. Moreover, as late as 1996, more than two-thirds of active clergy in the Tennessee Conference of the United Methodist Church were Vanderbilt graduates; additional strong representation of Vanderbilt graduates is found in contiguous conferences in Tennessee, Kentucky, and Alabama. In light of this history, the importance of a partnership in education for ministry between the Divinity School and the United Methodist Church can hardly be overestimated. These creative partnerships with supportive constituencies are indications of the important role the Divinity School plays in helping its university achieve its goal of providing excellent leadership for the major institutions of the society.

When I arrived at Vanderbilt in 1990, former chancellor Alexander Heard told me that the Divinity School had served from time to time as the conscience of the University. I assumed that he was referring to the so-called "Lawson Affair" of 1960. As our conversation continued, I realized that he had more than that in mind. There have been other occasions in Vanderbilt's history when the Divinity School has protested actions that the faculty, students, and administration of the school thought were morally questionable.

Yet it is wise not to claim too much. History chooses its agents of change much more often than the agents themselves decide to be chosen. In the case of the Divinity School, it was surely the special openness of the faculty that led to the admission of the first minority students to Vanderbilt, but significant leadership for these changes came from other University faculty members and administrators as well. To be sure, a divinity school that has the privilege of citizenship in a university will not serve its university well unless its members have the courage to stand for the principles it teaches. Those principles are by definition always open to persons on the margins of society and are grounded in the conviction of the value of every member of the human community. Yet those principles are not the exclusive possession of a divinity school, so it cannot alone be the "conscience of the university." The "conscience of the university" is the collective will of its courageous citizens in all the schools. The historical events that pushed the Divinity School to engage various issues at one time or another have etched themselves upon Vanderbilt's collective memory in the most dramatic fashion, but that is always a matter for thanksgiving rather than for pride.

Vanderbilt Divinity School in the Context of American Theological Education

Glenn T. Miller

MERICAN THEOLOGICAL EDUCATION COMPRISES MORE THAN ONE type of institution. Theological schools are diverse in their organization, theological commitment, social and racial composition, and aims and purposes. Although there are a few schools with large enrollments, most theological schools enroll a comparatively small number of students. Further, while theological schools serve the churches, they also often serve multiple constituencies that have their own histories and commitments. To place a school in the context of such institutional diversity is to identify some of the experiences that, while not unique, have made that school different from many others.

For Vanderbilt, the events that set the school apart from other theological schools tended to place it just a little ahead of the pack; that is, Vanderbilt has often passed through experiences, destined to be common to many other schools, before those changes affected other institutions. This location has not always been comfortable. Prophecy is never recognized until a later generation looks back and sees that some events pointed toward later experiences. At the time, prophets experience their location as a dislocation that alienates them from their immediate surroundings. In the case of Vanderbilt, the cost of being out of phase has been monetary. Historically, the Divinity School has had less financial support than its intellectual or ecclesiastical achievements would seem to merit. But that same dislocation has made for creative possibilities. In the sections that follow, I seek to place Vanderbilt in this larger institutional context by examining five topics and the issues and themes related to them.

An Important Decision

In 1866 and 1870 the Methodist Episcopal Church, South (MECS) engaged in a series of debates about the establishment of a theological seminary. Although there were some voices who warned that theological education was an invitation to heresy, the primary debate was over resources. Those who wanted a theological school admitted that such an institution needed three or more professors in order to operate at the highest level. That expectation, however, pointed toward the problem that most worried the opponents of seminaries: finances. The Civil War had left the Methodists, as well as other southerners, short of funds, and the church had substantial difficulty raising enough funds to support its three colleges, Randolph-Macon, Trinity, and Emory. A minority of the 1870 Education Committee claimed that the church was "in far more danger of losing position in the world of letters, caste in society, and human efficiency in preaching the Word of God, from want of first-class colleges, than from any present lack of theological seminaries."[1]

The minority report's diagnosis of the educational context was perceptive. An educational revolution was taking place in America, especially in the towns and cities that accompanied the burgeoning industrial revolution. This revolution began at the bottom of the educational ladder with an increasing demand for eight years of elementary education. Above this, the high school diploma—a middle-class substitute for the old academy—was gradually becoming the ticket to white-collar employment for both men and women. High schools, in turn, generated increased interest in colleges and professional education. In protesting theological seminaries, the authors of the minority report expressed their fears that Methodism, despite its apparent successes, would miss one of the most significant movements in contemporary American culture and lose its place in the center of American society. At a time when the general level of education was rising, why should the Methodists concentrate their funds on training a small, elite leadership?

Northern Methodists shared this concern. Although their liberal arts colleges were more prosperous, they felt a similar need to place the church near the head of the social forces shaping Methodist congregations. They, too, feared that theological schools might drain scarce resources that could be better used elsewhere. As in the South, the bishops did not worry that the church would fall behind in theological scholarship or in the development of the arts of ministry.

In their view, Methodism was theologically and ecclesiastically healthy. They did worry, as in the South, that theological schools might drain resources from the task of keeping up intellectually with the church's more socially and economically advanced members. They wanted ministers with an elementary education to minister to those who had finished the common schools; ministers with an academy or high school education to minister to those who had moved up slightly in the social order; and ministers with college training or the equivalent to minister to their members who had attained professional status. The goal, in short, was to serve America's growing middle classes.

What is remarkable is that Methodists in both regions hit upon the same solution at roughly the same time. In part, the solution was almost an accident. Things fell together in a way that seemed to be the result of good fortune, or, as the more religious would have said, God's hidden will. The new industrial world had produced money faster than conspicuous consumption could spend it. The holders of this new wealth were searching for ways to demonstrate their social acceptability. Many millionaires and multimillionaires began their careers as poor men, and they never lost some of their awe at the social sophistication of the gentlemen of "property and standing" they had envied as children and teenagers. John D. Rockefeller, for instance, was the son of a medicine man who wandered the Midwest hawking his wares; Cornelius Vanderbilt had to leave school at the age of eleven to work with his father; Daniel Drew began selling "watered" cattle in the city; and Johns Hopkins, son of a poor Quaker, had come to Baltimore almost penniless. Such men had strong opinions—about democracy, about opportunity, about ordinary folk—and their prejudices fit those of the Methodists to a tee. For the first time there were large numbers of people of great wealth who shared a common perspective with one of America's most populist denominations.

One cord that bound the new philanthropists most tied to Methodism was their dislike of the old social elite and its pretensions. In many ways the old-time college mirrored the worst of the old social distinctions. The literary schools were training grounds for "gentlemen" who did not have to work for a living and who were able to invest considerable money in the arcane study of the classics. Such places were a long way from the rough-and-tumble world of railroads, oil fields, and useful inventions. If, in a sense, theological schools had to be made more democratic to satisfy such men as Bishop George Pierce—who was, ironically, a strong supporter of Emory College,[2]—colleges had to be made more democratic to satisfy the people who earned great wealth in an industrial economy.

The answer was in a new style of institution, the university. The American university was a complex institution, inspired by many different antecedents and ideals. European precedents existed, of course, both in Germany and in England, and these had considerable influence on American educators. Equally important was earlier American dissatisfaction with the liberal arts college. Both Harvard and Yale had added scientific schools early in their histories, and the new state universities, beginning with the University of Virginia, had hoped to teach all of the useful arts and sciences in addition to the classics. In 1862, Congress provided land grants to endow institutions that would teach the mechanical and agricultural arts in addition to the more traditional college fare. The desire for universities was also formed, in part, by new expectations around the professions. Before the Civil War, the education of doctors and lawyers had been a haphazard affair, and many Americans believed that the time had come for more effective education for these occupations. Equally important, new occupations were claiming the prestige of the traditional professions, and universities had begun to offer the specialized training that these new occupations required. Often these new applications were based on the model of the relation between theory and application. Thus, engineering was taught as the application of science to specific industrial problems, and social work as the application of the social sciences, including psychology, to such human problems as poverty.[3] The professional was an expert who made things work.

The university had one further advantage. It was a flexible institution that could be established around a small core of courses and then expanded as the demand for higher and professional education increased. Most of the new universities began with little more than a liberal arts college and instruction in one or more other areas and then expanded as donors and students became available. Many never expanded but remained colleges in all but name. But much of the promise contained in the word "university" was that of an educational institution that could, like the new industrial firms, grow to fit larger markets. This aspect of university life particularly appealed to Methodists, who had triumphed in America partly through a flexible organization that provided religious services wherever they were needed.

The Methodist debate over whether a college or a seminary was the best way to educate the upper class of Methodist ministers basically ended in a draw. When Bishop Holland N. McTyeire made a motion at the 1872 Memphis Educational Convention, he did not propose a seminary or biblical institute. Instead, McTyeire proposed that the Convention move toward the establishment of a university "of the highest order" that would offer literary, scientific, theological, and professional studies. McTyeire's appeal to Cornelius Vanderbilt for the funds to begin the new institution was apparently as much patriotic as religious: a southern university would help to reunite the country.

The trustees quickly moved to name the new university after its patron and to formulate plans for its opening in Nashville. Naturally, it would include a "biblical department" or divinity school. But what type of divinity school did the Commodore's money found? Like the seminaries in the North, including the new but already influential Boston University, it had four faculty members who taught the principal divisions of theology: biblical studies, church history, theology, and practical theology. This arrangement of the theological disciplines provided students with an overview of the various disciplines as well as a sense of areas that had yet to be fully explored.

The Divinity School did not begin its career as a graduate institution. Like all Methodist schools, it was tied to the Course of Study of the denomination, a program of readings that prospective ministers were expected to complete before being accepted in full connection. In theory, a Methodist divinity school was a more advanced way for students to complete the same work that would have been required had they been probationary members of their conferences. This provided the seminary with a standard of ministerial competence that was related directly to the practice of ministry.[4]

The Methodist Course of Study functioned for Vanderbilt and other Methodist schools much like the "classical curriculum" of the Presbyterian and Congregational seminaries, which assumed that a person who was theologically educated had the foundation of training in the languages and scholastic theology. In the traditional understanding, the ideal minister was the learned "clerical gentleman," whose primary interface with the world was the study. Even after schools adopted more modern programs, this assumption tended to remain. In contrast, the Course of Study envisioned a minister who was a master of practical divinity and who could make an impact on the moral and religious life of the community. The ideal Methodist minister was, like a politically involved attorney or active business leader, a person of affairs, involved in the life and issues of the time.

The Course of Study's vision of practical divinity shaped all of the Methodist schools. Robert L. Kelly noted in 1924 that Methodist institutions, taken together, placed more emphasis on pastoral theology, with their programs intending "to relate the church to the present social order."[5] In other words, the Course of Study tended to start Methodist schools on a trajectory toward a more professional understanding of theological study.

The decision to establish a university that offered professional training for ministry rather than a seminary set the school's course. For one thing, ministerial education at Vanderbilt was never isolated from what was happening in the larger world. Ministers were trained in the same institution as teachers, medical doctors, lawyers, and researchers. Even had Vanderbilt's faculty wanted to avoid the contemporary issues, its location made that difficult, if not impossible.

While location outside of a university does not mean that a school will avoid contemporary issues, location inside a university exposes a theological school to the implicit modernism of an institution committed to preparing people for present-day employment.

Put another way, the old-time college was an institution primarily committed to the transmission of a cultural heritage. Its stock in trade, the learned languages, enabled a student to access the wisdom of the past. The very idea of a classic implied something that had perennial value as an exemplar. The antebellum seminary continued this style of education, with the Bible in the original languages replacing the classics at the center of the curriculum. In contrast, the university was devoted to the transformation of society through research. A similar passion for improved practice also shaped professional education, especially in medicine and law. The hope was that exposure to the best of contemporary practice would enable students to improve the art and pass those improvements on to the next generation. For modern medical education, for instance, it was not enough to know texts or even the best contemporary understanding of the body: a modern school had to have the laboratory, the clinic, and the hospital.[6]

Location and Modernity

The effects of location on theology were demonstrated almost as soon as the school opened. McTyeire wanted to construct a faculty for his university that was second to none. In geology, this meant recruiting Alexander Winchell, the vice-chancellor of Syracuse University. Winchell was almost a model of the Protestant man of science. A graduate of Wesleyan University, he had earlier taught at the University of Michigan before going to Syracuse. His publications included both scientific treatises and more popular works. Many of Winchell's studies dealt with the relationship between science and religion and sought to show that the supposed conflict between them was only apparent. If Winchell was not America's leading geologist, he was a highly competent, substantial addition to the new school.

He was also an evolutionist. For Winchell, the rocks and fossils that he collected so carefully told the tale of a planet that had been transformed over aeons and of the many forms of life that had inhabited it. It is no exaggeration to say that for Winchell, the record of the earth was as awe-inspiring as Kant had found the heavens above and the moral law within. Winchell's powerful Methodist experience led him to celebrate his discoveries with the joy of a convert relating his conversion to a class meeting. Indeed, conversion is an apt metaphor for what happened to Winchell and many other young Methodists when they encountered the larger world of science. One reason for the success of such early Methodist enterprises as Boston University, Northwestern, and the University of Southern California was the sense of freedom and liberation that many brought to their studies from their faith.[7]

Not all were persuaded by Winchell's reconciliation of science and theology. Thomas Summers, the first dean of the Biblical Department, was among those suspicious of such formulations.[8] What if Winchell's radical teachings were to overflow from the Department of Geology and corrupt the young men studying for the ministry? Working behind the scenes, Summers pressured for ousting Winchell, and in 1878 McTyeire told the geology professor that his contract would not be renewed. A newspaper war followed that was to influence the development of academic freedom in the United States. But that is not the point of this chapter. The fact of the matter was that Summers was right. Dangerous teaching any place in the university was a threat to the orthodoxy of people in the Divinity School. The MECS had created a form of theological education it could not control.

Methodist conservatives elsewhere were learning the same lesson about the effects of the university on divinity school education. For instance, the dismissal of Hinckley Mitchell at Boston University, though over different issues, was part of the same battle. A controversial Old Testament professor, Mitchell had awakened the ire of some within New England Methodism for some time. His views, perhaps, were not as radical or as advanced as either Mitchell or his critics thought. Be that as it may, when Mitchell's contracts came up for review in 1895, 1900, and 1905, students collected information designed to show that his teaching was not in line with historic Methodism. Mitchell was sustained by the Board and by the school's president, William Warren, in all three instances, but on the last occasion, the bishops exercised their right of veto. After a somewhat protracted dispute, the bishops' decision in the Mitchell matter stood, but the Methodist Episcopal Church in the North knew that it was facing a crisis. The bishops' right to veto faculty appointments was gradually withdrawn, first for existing faculty and, eventually, even for first appointments. Viewed from the perspective of Methodist history in the late nineteenth century, the check on the bishops' power over the school came at the end of a long and sustained development of the episcopal office. Nineteenth-century Methodism was marked by a tendency to centralize the administration and control of the church more or less on a business model.[9] In the Mitchell case, the bishops extended their power beyond their competence; both sides knew it, and once it was possible to do so without losing face, the bishops withdrew.[10] Incidentally, their withdrawal left them with more influence over the school and its direction than they would have retained had the school officially separated itself from the church.

The MECS would also eventually reach agreement with its universities. But before that compromise was attained, the crisis became more serious than it had been in the North. At Vanderbilt, Winchell's travails were the prologue to a sustained war of words. From the 1880s, the College of Bishops increasingly became embroiled with the administration of the school. In part, the battles between the bishops and the university administration were over theological matters, but they were more complex than that. They also involved questions of control, status, and subservience. These struggles climaxed during the administration of Chancellor James H. Kirkland. The immediate occasion for an escalation of tensions was Kirkland's nomination in 1904 of a professor of history and a Baptist, Frederick W. Moore, as dean of the Academic Department (later, College of Arts and Science). Whether Kirkland's decision was motivated by his contemporary negotiations with the Rockefeller-controlled General Education Board is not known, but once the issue was raised, he knew that repudiating a noted Baptist scholar could not help his cause. The issue became even more acute when Kirkland applied for funds from the Carnegie Foundation's program to establish retirement accounts for faculty members. The Foundation required participating schools to be non-sectarian in their trustee boards, hiring practices, and administrative regulations.[11]

Vanderbilt met the requirements of the Carnegie Foundation by removing the bishops from the Board of Trust. When the bishops appealed to the courts, they were restored as essentially a Board of Visitors without clearly defined powers. In many ways, this was the same solution that had been effected at Boston: the school was firmly under Methodist influence, but it was equally clearly in the hands of those with fiduciary power over its future. Had the Methodist bishops accepted this type of halfway agreement, the church and the university might have found ways to work together similar to those reached in the North. But the bishops were not satisfied. In 1910, they attempted to name new members of the Board of Trust to replace those whose terms had expired. The Board met this with an equally determined refusal to seat the new trustees. Another appeal to the courts followed.

In 1914, when the Supreme Court of Tennessee resolved the issue in favor of the University, it should not have been such a shock to Methodist leadership. The tendency of American courts had been to join supervisory and fiduciary responsibilities. What was unusual in the Vanderbilt case was the anger that greeted the decision. Vanderbilt was disowned by the MECS. Like a Victorian father dealing with a disobedient child, the church cut its ties with its school and gave its inheritance to others. The bishops acted quickly to transform Emory College into Emory University in Atlanta. Asa Candler, the Coca-Cola magnate, gave the refounded school more than $1 million to relocate. At the same time, the Methodists moved to establish Southern Methodist University in Dallas. Both new universities had divinity schools. Ironically, despite some friction between school and church, the relations of the Methodist church to these institutions remained amicable, in part because the bishops avoided the type of conflict that had poisoned their relationship with Vanderbilt.

As a cast-off school, Vanderbilt appears to be to unique. Union Seminary in New York, to be sure, separated from the Presbyterian Church over the Charles Briggs affair,[12] and Harvard Divinity School became nondenominational under Charles Eliot. But even in these two famous cases, one could argue that the separations were as much evolutionary as they were revolutionary, and in both cases many students and faculty members continued their personal relationships with their formerly sponsoring churches as before. More commonly, schools have slowly developed a nondenominational self-understanding. When denominationalism declined among mainstream Protestants after the 1950s, for instance, many seminaries moved to appoint faculty members from different backgrounds and to enlist students from different churches. In time, trustees would also be appointed from diverse traditions at these schools. But Vanderbilt's School of Religion had to adjust to a nondenominational status all at once and without the benefit of a period in which to experiment with its new identity.

One might be tempted to say that the rejection of Vanderbilt by the MECS was the best thing that happened to the School of Religion, but that would be too sanguine about the school's situation before the Sealantic grant in the 1950s. For much of its history, the school has had financial difficulties that might have been alleviated by a closer relationship with Methodism and with Methodist donors and students. Further, one suspects that a more gradual movement toward nondenominational status would have allowed the school to try alternate approaches to an ecumenical program.

Having noted the serious limitations imposed by the end of its relationship to the Methodist church, we should also note Vanderbilt's subsequent creativity. In part, the school had to struggle to find its clientele. The establishment of a strong Disciples Divinity House was a major step in this direction. In locating a Divinity House at Vanderbilt, the Disciples provided for their own ministry, helped Vanderbilt develop its own constituency, and forwarded their own larger ecumenical goals. If the Disciples represented one constituency, the more important new constituency was the "progressive" South. The South had all the elements of an American colony: its economy was rural and often based on the extraction of resources; many of its people were less educated than the national average; and it had little capital. The region was also divided racially, and segregation added to economic and educational problems. The sheer cost of maintaining two parallel school systems, for instance, was a major drain on an already poor region. Not surprisingly, southern religion often reflected the southern social order. In some churches, conservative theology and conservative politics combined to legitimate the status quo. This faith was often aristocratic, stressing kindness and personal concern, and intensely patriotic. Other southerners—white and black—had a "religion of the dispossessed" that often featured emotional release from the burdens of poverty and sickness. But there was a small, third group of southerners, many of them in the business and education communities, who were interested in modern business methods, the new agriculture, science, and the integration of the South into the national economy. The School of Religion at Vanderbilt became an important voice for the theological training of clergy to serve this segment of southern society.[13] The school also, in conjunction with the University's Graduate School, became a leading educator of southern college and university professors who, in turn, tended to strengthen southern progressivism.

The rejection of Vanderbilt by the MECS happened just as American denominationalism passed its apogee. Ecumenical sentiment in America had grown steadily since the Civil War, and such interdenominational organizations as the Young Men's Christian Association were found on almost all college campuses. The need for urban missions and for a clearer social witness inspired the founding of the Federal Council of Churches, initially a league of thirty-three denominations, formed around an activist program. Just as Vanderbilt was becoming independent, the Federal Council of Churches began to prove its worth to American Protestants by coordinating Protestant work in the armed forces. The value of ecumenical cooperation was further affirmed in the 1930s as the movement for a World Council of Churches, usually dated from the 1910 Edinburgh Missionary Conference, gathered steam. The conferences on "Life and Work" (1925 and 1937) and "Faith and Order" (1927 and 1937) were among the few opportunities for Christians of different denominations and nationalities to come together for dialogue, reflection, and fellowship as the world drifted toward World War II.

The ecumenical movement permitted Vanderbilt to make a small but highly significant change in its self-understanding by seeking to define itself as a non-denominational theological school. The 1915 catalogue listed these marks of the institution:

1. It magnifies religion and ethics rather than theology as the things of first importance in the training of those who are to be the religious leaders of our times.
2. It inculcates the reverent scientific spirit as the principle that should

guide in the discovery and application of truth in religion as elsewhere.

3. It interprets the fundamental principles of Christianity as given by
   Christ in terms of democracy.
4. It gives central place in its program to the great truths upon which
   Christian bodies agree rather than upon the things that separate, and
   it extends its advantages to all religious denominations on equal
   terms.
5. As stated above, its doors are open not only to those preparing for
   the ministry, but to social and religious workers of all types, recognizing that those who are called to be co-workers in the kingdom of
   God will be mutually benefited by the close association during their
   years of preparation.[14]

The ecumenical movement encouraged Vanderbilt to place a different emphasis on these important ideals. In 1956 another new name, "Divinity School,"
moved the school from seeing itself as the center of a liberal alternative to the
present church toward a self-definition as a school serving the church of the
future.

Perhaps the most visible sign of Vanderbilt's status as the ecumenical school
of the South came in 1955 when John D. Rockefeller, Jr., included Vanderbilt
among the institutions to receive part of a $20 million grant to theological
education. The other schools to receive funds were Union (New York), Yale,
Chicago, Harvard, and the Pacific School of Religion. The criteria stated that
grants would be given to a small number of schools that were multi- or nondenominational, standard-setting institutions that were liberal and related to a
major university, and schools whose programs made a regional impact; they
would be given in response to a clearly defined need and without reference to a
possible Rockefeller gift; and they should be used to raise the quality of the
ministry and to upgrade teaching in order to place those schools on a par with
other graduate schools.[15] After years of struggling to build a constituency, Vanderbilt was nationally recognized as the leading university-related theological
school in the South. If the numbers did not suddenly increase, the school's
confidence and its sense of direction did. The school began to seek faculty with
academic reputations that might match its new status.

The Cole Lectures and the Wider Theological World

In 1890, E. W. Cole, a Methodist layman, railroad executive, and treasurer
of the University's Board of Trust, gave $2,500 to endow a series of lectures at

Vanderbilt "restricted in its scope to the defence and advocacy of the Christian religion." Not until 1903, after Mrs. Cole added $5,000 to the endowment, were the lectures an annual event; initially they were given in alternate years. Outwardly, the Cole Lectures were not unique. At many other American seminaries, philanthropists were giving money to establish lecture series that would meet the particular needs of specific institutions. Dean Wilbur Fisk Tillett and the faculty impressed upon Cole the importance of the Bampton Lectures for Oxford University and for British theology; the Lyman Beecher Lectures on Preaching at Yale, established in 1871, would have been the most notable example in this country. These series enabled institutions to attract distinguished scholars and church leaders and to participate in a wider conversation on issues of the day, a conversation that was extended by the publication of the lectures, which also increased a school's visibility. In addition, theological schools always wanted to be public institutions; a lectureship offered a way to gather an audience of ministers and laypeople under the auspices of the school. By mid-century the Cole Lectures had become part of the social calendar for many people in the Nashville community.

While in the early years the Cole Lecturers included the obligatory Methodist bishops and denominational leaders, the series has consistently reflected the crucial issues in contemporary theology. During the liberal period in American theology, roughly 1900 to 1940, Vanderbilt's lecturers spoke to topics characteristic of the dilemmas that liberal theologians faced, including such issues as Christianity and progress, the nature of the modern world, contemporary problems of rural churches, and the relationship between Christianity and creativity. In the years 1907–25, nine of Vanderbilt's Cole Lecturers had also been or would later be Lyman Beecher Lecturers.

The middle decades of the century saw the existential questioning of America's "neo-orthodox" period, as American theologians and pastors tried both to get beyond the limitations of liberalism and modernism and to find newer ways to understand the tradition. One of the most important characteristics of these decades was the pairing of existential and cultural concerns, a dialectic perhaps suggested by the work of H. Richard Niebuhr, who lectured in 1961. The last three decades of the century in American theology had less thematic unity. Part of what changed was, of course, a new openness to women and to people of color. Another, less obvious, shift was that the lectures became more concerned with methodological issues, reflecting a growing self-criticism in the theological disciplines, than with the application of theology to broader social issues that had dominated earlier discussions. This also reflected larger shifts in American theological education.

Perhaps the most significant change in the Cole Lectures came in 1948 when the University ceased to guarantee the publication of the lectures. That decision was, of course, related to the increasing costs of theological education in general, as well as the decline in value of the income from the Cole Trust.[16] But it also reflected another long-range trend. While the content of major lecture series was as strong or stronger than before, the series themselves were attracting smaller and more specialized audiences.

The Profession of Ministry

Vanderbilt's emergence as an independent school and its interest in becoming part of the wider theological world contributed to its decision to adopt a professional model for its work. The word "professional" is hard to define in American English. In some respects, it refers to the classical professions of law, medicine, and ministry. Each of these required practitioners to master a basic literature that they would—to some extent—apply to their occupation. Somewhere in the late nineteenth century, the word acquired different connotations. For many, it was understood in terms of expertise. An expert was a person who had studied a specific area so thoroughly that he or she knew all its ins and outs. All experts could do something, and they could do it well. Expertise became part of the modern American understanding of professional. Some of the new academic and intellectual fields or disciplines also added a different connotation to the word "professional." In engineering, for example, a professional was someone who could apply science to a concrete problem; in education, the master teacher was someone who could apply the principles of teaching and learning to a specific class or school situation. In other words, professionals were people who used scientific knowledge and methods to improve human life.

American theological educators began experimenting with a new style of practical theology in the 1880s. Much of what was new came from the development of the social sciences, especially sociology, psychology, and education. The social sciences that entered the seminaries were not "value-free" examinations of human life. Many progressives seeking intellectual grounding for their programs of social and moral reform passionately embraced sociology, psychology, and education because they believed that knowledge furthered reform. Indeed, the progressive recipe for social change might have been written as follows: take a serious study of conditions (done by an expert), agitate to make those facts known, and then propose remedies. Progressive clergy tended to follow the same prescription. Thus, a minister might study the sociology of the family to see how the church could strengthen families; or, one might study the social consequences of alcohol to make the case for prohibition. Education has always been one of the most popular American reform movements. In the late nine-teenth century, the American system of schooling was developing its charac-teristic organization: kindergarten through eight years of elementary school, four years of high school, and then college and beyond. The new science of education was a natural handmaiden to these changes, and theological seminar-ies established departments of religious education to help spearhead similar changes in the churches' programs. A leading religious educator captured the spirit of this synthesis of reform, social science, and religious fervor when he described the work of religious education as "salvation by education."[17]

Many theological educators were convinced that there was a social science of ministry that paralleled the other social sciences and, like them, combined elements from many different disciplines. Between 1912 and 1916, Shailer Mathews, Gerald Birney Smith, and George Burman Foster of the University of Chicago published a series of articles on what Mathews called "church effi-ciency, i.e., the preparation of men trained to lead the churches to the perfor-mance of their particular function."[18]

Like other divinity schools, Vanderbilt fully participated in the new em-phases. Reading the school's catalogues from 1920 to the 1950s, one is struck by the expansion of the range of practical courses and the school's commitment to an education for ministry that dealt with the nitty-gritty aspects of the clerical profession such as religious education, counseling, and administration. The one area that suffered comparative neglect, at least before the 1950s, was field educa-tion. As in many American theological schools, field education would have its greatest period of growth at Vanderbilt after World War II.

The professional model had at least one negative consequence. Vanderbilt, like Yale and some other divinity schools, tended to segregate academic theol-ogy from the practice of ministry. This separation has a long history. In 1913, Mathews noted:

> Educationally considered a theological seminary is primarily a profes-sional school. It may offer advanced courses of scholastic quality for the benefit of its students who wish to become specialists; and if it is associ-ated with a university, it must carry on highly specialized investigative work on the part of its advanced students and its faculty. But in so doing it becomes a graduate school of theology rather than a theological school proper.[19]

At Vanderbilt, the separation of the two aspects of the Divinity School was institutionalized by the division of the Divinity faculty into those who also teach in the graduate school and those whose work was confined to the Divinity School. According to the 1945 catalogue, "Courses in the Practical and Sociological fields, being regarded as more strictly professional in character, are not included in the curriculum of the graduate school."[20] The basis for the separation was the idea that the study of theology and the practice of ministry are different academically and that they represent different modes of intellectual accountability. In the 1980s, Vanderbilt's Edward Farley provoked a wideranging discussion of the nature of theological education by arguing that theological study had lost its nature as a unity—a habitus—and had become a series of unconnected academic disciplines. At the same time, Farley suggested, theological study had lost its center as reflection on behalf of the whole church and had become narrowly defined as the intellectual and professional training for the clergy within the church.[21]

Despite the separation of theological study and practical ministry, Vanderbilt made distinctive contributions in two areas of practical theology at two different periods in the twentieth century: the rural church movement and the development of the Doctor of Ministry degree program. The rural church movement applied both the Social Gospel and the ideals of ministerial efficiency to the rural church. In 1928, Jerome Davis, who worked with the great sociologist of religion Henry Holt at the Chicago Theological Seminary, claimed that "every theological seminary should have adequate courses in rural work. When we consider that there are today over a hundred thousand rural churches in America and over thirty million farm people who must attend these churches or none at all, we can realize something of the importance of the problem."[22] Sociological studies of the rural churches, however, revealed serious problems: small churches, often rendered ineffective by denominational competition, with poorly trained and occasionally non-resident pastors, inadequate Sunday Schools, and little youth work.[23] It was as though the revival had burned out and left behind scorched ground. Further, the theology of rural America, often a blend of folk religion, revivalism, and radical individualism, did not lend itself to cooperative action against common problems. Hope was often for deliverance from a hell to come, not for salvation from present tribulations.

The desperation of the religious situation in the countryside was matched by changes in rural life. After the Civil War, American farms entered into a period of rapid expansion and mechanization that increased acreage and production while requiring less human labor to produce the crop. By 1920, the gasoline-fueled tractor, a relatively inexpensive tool, had become almost universal. In that same year, prices began to plunge, and agriculture moved into a serious depression. In turn, this depression accelerated the rate at which people left the countryside, which spurred further mechanization. When the rest of the American economy followed the farmers in 1929, the situation went from critical to catastrophic. To many disappointed farmers, it seemed as if America had gone from rural paradise to rural slum in less than a generation.

The rural church movement believed that effective Christian ministry to distressed rural areas required theological training of the most professional sort.[24] The minister entering a rural area needed to have a good grasp of what was happening to the population in order to help the churches find ways to meet human needs. This type of minister, however, was rarely attracted to rural work, and much of the energy of the movement went into recruiting. It hoped to inspire some of the most able younger ministers for rural work and sought to provide them, once inspired, with the tools they needed to do the task effectively.

Although rural church work flourished in some denominational seminaries, including Bangor and Andover Newton, divinity schools like Vanderbilt provided an ideal location for such studies. Most rural church theorists believed that the future of rural religion had to be ecumenical, or at least nondenominational, and most hoped that the churches could be centers for real reform. A good rural pastor needed to be able to harness public opinion, for instance, to support better public schools, to persuade governments to make advances in sanitation and electrification, and to provide guidance for rural young people who needed to be inspired to get further education. It was a grand dream. Unfortunately, most seminary-trained ministers, especially those with a more liberal and socially concerned theology, were inclined to minister to urban or suburban congregations (in part because of finances) or to work with urban social problems. Few model rural ministers were actually trained, but many clergy became more sensitive to the site of many serious American social problems.

Vanderbilt was also in the forefront of the movement to develop a professional doctorate for ministers, which attempted to address two basic problems. First was the problem of professional nomenclature for ministers. The twentieth century had seen the doctoral degree adopted as either a standard or a sign of excellence in many professions. Many school superintendents and principals held doctoral degrees, as did the leading people in professions ranging from chiropractic to engineering. In this social world, the ministers' Bachelor of Divinity degree was not very imposing and did not reflect the education that seminary-trained ministers had, in fact, received. While status was a major matter to some, theological educators had run into an impasse that was much more serious. The three-year program did not provide enough time for both sufficient pastoral practice and serious theological study, and many argued for a fourth year in order to provide the needed education. After a long and frustrating period of discussion in the Association of Theological Schools, Vanderbilt, Chicago, and Claremont announced that they would begin to enroll students for the new degree that would provide that fourth year.

Vanderbilt's Doctor of Divinity (D.Div.) degree, first offered in 1968, represented a substantial attempt to raise the standards of American theological education. The program followed its Master of Divinity program for the first two years and then branched off to include concentrated study in one area plus electives, substantial field education, and completion of a thesis.[25] Students who held the first theological degree from another school or from Vanderbilt could earn the D.Div. by completing a minimum of twenty-four course hours spread over a year and a summer, the latter to complete the field requirement of a summer intensive program. With the exception of the lack of a formal internship year, the Vanderbilt program summarized the best thinking about ministerial education over the previous forty years.

In many ways, the Vanderbilt D.Div. was a bridge too far. Many of the weaker schools in the Association of Theological Schools worried about whether they could absorb the cost of such a program and, equally important, whether their students could afford another year. Moreover, many theological educators were more concerned with finding a way to reward clergy for completing a program of continuing education. By offering a Doctor of Ministry degree, based on a period of active service, they hoped to meet this need. To others, the requirement of a thesis and a concentration sounded too much like a research degree.

Educational goals and purposes were not the only reason for the failure of the Vanderbilt D.Div. to become a standard theological degree. The D.Div. came near the end of the post–World War II renewal of interest in religion, which had been very good for theological schools. Their enrollments swelled, with many new students financed through the G.I. Bill. The three-year degree, long advocated by American theological educators, became standard, and the emphasis on the study of Western civilization in the colleges provided preseminary bachelor of arts studies with a rationale they had lacked in the more vocationally oriented 1930s and 1940s.

Then the boom burst. The 1970s was a decade of intense financial struggle for many schools, often accompanied by student and social unrest. Many schools, including Vanderbilt, adopted programs that were almost entirely elective in response to student demands that they be allowed to "do their own thing." D.Div. programs were among the casualties. By the 1980s, further, the mainstream churches that had appeared so strong earlier in the century were experiencing visible difficulties. Competition from the evangelical movement, shifting American demographics, the secularization of society, too many downtown churches—the list of usual suspects was long. However explained, the decline was real. Few schools had the leisure to seek higher academic standards for ministry; the D.Div. died, replaced by the Doctor of Ministry as a largely continuing-education degree for ministers.

The Lawson Affair

In 1960 the Divinity School was rocked to its foundations by the case of James Lawson, an African American Methodist who transferred to Vanderbilt from Oberlin in 1958. A participant in the work of the Fellowship of Reconciliation, Lawson became involved in the organization of the lunch counter sit-ins in Nashville. For his activities and his advocacy of nonviolent protest, he was expelled by the University. The Divinity School's faculty protested. Eleven of its sixteen members signed a declaration of conscience that said, "Whether or not we approve his strategy, we believe that Mr. Lawson has endeavored to follow his Christian conscience, and we see no adequate justification for his expulsion from the Divinity School."[26] Dean Robert Nelson and these faculty members eventually submitted letters of resignation in response to the incident. After a series of complex negotiations, Lawson was given the option of completing his final semester courses and receiving his degree, the faculty were allowed to withdraw their resignations, and the resignation of the dean was accepted. The incident was declared closed.

For all the sound and fury, the Lawson affair was only an incident. The school, strengthened by the Sealantic grant, continued to be strong academically, and, despite the tendency of some to flagellate themselves and others, to be a progressive and moral force in southern life. Like the earlier rejection by the Methodist Church, this event hurt many people in the Divinity School community, and yet it also helped the school face a more complicated, diverse future.

* * * * *

There is also a sense in which it exemplifies Vanderbilt's place in American theological education. The school has often been just a little ahead of its contemporaries. It faced the question of advanced professional education for Methodist ministers just before the denomination was completely ready for that alternative; the issue of evolution swept through the institution just before it became a passionate subject for theological debate in the 1880s; the school became nondenominational (later ecumenical) just before that movement became central to America's Protestants. Likewise, the Lawson case came just as the nation and its theological schools were on the verge of a season of unrest and radical social change. Shortly thereafter, almost all the nation's theological schools would have to deal with serious moral crises connected with civil rights, the Vietnam War, poverty, the rights of women and minorities, and other related issues. When the Lawson case is placed in this context, Vanderbilt handled the issue effectively and conscientiously. The faculty and the dean showed courage in demanding that Lawson's expulsion be revoked. In the next decade many other administrators and faculty members would face similar decisions.

Vanderbilt's tendency to be ahead of many of the trends in American theological education has often put the school at risk. Despite the Sealantic grant, the Divinity School has historically had to struggle to balance its budget, and it has not always had the funds to finance its dreams. The Divinity School has lived between the rock of its drive for excellence and the hard place of its limited means. At times, this position has meant that some talented faculty have moved on to higher salaries at better-funded institutions, but it has also meant that the school has attracted many adventurous souls who enjoyed its position on the edge of changing times.

PART II
School of the Prophets?

Vanderbilt's founders adopted a label for its theological institution that had been common in America since the eighteenth-century parsonage seminaries: "school of the prophets." Although it simply identified institutions whose primary function was the education of ministers, the expression carried with it serious intent and no little pretension as well. If in the eighteenth century the force of the term was directed more to the religious constituency than to the general culture, it nonetheless contained a clear argument: ministers could be educated for their work. In the revivals and awakenings of the eighteenth and early nineteenth centuries, which saw the emergence of a broad and varied evangelical spirit, the seventeenth-century expectation of a "learned" or educated ministry was severely challenged and its virtual opposite trumpeted. Many believed that capacities for ministry were inhibited by education because the individual would be tempted to put learning in the way of the inspiration and empowerment provided by God. Any denomination (and any school associated with it) that was part of the evangelical movement in America would have to contend with this issue. In the conservative South, where evangelicalism had become the dominant religious expression and where theological institutions had been slower to develop than in the Northeast, Vanderbilt's adoption of "school of the prophets," even in the latter part of the nineteenth century, asserted something that was not self-evident to much of its Methodist constituency. The chapters by Frank Gulley, Jr., and Richard Goode in this section illumine the tensions involved in these different perspectives on ministry, played out in such matters as financial support and institutional control. In time, a larger but less readily identifiable tension between the interests of academic institutions and those of the churches emerged, both at Vanderbilt and at other theological schools.

The regional context provided the more substantive engagement for the school's first two expressions as Biblical Department and School of Religion, in that it put the question of how and what "prophetic" meant in terms of the relation between religion and culture. It is the burden of every theological institution to consider how its education reflects or challenges the concerns of the surrounding culture, especially in relation to its broader constituency of support. Losing its Methodist association to become interdenominational and self-consciously liberal did not immediately change the school's basic relationship to southern culture. However, as issues of economics, social class, and race came to impinge on America, as critical study of the Bible became a hallmark of the school that was at odds with much of southern religion, and as the school's orientation was directed increasingly to the great northern interdenominational institutions, the word "prophetic" began to take on a more oppositional tone, creating tensions within the university as well as with the region. James P. Byrd, Jr.'s chapter, together with Richard Goode's analysis of the career of Alva W. Taylor, shows how uneasy the relationship between the culture and the university became in the second period of the school's history. The content of the expression "school of the prophets" had evolved well beyond its original meaning. If Vanderbilt's theological vision shared the ambition of the leading theological schools of the country to Christianize American society, the contours of that vision shifted considerably as the heady optimism of the social gospel movement was succeeded by world war, economic depression, and the civil rights movement.

In the Beginning:
The Biblical Department

Frank Gulley, Jr.

WHAT IS THE PLACE OF FORMAL EDUCATION IN THE PREPARA-
tion for ministry? This question was in great debate among southern Methodists in the years following the Civil War. The issue had
begun to present itself earlier in the nineteenth century as Methodists all across
America increasingly achieved middle-class status. Handsome church buildings
well appointed; comfortable seats; dignity in worship; reasoned, thoughtful
sermons eloquently delivered—all these meshed with concern for an educated
ministry and increasingly became the goal of the majority within the denomination. But the question of formal education did not receive focused attention
among southern Methodists until the close of the war.

The war had been a disaster for the Methodist Episcopal Church, South
(MECS). When the MECS was established in 1845 as the result of disagreements
with Methodists in the North, its future looked bright. Converts were made in
great numbers, impressive church buildings were constructed, new congregations were formed, and educational institutions at many levels emerged in strategic locations. The end of the war found the church, like most of the South, in
disarray. Many congregations had ceased to exist, bureaucratic offices no longer
functioned, church buildings and other church property had been severely
damaged and in many instances destroyed, ministers in many places were unable to make their appointed rounds. Many southern Methodists believed their
church could not continue. They did not, however, appreciate the depth of

determination of the leadership. Within months of the cessation of hostilities, steps were underway to pick up the pieces and move the church forward.

The supreme governing body of the church, the General Conference, convened in 1866 in New Orleans.[1] In the history of American Methodism this meeting was historic. Among other matters, in their "state of the church address" to the delegates, the bishops urged the establishment of an "institute," a seminary "for the proper training of our young preachers." The majority was set against such innovation, so that the recommendation was certain to produce controversy. Were not theological schools notorious for stifling the Spirit, teaching a style of preaching contrary to experiential religion? And what about heresy? Seminaries were known frequently to be the seedbed of erroneous teaching. Does not God give to those called to ministry all that is necessary to fulfill that mission? Is not Methodism's spectacular growth all across the land clear evidence that her preachers have all the requisites needed to fulfill their calling? Such were points frequently raised by the opponents of formal education for ministry. On the other side were those who had come to believe that formal education for the ministry was essential if southern Methodism was to appeal to the emerging middle class. An educated ministry, they were convinced, was an important key to the church's continuing growth and prosperity.

Contrary to the bishops' recommendation, the Conference delegates approved another solution for training ministers. The church's colleges, scattered across the South, were urged to appoint faculty to "biblical chairs" that could educate young men for ministry and offer other students appropriate insight into the faith. Having biblical chairs was something of an innovation for Methodists. On the whole, colleges did not routinely teach aspects of the religious tradition. Where religion was part of the curriculum, most often it was taught by persons with little formal training for the task, such as local ministers. In those years college administrators most often relied upon revivals, daily chapel services, and the personal examples of the faculty to instill Christian principles in the students. Nevertheless, the idea gained support because it also spoke to another concern—that money not be drained from local educational institutions and sent elsewhere.

Parallel to the concern for founding a theological school was interest among some that the southern church establish a genuine institution of higher education, a university. Before the war, Methodists had prosperous undergraduate institutions in every state of the Confederacy; at its end, all but one or two were closed. It was only by great effort that most of these found the resources to re-open, and when they did, most discovered their students ill-prepared for college-level instruction. The economic and social conditions of Methodism suggested that the resources could not be found to establish and sustain a university. Yet these advocates would not surrender their dream, and they quietly began to develop a constituency in support of such a project.

In 1871 the Tennessee Conference of the MECS[2] approved a resolution requesting that the bishop appoint a committee to ask other conferences to send delegates to a convention to explore the possibility of establishing a university. The next January, twenty-seven delegates from nine annual conferences convened in Memphis. Two bishops also were present, one of whom was Holland N. McTyeire, a visionary, progressive leader strongly in support of a theological school. At this gathering, the interests in ministerial education found common ground with those advocating graduate and professional education; the resulting "great university" would offer specialized instruction to match that of any northern institution. It is important to note that this project was not sponsored by the General Conference of the denomination, nor did it receive support of even a majority of the annual conferences. If the venture had limited backing, though, it had the support of persons of influence.

Within a few days of their gathering, the delegates produced a document that called for founding a university "of the highest order" composed of five schools: theology, literary and scientific, normal, law, and medicine. It was agreed that $1 million would be needed to set this institution on a firm footing and that at least half of that sum would be required before the university could open. Before adjourning, the delegates appointed a board of trustees for the new university, composed mainly of the delegates themselves. That body in turn organized itself, established the mechanism for raising the funds to make the dream a reality, and initiated the process by which the university could be incorporated under the laws of the State of Tennessee. The charter issued by the state empowered the Board of Trust, among other things, to purchase and hold property, to raise and disperse funds, to appoint persons to fulfill its mission, and to make by-laws for conducting business. It also gave the Board authority to determine its own membership in "perpetual succession," words that would become important in later debates about the founding of the university.

Upon adjourning, representatives of the Board of Trust traveled the South seeking funds for the new university. After months of effort, those in charge could report only modest results—approximately $30,000 in pledges and cash. At that rate, no one could anticipate the university's opening in the near future. Many came to believe the project was hopeless.

Then a chain of circumstances unfolded that some could only call providential. In February 1873, Bishop McTyeire went to New York City to consult a physician about a personal medical problem. While there, he was the guest of Cornelius Vanderbilt, one of the wealthiest men in America, and his wife. Vanderbilt's second wife, Frank Crawford, was related to McTyeire's wife, Amelia Townsend. Though distantly related, the two women were quite close, and it was natural that McTyeire would be invited to stay at the Vanderbilt mansion. He was there approximately two weeks, during which time he and the Commodore, as Vanderbilt was known by his friends, had many conversations. It is clear that the two came to trust and respect each other. McTyeire left New York with a letter from Vanderbilt to the Board of Trust offering the funds necessary for the opening of Central University, the name chosen by the Memphis convention.

Vanderbilt promised a gift of "no less" than $500,000, with any excess over the actual cost of buildings, books, equipment, and land to go into endowment. Before his death in 1877, he had raised his contribution to almost $1 million. Certain strings were tied to the gift, however. McTyeire was to be chairman of the Board of Trust for life and given virtual veto authority over actions of the Board. The university was to be located in or near Nashville, and all endowment funds were to remain inviolate.

Upon returning to Nashville, McTyeire called a meeting of the Central University Board of Trust and presented Vanderbilt's offer. In grateful appreciation, the Board agreed to the stipulations and changed the name of the institution to Vanderbilt University. They also authorized the necessary legal steps to change the name of the university. In that process the court conveyed to the Board of Trust certain powers including the "power . . . to increase and diminish the number of the trustees."

Within weeks McTyeire moved to fulfill the dream. Land was purchased, architects secured, contracts let for building construction, faculty and staff hired, equipment and books ordered. On October 3, 1875, the University opened.[3]

The Biblical Department: The First Decade

In Vanderbilt's first decade, Bishop McTyeire was clearly the dominant figure in shaping the Biblical Department. While he had a deep commitment to the whole University, the Biblical Department was the "apple of his eye."[4] Sharing with him in this enterprise was Landon C. Garland, one of the teachers under whom McTyeire had studied at Randolph-Macon College, and who became Vanderbilt's first chancellor. Together they would shape the program for ministerial education, but it was McTyeire who was the guiding hand.

Neither McTyeire nor Garland were graduates of theological "institutes" and thus did not have direct experience with theological studies programs. They would be guided by the experience of similar northern institutions—Harvard's and Yale's, for instance—but at the same time they had to be sensitive to the Methodist tradition, its values and ways of being in southern culture. While not necessarily antithetical, these two concerns were not always compatible. So

McTyeire and Garland were forced to walk a tightrope—offering a program of theological studies that would capture the attention of the educated elite and thereby establish Vanderbilt's reputation nationally, but at the same time provide Methodist students with the resources to be effective in ministry and in so doing gain the respect and confidence of the Methodist community. Accomplishing both objectives was not an easy task.

The name "Biblical Department" seems not to have been preferred by McTyeire and others. Most often in correspondence and in official minutes, this part of the University was referred to as "the theological department" or "the divinity school." "Biblical Department" seems to have been a concession to fears among some in the church that this venture was going to develop theological sophisticates who could not communicate with the common people. It offered those unfamiliar with programs of theological education a vague clue, at least, of what this enterprise sought to accomplish. So it remained the Biblical Department until the break with the church in 1914.

The academic officers held their responsibility to be that of educating the whole person; they were "to train a body of gentlemen in knowledge, virtue, and religion," preparing them to make solid contributions to civilized society.[5] To accomplish that objective the University's programs were designed to care for the spiritual and physical health of students—their values as well as their bodies and their minds. The Biblical Department was to fulfill this objective in ways appropriate to its special mission. The University's first catalogue stated that the Biblical Department sought "to furnish the church ministers who in addition to a sound Christian experience, humble piety, and consecration to God, are learned in scripture, sound in doctrine, refined but simple in manners; earnest, direct, and plain in the presentation of the truth, and ready for any field of service to which the church may assign them."[6]

To achieve these results, certain structures were put in place—some common to any theological school, others peculiar to Methodism. Daily chapel services (weekends included) and student-led prayer meetings each evening would nurture the spiritual lives of students, as would the once-weekly "class meetings" peculiar to the Methodist tradition.[7] Meetings of the missionary society would provide occasion for students to become better informed about and share in the work of foreign and domestic missions.[8] On weekends students might visit the Nashville prisons and orphanages and share in the work of city mission projects, places where students could testify to their faith and lead others to commitment. In their academic work, students in the Biblical Department, as in other parts of the University, were to adhere faithfully to the Honor Code. Over all these expectations the faculty presided, giving encouragement when needed, chastising those who did not seem serious about their studies, and disciplining those guilty of serious breaches of the rules.[9] Clearly, the University aimed to create an environment wherein the young preachers could grow and mature in the faith, even as their minds were to be stretched and prepared for the work of ministry.

The initial curriculum of the Biblical Department reflected the Germanic pattern of a four-fold division, with one professor appointed to teach each of the subjects: systematic theology, exegetical theology, ecclesiastical history/introduction to the Bible, and practical theology. Because this was a Methodist institution, that tradition was prominently set forth at appropriate points, most visibly in the lectures on systematic theology. Using the Articles of Religion,[10] the professor argued the validity of Methodist theology against all its detractors, especially Calvinists. By 1875 American Methodists had not yet established a strong theological tradition; hence, students in systematic theology focused on the scholarship of English Methodism, especially the writings of John Wesley, Adam Clarke, and Richard Watson, but with increasing attention to such American authors as Nathan Bangs, Wilbur Fisk, and, in time, John Miley and Daniel Whedon.

Methodists were known to be people of one book, the Bible. Young preachers arriving in Nashville in the 1870s to begin their studies probably thought themselves well acquainted with the biblical content and message. Little did they realize what was before them. The faculty was convinced that a true understanding of the Bible required that the text be read in its original languages—Greek and Hebrew—studies that would try the souls of most because their knowledge of the English language was so meager. Students were then told to read these ancient books using textual criticism. Scholarly approaches to the Bible had arrived in Tennessee, but probably in their mildest form. The inspiration of scripture would not be denied!

Although the curriculum required that students be introduced to church history, the subject seems not to have loomed large in their studies. They were required to read Philip Schaff's history of the church, and especially to become familiar with the history of the Methodist tradition, both English and American, a subject important to McTyeire.[11] The professor of church history also taught other subjects, such as the formation of the biblical canon and the insights for Christian faith gained from biblical archaeology.

"Practical theology" seems to have been something of a catchall. Here students studied homiletics, denominational polity, and "pastoral charge" (later titled "pastoral theology" or "ministerial office"). Invariably, the holder of this teaching position was a person who had gained prominence in the church and could speak out of experience about the practice of ministry. Doubtless, many students thought these subjects the most important of all.

Subject areas were not divided into required and elective courses. Students had to study with the professor in each area, attending all the lectures on all the subjects in the curriculum. One exception was that students in the English Curriculum did not study the ancient languages; upon completing a two-year program, they were given a certificate. Most students opted for this program of studies.[12] Fewer students were enrolled in the three-year Classical Curriculum that covered all subjects taught, languages included, and for which they were awarded a diploma.

Initially, students enrolled in the Biblical Department were not awarded degrees, a common practice in theological education of that time, but in time that changed. Those with bachelor of arts degrees from reputable colleges entering in the fall of 1881 could enroll in a program leading to the Bachelor of Sacred Theology (S.T.B.) degree.[13] Students in this program had to complete the Classical Curriculum, including examinations in Greek and Hebrew, and present an acceptable treatise on the doctrine of the atonement. With the catalogue for 1886–87, a Bachelor of Divinity (B.D.) degree replaced the Bachelor of Sacred Theology. Meanwhile, those entering without undergraduate degrees— the overwhelming majority—could continue to enroll in the English and Classical programs.

Only one criterion seems to have been essential for the faculty—those appointed had to be ordained Methodists. For McTyeire and Garland it was natural that the name of Thomas O. Summers would quickly come to the head of the list. He was appointed dean and professor of systematic theology in 1875.[14] Summers was probably the best-known scholar in southern Methodism. Although his formal education was minimal, he read widely and was regarded by those who knew him well to be a walking encyclopedia. He was the author of biblical commentaries and works on theology, served as editor of several journals, and for thirty-two years was book editor for the denomination. As a theologian he was rigidly orthodox; one of his greatest pleasures was to confront those, especially students, whose theological views deviated from the Methodist straight and narrow. As a teacher he was dull and as a preacher even more so. McTyeire probably got it right when he said that Summers was "a vat into which all learning had been poured, as incapable of originality as of sin."[15] McTyeire's other appointments were similar—persons with solid church credentials, orthodox in their theology, reasonably competent as teachers and scholars, but not capable of shaping their disciplines—that is, men like McTyeire himself.[16] That was what the church needed, McTyeire believed.

McTyeire and Garland had high hopes for the quality of students the new university would attract. They saw Vanderbilt as the capstone for Methodist higher education in the South—the institution to which the many Methodist colleges would send their brightest and best-prepared graduates. Even before the first class arrived, however, they were forced to lower their sights. Those presenting themselves were in most instances ill prepared for the level of instruction proposed.[17] An embarrassed McTyeire would later lament, "If we had stood firm by our rules, we should have rejected fully two-thirds of those who presented themselves for matriculation."[18]

The situation facing the Biblical Department was similar. Many applicants lacked a rudimentary secondary education. Most could not speak or write the English language adequately, and their reading skills were woefully deficient, leading the faculty to complain repeatedly of their students' lack of "culture of mind." What should they do? They saw no alternative but to admit most of those applying—provided they could present a testimonial of good moral character and a letter of endorsement from a church official. Practically speaking, there was an open admissions policy.[19]

Within days of the opening of classes, the faculty realized they faced a major problem. Students were unable to understand their lectures or complete the reading assignments. At every turn students were failing. Quickly the word spread throughout the University and, in time, across the church. The University's image was tarnished. It was reported that some of the more capable and well-prepared students "left in disgust," while those who were dismissed for failure departed in sharp criticism of the school. The most significant step to address the problem was the institution of classes in English grammar for all students found to be deficient. As discussed below, it was not until 1885, however, that this issue was directly confronted and resolved.

Although McTyeire and Garland initially opposed the construction of dormitories at Vanderbilt, plans were developed early on to construct a building to house the Biblical Department that would also include living accommodations for students. Wesley Hall, occupied in the fall of 1881, came from the generosity of William H. Vanderbilt, son of the Commodore, who contributed $145,000 for its construction.[20] This majestic, five-story structure was built on an elevation near the center of the campus with a commanding view of the city of Nashville.[21] Those entering Wesley Hall immediately discerned its purpose. Above the main door chiseled in stone were the Latin words *schola prophetarum*, "school of the prophets." The Biblical Department's mission was clear—to prepare men to speak for God in a world alienated from God. The building was constructed to serve all the needs of the Biblical Department community. In the ground-floor dining hall students took their meals, prepared by the black servants, "Aunt Mary," the cook, and her associate "Uncle Josh." In the beginning the food service was contracted out, an arrangement in time found to be too costly (more than eleven dollars per month per student). Eventually the Board of Trust authorized the implementation of "the messing system," wherein students carried major responsibility for the food service.[22] In time they could report that the cost per student per month was in the range of eight to ten dollars. While this arrangement did not solve all the problems, students year after year voted for its retention.

The main floor of Wesley Hall was given to the principal activities of the school. Here students gathered for worship in a small chapel, attended classes each day (Saturday included) in the four lecture rooms provided, utilized the services of a small library (open only four hours per week in the beginning), and found opportunity for relaxation in the parlor and reading room. This floor also provided a small apartment for the manager, accommodations for a few faculty and students, and a room called the "sanitarium" for ill students.[23] Most students lived on the top three floors, with one or two students per room. For the comfort of all, the new structure provided central heat and lighting, great luxuries for which students were charged five dollars per year. Because the building was made of wood throughout, and evidently not well constructed, the administration constantly worried about its vulnerability to fire. Small fires were frequent, especially in student rooms and in the ground floor kitchen. An early effort at developing a fire brigade among the residents proved ineffective. In time fire escapes were constructed on the outside of the building, to the relief of many.

One cannot read the records from this period without being impressed with the poverty of the students. Although by 1875 the membership of the MECS was mainly middle class, its ministers tended to come from the lower ranges of the economic scale. They were poor, and their families were poor, and they arrived at Wesley Hall with little more than the hope that the Lord would somehow provide for their education.

Theological schools across the country in this period regularly subsidized the studies of their students, offering free tuition and, in many instances, financial assistance to cover other costs. For students enrolled in the Biblical Department there was no charge for rooms in Wesley Hall or for tuition, an arrangement that would remain for nearly forty years. The only sums requiring payment, beyond the cost of food, were a matriculation fee of twenty dollars per year, a five-dollar library fee (apparently the sole source for book acquisitions), the cost of "fuel, light, and washing," and books, estimated to cost ten dollars. For most of the students, the money to cover even these charges was difficult to find. As late as 1901, the dean asserted that "homes of economy, self-denial and poverty seem to be the nurseries where young ministers are reared."[24]

The Biblical Department: Tillett at the Helm

Summers's administration came to an end in the spring of 1882 with his sudden death from a heart attack. He had not been well for many months. He arrived each day at Wesley Hall exhausted after slowly walking from his home on campus. During the last weeks students carried him up the steep staircase to his office, where he would rest before beginning to teach.

He was succeeded by A. M. Shipp, an ordained Methodist and member of the Biblical Department faculty from its inception, who before arriving at Vanderbilt had been president of Wofford College. He held the post until 1885, when, according to him, he resigned. McTyeire, however, reported that Shipp was fired for "inefficiency as an officer and his incompetency as an instructor."[25] All of this became common knowledge, appearing in the local press when Shipp publicly attacked McTyeire, who responded in kind. There was no permanent dean for the Biblical Department during the 1885–86 academic year.

We know nothing of the process used by McTyeire and Garland in selecting the next dean. The record states simply that Wilbur Fisk Tillett was given that responsibility beginning with the 1886–87 academic year. For the next four decades, until his retirement in 1919, Tillett was to be instrumental in shaping the Biblical Department by his vision and guidance.

Tillett came to Vanderbilt in 1882 at age twenty-eight as chaplain to the University, part-time instructor in theology in the Biblical Department, and minister to a newly formed Methodist congregation on the edge of the campus specifically organized to meet the spiritual needs of the campus community. Nothing in his record to that point suggested an unusually bright future for him, nor is there evidence to suggest that his four years at Vanderbilt were so outstanding as to merit his appointment to such an important post.[26] Tillett inherited a Department in disarray. One issue stood out—the academic quality of the students admitted to the school. As already mentioned, most arrived ill prepared for the level of instruction offered. The matter was given special attention by the Board of Trust at its meeting in the spring of 1885. A special committee chaired by Chancellor Garland sharply criticized the open admissions policy. Because so many poorly prepared students had been admitted, Vanderbilt's reputation among Methodists generally, and especially among Methodist college faculty, had been tarnished. "This has degraded the theological course not only in the estimation of the graduates of those colleges who have entered the Theological Department . . . but in the estimation of our own pupils. In this state of things we can never attract the graduates of colleges, and it is easy to see why the few who have come, have either left in disgust or have entered the literary and scientific department [Vanderbilt's arts and science faculty] exclusively."[27]

After much discussion, the Board approved a plan that seems to have originated with Tillett, but was presented as the committee's report to the Board of Trust. Henceforth, students admitted to the Biblical Department would be required to have completed at least the sophomore year of a liberal arts program, a level acknowledged to be low, but "the best that can be expected at the moment." Those applying without such preparation would be admitted as "young men studying for admission to the Biblical Department" but enrolled in the Academic Department, where they would receive most of their instruction. These students, called "candidates," would be enrolled in the Biblical Department only after they had achieved the equivalent of sophomore-level status.[28]

For a year or two following this decision many in the Department were anxious over its implications for the future. How would enrollments be impacted? How would the church respond to such action? "Candidates" substantially outnumbered the other students, but within three years that situation began to reverse. Meanwhile, with those ill prepared removed from classes, the learning environment improved dramatically.

As noted previously, many students at Vanderbilt came from poor families and had little money for their education and other needs. At that time there were virtually no part-time student pastorates. While some students were fortunate enough to secure part-time employment in Nashville, that was not a reliable source of revenue. To Tillett and others it was clear that if the Biblical Department were to have an adequate enrollment, a loan and scholarship program was required. A Sustentation Fund was in existence by 1880, composed of all those contributions to the Biblical Department designated for student support. In most instances the contributions were modest—small checks from individuals, an offering from a church. Tillett was indefatigable in presenting the needs of students to individuals, congregations, and the many annual conferences he visited each year. The money that came in was distributed to students on the basis of need. In any year an average of twenty-five to forty students received interest-free loans that they were obligated to repay upon leaving the University. A note in the Board of Trust minutes indicates the importance of these being loans and not gifts: "Christian manhood" holds that "it is better for a young man, who really needs it, to accept *help* than a *gift*. To pay back in small installments, as he may be able, will not embarrass him, while habits of economy and self reliance are cultivated."[29]

In time the Sustentation Fund was also tapped for another purpose—scholarships for capable college graduates. Tillett was aware that other theological schools used scholarships to attract quality students. So beginning with academic year 1887–88, fellowships in the amount of $100 per year were offered to graduates of select academic institutions that Tillett and the faculty thought would enhance the academic level of the Biblical Department. Tillett reported to the Trustees in 1894 that twenty-three students were enrolled with these scholarships.

By the early 1890s, Tillett and others in the University realized that very few graduates were repaying their loans. The anticipation had been that the monies repaid would be recycled through the Sustentation Fund for others to borrow. By 1895 the Chancellor reported to the Board of Trust that the Fund was exhausted. Reminders were mailed to all with loans outstanding, a strategy that produced modest returns in the first year, but these grew larger as the years passed. Starting in 1900, those borrowing had to pay interest and, for the first time, loans were restricted to Methodists.

From its inception in 1875 the Biblical Department had not been narrowly sectarian in its theological orientation. To be sure, it was decidedly Methodist in its ethos, but students of other denominational traditions were welcomed. Indeed, in the very first class one person from the Cumberland Presbyterian Church enrolled for study. Evidence suggests that in every way non-Methodists were given the same privileges and had the same expectations laid upon them as the Methodists.

The last fifteen years of the nineteenth century were something of a watershed in American religious history, with the growth of liberal theologies and the emergence of the Social Gospel movement. Although these developments were slower to arrive on the southern religious scene, they were clearly present by the turn of the century, and the Biblical Department appears to have been a major source of their introduction. The clearest evidence for the changing theological perspectives in the faculty is in the thought of Tillett himself. He arrived at Vanderbilt steeped in the writings of English Methodist theologians and at home in the American Methodist theological scene, which, in the early 1880s, had not strayed far from the views of John Wesley in the eighteenth century. By the turn of the century, however, many Methodist theologians heretofore thought to be faithfully evangelical were entertaining new perspectives. That is Tillett's story. During the last decade of the nineteenth century and the early years of the twentieth, he was uncomfortable with theology's new direction. He spoke of it as a fad that would soon pass away.[30] But in time he became a convert, at home with the presuppositions and vocabulary of the new liberal theology—at least in its most moderate form. He was unwilling completely to jettison the old for the new, but sought to blend the best of both. He expressed that aim in his *magnum opus*, *The Paths That Lead to God*: "The author considers himself a modern-minded man, possessed of an open attitude towards the results of modern scholarship. . . . But he has not so far reacted from the views of the fathers of the past generation as to feel . . . that it is best to abandon entirely the time-worn arguments of the old theologians."[31]

In his report to the Board of Trust in June 1904, Chancellor James H. Kirkland had occasion to speak of the "radical changes in the course of the Biblical Department."[32] In comparison to the previous generation, developments under way were, indeed, radical. New theological perspectives were being entertained, new fields added to the curriculum (bringing with them an expanded faculty), and new requirements established for students. For all concerned this was a turbulent and exciting time.

A course titled "Applied Christianity" first greeted students in 1899, taught by a professor of sociology who also held appointment in the Academic Department. In this course, almost immediately required of all students, one was introduced to "the social teachings of Jesus and the application of Christian principles to present-day social problems," such as poverty and crime.[33] A year later, students were invited for the first time to study the "History of Religions," taking a comparative look at Christianity and the other major world religions—concluding, of course, that Christianity was superior to the others. In the bulletin for 1904–5 "Religious Education" appeared as an area of study. Students were to learn that coming to faith was a process that took time and that being nurtured in the tradition, using the latest insights of pedagogy, was an important part of the process of making Christians. These changes took place amid the increasing conviction that ministers needed not just the insights that came from courses in the Biblical Department, but that courses in other parts of the University were important as well. What the churches needed were ministers broadly educated, for only with such a background could they be effective evangelists among middle-class people.

By the turn of the century Tillett and Kirkland were not a little discouraged.[34] They had hoped that as the years passed more Methodists committed to ministry would seek admission to the Biblical Department and enrollment would steadily increase. That was not happening. As late as June 1902, only thirty-nine students were enrolled, with another twenty-six "candidates" preparing for admission but enrolled in the Academic Department. Tillett and his colleagues hit upon a multifaceted strategy to show to the church, which still harbored reservations about the importance of theological education, that the Biblical Department could serve the needs of the ministry. The key to this new effort was the establishment of the Correspondence School. This was aimed primarily at that large body of young ministers preparing for ordination through enrollment in the Conference Course of Study, a program administered by the church but which church leaders increasingly came to view as inadequate. It was unevenly administered across the denomination by persons who were themselves not well informed. Most of the candidates, on the other hand, favored this system because it was the least costly alternative open to them and permitted them the opportunity to serve as ministers while engaged in this minimal educational venture. A Correspondence School, then, was an advance over the old system in addressing the problem of ministerial education.[35] It was approved by the General Conference of 1900 and became part of the program of the Biblical Department in 1902.

Under the direction of J. L. Cuninggim, the new program embraced five different "methods," as they were called; the most important were a summer Biblical Institute, the establishment of an extension library from which books could be mailed to ministers on request, and a series of correspondence courses aimed at both laity and clergy but primarily directed at the latter. The faculty designed the courses, read the weekly papers prepared by students in the early years, and graded the examinations at the end of each course. The program was an immediate success, boasting an enrollment within five years of 1,017 persons in thirty-two different courses. In time the courses were graded: four or five "popular courses" for the laity, a four-year sequenced schedule of foundational courses for beginners in ministry, and several advanced courses for those who had completed the foundational work. By 1904, most annual conferences had decided that completion of the program and receipt of a certificate from the Correspondence School satisfied the educational requirements for ordination.

A second part of the Tillett/Cuninggim strategy was the establishment in 1899 of the Vanderbilt Biblical Institute, bringing ministers to the campus for one week in June to hear lectures by members of the faculty and other national leaders and to participate in discussions on the practice of ministry. Although intended for ministerial candidates in the vicinity of Nashville, it quickly evolved into a major gathering of ministers from across the church and in time was attracting many non-Methodists as well. In 1911, with more than 200 persons registered, it was reported that "at several sessions a Jewish rabbi, an Adventist preacher, Episcopalian rectors, Presbyterian ministers, Baptists, Disciples, Lutherans, and Methodists were so in evidence that the meeting had the spirit of a great religious congress."[36] Increasingly, the Biblical Department appealed to persons from all Christian traditions, one of the evidences that Tillett and his staff would point to later, when the Department sought to become a School of Religion, open to persons of all religious faiths.

Movement toward Crisis

From the school's inception, many southern Methodists had ambivalent feelings about Vanderbilt; as the years passed, those feelings did not change. On the one hand Methodists were proud that this institution, which had cost them almost nothing, was increasingly recognized nationally for the excellence of its programs. University officers had worked hard at binding the University to the church. Bishops had been prominent in the leadership on the Board of Trust; Chancellors Garland and Kirkland had taken active leadership roles in the church; Tillett was highly respected across the denomination; members of the Biblical Department faculty tirelessly traveled the church lecturing, preaching, and teaching. Every effort was made to establish the University in the hearts of southern Methodists as an institution of which they could be proud and which they could trust.

But the best efforts of Kirkland, Tillett, and others did not erase all doubt. Suspicion remained, born of the gulf between the church's membership, which knew nothing of life in a university, and the faculty, who sought to work on the frontiers of knowledge, unencumbered by past traditions. Church members knew something of the controversies that universities "up north" had provoked. Would Vanderbilt be any different? The Winchell case (see Chapter 2) confirmed the suspicions of those Methodists who wanted to believe that universities generally were antithetical to the interests of genuine Christian faith; his dismissal by the Board of Trust in 1878 did little to assuage those views. Other concerns sustained those suspicions, such as the appointment of non-Methodists to the University faculty. The Board of Trust had never insisted that only Methodists be appointed; indeed, from the beginning, non-Methodists were given teaching posts. But the matter came to a head in 1904, when the renewal of a faculty position for Herbert Z. Kip came before the Board of Trust. Kip, a Presbyterian, had been appointed in 1901 as adjunct professor of German. In every way he had fulfilled his contract acceptably, leading Kirkland to recommend his reappointment. Some Board members, especially conservative Bishop Warren A. Candler, expressed reservations, pointing to his Presbyterian church affiliation. By their count, there were many more non-Methodists on the faculty than Methodists. "We are not illiberal or bigoted," they insisted, "but we submit that this is out of all proportion, and must necessarily tend to estrange the University from the church and the church from the University."[37]

The matter was resolved in Kip's favor when Kirkland cast his affirmative vote, but that did not end the matter. The more Kirkland reflected on the debate within the Board, the angrier he became. He decided he had no alternative but to resign. This he did in a communication to the chair of the Board, Bishop Robert Hargrove. Aghast at the prospect that the University might lose its beloved chancellor, Hargrove immediately called a special meeting of the Board. Kirkland explained that his policy had always been, all other things being equal, to appoint Methodists, but that ultimately he was concerned to appoint the most competent faculty the University could attract. He interpreted the close vote as one of no confidence in his leadership. The minutes of the meeting do not provide insight into the debate, only the decision that was reached. Henceforth, faculty appointments would be made without regard to denominational affiliation, except in the Biblical Department. Kirkland had won, but Candler and others in the church saw this episode as evidence that the church needed further control of the institution.

Meanwhile, the MECS was experiencing significant membership growth and geographical expansion, causing its thirteen episcopal leaders to call for an expansion of their numbers. Such a proposal had implications for the Vanderbilt Board of Trust. From 1894 all bishops were *ex officio* members of the Board.[38] Although many of them were not active participants in its deliberations, the possibility existed that at some future time they could become a controlling block, especially because the Board was limited by Tennessee statute to thirty-three members. At the same time Kirkland increasingly felt the need to expand the number of businessmen and lawyers on the Board, not to mention alumni who pressed him for representation.

At the Board of Trust meeting in June 1905, Kirkland proposed that the University seek a new charter from the state. Above all he wanted to clarify the relationship of the University to the church. He intended to establish the complete autonomy of the Board and thereby divest any claims that all members of the College of Bishops might have to Board membership. He proposed that five of the bishops, those most senior in service, be elected to regular membership, with limited terms like all other members. The proposal went to a five-member committee that included three bishops; it supported Kirkland's recommendation, as did the full Board later without a dissenting vote.

This action of the Board further fueled the suspicions of many within the leadership, including a minority of the bishops, that the University was not "thoroughly loyal" to the church and was on a trajectory toward secularization. Bishop Elijah E. Hoss, a former member of the Biblical Department faculty, emerged as the champion of this view. He had been out of the country when the Board made its decision. When he heard of the action, he was furious and launched a crusade to reverse the decision, which if successful would require action of the next General Conference of the denomination.

The "Vanderbilt situation" was a hot topic at the General Conference of 1906. It was inevitable that it would reach the Conference floor for debate. In the end, cooler heads prevailed; the Conference decided that it could not resolve the many questions in dispute and that those questions needed the attention of legal experts. A committee of five Methodist lawyers was appointed. The membership of the "Vanderbilt Commission," as the group became known, pleased Kirkland. He was convinced that the action of the Board of Trust would receive a sympathetic hearing.

Two important issues came before this body.[39] The first was the legal relationship of the church to the University. The Board of Trust's position was that the founder of the University was Cornelius Vanderbilt, not the church. Consequently, the Board was within its power to determine its own membership. But the Commission insisted that the University's founder was the church, through the representatives of the nine annual conferences that convened in Memphis in 1872. Hence, the church, through its agency the General Conference, had authority over the Board of Trust and could determine the Board's membership. The second related to the "charter rights" of the bishops. While the Commission agreed with the Vanderbilt position that the bishops did not have *ex officio* membership on the Board of Trust, it maintained that the College of Bishops could legitimately function as a "board of visitors" with authority to veto actions that it believed were antithetical to the interests of the church. Attributing such powers to the College of Bishops rested upon a long legal tradition derived from English common law.

Kirkland and members of the Board were heartsick over the Commission's conclusions. Hoss, Candler, and their supporters were elated. How would these conflicting views be reconciled? The meeting of the General Conference in 1910 became the arena of conflict. Meanwhile, those bishops who had been active participants in the governance of the University through membership on the Board of Trust resigned their positions. It was clear that their first loyalty had to be to the church; for two or three, being forced to divide their loyalties was a bitter pill.

Even before the 1910 General Conference convened in Asheville, North Carolina, it was clear that the church would seek to exercise its authority over the University. Resolutions from many annual conferences urging the General Conference to reclaim Vanderbilt for the church made clear the eventual outcome of the struggle. Confrontation could be avoided only if Kirkland and the Board of Trust renounced their position, which they refused to do. In due course the Vanderbilt Commission's report reached the floor and was adopted. Believing they had authority to name the Vanderbilt trustees, the Conference delegates elected three men to fill vacancies on the Board. The Conference also gave the College of Bishops and the church's Board of Education authority to sue in court in defense of the rights of the church if necessary.

At its annual meeting a few weeks later, the Board of Trust formally received the action of the General Conference. Two of the three men elected to the Board by the Conference attended. While their presence was courteously acknowledged, the Board refused to seat them. Instead it moved to elect other trustees to fill all vacancies and then took the unprecedented step of refusing to submit the names of the newly elected members to the Board of Education for ratification. This was followed by a vote to rescind the by-law requiring that the names of trustees be passed before the Board of Education for ratification. In effect the University had declared its autonomy from the church.

For months the whole of southern Methodism and, increasingly, many outside that fold, especially in higher education, watched with fixed attention the events surrounding the Vanderbilt controversy. As is so often the case, the merits did not always decide which side individuals took. For weeks emotions ran high; neutrality was virtually impossible. Some stood with Vanderbilt against what they believed was a move by a backwater church, led by Hoss and his supporters, concerned to stifle the advancement of truth. On the other side Kirkland was portrayed as the devil stealing from God's people what rightfully belonged to the Lord and planning to develop a secular university robbed of faith's rightful place. Between these polar positions were many who were concerned with the legal merits of the case and others who desperately looked for a mediating position between the extremes, one that would hold the University and church together. The struggle was no local affair: it had significant and far-reaching implications for religious education in the United States.

The refusal by the Board of Trust to seat the trustees elected by the Conference produced the expected results. In October 1910, suit was filed by representatives of the church in the Davidson County Chancery Court. Underlying the particulars were two important issues: the right of the Board of Trust to determine its own membership, and the relationship of the University to the MECS. On February 21, 1913, the Chancery Court decided in favor of the church—the church owned Vanderbilt and had the right to name its trustees. All actions of the Board of Trust contrary to these assumptions were declared null. As expected, Vanderbilt appealed. A year later, on March 21, 1914, the Supreme Court of Tennessee handed down its decision. Overturning the judgment of the lower court, it ruled that the Vanderbilt Board of Trust had authority to name its membership (subject to the long-standing practice of passing the names of newly appointed members before the Methodist Board of Education for confirmation), that Cornelius Vanderbilt was the founder of the University, and that the College of Bishops had no visitorial powers over the University. The Court also stated that if the church refused in good faith to abide by this ruling, its participation in the management of the University would close and the Board of Trust could proceed as an autonomous institution to conduct its business.

Approximately three months later, the General Conference of the MECS opened its quadrennial meeting in Oklahoma City. Some were so angered and bitter that they saw no alternative but to sever all ties with the University; others of a more generous spirit argued that the church's relationship to Vanderbilt should go forward as before; a few wanted to press further legal remedies and appeal to the U.S. Supreme Court. A special committee was appointed to bring forth a recommendation, and both a majority and a minority report were eventually presented. The majority report recommended that all relations between the University and the church be abrogated and that the church take steps to

found two new universities.[40] The minority report called for a continuing relationship between the University and the church and recommended that the
Conference assert its right in the confirmation of trustees and in time work
toward changing the leadership of the University. On the floor of the Conference, angry, emotional speeches presented the many sides of the matter. The
final vote was 151–140 in favor of the majority report's recommendation. The
die was cast; from that day forward the formal relationship between Vanderbilt
University and the church was severed.

Even during this period of turmoil, enrollment in the Biblical Department
continued to grow, reaching a peak in 1911–12, when 119 degree students were
enrolled, along with 15 candidates in the Academic Department. Students arrived from virtually all annual conferences with bachelor degrees in hand, signs
that Vanderbilt was more and more seen as the place where prospective ministers
could prepare themselves. The Biblical Department was able to function more
clearly as a graduate professional institution than ever before. Adjustments were
also made in course offerings and degree requirements. Beginning in 1907,
students no longer could earn a certificate by completing the English Course.
Those entering without an undergraduate degree could still receive a diploma
upon completing the Classical Course, but most came prepared to fulfill the
B.D. requirements. In that same year the "elective system" became a feature of
the curriculum. The increased size of the faculty meant that students no longer
could be expected to study with all the teachers. From 1908, persons could earn
the B.D. degree having studied only one of the biblical languages.

We have very little evidence of how students and faculty of the Biblical
Department viewed the crisis that engulfed the church and the University. We
can assume that it was a subject of increasing concern as the issue rolled toward a
climax. Tillett's papers are amazingly silent about the matter. Only once or
twice did he betray his own concern and his hope, indeed his expectation, that a
catastrophe would be averted. In his report to the Board of Trust in June 1914,
following the action of the General Conference, he wrote:

> I can but believe that the Biblical Department . . . which has now in the
> active work of the Methodist ministry at home and abroad about 850 of
> its former students will accomplish a yet greater work for the Church
> [i.e., MECS] in the future. I am glad to believe that the emblem of the
> cross with its inspiring words "in hoc signo vinces" has never yet be-
> come less but rather all the more an emblem of victory when, wrapped
> around with the black and the gold, the colors of their Alma Mater, it is
> borne forward in faith and fidelity by our Vanderbilt boys and planted
> in all places where God has called these boys to preach the gospel.[41]

That was not to happen. Never again would the Biblical Department have formal ties with the MECS.

Following the action of the General Conference of 1914, the University was confronted with several questions: Should it continue its program of theological education? Was such a venture even thinkable without a church constituency feeding students into the program? If continued, how would it be funded? What would be the shape of such a program? Answers did not come quickly. After the dust of controversy had settled a bit, Chancellor Kirkland, with Tillett's blessing and urging, decided that while the University was no longer formally tied to the MECS, there was no reason why a special contract could not be reached between the University and the church whereby the Biblical Department would be the joint responsibility of both parties. Such an arrangement would require each to contribute to its financial support and share in its governance. Kirkland made it clear that the University would continue to contribute the sums that it had in the past, but more than that it could not do. The church, which had been quite stingy in the past, would now have to pick up the balance.

Tillett most likely was the individual selected to float this possibility before the church's leadership. In the end, the idea came to naught. The church would have nothing to do with any part of Vanderbilt, and Methodists who had any ongoing relationship to the institution were viewed almost as traitors. Students enrolled in the Biblical Department were the most vulnerable to such pressures, and they defected in large numbers. In 1914–15 their numbers declined by 60 percent from the previous year, to thirty-eight students. Even Tillett did not survive untouched. The bishop presiding over the Tennessee Conference refused to appoint him to the deanship; he was appointed instead as "assistant pastor of the West End Methodist Church"; he continued to function, of course, as dean of the Biblical Department.[42]

A new vision was needed for the Biblical Department, one that offered a genuine prospect for the future. Doubtless it emerged in time through extended conversations with many people, but Tillett was clearly a major contributor. Our first glimpse of that vision comes from Chancellor Kirkland's report to the Board of Trust in June 1915. He proposed that the Biblical Department become a nondenominational School of Religion; that its faculty be expanded to include scholars of differing denominational commitments; and that it broaden its mission to include, not only the training of men for ministry, but persons for specialized religious work, such as social workers, directors of YMCA programs, and Sunday School workers. It was a bold vision, unprecedented in the South, though there was some precedent in the North. Would it work? Only time would tell. With Tillett still at the helm, though, it had a better than even chance.

4

Charting a New Vision:
The School of Religion

James P. Byrd, Jr.

THE SCHOOL OF RELIGION AROSE AT A MOMENT IN AMERICAN theological education when major divinity schools sought no less than to redeem the nation and to inaugurate the Kingdom of God. As Conrad Cherry expresses it, the theological schools at Yale, Harvard, Chicago, and Union (New York) were "hurrying toward Zion" in the late nineteenth and early twentieth centuries. Not satisfied with serving denominations, these schools intended "to shape the culture of the nation" by joining "the mission of the church with the educational venture of the emerging modern university."[1] This university context was crucial for theological schools that sought to influence an educated, modern America. With the intellectual leverage of the modern university behind them, theological educators such as Charles W. Eliot of Harvard and William Rainey Harper of Chicago endeavored to liberate theological truth from the confines of the churches and apply it to modern society.

This agenda required a reformulated version of Christian theology that could meet the standards of all modern forms of inquiry within the university, especially scientific method. Furthermore, if theology were to influence a nation rather than merely a particular church tradition, it had to be liberated from the restrictive demands of the denominational seminary. The location of theology strictly within the confines of a denominational school smacked of "sectarianism," which limited theological truth within a specific tradition.[2] Meeting the needs of society required more than narrow focus on doctrine; it demanded that theology speak to the broader ethical issues that confronted an urbanized and industrialized American society. Therefore, equipped with a theology that was ecumenical in scope and ethical in application, interdenominational divinity schools strove to reform American society, hoping to inaugurate the Kingdom of God in the twentieth century.[3]

The School of Religion adopted this vision, noting in a 1916 issue of the Vanderbilt *Alumnus* that the newly independent and newly named school intended to be a southern representation of the theological "mission" that guided Union, Yale, and Chicago.[4] While this vision would undergo minor changes over the next forty years, the central purpose remained constant: the School of Religion devoted critical religious inquiry to the task of improving American society, not just the American churches. It endeavored to apply a northern, nondenominational, liberal vision to the conservative and denominational South. This presented the greatest challenge, for the faculty and administration of the school knew that Nashville was not New Haven. Throughout its history, the School of Religion faced the conflict between its vision and its southern context.

The Costs of a Southern "Zion": Financial Crisis and the Aftershocks of 1914

The School of Religion originally embraced this nondenominational vision as a survival tactic in the aftermath of 1914. In his report to the Board of Trust in June 1914, Chancellor James H. Kirkland proposed either that "a new adjustment" be worked out between the School of Religion and the Methodist General Conference or that the Board of Trust consider discontinuing the school.[5] In the hope of continued cooperation, the Board of Trust resolved that, despite the dissolution of ties with the church, Vanderbilt University remained committed to the conviction that all "learning" should be "dedicated to the highest service of God." Furthermore, the Board desired that the "technical" division would not "destroy the friendly association between the University and the Methodist Church." The most urgent need for a continued "friendly" relationship was in the Biblical Department, which depended on the denomination for funding and students more than any other department in the University.[6] Only after the church refused continued cooperation did the Board of Trust announce the name change to the "School of Religion" and the accompanying reorganization of the school on an interdenominational basis. As Kirkland reported in 1915, the events of the previous year "forced" the Biblical Department to adopt "a more general program which we have indicated under the title of a 'School of Religion.'"[7]

After one year, however, the future of the new school was in peril. Kirkland reported to the Board of Trust that the School of Religion had the financial means to operate for only two more years, thanks to additional funds that the Methodist Church still owed the school from a previous commitment. However, he asserted that the Board need not wait two years to consider the long-term financial viability of a nondenominational school in the South. In Kirkland's view, such a school would need to surpass the former Biblical Department in both the size and denominational diversity of its faculty. In addition, a respectable nondenominational school would need the means to offer broader programs of study to train students to serve in social ministries outside the confines of the parish. Kirkland regarded the present faculty as too Methodist and too focused on traditional ministerial training to readjust to this broader challenge. Furthermore, he believed that an interdenominational school would need a "regular publication" to call attention to the school and its programs. All these aspects demanded funding that far surpassed that of the former Biblical Department. He estimated that such a school would need an endowment of at least $500,000, an amount that the School of Religion had little hope of raising without the help of a generous benefactor. Even if that amount were secured, it might still be insufficient for so grand an enterprise. Kirkland noted that Yale's endowment of $1 million was not wholly adequate for its Divinity School. His point was clear: if the Vanderbilt School of Religion wanted to establish itself as a southern Yale, it needed to attract comparable funding. Kirkland's inclination was to abandon the effort. He believed that Vanderbilt should consider discontinuing its theological school "with honor rather than to perpetuate a department of work so crippled as to be of little service and no credit."[8]

Kirkland continued to be discouraged throughout the 1915–16 academic year, as the School of Religion, depleted by the Methodist exodus, hobbled along with only forty students.[9] The school survived the year because of the annual $12,000 contribution from the University, $3,500 in gifts, $2,000 that the Methodist Church had previously committed, and $2,000 in rental income from Wesley Hall. More important, it survived because of the diligent efforts of Dean Wilbur Fisk Tillett. Kirkland acknowledged that "no sacrifice has been too great, no labor too arduous" for Tillett and the School of Religion faculty in their efforts to keep the school alive.

Among the survival tactics that Tillett engineered was the development of a summer school in 1915 and 1916. In order to strengthen the School of Religion, Tillett and his faculty volunteered their services to hold the summer school in conjunction with Peabody College. While Kirkland applauded their intentions, he disapproved of a summer school that did not attract serious students, but rather "a less meritorious clientele" composed primarily of women who sought "entertainment" or "culture" during the summer. He also thought it inadvisable for professors to neglect their vacation time to teach summer school without remuneration. Finally, he disapproved of developing a summer school when the University was still "wholly undecided as to the future of the department during the nine months of the college year." However, since the faculty did not ask for additional funding for the summer school, Kirkland could hardly forbid them from volunteering their time. Regardless of his qualms about the future of the school, Kirkland praised Tillett and the faculty for their efforts to save Vanderbilt the blow "to its pride and prestige that would have come from a forcible closing" of the school. However, he reasserted his pessimistic judgment that, "pride and prestige" aside, the University still had to face the hard reality that Vanderbilt may not have the means to support an interdenominational school.[10]

Kirkland's comments reveal an ambivalent attitude toward the School of Religion. From one perspective, he welcomed a departure from a Methodist-controlled Biblical Department, for he believed that denominational ties embarrassed northern contributors and improperly restricted any modern university.[11] He seemed buoyed by the prospects of a school that, as he put it, "stands for the Kingdom of God rather than for any denomination, that emphasizes religion rather than theology, service rather than creeds, that approaches its problems from the standpoint of science rather than of authority, that prepares workers not for the ministry only, but for all lines of social and religious activities."[12] From another perspective, however, Kirkland despaired of the prospect of such a school in a conservative, southern context. He recognized that abandoning the School of Religion could actually prove favorable to the rest of the University by softening "some of the enmity felt against the University in Methodist circles." Specifically, he expressed concern that the Methodist Church viewed the school as "an effort to entice Methodist preachers away from their denominational" institutions. During this early period, he seems to have preferred incorporating the School of Religion into a small department of religion in the College.[13]

In the face of Kirkland's pessimism, the faculty persevered in their attempts to save the school. In 1916, a committee composed of School of Religion faculty members convinced the Board of Trust to postpone discussion of the future of the school. The committee argued that, even at the cost of financial strain, the prospect of an interdenominational school in the South remained "a highly important and promising experiment." The committee pointed to the growth of liberal, nondenominational divinity schools in America and their prophetic role in the nation, and it reasoned that this held great promise for the future support of a similar school at Vanderbilt. In support of this bright prospect, the committee presented letters that Tillett had secured from leading religious educators in America who applauded "the ideals of the School" and predicted its eventual emergence as a "prophetic" voice in the South. Further, it reminded the Board of Trust that "a divinity school was fundamental in the thought of the two men who originated Vanderbilt University—[Holland N.] McTyeire and Cornelius Vanderbilt."[14] The Board of Trust approved this report, thereby suspending the death sentence of the school.

The school's survival remained questionable in 1917–18, when enrollment dipped to thirty-seven, and its chances declined even more when only twenty-one students arrived for study the following fall. In June 1918, the Board of Trust ordered the Executive Committee to undertake a year-long study to ascertain whether the school should continue.[15] In all likelihood, the Executive Committee would have decided to close the school had it not been for the intervention of the Young Men's Christian Association (YMCA). During the following school year, a committee of the YMCA, chaired by W. D. Weatherford, proposed that the School of Religion serve as the site for a southern "School for training YMCA Workers." This proposal added at least fifty students to the struggling School of Religion, and Weatherford promised to assist the school in its search for a $500,000 endowment. Kirkland was optimistic that the YMCA would bring "a new impulse and a new life" to a declining operation. Due to this new prospect, the Board of Trust again postponed discussion of abandoning the school.[16] Not only did the YMCA save the school from dissolution, but its participation also provided avenues for the school to pursue its mission of training students for careers in social work.

As this new initiative took shape, Tillett resigned the office of dean after thirty-three years, opting to continue teaching systematic theology as a member of the faculty. Tillett had kept the school alive until the YMCA intervened to delay its closing. However, the battle for its survival was not over. Kirkland appointed Oswald E. Brown, professor of church history, to succeed Tillett; the school's tenuous position probably led Kirkland to name an inside person. Although the intervention of the YMCA postponed discussion of the school's survival, the issue remained undecided as the new dean took office.

The Struggle for Survival in the 1920s

The School of Religion's struggles continued in the early 1920s. The YMCA College brought a much needed enrollment boost. Other support came from rentals in Wesley Hall, profits from a new cafeteria, and the annual $12,000 allowance from the University. Questions remained, however, about the need for an interdenominational school in the South. The graduation of only four

B.D. students in 1923 provided evidence of the apparent lack of interest in the school's ministerial programs. Indeed, nearly half of the twenty-three students enrolled in 1923 were pursuing an M.A. in the College. As Paul Conkin put it, many of these students were taking courses in the School of Religion "as an easy back door into the graduate program of the College."[17] The faculty of the School of Religion encouraged this practice and proposed that these students be allowed to take all of their course work there and still receive the M.A. This practice irked Kirkland, who regarded it as "turning the School of Religion into a graduate school" of Arts and Science. He remarked that "if the Bachelor of Divinity program has lost its attraction," then the School of Religion has lost its "drawing power" and perhaps its usefulness to the University.[18]

In response to such questions about the School of Religion's viability, Brown and Tillett published an article in the 1924 *Alumnus*, arguing that it had played a primary role in the history of Vanderbilt University. This article reminded the Vanderbilt community that "in the minds of those who brought about the establishment of the University, the theological or biblical department held the foremost place."[19] But statements of the school's historic place in the University would have been irrelevant had it been unable to locate adequate funding. That task fell to Henry B. Carré, professor of Bible. As director of the School of Religion Expansion Fund, Carré highlighted the ambitious mission of the school, as in the attractive brochure entitled "The Vanderbilt School of Religion: A Statement of Its Place in the Field of Theological Education, as Well as of the Reasons Why It Should Be Adequately Endowed and Equipped" (1924). In his case for the support of the school, Carré placed it alongside Harvard and other major divinity schools that had outgrown denominational roots to embrace a nondenominational vision. He even painted a rosy portrait of 1914, arguing that the nondenominational status of the school resulted from a "fortuitous" battle between the University and the Methodist Church that allowed the School of Religion to achieve nondenominational status without "becoming a storm center" of theological controversy, which would have alienated churches and caused bitterness in the region.[20]

In keeping with the social vision of the major divinity schools, Carré argued that the School of Religion deserved an increased endowment because it served not only churches but the society as well. He emphasized that religious training was vital to "the advancement of civilization" in the twentieth century because religion served to control "unregulated passions," the chief causes of human suffering in the world.[21] No doubt this concern motivated his own work as the seventeen-year chair of the Anti-Saloon League of Tennessee.[22] He stressed the need for schools that would properly train religious leaders, who in turn would guide the emotional life of the nation and encourage "the progress of society in the future of America." Carré also called for a "Kingdom of God" that would incorporate modern science and eliminate "war, race antipathies, and class antagonism," the emotional maladies that imprisoned millions of people, "consigning them to ignorance, poverty, disease, and crime." He appealed for funds on behalf of this "Kingdom" that the School of Religion sought to build, both in human hearts and in "social institutions."[23] He could hardly have presented a better statement of the school's effort to join better-established divinity schools in pursuit of the reformation of American society.

Carré realized that the School of Religion was distinctive because it was southern. It was a pioneer institution that promised to adapt the vision of the "Big Four" schools of the North (Yale, Harvard, Chicago, and Union) to the educationally deprived South. To emphasize this identification with the agenda of the "Big Four," he included in the brochure a letter from Shailer Mathews, dean of the Divinity School of the University of Chicago, in which he praised the School of Religion because it sought to instigate a "modern view of religion in the South."[24]

Mathews's endorsement notwithstanding, the success of the project depended upon Carré's ability to prove that the South needed the "modern view of religion" that the School of Religion offered. To support his argument, he seized upon two pressing problems that plagued the South: denominationalism and racism. First, he argued that the interdenominational school would provide a positive force in a solidly denominational context. Due to its "rigidity and fixedness," the South needed ministers with training in an "interdenominational atmosphere" who could "lift" the South "out of its hard and fast denominational lines." Second, Carré referred to "the race problem" that marred the South more severely than any other region in the nation. By educating ministers in an "atmosphere of toleration and fraternity," he argued that an interdenominational school could loosen racial animosities and promote peace and unity. He called upon Mrs. Booker T. Washington to support his claim for the school's treatment of the race problem. She obliged him by writing a letter that expressed the need for classes on interracial understanding such as those proposed by the School of Religion. F. A. McKenzie, president of Fisk University, also wrote in support, calling the school a prophetic voice of "peace and reconciliation" in race relations. These and other letters testified that the School of Religion, in proclaiming the social witness of the Christian Gospel, would do a great service to southern culture.[25]

Largely due to Carré's tireless efforts, John D. Rockefeller, Jr., responded to the need and promise of the school by donating matching grants of up to $25,000 annually for five years.[26] Rockefeller considered the gifts an experiment on the question of whether an interdenominational School of Religion could

successfully carve out a niche for itself in the South.[27] His generosity both
encouraged and challenged the school. An annual matching requirement of
$25,000 was a monumental undertaking for a school struggling to survive.
Nevertheless, it accepted the challenge by launching a campaign to raise the
funds to match Rockefeller's annual contributions.

In this expansion drive, the focus of attention turned to the founding of an
annual Rural Church School that would educate rural ministers in the South.
This project fit perfectly with the vision of an interdenominational school that
served the social needs of the South, and it coincided as well with one of
Rockefeller's interests. Beginning in 1927, it was open to rural ministers regardless of denominational affiliation and provided short courses on subjects
such as Farm Problems, Auto Mechanics, the Church as a Community Center,
Social Messages of the Prophets, the Church and Rural Life, and other topics
that concerned country preachers. In keeping with the concern of the School
of Religion to emphasize social ministry and ethics rather than doctrine, the
Rural Church School trained ministers to "act as social leaders" who were more
than "interpreters of doctrinal standards" in their communities. Its success provided an unprecedented and unexpected boost to the School of Religion. In
1928, it enrolled 370 men and 5 women representing 17 states and 20 denominations. By 1929, it had blossomed to the point that it had to turn down hundreds
of interested applicants. This success attracted the Atlanta Theological Seminary, a small Congregationalist school, to move to Vanderbilt in 1929, continuing in the School of Religion as a separate foundation under the direction of
William J. Campbell that supported persons of that denomination studying for
the ministry.[28]

The Rural Church School brought greatly needed publicity to the School
of Religion. The *Chattanooga Times* called it a progressive influence on the
South that combated denominational divisiveness and, in uniting the churches,
promised to increase Christian potential "for the healing of the nation." Word
about the programs even reached the Southwest, where the *Tulsa Tribune* encouraged ministers in rural Oklahoma to attend so that intellectual enlightenment would improve their ability to minister in their communities. This
increased publicity stimulated the School of Religion Expansion Campaign
considerably and secured pledges for $164,000—more than enough to match
Rockefeller's five-year gift.[29]

Despite the excitement, publicity, and increased pledges generated for the
School of Religion, Kirkland remained skeptical. He appreciated that the Rural
Church School had served rural ministers and had "seemed to fire the imagination of all classes of people." However, Kirkland insisted that this program was "a
very superficial task" that remained "outside our regular University work" and

could not become "a permanent part of our School of Religion." He also complained that social work had dominated the School of Religion, eclipsing its more important scholarly work.[30]

The School of Religion and Fundamentalist Opposition

The most visible affront to the school's liberal stance arose when Tennessee became the site of fundamentalist opposition to the theory of biological evolution. In March 1925, the Tennessee legislature passed a bill that prevented public school teachers from considering the theory of biological evolution in the classroom. The violation of this law by John T. Scopes, who taught science in Dayton, Tennessee, initiated a trial that captured media attention across the country. Clarence Darrow defended Scopes against William Jennings Bryan, an avid anti-evolutionist, in the so-called "monkey trial." Although Scopes lost the trial, Darrow humiliated Bryan in court, turning him into a laughingstock, and depicting his stand against evolution as intellectually indefensible. After the trial, the fundamentalist movement became the object of national ridicule, with reporters characterizing fundamentalists as ignorant, southern hicks.[31] As Conrad Cherry put it, the Scopes trial "routed" fundamentalism's status "as a significant cultural power" in the nation.[32] Fundamentalism, however, retained much of its power in Tennessee.

As Tennessee's only university of national reputation during the Scopes debacle, Vanderbilt provided an easy target for southern fundamentalists. Many southerners apparently agreed with a letter to the *Tennessean* in 1925 arguing that the evolution law was necessary to protect youth against "professors and preachers" who "have been poisoned with the deadly nightshade of infidelity, parading under the habiliments of science."[33] Such a statement showed the ideological chasm that separated Vanderbilt from much of the South—the very people whom the University sought to serve by advancing modern science and liberal religion.

The fundamentalist controversy posed an especially acute challenge to the School of Religion. As the chief advocate for liberal theology in a largely conservative South, it faced criticism from the local population. The media attention of the Scopes trial strengthened the school's argument to northern benefactors that the South sorely needed a liberal school of religion. At the same time, a school that claimed to be a proponent of critical religious inquiry in the South could not remain silent in the face of rampant fundamentalism. As Kirkland put it, the debacle at Dayton called for a School of Religion that espoused "the strength of a common faith and the glory of a universal worship" against "a narrow sectarianism and a belligerent fundamentalism."[34]

Vanderbilt struck its chief blow against fundamentalism in *God and the New Knowledge* (1926), a book that contained essays by Kirkland, Dean Brown, and Edwin Mims from the English Department. These essays derided fundamentalist parochialism and asserted the compatibility of modern science and liberal Christianity. *God and the New Knowledge* denied the claims that belief in evolution necessarily led to materialism that "abandoned faith in God for the findings of modern science" and that modern biblical interpretation robbed the Bible of "sacredness" and authority. Brown's essay presented a textbook modernist attack on fundamentalism. On the issue of evolution as a challenge to Christianity, Brown argued that "scientific truth" is compatible with "spiritual truth." In addition, he insisted that traditional creeds were limited statements that needed periodic revision rather than legal documents that defined orthodoxy for all time. On the thorny issue of biblical interpretation, Brown shocked fundamentalist sensibilities by suggesting that God intentionally allowed some errors in the Bible in order "to challenge and stimulate faith," since an "absolutely plain and simple" Bible allowed no room for faith.[35] With *God and the New Knowledge*, Vanderbilt, and especially the School of Religion, openly aligned itself with the forces of American liberal Protestantism and served notice that it intended to represent in the South the vision of Yale, Harvard, Chicago, and Union.

Financial Depression and Curricular Compromise in the 1930s

While the Rural Church School and the fundamentalist controversies brought publicity to the School of Religion in the 1920s, this heightened visibility concealed deep financial problems. The school had succeeded in raising the $125,000 to match Rockefeller's gift. However, most of the funds supported the Rural Church School. At the end of the five years, the School of Religion owed $57,000 to the University. In 1928, during the height of the campaign, Carré died, leaving Dean Brown in charge of the fundraising. Brown believed that the growth of the School of Religion during the five-year period, especially the popularity of the Rural Church School, would convince Rockefeller to donate at least $500,000, perhaps even $1 million, for the endowment. In pursuit of this additional help, Kirkland and Brown wrote to Rockefeller in March 1930, reporting on the progress of the school and asking for a gift of $1 million for an endowment. Rockefeller rejected this request, but he offered to renew the annual matching gifts of up to $25,000 for five additional years (1931–36). In addition, Rockefeller offered to match any gifts toward endowment up to $500,000 during the same period.[36] Thus, the School of Religion faced the continuing problem of raising matching funds in the midst of a national economic depression.

A change in leadership accompanied these financial straits. A decline in health forced Brown to retire as dean in August 1930. At Brown's request, Tillett stepped in as acting dean until his own ill health forced him to resign only two months later. Kirkland's doubts about the survival of the school prompted him again to forgo a major search for a new dean. Instead, he appointed George B. Winton, lecturer in history of religion and Christian missions, as acting dean in October.[37]

The economic depression of the early 1930s nearly forced the School of Religion to close. Kirkland reported in 1932 that the school had little hope of matching Rockefeller's gifts for four additional years. In an act of desperation, he suggested a further appeal to Rockefeller, requesting that he soften the terms of his donations.[38] A few weeks later the desperation of the school multiplied when a devastating fire destroyed Wesley Hall, its home since 1881. The fire began on Friday afternoon, February 19, and raged until late that evening, destroying the interior, including the library and its 15,000 volumes, despite the efforts of students who rushed into the building and carried or threw out as many books as they could. Since Wesley Hall also served as a dormitory, its destruction displaced ten faculty and seventy-five student residents.[39] Most of these displaced residents found temporary homes in Kissam Hall, and the faculty relocated their offices to Neely Auditorium. The school endured these temporary facilities until 1936, when Vanderbilt acquired the old YMCA building and dedicated it as the new Wesley Hall.[40]

Coupled with the dire financial condition, the burning of Wesley Hall was almost the last straw. Yet the faculty and administration viewed the fire as an encouragement to increase their efforts on behalf of the school.[41] In their appeals for its survival, the constant refrain was the school's original vision that critical religious study played an essential role in the improvement of American society. The 1933 *Bulletin* appealed for support by arguing that "religion is basic for an enduring civilization" and "is the foundation of the social order." It warned that, without religious leadership, the "national character" would deteriorate. Therefore, money donated to liberal theological schools was "the finest social insurance" because these donations "will guarantee progressive reconstruction of our civilization." In light of these convictions, the *Bulletin* proclaimed confidence in donors who would support the attempt to provide "spiritual leadership," which is "the only stabilizing force against the overthrow of our civilization."[42] Consequently, during the time of its most urgent financial need, the school clung to the pursuit of Zion in America as the greatest justification of its existence.

The year 1936 loomed large as the beginning of the School of Religion's life without the matching gifts from Rockefeller. In order to survive, it had to reorganize itself, trimming its programs and realigning its budget. The major changes were the dismissal of Professor Alva Taylor and the dissolution of his

Department of Social Ethics. Taylor's arrival in 1928 had made perfect sense in light of the social vision of the school. He was an avid proponent of the Social Gospel, an ally of liberal theology in the drive to create a Christian America in the late nineteenth and early twentieth centuries. In expressing this hope for an American Zion, he asserted that "when science gives the technique and the Church gives the social passion, we will possess the power to make the world over into the kingdom of God."[43] Taylor brought these optimistic convictions to a receptive School of Religion, where he taught courses such as "The Ethics of Human Relations," which emphasized "the moral obligations of the United States as a Christian Nation." Taylor's zeal to Christianize America was somewhat at cross-purposes with Kirkland's attempt to build the school without alienating the Board of Trust and the wider community. Taylor's goals included reforming the nation's industrial system, pursuing world peace, and striving for the rights of African Americans.[44]

Kirkland denied that Taylor's radicalism played a role in his dismissal. When one of Taylor's supporters later wrote to protest his treatment, Kirkland replied that "Taylor was not removed from the Chair of Social Ethics, and no question of academic freedom was involved." He insisted that the financial crisis required a "complete adjustment of the School of Religion curriculum" and that the school determined that social ethics was expendable since the College offered courses in sociology. Led by Frank D. Alexander, secretary-treasurer of the School of Religion Alumni Committee, sixty alumni/ae submitted petitions to the Board of Trust in support of Taylor and his work. Offering to raise the money themselves to keep the chair, the alumni/ae argued that the Department of Sociology could not compensate for the loss of social ethics in the School of Religion, as Chancellor Kirkland suggested, because the courses were not congruous: "Courses offered by Dr. Taylor are taught from the Ethical, Christian point of view while in the courses in the Sociology Department the facts are studied without any religious evaluation." Additionally, the alumni/ae pleaded that the minister "must be acquainted with the total culture of his community." Ministerial candidates could not acquire that knowledge from Kirkland's reorganized curriculum.[45] Taylor offered the most practical pre-professional training in the School of Religion, alumnus John C. Granberry argued. "Especially at this time," Granberry pleaded, "our Southern Schools need men who are capable of interpreting events in a broad manner, in harmony with the welfare of the masses of people and with the demands of the new day."[46]

The Vanderbilt administration avoided publicly debating the need for social ethics, choosing instead to respond to the financial issues of the case. The Board discussed the petitions at its June 1936 meeting and referred the matter to the Executive Committee "with power to act." The Executive Committee then authorized Chancellor Kirkland to inform Frank D. Alexander that the alumni/ae offer failed to "relieve the University of definite financial responsibility."[47] Consequently, Kirkland dismissed "any effort to make [Taylor] a martyr to persecution" as "unfair and unfounded."[48]

Taylor disagreed, insisting that his liberal social teachings provoked his dismissal at the hands of Kirkland, whom Taylor called a "hard boiled old Czar."[49] In his study of the controversy, Conkin agreed with Taylor, claiming that Kirkland had become "increasingly authoritarian" and "almost paranoid" by the mid-1930s, and that the financial crisis merely provided Kirkland with "a good opportunity to be rid of Taylor."[50] To be sure, Kirkland had never fully supported the school's social vision, as demonstrated by his opposition to the Rural Church School despite Rockefeller's support and interest. Nevertheless, Kirkland's dismissal of Taylor had the support of Tillett, although Winton and Brown supported Taylor.[51] During the fundamentalist controversy, the School of Religion defended its vision of theological education against a hostile South. However, the financial crisis, coupled with Kirkland's bias against Taylor, prevented the school from mustering such fortitude in the Taylor case. With the dismissal of Taylor, the school lost an important component in its social mission to Christianize American society.

In 1936, the school appointed a new dean to guide it though the financial crisis. Umphrey Lee, who came to Vanderbilt from Southern Methodist University, embraced the school's mission to provide much needed religious guidance to America. He bemoaned the rise of secularism and the decline of the significance of theology in modern society. In Lee's assessment, a secular, scientific worldview had captured the allegiance of modern society, prompting "educated people" to turn from religious leaders to scientists and philosophers for authoritative guidance. He believed that Christianity's survival depended upon schools that trained "intellectual leaders in religion" who combined "knowledge of the Christian tradition" with an equally competent knowledge "of the social and intellectual world" in the twentieth century. This was the ambitious goal of the Vanderbilt School of Religion, even in the midst of financial crisis. Lee perceived that the school's best opportunity for success was to bypass "the easier way" and embrace "rigorous standards" of admission. These increased standards included for the first time an annual tuition fee of $150, beginning with the 1937–38 academic year. Lee realized that tougher standards meant lower enrollment. However, he reiterated that "the popularity of a correspondence school cannot be coupled with the demands of severe graduate training."[52]

John Keith Benton and the Recovery of the School of Religion

The late 1930s brought transition to the University and the School of Religion. In 1937, Kirkland resigned after forty-four years as chancellor and the

Board elected Oliver C. Carmichael as his successor. In the School of Religion, Dean Lee resigned in 1939 to accept the presidency of his alma mater, Southern Methodist University. Chancellor Carmichael chose John Keith Benton, an Alabama native with degrees from Yale and Edinburgh, to succeed Lee. Benton had a wide range of experience with Methodist higher education, coming to Vanderbilt from Duke, where he had been a visiting professor, after serving as professor of philosophy and psychology at Drew University for eight years.[53]

Benton brought a firm commitment to the academy and the church. Under his leadership, the School of Religion veered more toward training students for the parish ministry, with less emphasis on training for social work. Benton's emphasis on ministry elicited positive responses from denominations. A clear victory came in 1941, when the University Senate of the Methodist Church granted full accreditation to the School of Religion. Hence, the Methodist Church regarded ministerial training at the School of Religion equivalent to that of a Methodist school. Almost immediately, student enrollment increased. By 1942–43, seventy-four students were enrolled in the School of Religion, as compared with only twenty-five in 1937–38.[54]

Another indication of the School of Religion's recovery was the development of the library. After the devastation of Wesley Hall, the surviving books were stored in Buttrick Hall until they could be moved to the school's new location. In 1936, John Kesler, Professor Emeritus of Religious Education, secured a grant of $6,000 from the Carnegie Corporation for an extension library to serve rural ministers. Together with librarian Grace Newell Teague, Kesler oversaw the growth of this library to a circulation of more than 87,000 volumes by 1945. The library also found a new home, moving in 1941 to the new Joint University Libraries building. This move gave Benton the luxury of advanced library facilities at no added expense to the school.

Benton and the school received a powerful ally with the arrival in 1946 of Vanderbilt's fourth chancellor, Harvie Branscomb. Before coming to Vanderbilt, he had served for two years as dean of the Divinity School at Duke University. He was an accomplished scholar in New Testament literature, with publications that included *Jesus and the Law of Moses* (1930), *The Teachings of Jesus* (1931), and *The Gospel According to Mark* (1937).[55] From the beginning of his career at Vanderbilt, Branscomb proved to be an advocate of the School of Religion. At the June 1947 meeting of the Board of Trust, he decried the fact that financial crises had forced the school into a "threadbare existence." He called it one of Vanderbilt's "most distinguished schools," praising its great service to the South and to the world at large through the training of missionaries for various denominations. In addition, Branscomb credited the academic leadership of the school with preventing the Methodist Episcopal Church, South from retreating into fundamentalism in the 1920s. Branscomb worked closely with Benton to strengthen the school's program of training students in practical, ministerial skills. He praised the independent standing of the school, but cautioned that "nondenominational" did not denote non-affiliation and isolation from "denominational contacts," such as the associations already held with Congregationalists, Disciples of Christ, and Presbyterians.[56]

The Benton and Branscomb years brought an end to serious questions about the survival of the School of Religion. A new optimism emerged, despite a period of low enrollment in the late 1940s. Branscomb acknowledged that the enrollment of fifty-three students in 1947 was "a very small number for a School endeavoring to serve all Protestant Churches." However, the pessimism of the Kirkland years was gone. In 1948, Branscomb calmed anxieties about low enrollment by insisting that the school only needed "some strengthening in the department of Practical Church Work," coupled with added publicity, and the enrollment problem would dissolve.[57]

Branscomb's prediction came true. By any standard, the School of Religion strengthened in the 1950s. By the beginning of the decade, enrollment had soared to 128 students. More importantly, the quality of enrollment increased, with more students coming from major colleges and universities. These years also saw an increase in the scholarly work of the faculty. Examples included J. Philip Hyatt, who gained attention with his service on the Revision Committee for the Standard Version of the Bible, and Samuel E. Stumpf, whose book *Democracy and the Christian Faith* (1950) was widely read. Renowned theologians such as Rudolph Bultmann and Paul Tillich visited as Cole Lecturers. In addition, Benton continued to nurture relationships with regional churches. In April 1951, some five hundred ministers from several denominations attended a spring convocation at the school. All of this impressed Branscomb, who applauded the "unique contribution" the school made as a liberal, interdenominational institution in the South.[58]

The addition of prominent faculty members and the steady increase in enrollment in the School of Religion paralleled the rise of the University as a whole beginning in 1947. Conkin observes that the late 1940s and early 1950s saw Vanderbilt's "great leap forward" in which the University began "to outgrow its provincial roots" and gain a national identity. However, as Conkin argues, this period of growth in national prestige elicited resistance from longtime supporters of the University who held "narrowly provincial" convictions. One of the most severe rifts between the national identity of the University and its southern roots emerged on the issue of academic freedom. Early on, Branscomb recognized that the University had to embrace an unequivocal commitment to academic freedom if it were to recruit prominent scholars from major universities. This commitment would be a hard line to hold for a University located in the conservative South.[59]

The School of Religion became one of the major battlegrounds between this ideal of academic freedom and the convictions of conservative Protestants. The crisis emerged from Benton's efforts to recruit a first-rate faculty. Benton and Branscomb agreed that a distinguished faculty was essential if the school were to continue its ascent. In pursuit of this goal, Benton appointed Nels Ferré, a professor from Andover Newton Theological School, who had impressed the Vanderbilt community when he delivered the Cole Lectures in 1949.[60]

The school viewed Ferré as an attractive addition because his theological perspective mediated between traditional Christianity and modernism. The *Alumnus* praised him for welcoming modernism's advocacy of scientific inquiry while maintaining "distinctively Christian viewpoints and values."[61] He was a respected theologian who brought academic prestige to the school without alienating denominational leaders. In any other major theological school, this expectation would probably have come to fruition. However, Ferré's turbulent career at Vanderbilt reminded the school that fundamentalism still held powerful sway in the South, even if it had lost ground in other regions.

Upon Ferré's arrival, he became the target of a vast array of fundamentalist preachers and writers who labeled him a communist and an atheist. The charge of communism was serious in the postwar "McCarthy era." In the early 1950s, the fear of communism permeated much of American culture, and it affected major universities that sought to uphold standards of academic freedom. At Vanderbilt, there was a pronounced tension between a stance against communism and in favor of academic freedom. For Branscomb, academic freedom reached its limits when professors attempted to practice or to promote communist teachings. Even in his appeal for academic freedom in 1950, Branscomb identified communism as the major exception to tolerance because communism was itself a system of thought that threatened the freedom of others. Again in 1953, Branscomb cautioned that commitment to academic freedom notwithstanding, schools of higher learning could not provide "temples of refuge for disloyal citizens."[62]

Branscomb did not consider Ferré a radical communist who threatened the American social order. Rather, he saw Ferré as a scholar who engaged in a theological critique of some aspects of modern capitalism. If Branscomb needed any reassurance, Benton provided it, asserting that it was "inconceivable" to regard Ferré "as a communist" or one who entertained "disloyal thoughts" toward the nation. Benton admitted that Ferré was "a creative genius" who did "not fit into regular patterns" and often said "things in unusual ways."[63] In other words, Ferré was the perfect target of fundamentalists who wished to pick apart his writings in search of material that was objectionable to their sensibilities.

Benton and Branscomb spent a great deal of time responding to rumors of Ferré's communist leanings. In one of his typical denials, Branscomb asserted that the problem was purely one of semantics. He explained that the form of "communism" advocated by Ferré was not the modern political system but rather a theological understanding "of social solidarity and community [that] is vital to Christian teaching." Branscomb assured anxious inquirers that they "need not worry about Nels Ferré at Vanderbilt preaching communism. He is a Christian prophet and as such is a bit uncomfortable for us at times, like all prophets are. He is more concerned with ethical principles and he understands them better than practical applications." Branscomb reiterated that Vanderbilt stood "for sanity, stability, and change by means of orderly progress" and not "by revolution." He admitted that Ferré could "make some of the most unnecessary remarks, which makes it frightfully easy for people to make him out as an atheist and skeptic."[64]

One of Ferré's "most unnecessary remarks" concerned the virgin birth of Jesus. In *The Christian Understanding of God*, Ferré briefly cited an old Nazi legend that Jesus' biological father could have been a German soldier, stationed at a nearby Roman fort. He did not argue for the historical legitimacy of this legend. Instead, his point was to disregard the theological importance of the virgin birth for the Christian faith.[65] However, despite Ferré's benign intentions, conservative Christians throughout the South seized upon this passage as evidence of his radicalism. An example of such attacks came from the fundamentalist journal *The Sword of the Lord*, published by J. R. Rice. It called Ferré an "enemy of Christianity" and cautioned that "any school that hires" him "is not worthy of Christian support."[66]

Such attacks aroused suspicion about Ferré to which Benton and Branscomb felt forced to respond. Ferré's most serious enemy was Vance Alexander, an influential Memphis banker and a member of the Board of Trust. Alexander inundated Branscomb with complaints that derided Ferré as "not the type [of] man we want teaching at Vanderbilt," because he has no "religion"—or at least "not the type I was raised on." Alexander continually complained to Branscomb about Ferré's liberal religion, communist convictions, and subversive pacifism.[67]

In responding to the critics, especially Alexander, Branscomb encountered the tension between the University's commitment to academic freedom and the need to appease powerful constituents.[68] Writing to Alexander, Branscomb admitted that Ferré "made one almost inexcusable mistake" in the much-quoted "Nazi legend" about Jesus' conception. Branscomb acknowledged to Alexander that anyone "born south of the Mason-Dixon line would have had more sense than to use that language." He also asserted that "if this kind of tactlessness were frequent, I would have a clear responsibility to do something about it." While Branscomb advised the Board of Trust not to take punitive action, he allowed that the Board may wish "to warn" Ferré against writings that "his critics" can "take out of context."[69] This letter was typical of Branscomb's apologies on Ferré's behalf. He continually attributed the problem not to Ferré's radicalism, but to his tactlessness and imprecise language. As Branscomb wrote to the concerned mother of a prospective student, Ferré's unfortunate remarks about Jesus' conception resulted from the fact that he was born in Norway and consequently "never learned to write in English with the clarity and ease which I could wish he had."[70]

The controversy grew to such a level that, in 1955, the Methodist board at the Lake Junaluska Assembly in North Carolina cancelled a scheduled teaching engagement by Ferré. The cancellation received a surprising amount of publicity, with stories in both of Nashville's newspapers.[71] Even the *Christian Century* entered the fray with an editorial that chastised the Methodist Church for succumbing to public pressure that came mostly from Southern Baptists. The editorial called the attacks on Ferré "ridiculous," since those who read his books more extensively than a brief passage on the virgin birth understood the great importance he placed on the Incarnation, and it described Ferré not as a true radical, but only a "fundamentalist bogey" in the tradition of Harry Emerson Fosdick.[72]

The controversies over Ferré's supposed radicalism ended in 1956, when he resigned to return to Andover Newton. The resignation was welcome news to Branscomb, who made no effort to persuade Ferré to stay. Throughout the controversy, the School of Religion experienced a vivid example of the costs of representing liberal theology in the conservative South. Despite the school's pledge to liberal theology and the University's advocacy of academic freedom, the pressure of holding these views in the region was great. Branscomb came very close to compromising his commitment to academic freedom due to pressure from many churches and from persons on the Board of Trust.[73] Instead of standing by Ferré, Branscomb promised Alexander that he would monitor Ferré's activities and bring him into line if necessary. Like Taylor's radical Social Gospel, Ferré's theological writings tested the commitment of the school to building an academically respectable theological institution in the South.

Sealantic Deliverance

The progress of the School of Religion in the early 1950s was accompanied by an increased need for funding. Branscomb exclaimed in 1951 that the only limit to the school's possibilities was financial.[74] However, the efforts of Branscomb and Benton to arouse the interest of wealthy benefactors had little success in the early 1950s. The pivotal moment arrived in January 1955, when Benton read a *New York Times* article that reported a gift of $20 million by John D.

Rockefeller, Jr., to develop the Sealantic Fund to benefit Protestant theological schools in America. Benton, who was in Ohio when he heard the news, immediately contacted Branscomb and asked him to begin lobbying for the present needs and future promise of the School of Religion. Branscomb had previously informed Rockefeller of the school's ambitions. As recently as 1952, Rockefeller had denied Branscomb's request for additional funding. However, in a letter to Branscomb, Rockefeller agreed that the school held "great possibilities for widespread usefulness" and offered the possibility that he could do something to assist it in the near future.[75] This hope came to fruition with the Sealantic Fund.

In April 1955, the School of Religion submitted a memorandum to the Sealantic Fund that identified the improvements needed to build "a school of national significance and broad regional influence." The document first proposed an increase in enrollment to match that of the divinity schools at Yale, Harvard, Chicago, and Union. Regarding the enrichment of curriculum, the school proposed enlarging its programs in practical ministerial training, including preaching and church administration. It also expressed the need to expand programs on issues such as religion and the fine arts, the relationship between Christianity and democracy, and the library for rural ministers. Branscomb closed the statement with "a personal word," revealing his convictions "that the greatest educational need in the South is for a distinguished interdenominational divinity school" and that the improvement of the School of Religion "would represent the culmination and ample reward of a lifetime devoted to education in the South."[76]

Branscomb took care to ensure that the ongoing controversy regarding Ferré did not obstruct the Sealantic proposal. Dana Creel of the Sealantic Corporation contacted Branscomb to request information about the issue. Specifically, Creel wanted to know about Ferré's supposed sympathies with communism. In response, Branscomb quickly dismissed the claim that Ferré taught "Marxist socialism" at Vanderbilt. He reassured Creel that the real issue was theological, not political, and that the disruption occurred when fundamentalists misunderstood passages from Ferré's books. In identifying the controversy as purely theological, Branscomb contended that the dispute was neither radical nor new. Rather, it was merely the latest resurfacing of fundamentalist controversies that started in England in the 1870s, moved to America with disputes surrounding Charles Briggs and Harry Emerson Fosdick, and most recently plagued Vanderbilt.[77] Thus, Branscomb presented the Ferré controversy as one of many debates that occasionally ignited in liberal divinity schools, not one that should provoke undue concern. Indeed, he indicated that the disruption over Ferré was a status symbol that placed the School of Religion in the company of schools at the forefront of theological education.

In December 1955, Branscomb received the good news from Creel. The

Sealantic Corporation agreed to grant $2.9 million to the School of Religion over a three-year period. The main stipulation required that the University provide $1 million for new facilities for the school.[78] Two days after receiving the letter, Branscomb invited the school's faculty to his home for the announcement, where he informed them that the grant was the largest that the Sealantic Corporation had given to any school. Vanderbilt's unique situation in the South undoubtedly accounted for the size of its grant.[79] Benton and Branscomb had successfully made the case for a liberal, interdenominational school in the South.

Vanderbilt and the Race Problem in the 1950s

In contributing to the School of Religion's endowment, Rockefeller demonstrated his support for its progressive social vision. This entailed support for its stance on racial segregation, by far the most divisive social issue that the school encountered during the grant process. Conkin observes that this prophetic stance impressed Rockefeller to the point that the decision of the School of Religion to admit black students was an "unspoken" although "necessary condition" of the Sealantic gift.[80]

Its liberal social vision empowered the school to move ahead of the rest of the University in attempting to deal with racial injustice. Conrad Cherry correctly observes that the School of Religion "functioned as a kind of conscience" within the University on race-related subjects, thereby "raising issues on religious and moral grounds and volunteering to lead the way in the integration process."[81] Even so, the witness of the school against racial injustice took several decades to develop. While Alva Taylor's radical position provided glimpses of future possibilities, the school did not take even a modestly prophetic stance on race until the 1950s.

In 1952, the faculty of the School of Religion adopted a groundbreaking resolution to admit African Americans. In a unanimous decision, it resolved that the "Christian Gospel" required that "the fellowship and instruction of the School should be open to qualified students without reference to their race or color." Branscomb emphasized this pivotal resolution in his correspondence with Rockefeller in 1952, couching this progressive policy as evidence of the prophetic voice of the school in the South on racial issues. Rockefeller responded with praise, commending the school on this pioneering effort that would "have far-reaching results." Earlier in the year, Branscomb had informed Rockefeller of the school's plan to lead the way in racial issues in the South. He believed that, by voluntarily opening its doors to black students, the school would have a great effect on "the psychology and outlook of the South" concerning race relations.[82]

Events in 1953 tested the school's stance on the admission of African Americans. Early in the year, it allowed the attendance of two black students who had previously enrolled at Scarritt College for Christian Workers. The basis for their acceptance was a cooperative agreement between the Scarritt and Peabody Colleges and Vanderbilt that allowed students enrolled in one of these institutions to attend classes held at the other two. The Board of Trust used pious language in extending this arrangement to the two black students, stating that "Christianity is not the sole possession of any one race or nation." Even so, it refused to issue a policy statement on the admission of African Americans in the University.[83] Later that year, the School of Religion enacted its new open admissions policy by accepting Joseph A. Johnson as the first African American to enroll as a regular student at Vanderbilt. In response to Johnson's admission, the Board of Trust decreed that Vanderbilt should not admit black students "to courses of study which are already available to them in this vicinity" through other institutions. However, the University allowed Johnson's admission because "no Negro graduate and accredited school in the field of religion" existed in Tennessee.[84] To be sure, the Board was not ready to throw open the doors of the other schools of the university to black students in 1953, regardless of the progressive policy enacted by the School of Religion.

The open admissions policy of the School of Religion was hardly easy to implement. In light of Johnson's impending arrival, Vice Chancellor Madison Sarratt sent Dean Benton a copy of the code of Tennessee that declared it "unlawful for white and colored persons to attend the same school." Any teacher who violated the law was guilty of a misdemeanor, which carried the penalty of a fifty-dollar fine and imprisonment of one to six months. Sarratt informed Benton that "two distinguished alumni" had mailed copies of this law as an intimidation strategy in response to the intention of the school to admit African Americans. Sarratt wryly noted "with some relief that the penalties" applied only to teachers and not to administrators. Still, he suggested that Benton post these codes in the school as a warning to faculty members who were "contemplating breaking the law."[85]

The fact that the rest of the University had no admissions policy regarding black students complicated the prophetic intentions of the School of Religion in this area. Benton emphasized the practical difficulties in his letter to Dwight W. Harwell, a prospective black student in 1954. Benton informed Harwell of his acceptance for the 1954–55 academic year, but he cautioned that "Vanderbilt is in a transition period in regard to the admission of Negro students." The problem was that, while Harwell could attend classes in the School of Religion, no other school in the University extended the same right to him. Benton also pointed out that while Harwell was welcome in the "instructional facilities" of the School of Religion, he could neither take his meals in the dining room nor live in the dormitory, for the University did not have separate eating and sleeping facilities for black students. Such facilities did not open to black students until the 1955–56 academic year.[86] Therefore, in admitting black students, the School of Religion assumed a prophetic stance that placed it in an awkward position in relation to the rest of the University, as well as to southern culture.

To the school's credit, its faculty remained steadfast behind its commitment to racial justice. A particularly thorny situation that tested this commitment arose in 1954, when Kate Tillett Smith, daughter of former Dean Tillett, willed to the school an estate called Dearmont, located in Highlands, North Carolina. She desired that the house serve as a vacation home for the faculty and dean of the school. However, she stipulated in her will "that no member of the Negro race, whether a student in the School of Religion or not, be entertained at Dearmont as a guest." This stipulation was unacceptable. While the Highlands home was attractive, to submit to this racial requirement would have been the height of hypocrisy, contradicting the progressive statements of the school. Therefore, faculty members refused the use of the property, choosing instead to maintain their witness on the issue of race in the 1950s.[87]

Vanderbilt Divinity School: The Redemption of the Vision

Benton called 1955 "the finest year" in the long history of the School of Religion. Significantly, he made this statement several months before the Sealantic grant became known. He had several reasons to be pleased with the school's progress. In that year, it had a record enrollment of 219 students, and the Bachelor of Divinity graduating class of 42 was the largest ever.[88] It boasted a strong and productive faculty that brought visibility and academic respectability to the task of interdenominational education in the South. It also enjoyed the support of several denominations. One particular victory in 1955 came when the Tennessee Conference of the Methodist Church requested a closer cooperation with the School. Branscomb noted that this unsolicited request from the Methodist Church resulted both from the recognition that the School of Religion had trained many Methodist clergy in the area and from the church's respect for Dean Benton. Despite these achievements, Benton did not believe that the school had reached the apex of its ascent, but rather stood "on the brink of a new and great period in its history."[89] The news of the Sealantic grant at the end of the year more than confirmed Benton's assessment.

In 1956, the School of Religion punctuated its ascent by renaming itself the Vanderbilt Divinity School. As Branscomb said at the time, the school changed its name to conform to "established academic usage."[90] Since 1915, the School of Religion had sought to build itself into an institution that would do for the South what Yale, Harvard, Chicago, and Union did for their respective regions. Finally, in 1956, backed by the Sealantic grant and the growth of the school under Benton's leadership, the faculty and administration believed that the School of Religion was now a major, interdenominational institution that would soon rival the best in the country. The change of name signaled that this institution was a peer of other divinity schools at Harvard, Yale, and Chicago.

This stage of development closed with Benton's death on August 21, 1956. The *Nashville Banner* reported that Benton died as the School stood "on the threshold of a new era" in service to the region. In praise of Benton's leadership, the faculty of the Divinity School resolved that "Benton was the Moses who led this School through memorable days of struggle and grace." And, like Moses, Benton died before leading his people "into the new land" of a promising future.[91]

J. Philip Hyatt served as acting dean the following school year, but the difficult task of replacing Benton fell to thirty-six-year-old Robert Nelson, who came to Vanderbilt in 1957 from the World Council of Churches in Geneva. Nelson was an appropriate choice for the Divinity School. His ecumenical work as secretary of the Faith and Order Commission prepared him to lead a school that remained proud of its interdenominational heritage in the South.[92] Under Nelson's leadership in the late 1950s, the school continued to expand. Construction was begun on a new divinity quadrangle, across Twenty-first Avenue and adjacent to the University Library, which would become the school's new home in 1960. The Board of Trust dedicated $1 million for the construction, in accordance with the stipulations of the Sealantic grant.[93] The new facilities, including classrooms, faculty and administrative offices, dining services, and a chapel, would replace Wesley Hall.

The support of the Sealantic Fund and the prospect of new facilities buoyed Nelson and the faculty in their drive to expand the school beyond its current bounds as a "local institution" that primarily catered to Methodists and Disciples. James Sellers, then assistant dean and assistant professor of theology, documented these concerns in his "Recruitment Proposals for the B.D. Program" in early 1958. Sellers outlined the problems succinctly: the school needed to attract higher quality students from a broader spectrum of geographical and collegiate backgrounds. It also desired a student body that represented more denominational diversity, with proportionately fewer Methodists and more Presbyterians, Lutherans, Episcopalians, and American Baptists. The concern was that, even with the advances spearheaded by Benton, the school lacked a national reputation that could draw students beyond the southern states. In its attempt to address this problem, the Sellers memo reflected the school's ambition to be not only an interdenominational institution for the South, but for the nation as well.[94]

Continuing its efforts to provide a prophetic voice in the South on social issues, the Divinity School sought Rockefeller funds for a conference on race relations.[95] This attempt to take a prophetic stance on racial justice in the late 1950s testified to the school's continued objective of providing a critical, theological witness to society, which had been an essential objective of the School of Religion since 1915. The history of the school amply demonstrated the costs of pursuing this objective in the South. Its tribulations with the Social Gospel of Alva Taylor, the fundamentalist controversy, Nels Ferré's outspoken liberalism, and the pioneering admission of black students had threatened its viability and vision. The events of the early 1960s would demonstrate that the drive to be a prophetic voice within the University as well as in the larger southern culture continued to provoke costly struggles for the Divinity School.

5

A School for Prophets of the New South: The Dilemma of Engaging Southern Culture

Richard C. Goode

IN 1869, THE *NASHVILLE CHRISTIAN ADVOCATE*, THE PAPER OF THE Methodist Episcopal Church, South (MECS), opened a discussion on ministerial credentials in the denomination. Obviously, some Methodist sentiment had changed from the days of frontier camp meetings. In February, for example, it reprinted an editorial from the *Memphis Christian Advocate*, which warned, "While it was wise and proper for Methodists to insist every candidate for the ministry" have a "personal knowledge of pardoned sin, the consciousness of the love of God abiding in their soul, evidences of inward grace, an outward holy life," it was unfortunate that the MECS had failed also to stress "mental culture and literary attainments." Due to this oversight, the church had ordained those "notoriously incompetent to discharge the functions of so sacred and important an office." The congregations were crying, "Send us an educated man!" and the editor pleaded, "something more than a preliminary education is necessary to full success." That *something*, the editor announced, "is the prosecution of theological studies by our young men, under the eyes and by the direction, and with the assistance of the Gamaliels of the Church. We must have our schools of the prophets."[1]

Landon Garland, a Southern Methodist leader and eventually the inaugural chancellor of Vanderbilt University, concurred and went further. According to Garland, increasing the demands of theological education would serve as merely one phase of an overall social upgrade of the Methodist church. "A decent and proper conformity to the usages of polite society is required by both [vital piety and correct taste]," he argued. If salvation depended upon "discomfort and filth," southern Methodists would humbly submit, Garland admitted. Much good, however, could come to the church that utilized "long-drawn aisles, fretted vaults, and fluted columns—sanctuaries in harmony with the refinements and cultivated tastes of society." Antebellum Methodists could be excused for a "disregard of comfort, cleanliness, and taste" when most lived in log huts, "but as the country advanced in population, wealth and refinement, we did not advance with it in the comfort and neatness." The church should "advance with society."

In Garland's estimation, a refined, well-educated minister served as an accessory to dignified architecture and other liturgical aesthetics. "It is shocking to see a minister in the pulpit in a garb that would mortify us in the parlor," he lamented. "Linen soiled—collar opened—neck without a tie—vest not reaching to the waistband, exposing the underclothes—shoes unpolished—coat unbrushed, and unclerical in cut and color." Both in and out of the pulpit, the minister should personify cleanliness and neatness in a "manner becoming a gentleman." So important were these details to Garland that he was "disposed to question any man's religion which does not embrace soap and water."[2] Garland's comments struck a nerve in the denomination. Later in 1869, the *Advocate* ran an article under the heading "Decorum in the Church" decrying "harsh, uncouth, funny, and eccentric" language that illustrated the southern Methodist clergy's "want of good breeding."[3]

The "New South" Thesis

What explains such social elitism on the part of these MECS spokespersons? Why were they so harsh on their own clergy? Had not these common, unkempt, itinerant preachers made Methodism the largest Christian denomination in nineteenth-century American society? We might expect, therefore, commendation rather than condemnation. In this chapter, I suggest that behind the rhetoric belittling the clergy lay a much larger social and cultural dilemma. At Vanderbilt's inception, southern Methodism was struggling to define an appropriate strategy for engaging the New South. Some factions wanted to resist change and maintain the ministerial system that had provided success and stability. Others argued that social responsibility and continued growth demanded adaptation and assimilation to the New South. As an offspring of the MECS, and originally a school for the training of MECS clergy, the Vanderbilt Biblical Department inherited this dilemma. In some ways the term "school of the prophets" became a catch phrase for describing and engaging the dilemma.

As representatives of the first generation, Bishop Holland McTyeire, Landon Garland, and Thomas Summers typified those who understood Vanderbilt's prophetic role as leading the MECS out of its perceived southern backwardness, embracing the promise of the New South. They designed their school of the prophets to acculturate southern Methodism to the New South. In the second generation, Wilbur Fisk Tillett stood for those who envisioned Vanderbilt's prophetic role as preparing and empowering New South clergy for the propagation of a Christian America. As illustrated in his life's work, Vanderbilt progressed in its second generation from cultural accommodation to cultural chauvinism. Foreshadowing generations to come, rather than personifying the official vision of the school during his brief tenure, Alva Wilmot Taylor represented yet a third definition of "prophetic" theological education at Vanderbilt—cultural criticism. Although the one individual from this list who did not use the phrase "school of the prophets" to describe theological education at Vanderbilt, Taylor, by comparison, was the most antagonistic toward the New South—advocating unpopular positions on such issues as racial respect and reconciliation, women's rights, and economic justice.[4]

The term "New South" refers to the period after the Civil War and Reconstruction when southern communities began to reclaim control of their society from occupying Union armies and governments. Southerners self-consciously chose the moniker to describe the changes they foresaw and probably desired. To be sure, the epithet was not a repudiation of the past. Most citizens of the New South respected the Old South, yet realized they could no longer live in the past. As J. C. C. Newton noted, the term "New South" meant "that the South has entered upon a new era. It means that the time is fully come when our people look, not backward *only*, but also forward; that the South is to have a future. The flesh and blood of the old body cannot enter this new kingdom."[5] Optimism ran high. The Civil War and Reconstruction represented for the South a kind of cultural wandering in the wilderness, a painful experience that had figuratively created and purified a new people. With the overthrow of Reconstruction, the South had crossed its Jordan River and was entering an economic, racial, and political promised land.

Historians most often associate the term "New South" with Henry Grady. Both in the editorial pages of the *Atlanta Constitution* and in various speeches (e.g., his famous 1886 "New South" address before the New York New England Society), Grady painted an optimistic picture of the New South's growth and prosperity through industrialization and laissez-faire economics. In addition to unrestrained capitalism, racial segregation, and one-party politics, Grady's regional boosterism served as a trademark of the New South ethos. C. Vann Woodward defined Grady's New South ideology as the belief that not only had "acquisitive instincts" become "respectable," but "ambition" had become the southern vogue.[6] Although he was less certain than Woodward that the New South's acquisitive dream of progress was evidence of a "change of heart," W. J. Cash admitted that this emphasis on progress did "manifestly abandon the purely agricultural basis from which the Southern world, and ultimately the Southern mind, had been reared." Yet the adoption of the New South creed in the last quarter of the nineteenth century was a tactical decision. The New South could earn and guarantee its distinctive autonomy by successfully competing in the materialistic quest of the Gilded Age.[7] Paul Gaston interpreted the New South ideology less as southern strategy for beating the materialistic Yankees at their own game than as an embracing of the American Dream. This doctrine, Gaston argued, filled southerners with hope and told them that their goal of status and respectability was both right and achievable. Imagination and aspiration fused into a dream that became a powerful force in southern history.[8]

Gaston was correct. The New South myth was such an inexorable cultural force that, to an extent, it no longer mattered which myth individual southerners chose—Old or New South. Social transformation was taking place. Thus, as Newton explained, the MECS had to address such questions as "What has the Church to do in building up this New South? Does the Church incur special responsibility in view of the future developments awaiting this southern country? . . . Is the Church of Christ to have a voice or not in determining whether the new culture of the South shall be in harmony with the Spirit of Christianity, or hostile to it?"[9] Instead of wasting time and energy resisting the inevitable, MECS progressives wanted to get in front of this cultural evolution and direct it along paths they saw as consistent with, or at least amenable to, their understanding of a Christian civilization. As members of the largest Christian denomination in the region, many southern Methodists assumed that cultural stewardship fell to them. This meant, however, that the church had to invest in the New South vision. It could not assume the voice of cultural critic. It first had to acculturate, and then to lead the New South from inside the course of events. Education provided key means toward that end. If the church, through its clergy, could grow and guide the new generation of southern business, political, and intellectual leaders, then the New South would emerge as a Christian civilization. Utterly essential to this response to the challenge of the New South, therefore, was the appropriate training of the Methodist clergy.

The creation and evolution of Vanderbilt University's Biblical Department/ School of Religion/Divinity School is a case study in how theological education often reflects and/or challenges the concerns of the surrounding culture. From its inception in the minds of a few MECS leaders in the late 1860s through the first half of the twentieth century, theological education at Vanderbilt personified the values of an elite southern culture. Though challenged from time to time, this mission lasted until the late 1950s when the civil rights movement, among other forces, moved the Divinity School away from its close alignment with elite New South conservatism. Only then would the school understand its mission as a "school of the prophets" to engage southern society critically. Not surprisingly, such a move alienated the institution from its surrounding culture.

Garland's Call for a Cultivated Clergy

In 1866, the MECS bishops publicly lamented, in their *Journal of the General Conference*, a "disparity between the intellectual acquisition of our young ministers and the people they are sent to serve." To rectify the clergy's deficiencies, they desired "a thorough knowledge of all those ordinary branches of education which bear directly on their pulpit performances." Toward that end, the bishops affirmed, first, education "as an indispensable part of our vocation as a church." Second, the highest grade of instruction should be secured, combined with the constant inculcation of evangelical religion. Third, the period had fully arrived when it was the duty of the church to provide specific means for the education of young preachers. Finally, they committed themselves and the denomination to the establishment of a theological institute.[10] Due to post war financial realities, the MECS initiated little or no action to implement the bishops' recommendations.

In October 1869, Landon Garland published his six-part open letter in the *Advocate* championing the cause of "cultured" theological education. Trying to placate traditionalists by admitting that the poorly educated, spirit-filled, itinerant circuit rider had sufficed for the old southern culture, Garland argued that the time had arrived for the creation of an institution "whereby a higher intellectual culture may be imparted to its ministry." Still, Garland undoubtedly offended many democratized southern Methodists when he rhetorically asked, "Does the Holy Ghost fill with knowledge the minds of the stupid and the indolent?" The Holy Spirit will never teach us anything revealed in the Scriptures, he warned, "unless we give our minds" first to academic pursuits. Garland was convinced that the New South was a more intellectually challenging and dangerous place for Christians than the antebellum world had been. Where once a devout but poorly educated minister could meet the needs of his society, now the minister had to engage a sophisticated foe. Moreover, the Methodist clergyman often found himself the intellectual inferior of his parishioners. The professionalization of various vocations during the century had facilitated the education of many Methodist lay members, but because the ministry had not followed suit, the minister was left behind and could no longer lead and nurture those who held him in low esteem. Thus on both pastoral and apologetic grounds, "we want a minister to be educated, that his mental faculties may receive that expansion and training which are essential to the profound and accurate investigation of truth. That when he opens his mouth it may be in wisdom and simplicity. That thus profoundly studying the truth, he may be the more deeply impressed with its value, and may the more earnestly enforce it upon others." These provided more than sufficient grounds for a "higher standard of ministerial culture."[11]

Garland knew his Methodist colleagues well enough, however, to anticipate a typical response. " 'But if he is called of God to preach, how can we keep him back from his Master's work, to be educated'?" Garland asked, mimicking the traditionalists. He believed the practice of encouraging and empowering an individual to preach, without delay and based merely upon a "call," was unbiblical. Samuel, the Hebrew prophets and priests, and the apostles, for example, all had some study and preparation before being sent upon their respective missions. "When God calls a man to preach," Garland assured, God "calls him to the use of all the means by which he may become an efficient preacher. This rushing into the ministry, like a 'horse into battle,' is unbecoming the man, and contrary to the economy of God." Nevertheless, Garland was sensitive to the charge of "manufacturing preachers." He had no intention of "usurping the functions of the Holy Ghost" in calling individuals to the ministry. But he had every desire of taking those called by the Spirit and "holding them back in order to prepare them for larger usefulness," a plan he defended "upon the score of common sense."[12]

The caricature of the theologically trained minister as cold and formal in the pulpit was a serious threat to Garland's vision of theological education. He conceded that the practice of some denominations in "muzzling every mouth which has not been filled in her theological schools" might extinguish the Spirit's fire in the pulpit. But he denied any necessary connection between advanced theological education and an "abstract and metaphysical preacher" devoid of fervor. In fact, depth of spiritual devotion, Garland proposed, was more likely attached to the accuracy of perceptions, which education would only enhance.[13]

Garland deemed it best not to create a series of regional seminaries, nor to hand the responsibilities off to undergraduate institutions. Instead, he envisioned one seminary for the MECS, and he wanted it located in Nashville, Tennessee, because Nashville embodied the culture Garland wanted instilled in the southern Methodist preacher. "It is a city of refinement and taste," he argued, "living in the midst of families of piety and cultivation." Consequently, if ministerial candidates lived long enough in Nashville, they would become appropriately socialized and cultured, and "their asperities of manner worn down." With a large dose of paternalism coloring his vision, Garland depicted the seminarians living not in dormitories on campus, but with designated "cultivated and refined" Nashville residents.[14] Such a residential "outing" program would serve as a kind of field education.

Garland represented a key constituency in the MECS, and responses to his series illustrate the popularity of his vision. Just a few weeks after Garland's plan for theological education ran in the *Advocate*, the journal published an anonymous letter affirming Garland's proposal. If it was ever "necessary to accept into the ranks of the ministry and send forth as preachers of the gospel, an uninformed, uncultivated, uncouth man," the letter read, "that time has passed."[15] A series of letters signed "Holston" also put a fine point on Garland's articles. Holston rhetorically asked whether "a first-rate theological school, in the bosom of the Methodist Episcopal Church, South," was consistent with the MECS call to ministry?[16] Would any dare ask, Holston wondered, "whether it is any help to a mechanic to have served an apprenticeship, or for a physician to have studied the art of healing?" "Men, when called to the ministry, are either inspired—sum and substance, matter and form—with ready-made sermons, replete with instruction, faultless in style and method, together with graceful property of manner, or else they must come at these items in some other way." And Holston was convinced that of all disciplines and professions, theology required extraordinary preparation and study. Yet Holston, like Garland, made theology an intellectual means to a social end. Although theological education was necessary to mine God's truths, the ultimate desire was for a "more thorough and efficient" method of presenting those truths. "In order to do this, it is self-evident that the people must be entertained. If so, the preacher must be entertaining." Otherwise, the minister will "preach to empty benches."[17] To promote "actual, broad, liberal" theological education in the MECS, sufficiently powerful to "command the respect of the whole Church," and to drill candidates in the arts of entertainment, Holston envisioned the creation of an "ecclesiastical West Point." Certainly God would provide the initial call to service, but Holston begged the MECS to commission no minister below the rank of "a captain—lieutenant at the lowest" to lead the church. As with West Point, such professional training would stress the improvement and refinement of manners in addition to technical skills.[18]

"Progress," a frequent contributor to the *Advocate*, demonstrated that many within the MECS were eager and poised to "advance in influence and power" in the New South and thought, in fact, that God had commissioned the MECS to lead the New South.[19] With opportunities, however, came responsibilities, Progress warned, and only well-trained and -drilled ministers would help the

MECS "hold the place we covet at the head of Christian civilization." The MECS could not "reasonably hope to advance in such a path of glory" as long as its young ministers had to "supplement their intellectual culture" elsewhere. Thus some of the original impetus behind the creation of theological education at Vanderbilt was the desire to fashion "an institution the civilized world will view with respect, where a large number of the greatest minds shall be gathered as teachers; where great libraries and costly accumulations" will attract the most "ingenious and aspiring student." Combining such profound resources and "erudition" would grant the MECS an "authority" that would only "enhance our respectability before the world." Having earned that respect, they could control the direction of the New South and beyond.[20]

Some, however, questioned the social vision of Garland and other proponents of theological education. "What are we working for?" asked "Timothy." "Glory?" If that was the mission of the MECS, then "educate, to the highest point, *every* young man," Timothy declared. "But if for the conversion of souls, then let us have 'some learned; but not many.'" The detractors of theological education, like Timothy, admitted that a few top-notch MECS theological scholars were necessary, but thought such men should not constitute the rank and file of MECS clergy for several reasons. First, the divine call to ministry took priority, such that the best credentials were moral fitness, assurance of pardoned sin, purity of heart and life, as opposed to "adventitious" academic qualifications. Second, many preachers were called later in life and already had significant family responsibilities, thus lacking the leisure necessary to pursue education. Finally, an educated audience needed educated ministers, but uneducated lay members did not. Like any army, Timothy reasoned, the Kingdom of God needed more rank-and-file troops than it needed officers, because these regulars functioned as the true forces who "battered down the forts of infidelity, and the boys [who] with their muskets make sad havoc in the demoralized ranks" of the enemy. So, playing off Holston's call for the creation of an ecclesiastical West Point, Timothy recommended that the ministerial "privates learn the squad-drill," and leave the MECS's theological academy graduates to function as the select few colonels and generals. Switching back to biblical metaphors, Timothy admitted that "we need men of mighty, polished minds; yet this does not prevent us from having men who are not so well educated. We want our Isaiah; yet let us not reject Amos because he is not brought up in the school of the prophets."[21]

The debate over the MECS seminary involved more than competing educational philosophies. It served as something akin to a referendum on the future of the denomination, determining which social and cultural vision would dictate the direction of the fellowship. To support the seminary and professionalization of the clergy was a vote for the New South and its progressive, optimistic, acquisitive aspirations. To fight the seminary was to cast a vote against acculturation to the New South creed and to protect the democratic power that had made humble Methodism the religious success story of nineteenth-century America.

If historian Robert Wiebe is correct, the populist outsiders were doomed to lose the contest for the control of the denomination from the outset. America, and especially the South, had built a society premised on local autonomy in the early nineteenth century, but in the last quarter of the century that independence and isolation proved untenable in the face of contemporary social, economic, and political forces. "By contrast to the personal, informal ways of the community" that previously governed life, Wiebe argues, "the new scheme was derived from the regulative, hierarchical needs" of modern society. The "progress" permeating American culture in the late nineteenth century required the centralization of authority and the bureaucratization of professions. The decision the church had to face—whether to create a seminary and require theological education—was, therefore, a specific example of a phenomenon impacting all American communities and denominations.[22] To what extent would the MECS reconceptualize its organizational and ecclesiastical structures to meet contemporary cultural challenges? Resistance could doom the denomination to cultural irrelevance. Unaware of the scale and scope of the forces they were up against, the MECS populists mounted a vigorous offensive.

The Populist Rationale

As the campaign for the seminary gained momentum, Bishop George F. Pierce announced that "every dollar invested in a theological school will be a damage to Methodism. Had I a million, I would not give a dime for such an object." As arguably "the most powerful figure in the College of Bishops," Pierce spoke for many in the denomination who, having read Garland's apologia for a theological school, were likewise insulted.[23] J. G. Wilson, from Huntsville, Alabama, complained that proponents of theological education portrayed most Methodist ministers as "a set of ignoramuses, incapable of understanding or opposing infidelity, or instructing our highly-educated people," and whose only real contributions were "pulpit pyrotechnics and flashy rhetoric." Beyond interpreting the push for theological education as a personal affront, detractors challenged the seminary on several grounds. One line of attack warned of the damage theological education would do to the clergy. George Stewart of Pearisburg, Virginia, wondered who would set the standards. "A mere call to preach is a sufficient qualification" for ordination in God's system, he claimed. J. M. Boland, also of Huntsville, concurred. Despite the lack of educational creden tials, most Methodist ministers had developed "strong native intellects, who have, now, a mental discipline, a fund of information in literature and systematic theology that makes them the equal to a theologue just from the molds of a theological university." Better yet, practical field experience and common sense had helped many a minister acquire in just a few months what it would take "one of those theologues ten years to acquire, if he ever becomes their equal in this department." About the only thing a seminarian could gain from all the assigned reading, Boland scoffed, was "dry, musty love."[24]

Another reader, Samuel Weber of Bishopville, South Carolina, added one other lesson seminary students might learn. "Graduates of theological seminaries almost invariably come from the seminary into the active ministry with offensive pulpit mannerisms, resulting from an unconscious imitation of the style and manner of their teachers." Itinerancy as traditionally practiced in the denomination, Weber argued, was "the best school for the cultivation of a natural and forceful pulpit oratory." Bishop Pierce agreed. "I do not want a man shut up in a seminary, lectured, and molded by a given pattern, till all individuality is destroyed." If the church moved forward on theological education, he predicted, those candidates who could not avail themselves of the prerequisite training would squelch their call, "and thus imperil their souls and bereave the Church." That some preferred to complicate matters by moving away from the church's "fresh, prompt, always available mode" of ordination was "amazing" to Pierce. The "old plan" of mentoring ministers, Pierce recalled, took a "timid, awkward youth" and put him on circuit that compelled him to preach every day, lead classes, then ride to the next church for a prayer meeting the following evening. The young novice had no time for reading and studying. Nevertheless, "out of this old plan, with all its hard work, and with few books, mingling all the while with the uncultivated, came the men who shook heaven, earth, and hell." So, Pierce concluded, "the man who does not make a preacher out of this [old] plan is a hopeless case. No culture, high or low, will make anything valuable out of him." To illustrate his point, Pierce pointed to McTyeire. "It would be hard to exaggerate [McTyeire's] value to the Church," Pierce noted. "But he would have been utterly spoiled by three years' arbitrary training in a professional school. He would have been stiff, cold, dry, and powerless."[25]

Detractors not only warned of the damage theological education would do to the ministers, they also cautioned about the stultifying effect it would have on the MECS's mission to common southerners. Pierce argued that the MECS was a "plebeian sect," with a "mission to the masses of society—not to the select few—a favored class." He had no intention of allowing any "scholastic isolation" of the MECS clergy to separate the denomination from its "sympathy with the masses and multitude of mankind." The old plan was right in taking common men, "however despised and berated," and encouraging them to speak in common language to common folk. Consequently, the Methodists were able to evangelize "rude settlements" without embarrassment, and to "keep company among common people" because the ministers and the denomination embraced their lowly social roots. Such was the "secret of our strength and progress," Pierce surmised. Southern Methodists were not called to market the gospel to the "cultivated and refined." "Preaching that is fixed up for the 'cultivated and refined' is very poor preaching," he lamented.[26]

Listing what made the MECS distinctive opened the door for comparison with other denominations and their ministerial training. Pierce dismissed the Presbyterian model, for example, as "too slow and stiff to meet the urgent and diversified calls of a promiscuous population." His real fear, however, was not that the MECS would become too Presbyterian, but that it would become too Episcopalian. When proponents of the seminary started talking about culture and social refinement, Pierce and other opponents assumed theological education would make the MECS more Episcopalian—a tradition "too delicate for country fare. It must dwell in town."[27] But what other denominations required in theological education concerned Pierce little. His standard yardstick of ministerial success was statistical. On this account, the MECS clergy bested their competitors in such categories as converts and church attendance. More to the heart of a populist understanding of what southern Methodism ought to be, an anonymous author warned, "sadness will come hand in hand with her espousal to formalism. There is not a Church in existence but has degenerated spiritually as they have courted an educated ministry."[28]

In a more philosophical moment, Pierce admonished readers of the *Advocate* that education was not an unquestioned benefit. Education was a skill, or "an edged tool, and whether it works mischief, or concrete value, depends on who handles it." From Pierce's perspective, too many in the MECS tradition, like McTyeire, uncritically adopted "the fashion to glorify education," and as a result "everything said in its favor is wonderfully admired and greedily swallowed." Once credulously embraced, education irrevocably altered ministerial practice. He complained, for example, that educated ministers often squandered pulpit time "reconciling Moses with modern science, instead of preaching repentance and faith," or went "so deep into geology as to show that Adam was not the first man—that the deluge was a little local affair." He preferred ministers who experientially knew that "breaking hearts with the hammer of words is better employment than splitting hairs with metaphysical acumen. I do think evangelical sermons better than critical lectures." To a point, Pierce perceived the situation correctly. MECS progressives were using education to make a cultural, social statement, and he implored his fellow southern Methodists not to yield to cultural temptation. "We are beginning," he feared, "to deify talent, and talk too much about the 'age' and 'progress,' and the demands of the time, for the simplicity of our faith, or for the safety of our Church. Not by might and power, but by my Spirit, saith the Lord." Thus Pierce self-consciously assumed the responsibility of putting the "brakes on the wheels" of MECS cultural "progress" and "innovations" like theological education.[29]

Progressive Rejoinder

A seminary proponent, "Filius Yalensis," offered one of the starkest contrasts to Pierce's position. In the new MECS "school for the prophets," he announced, theological education should, "like commerce, be governed by the laws of supply and demand." And the New South's law of social commerce demanded "the establishment of a school to elevate the standard of our ministerial culture" and to "better the culture" of those who desire the ministry. Even with such a culturally inspired justification, champions of theological education were not ready to concede the populists' monopoly on the Holy Spirit. Joseph Cottrell scoffed that whenever a new program or position was proposed, the populists "apprehend a departure from reliance upon the direct agency of the Holy Spirit. They fear a resort to substitutes for that agency which only God bestows." But Cottrell failed to see the necessary connection. "It occurs to me," he declared, "that the Holy Ghost might utilize an institution of larger proportion; and that reliance upon God is measured by the largeness or smallness of our undertakings for him." W. L. C. Hunnicutt of Yazoo City, Mississippi, thought ministerial candidates could be trained either "to suppress or cultivate their emotional feelings at pleasure." Academic training had no necessary or essential bearing on one's use of passion in preaching. If education presented no inherent harm, but offered significant social potential, why not, reasoned Hunnicutt, require seminary training?[30]

For Bishop McTyeire, however, MECS ministers were already harmed—not by quenching the Spirit with education, but by the failure to progress with current social forces. Responding to Pierce's challenge that McTyeire himself would have been harmed by theological education, he noted that under the old plan itinerants were like preaching apprentices. At each stop on the circuit, the apprentice repeated his sermons until he became skilled. "Not so now. Railroads, turnpikes, and telegraphs have cut up the work. The people demand Sunday preaching and the pastor to live among them. The times, the age, lead to stations and small circuits." Raw, untrained, and untried young ministers now lacked the time to develop experience and refine their sermons. The laity expected even young ministers to teach and govern with facility, sophistication, and wisdom as soon as they arrived at their first congregational appointment. To apply Pierce's old plan rigorously under these new circumstances "smothered" young preachers. "Without preparation," McTyeire warned, "to be thrust into the thick of the fight; to be placed where more sermons and services are called for than he can render" was the greatest of all dangers to the young minister. "The old plan of bringing in workers is gone," McTyeire retorted. "You can't fetch it back—no use trying."[31]

Of greater concern to McTyeire, however, was the way Pierce's old plan hamstrung the denomination and prevented it from keeping pace with cultural norms. McTyeire wanted no part of a fellowship that preferred to focus its labor on the lower social classes. "Give up a scheme for broader and higher literary and ministerial training in our Church, and what then?" McTyeire asked. "We must be content with a lower and restricted sphere of usefulness." But, he countered, "I am not resigned to that condition, either for myself or my brethren. I claim for Methodism a mission to all classes."[32] David C. Kelley offered McTyeire some historical support. John Wesley, he noted, was the "master of learning of his age." Thus, although Methodism may have initially emerged from, and for a long time appealed to, the lower classes, Kelley thought the real genius of Methodism was found in the movement's ability to assimilate and "adapt to the surroundings." As for McTyeire, Kelley's ultimate desire was that the MECS "crush out the sneer of the educated classes, and make them ashamed to libel us as ignorant." But he knew that southern Methodism had a long way to go to silence its cultured despisers.[33]

In June 1872, Thomas Summers, editor of the *Advocate*, entered the debate more intentionally and forthrightly. He noted that both sides had good and well-intentioned reasons. Nevertheless, as others had noted, the time for dialogue was passed. The pulpit had already lost significant social power and influence in the New South; if the pulpit were to reverse the decline and reclaim its authority, the MECS "must stand in the advance of the intelligence and culture of the new emerging culture." So long as the church yielded to the "tendency to a lower culture as a preparation for the ministry," it was doomed to cultural isolation and irrelevance. Or, as an open letter to several regional conferences in the *Advocate* encouraged, moving forward with theological education was a necessary step for the MECS because "no glorying" in past MECS successes will "achieve what remains to be done. No advance of time will diminish this demand; but on the contrary, increase of time will demand new increments of knowledge." Simply stated, theological education was essential "for the advancement of the cause of Christian culture."[34] Proponents of Vanderbilt foresaw only two choices for Methodism in the New South—either push forward and try to lead in the creation of a Christian culture in the South, or become isolated and insignificant. Defined in those terms, the choice was clear.

Summers and the Aesthetics of Theological Education

Thomas Summers was the ideal dean for the new Biblical Department at Vanderbilt for two reasons: he avoided the cutting-edge theological liberalism that would have frightened away the MECS's New South constituency, and he manifested the cultural progressivism McTyeire desired for the denomination.[35] He was literate, cultured, and aesthetically astute. "Where did this man who never enjoyed the advantages of regular classical instruction, get the knowledge of the art of versification, the purity and severity of taste, the delicacy of ear, the microscopic attention to detail?" his biographer, O. P. Fitzgerald, asked. He surmised that Summers's own "genius" provided the answer. In other words, in good Methodist and American fashion, Summers had lifted himself by his own bootstraps and simply would not turn away from a subject before he found the answer he wanted. Like many self-trained individuals, however, his education was uneven and he could become quite dogmatic about the truths he had discovered. "He blazed with virtuous indignation," Fitzgerald noted, "alike at the tampering with grave theological dogmas, important historical facts, or a question from a polemic or hymnologist. . . . His mental glow never cooled or fell below a red heat."

Summers's doctrinal conservatism helped McTyeire calm the fears of Methodist populists, for under his direction the Biblical Department would not be theologically progressive. During these conflicted, anxious times of the New South, Summers's "very failings leaned to the side of safety. And so he stood, like a sea-wall, to resist the advancing tide of radicalism in thought and in legislation. He was eagle-eyed to discern the least tinge of error according to the existing standards, and swift to expunge or refute it." Sounding almost as if he were describing Princeton's Charles Hodge, Fitzgerald admitted that originality was not Summers's strong point: "The criticism has been made, not unkindly, that he [Summers] originated nothing as a theological teacher and author. This is certainly true. No one would have more readily conceded the fact than himself. He felt he had no function as an inventor or revamper of theology—he made no effort in that direction. When he settled a question, it stayed settled for him, and was no longer open for doubt or debate in his own mind."[36] Under Summers's direction, theological education at Vanderbilt focused more on assent to a body of doctrines than probing the assumptions behind those doctrines.

Not only was Summers the safe choice to allay populist MECS fears, he was also the appropriate candidate to address the aesthetic concerns articulated by Garland and McTyeire. Although not an original thinker, Summers was a gifted and sensitive liturgist. According to Edward Philips, Summers and his Vanderbilt students helped transform Methodist worship from what a century later would be called "seeker-oriented services," where the focus was on effecting a conversion experience in the unbelieving through raucous, unorthodox services, to a refined and thoughtful "perpetual thank-offering of believers." Worship, as Summers understood and taught it, was not something for Christian neophytes, but best planned and directed by mature disciples. As Fitzgerald noted, Summers was less concerned about being popular than about elevating the religious taste and character of the MECS—especially hymnology and other forms of worship. He believed, for example, that the temperance crusade's "recent innovation" of substituting grape juice for wine in the eucharist denied the sacrament its full aesthetic import. For Summers the visible forms of worship had to coincide with and support its spiritual intent and significance. "He maintained," noted Philips, "that the liturgy deserved solemn care in order to be the appropriate worship of the people of God, and this meant that the minister must be aware of the aesthetic dimension of public prayer." This required more than "saying beautiful words; it also meant paying attention to how the liturgy was performed." Summers sought to train Vanderbilt students for aesthetic, liturgical excellence, and in the process to identify with the tastes and preferences of the New South's cultural elite.[37]

Summers also held the right view concerning the social role of education. Higher education's primary function was not the pursuit of theoretical answers to obscure discipline-specific questions. Rather, it existed to lead society in particular directions. For Summers this explained why religion held a vital stake in any future of education. In editing Josephus Anderson's denominational manual, Summers concurred that "knowledge is power, and Christianity must lay hold on that power, sanctify it, and employ it for blessing the world." Unrestrained and unsanctified education had a history of great social harm (e.g., the French Revolution). By controlling the forces of education, Christians could control the government, the press, the arts and sciences, industry, and the economy. Higher education also provided the best, if not the only, means to "control public sentiment, and thoroughly Christianize and sanctify all departments of life." In other words, by presiding over the intellectual formation of society's thinkers, Christianity could transform the larger culture.[38]

On this point Summers and Newton agreed. With the advent of the New South, the church had lost its privilege to speak *ex cathedra* on southern life and culture. Newton asked, What should the church do? Should it back away from the New South dilemma and surrender its cultural responsibility forever? Or should it engage society and aggressively promote the truth it understands at that time? "The church of Christ cannot retreat and surrender this territory without treachery to her Lord," counseled Newton. "She can and must conquer a peace by making of any who may be enemies either friends or captives." Theological education provided a vehicle for preparing the rising generation to assume responsibility and secure its influence for the best interests of society and humanity. It was incumbent upon the denomination, Newton urged, to "conserve the intellectual life of the country" and "save the age" by securing an attitude among the New South's leaders that "humbly recognizes Christ as the world's Great Master."[39]

Tillett and the Myth of a Christian America

The difference between the prophetic vision of McTyeire's first generation and that of Wilbur Fisk Tillett and his generation was not so much one of kind, but of degree and scope. Garland, McTyeire, and Summers had created a school at ease with the New South and a program intentionally oriented toward its cultural goals and ambitions. With that foundation established, Tillett could now oversee a program of theological education that maintained and advanced that comfortable cultural relationship. Tillett fully intended Vanderbilt-trained ministers to continue supporting the New South. In return, as the New South's power and influence expanded, Vanderbilt would play an integral role in the creation of a larger Christian culture. As dean he announced that his "school of the prophets" would now regard "the world as its parish."[40] Bishop Atticus Haygood's address to the Vanderbilt community in 1890 illustrated something of this self-perception at the University. Haygood took his audience back for a brief glance into pre-Columbian America, but only to establish that "till the English-speaking and God-fearing colonists came there were none who dwelt on this continent who had thoughts worth keeping alive in the world. If all the ideas our forerunners had were utterly dropped out of history men would not miss them." With the Native peoples of America summarily dismissed, Haygood introduced the "Anglo" people into America's history, asking rhetorically, "what are we here for? We are here to build a Christian Nation." Then Haygood brought the lesson home, focusing on the University's role in this process. It would providentially serve the South by "leading the people in the best ways of thinking and living" with their newfound wealth. "The training, culture, and inspiration a true Vanderbilt man" could return to society would help make America's Christian culture "truer and richer."[41]

Tillett propagated this mythic reading of America's existence. He believed himself able to forge ahead with this ambitious goal for theological education because the New South created not only new opportunities but, more importantly, a new type of southern student. The Old South's commitment to chattel slavery had placed a check on the moral development of the white man by pandering to his wants and needs. Consequently, antebellum whites degenerated into "idle do-nothings," who themselves were held in "bondage to leisure." Thanks to the Civil War and Reconstruction, however, the southern white man "was thrown upon his own resources." Thus, in the last quarter of the nineteenth century southern whites quickly overcame their contempt for labor, embraced their newfound liberty to compete for material prosperity, and "joined the other freemen of the earth in running a nobler and better race." They also took more interest in the Christian religion and built "neater and finer churches" than southerners had constructed during the best of times in the Old South. Tillett admitted that the South was still on probation to the rest of the United States. Nevertheless, he was optimistic that the New South had progressed sufficiently to model America's Christian civilization to the rest of the world and "bless the race."[42]

Liberated from the culturally stultifying effects of slavery, the white South joined the providentially produced chain of events that created a Christian America, stretching from the voyages of Christopher Columbus, through the founding of the English colonies, the establishment of independence, and the preservation of the Union in the Civil War. The New South, therefore, was part of the unique Christian enterprise known in world history as "America." In addition to historical examples of God's overruling providence, Tillett argued in 1923 that America was distinctly Christian because it "constantly manifested in its history deeds worthy of such a high claim." Of all of America's good deeds, those motivated by altruism most clearly defined the nation's divine commission. According to Tillett, the United States had recently manifested its altruistic compassion for the world in three military engagements. The Spanish–American War, the Chinese Boxer Rebellion, and the Great War served merely as initial providential means for global progress in the twentieth century. "What is the vocation of the American nation?" he asked. "What is the task which Providence has assigned to us, discharging which we will fill our place among those favored nations who are 'the called according to God's purpose'?" The mission was none other than "to maintain in the world" the form of social, political, and economic organization that God desired. To uphold its divine imperialistic mission, Tillett called on America to commit to a patient, firm, and vigilant cold war against an unnamed enemy, in which the U.S. provided an adroit providential counterforce for progress wherever and whenever needed. "To win this ceaseless fight for moral progress, and to keep it won," he asserted, "demands nothing less than the full moral equivalent of war."[43]

From our perspective, it is hard to believe that a former dean of the School of Religion would think, let alone publish, such words. Why would people believe such an interpretation of history? What did Tillett's schema suggest about his view of society and Vanderbilt's role in it? That he could equate Christianity and America should not, in retrospect, be entirely surprising. As Henry May noted, "in 1876 [the year after Vanderbilt opened] Protestantism presented a massive, almost unbroken front in its defense of the social status quo." Henry Steele Commager agreed. American Protestantism near the turn of the century had so adopted the social commitments of the larger culture that there was little left to distinguish American mainline denominations from the culture or even from each other.[44] According to Robert Handy, the advancement of America's supposed Christian civilization became for many Protestants the chief mission of their faith. Inextricably intertwined, the American church and state had one and the same purpose—the propagation of Christian civilization.[45] At the turn of the century, the "Christian civilization" ideology provided a win-win scenario for the American church and state. With the "Christian America" thesis as popular national policy, the church would sanctify the social status quo for the state, and the state would guarantee the church's continuing social role in a rapidly transforming culture. It is little wonder, therefore, that the "Christian America" premise found acceptance in the New South in the midst of its own transformation. The Christian America myth, for Tillett and others, justified a social conservatism.

Along with his sanction of some of the United States' most aggressive military conquests, the social chauvinism underwriting Tillett's plan came through in his writings on race and economics. On the matter of race, Tillett did not fight the New South's Jim Crow laws, but expressed his wish, as had Newton earlier, that God would make some of the "Negro race the ultimate intellectual, moral and social good of their entire race, not only here, but in darkest Africa." Tillett envisioned a separate-but-equal providential mission for African Americans. On a different racial note, Tillett sounded like Josiah Strong, who nearly forty years earlier published his "Christian America" manifesto, *Our Country*. Like Strong, Tillett was more eager to have Americans be altruistic "over there" than to have immigrants come "over here" and threaten the Anglo-Saxon racial composition of "God's country." When discussing recent immigration patterns from central and eastern Europe, for example, Tillett cautioned, "the contrast in character between these earlier settlers, between these heroic and high-minded men and women who came to these shores and created our republic, and the human riffraff that is now drifting into this 'melting pot' of the Western world is painful to contemplate." Thus Tillett urged "the widest possible legislation, lest we as a nation in discharging our duty to others find that instead of our lifting these immigrant hoards up, we allow them to pull the nation down with their low, God-less, un-American ideals and social vices." Tillett's Christian America was also economically conservative. Two elements were necessary for America to implement its God-appointed mission, "money and men." "Money is needed and much of it," Tillett warned. "This means that it is the duty and providential mission of some men and some nations to make it, to make it that it may be used for the service of humanity. The commercialism whose accumulated coin is turned into currency for the service of mankind is in its ultimate aim ethical and altruistic."[46] Here was a message designed to sanctify a prosperous, acquisitive society. The successful, albeit charitable, capitalist fulfilled a necessary vocation in America's Christian civilization by underwriting the endeavor.

In addition to race and economics, Tillett manifested his social conservatism in his teaching on "progress." For him, social progress was essentially synonymous with providence. The plot of history, for example, "is a revelation of God's nature and of his providential government of men," a study of "the hand of God, as seen in the life of men and nations."[47] Because history is providential, and providence is progressive, Tillett reasoned that twentieth-century Americans were better prepared to lead a Christian civilization than any previous people or nation; God's "power and love and care" guided the maturation of the United States down to the "minutest details of our life." So, with some caveats imposed, Tillett concluded that America was at this particular moment the current pinnacle of God's civilization. His reasoning was almost Darwinian—that which exists now must be the most fit because it is the reigning champion of perpetual development.[48] Moreover, providential progress for Tillett could never end. Any cessation of progress would encourage stagnation, which would lead to decline and eventual death. That explained why the church had "to change and does change, ever adapting itself to the world's deep needs, that it not only lives but grows with the promise and potency of endless progress."[49]

Tillett's reasoning would have pleased McTyeire, Garland, and other initial supporters of theological education at Vanderbilt, since it supported the view that the inevitable, inexorable progress of society required a better-educated ministry. In other words, because God guided human existence through progress, God's prophets had to be vanguards. For Tillett, the three overlapping characteristics of efficiency, usefulness, and knowledge enabled prophets to fulfill their commission. Theological education provided the best opportunities for developing these traits.[50] Citing one unnamed MECS conference, Tillett found that 60 percent of the educated ministers were judged by members of their conference as "acceptable and successful" preachers. On the other hand, while only 20 percent of the educated ministers "were classed in a rank representing inferior usefulness," 60 percent of ministers lacking theological education were deemed of "inferior usefulness." In addition to having a higher approval rating, Tillett argued, theologically educated ministers had better results. His study suggested that MECS clergymen with theological education "show an average of 50% better results in that which constitute an average and successful ministry."[51] Employing a rural analogy, he described how a workman who invested thirty minutes in the morning sharpening his axe would still fell more trees in a day's time than another who launched quickly into his labors with a dull axe.[52] As Tillett told an audience at the Southern College of the YMCA, education sharpened the individual for greater, harder, and better work. Because a vital connection existed "between education and usefulness," which the history of the Christian church more than abundantly proved, ministers required theological education as it "increased influence, supremacy, and power." Usefulness was almost "exactly proportioned to intellectual strength."[53] In the end they all affirmed the cultural course of events already in place, because the status quo defined what was efficient and useful.

Samuel P. Jones's mockery of the "Rev. Supremus Eruditus" as a "theological dude" who sermonized on "the firstly's, secondly's, and thirdly's," and whose theological education "never added an ounce of weight to [his] brains or common sense," provided Tillett all the more reason to promote a high view of education.[54] The Christian church needed "trained, brainy, scholarly, aggressive, and consecrated" preachers whose "chief and ultimate aim" was the "building up of moral character, the making of cultured Christian manhood and womanhood—this is the end of all preaching." Only the theological seminary could "train men for preaching, for teaching, for ministering in a way to meet the conditions and needs of today." Furthermore, if the church were to fulfill its mission to support America's ever-progressing Christian civilization, ministers were needed who could effectively, efficiently, and knowledgeably advise each generation's social and intellectual leaders—those who set the tenor of the age. In light of the clergy's wide-ranging social responsibility, he viewed the ministry as the vocation requiring the most professional preparation. To make his case that future American progress depended upon a well-trained clergy, Tillett delved deeply into history, arguing that "nearly everyone of the illustrious prophets and preachers of righteousness, whose names find an honored place in the history of the church [e.g., Moses, Paul, Chrysostom, Luther, and Wesley], obtained, in preparation for his holy calling, the very best education that was possible in the age and country in which he lived—and most of these men had special extensive training in theological studies in addition to their general education, and their preparation fitted them for understanding and meeting the special needs of the day in which they lived."[55] In this light, Tillett labored to make Vanderbilt a "school of the prophets equal to the best and strongest in America."[56]

Taylor: Vanderbilt's Prophet in Residence

Despite the University's separation from the MECS, Tillett provided continuity, carrying key elements of McTyeire's social vision for theological education at Vanderbilt into the twentieth century. McTyeire's "school of the prophets" sought to better acculturate Christianity to New South standards. Under Tillett the School of Religion maintained and advanced that relationship to better Christianize the New South and America. In 1928, however, a dissenting voice emerged when Alva Wilmot Taylor joined the faculty of the School of Religion. Not quite sixty years old when he arrived in Nashville, Taylor had already developed a career noted for genuine prophetic flair. He had done graduate study in sociology at the University of Chicago under Graham Taylor and had worked with Jane Addams at the Hull House. For his doctoral dissertation, Taylor lived among Irish wage-earners and observed relationships between landlords and tenants. Returning to the United States, he joined the faculty of the Bible College of Missouri in 1910, where he taught such courses as "The Social Teaching of Jesus," "The Social Message of the Old Testament," "The Social Work of Christian Missions," "The Social Aspects of Religious Education," and "The Social Function and Work of the Church." As a member of the Interchurch World Movement, he drafted the report on the 1919 steel strike that helped reduce the twelve-hour workday required of many steel workers. In 1921, Taylor became secretary for the Board of Temperance and Social Welfare Committee of the Disciples of Christ, which investigated and recommended policy—through publications and lectures—on race relations, labor disputes, and international relations.[57]

On the surface, Taylor affirmed Tillett's prophetic call to create a Christian America. Tillett, for example, would have supported Taylor's thesis that the "greatest mission" of the church was to "help transform civilization itself from a pagan to a Christian social order" and that the primary responsibility of the church was to "Christianize law and custom, business and diplomacy, racial feeling and international relationships." But at the heart of Taylor's thought and work were two primary questions that separated him from Vanderbilt's tradition in theological education. The first "big question," for Taylor, was "What is the genius of the Christian message?" He could not imagine that either personal salvation or institutional affluence ever adequately demarcated what was "Christian." As seen in the Sermon on the Mount, Jesus came to reorient radically all human relationships—favoring the poor and marginalized of society. No disciple, therefore, was truly Christian who failed to implement the "principles of the Sermon on the Mount in all his social relationships." Less certain than Tillett that the southern church had the right message to proclaim to America, Taylor spoke prophetically first to persons in the churches themselves. For Taylor, "the single greatest task of Christians is to integrate [the Sermon on the Mount's] teachings into the social order. The greatest single task of the church is to widen their small and limited brotherhoods into the brotherhood of all men."[58]

The second question focusing Taylor's thought and work was, "For whom does the church speak?" Like many Christian social reformers, he appealed to the ethical teachings of Jesus, who "called the social order into the free fellowship of a common brotherhood under the love of an all-compassionate Father. There can be no artificial privilege, no petty aristocracy where his spirit rules." Thus the church and its clergy existed to "lift the lowly and bring down the mighty from selfish privilege" and to imitate Christ "whose path and position is ever with the common people." In fact, the degree to which the church uplifted the lowly served as the measure of its success for Taylor.[59] Believing that the church had failed on these grounds, he was not surprised that society's humble had abandoned the church.

As a writer, educator, and activist, Taylor labored for nothing shy of the Kingdom of God on earth. Committed to a "kingdom of right relations" where humanity understood itself as one great family with a common "Father," he imagined that each member of the family would contribute more than he or she received. The color line would be erased. War would cease. Exploitation of the weak by the strong would stop. Laissez-faire capitalism would disappear. The spirit of service and sacrifice would become the overriding attitude. Taylor bristled when fellow Christians dismissed his vision as a "mere pious wish." This desired kingdom was the "concrete, practical, and daring undertaking" of Jesus Christ to which Christianity had committed itself at its inception, Taylor demanded. Christians, therefore, had no choice but to "live righteously for righteousness' sake, seek no worldly reward, hunger and thirst after righteousness where men of the world hunger and thirst after power, prestige and wealth." Once transformed into a Christian community, employers, politicians, and educators would understand their positions as a sacred public trust, charged to "see that the masses of mankind have enough of the necessities of life to make life worthwhile and not just endurable," and to guarantee that "brotherly love" was "markedly manifest." The compensation to society's leaders for their ministry? "Just to have battled valiantly for the rights of others," Taylor wrote, was "within itself enough reward."[60]

Why did someone as socially liberal as Taylor come to the School of Religion, especially in light of the fact that he had to absorb a nearly 50 percent pay cut to teach social ethics? As he told his brother-in-law, "my mission is to teach young men for the ministry." Yet he could have fulfilled that mission at any of the schools that invited him to join their faculty. Why Vanderbilt? First, it was the only nondenominational, theologically progressive school of religion in "the NEW South."[61] Second, Taylor found the South's social problems "so acute," so "very critical," and in such "great need of constructive Christian social approach," that the challenge "lured" him to the region—a region "still greatly influenced by the religious approach." Basically Taylor wanted to practice what he preached by serving the humble of the South in the creation of a truly new, that is to say radically reformed, South—a South progressing toward the Kingdom of God. In addition, he told Sherwood Eddy, his personal activism could model for young ministers appropriate methods for facing the social problems "down here." Then he could sow his students "all over the South with their social vision enlarged." In a letter marked "confidential," Taylor explained to Eddy, "The biggest thing I can accomplish for the kingdom for the remainder of my days is to hold this strategic position right here in this great old university and help both to redeem it to a progressive attitude and to put this nondenominational school of religion on its feet with a social direction in the training of the New South's religious leadership." His ministerial students in the School of Religion affirmed his decision. Although he worked for what he considered "starvation wages," Taylor found "eager young chaps going into the ministry," ready to push the racial and economic rights agenda in the New South.[62] According to Taylor's own calculations, 80 percent of the School of Religion's student body took classes with him in 1933, and 40 percent of the graduate theses in 1936 were written under his direction. He also claimed that his courses had two to three times the average enrollment. Aware that some wealthy contributors to the school might take offense at his social interpretation of Christianity, Taylor reminded Dean Brown of potential fallout. According to Taylor, Brown acknowledged the danger of Taylor's perspective to the institution, but responded, "There is no use of getting money if we cannot teach the truth."[63]

Taylor designed his courses to respond to current events, offering classes such as "Christian Ethics," "Rural Sociology," "Ethics of Human Relations," and a seminar titled "International, Racial, and Industrial Relations." He also planned future seminars such as "The Social Function and Work of Religious Institutions" and "The Social Basis of Moral Action." His publications were aimed more at a popular than an academic audience, denouncing nearly every noteworthy New South issue of the time. On the topic of war Taylor argued that class interest, propaganda, and half-truths inspired armed hostility, mobilizing even spiritual forces for human destruction. Because the "greatest need of the world today is that of Christianizing our organized relationships," he argued, "wholesale killing by war must be made a social crime just as personal killing has been made a crime"—otherwise "modern, scientific war killing will exterminate the race that is taught not to kill."[64] On the sensitive issue of race, Taylor publicly argued that race prejudice was more cruel and abominable than any other source of error in the world. For "anyone who takes his gospel seriously," he protested, "the most elementary application of the principles of Christianity" required the eradication of the color line, "and the granting of equal opportunities to those of all races."[65] Throughout his frequent editorials in the *Christian Century*, Taylor protested for human rights advances in the South by keeping before the readers lynching statistics in the 1930s; promoting integration in the churches, education, and social services; and advocating economic and voting rights for African Americans.[66] For the Disciples' Board of Temperance and Social Welfare he published the magazine *Social Trends*, which had as its mission "the promotion of every form of church activity that touches social welfare, and to educate in the use of ways and means to promote social justice." He edited a memorial edition of Walter Rauschenbusch's *Prayers of the Social Awakening*, and co-edited and authored other books while on the School of Religion faculty.[67]

In addition to teaching and writing, Taylor modeled his prophetic call for Vanderbilt's ministerial students in both symbolic and direct ways. He challenged the New South social code by holding a dual church membership in an interracial church at Fisk University and the Vine Street Christian Church and by entertaining Fisk students in his home.[68] He coordinated with Howard Kester the 1932 Nashville Conference on Unemployment, co-sponsored by John Dewey's Joint Committee on Unemployment and the local chapter of the Fellowship of Reconciliation. As chairman of the Church Emergency Relief Committee, an agency of the Federal Council of Churches, he became deeply involved in the Wilder, Tennessee, coal strike in 1931.

Involvement in the Wilder strike, however, may have been the beginning of the end for Taylor at Vanderbilt. Although his Church Emergency Relief Committee formally offered food, clothing, and shelter to all those impoverished by the strike, behind the scenes Taylor worked aggressively with the miners' union. "We are doing our part," Taylor privately told supporters, "to give the bosses a damned good licking." Additionally, he solicited his students and colleagues (e.g., C. C. Haun) to participate in his work at Wilder, anticipating full well the reaction of the Vanderbilt administration to his labor agitation. "If you ginks think I'm getting old and conservative," Taylor responded to friends, "just note that I'm helping garment and textile workers organize here in the realm of John Edgerton and that Saint John is Chairman of the University Board's Committee for the School of Religion. As George Pickett of the Llano Coop colony says, 'It's a hell of a job to try to bring in the Kingdom of Heaven.' " The situation turned gravely serious when Barney Graham, president of the local United Mine Workers chapter at Wilder, was ambushed and his bullet-ridden corpse found "nearly brained."[69] Violence did not deter Taylor, however. He became more involved in the Wilder situation, working closely with Kester.

An outspoken proponent of President Franklin D. Roosevelt's New Deal program, as seen in Taylor's writing and work as a liaison for the Tennessee Valley Authority (TVA) in Nashville, Taylor piqued the ire of Chancellor James H. Kirkland. Taylor felt that his personal support of the New Deal "does not help to keep my job secure," because "our old Chancellor is for everything that was of yesterday and most of all for the [laissez-faire] scheme that gave this University millions."[70] If Kirkland was the "the old-time Southern aristocrat" and "Old Bourbon" whom Taylor depicted, Taylor undermined what job security he had by frequently including reports of School of Religion events with running social commentary on the failures of southern conservatism in his editorials in the *Christian Century*. He left the impression among the periodical's national audience that Vanderbilt operated a radically progressive School of Religion.[71]

Taylor's position in social ethics existed on a grant from the Rockefeller Fund. But the grant neared completion in 1934, and with financial woes compounded by the Depression and a consequent drop in enrollment, Taylor feared that the situation "affords an excellent time to let the 'troublesome' fellows out."[72] Instead of immediately releasing him, Kirkland informed Taylor that his position would continue only if he raised half its cost, a move that Taylor interpreted as an unquestioned "stab at liberal social teaching." Scoffing at Vanderbilt's commitment to truly progressive theological education, Taylor seethed, "It's great to teach Christianity, *IF* you are never called upon to practice it." Thanks to the work of "Negroes, labor unions, Jews, and progressive businessmen," Taylor's friends raised enough money to secure his position for the next two years, literally underwriting his social agenda at Vanderbilt.[73] Honored by their efforts, Taylor knew their funds were only a temporary solution. He predicted that Kirkland would "garrote" him before long because, as he had suspected for some time, Kirkland wanted to purge the school of all but "the old guard."[74]

For the rest of his life Taylor felt blacklisted from theological education because he prophetically offered radical Christian solutions to New South social problems. Far from failing as a classroom instructor, Taylor believed he had succeeded all too well in establishing a prophetic voice in the School of Religion. The Vanderbilt administration, however, did not want the institution's name attached to Taylor's culturally subversive message.[75] In Taylor's own estimation, however, he could not have acted otherwise and still "kept his soul." He believed he exercised more discretion than necessary, even appropriate, all to "maintain my University work in this very strategic situation facing the conservative old South." So, although he found his "adventure" of helping ministerial candidates in the School of Religion "to face the New South" energizing and "fascinating," Taylor could not avoid running afoul of that "old Southern Bourbon" chancellor who "hates Roosevelt, deplores the TVA, sees no use of Social Ethics," and "has ruled the campus like Mussolini for forty-three years." Unable to find another permanent teaching position, Taylor tried to remain optimistic, noting that "worry kills and bitterness ruins the spirit, so I am indulging in neither but plowing ahead trusting the Lord and the New Deal."[76]

Conclusion

A quick walk around the exterior of the Divinity quadrangle today provides two examples of the power of communal identity. On the northwest corner—between the Divinity School and Garland Hall—is the gravesite of, among others, Bishop Holland McTyeire and Thomas O. Summers. On the western wall of the quadrangle's interior courtyard is the lintel from Wesley Hall, inscribed "Schola Prophetarum." Over the years the Vanderbilt community has deemed these personalities and phrases so intrinsic to the historical development of the institution's ongoing experiment in theological education that they have earned a place in the physical landscape. And yet the meaning of their presence is open to interpretation. What do these icons symbolize? What did those who decided to erect them intend to communicate to future generations? The motto "school of the prophets" may be the most puzzling, for it still begs the questions, as it always has, "Prophets to whom?" and "What kind of attitude toward culture will these prophets take?" Bishop McTyeire and the founding generation wanted conservative prophets to emerge from their school. Imbued with the New South ethos, and well connected to the South's upper echelon, McTyeire's prophets would raise the social standing and power of the church. The Biblical Department did not exist to criticize, but to advance a particular kind of southern culture. It is noteworthy that this sense of mission did not die with the first generation. Tillett's second-generation prophetic vision was no more critical of the New South. In fact, he built on the successes of McTyeire's acculturation to southern society by developing the prophetic vision into a cultural chauvinism. His school of the prophets, therefore, trained ministers in efficiency, usefulness, and knowledge. With these skills they could help refine and perfect the South and the United States for the larger altruistic, providential mission of the Christianization of the world. Taylor also believed that the propagation of Christianity would better the state of humanity, but found the church and the South unprepared to lead this mission. Both required fundamental reorientation. The church needed to reclaim the countercultural ethic in Jesus' teachings and then hold society up to greater scrutiny. For the time being, the church should be the New South's primary critic, rather than partner.

The prophetic understandings of McTyeire and Tillett allowed Vanderbilt to maintain a comfortable relationship with the South, as each affirmed the other. Stated otherwise, McTyeire and Tillett assumed the New South to be normative, while Taylor's understanding of Christianity functioned as the corrective to society's norms. Obviously, Taylor's version threatened to alienate the School of Religion from the surrounding society—the heart of recruiting and fund raising. Although he lasted only eight years, in some ways Taylor foreshadowed the prophetic understanding that would define the Divinity School in the latter half of the twentieth century. More iconoclastic, more antagonistic toward the New South, the Divinity School since 1960 has trained ministers as theologians to challenge prophetically southern society's assumptions on matters of race, gender, sexual preference, and economic class.

Wesley Hall, East Front; home of the Biblical
Department and the School of Religion from 1881 to
1932. This five-story building housed students and faculty
and provided classrooms, offices, a dining hall,
and the library.

From "School of Religion, Half-Tone Views,"
Special Collections, Vanderbilt University

Wesley Hall Library.

From "School of Religion, Half-Tone Views,"
Special Collections, Vanderbilt University

Campus gravesite and monument.
Three Methodist bishops (William McKendree,
Joshua Soule, and Holland McTyeire) and the first chancellor of
Vanderbilt University, Landon C. Garland, are buried here.
In 1876 McTyeire oversaw the reburial of McKendree and
Soule, who had died earlier in the Nashville area.
McTyeire died in 1889 and Garland in 1895. Only with the
completion of the Divinity School quadrangle in 1960
did the two sites stand side by side.

Photo by Neal Brake

Faculty and students of the Biblical Department, 1908–9,
on the steps of Wesley Hall. The lintel above the entrance
reads "Schola Prophetarum."

Dean Tillett is in the first row just to the right of the fold;
Chancellor Kirkland is immediately to his left.

Faculty of the School of Religion, 1931–32
(includes regular faculty, lecturers, and Kenyon Butterfield,
the Cole Lecturer for 1932).

*From "The Burning of Wesley Hall" [1932],
Special Collections, Vanderbilt University.*

Wesley Hall in flames, February 19, 1932
(photo touched up to provide additional flames).

From "The Burning of Wesley Hall" [1932],
Special Collections, Vanderbilt University

The new Wesley Hall, home of the School of Religion
and the Divinity School from 1936 to 1960.

Photo by Jack Corn; Photographic Archives,
Vanderbilt University

School of Religion faculty, 1951–52
(left to right, first row:
Batten, Sandmel, Benton, Hyatt, Mayhew, Ferré;
2nd row: Ramsdell, Henley [lecturer], Norton,
Grobel, Stumpf; not pictured: Hawkins).

Photo by Ken Spain; Photographic Archives, Vanderbilt University

Bishop Joseph A. Johnson (1914–79), the first
African American student in the School of Religion and
Vanderbilt University; he was elected bishop in the
Christian Methodist Episcopal Church in 1966.

Vanderbilt Divinity School

PART III
Transformations

As the Divinity School opened the 1959–60 school year and looked forward to occupying its new quadrangle, the most visible sign of its ambitions for the future, no one could have anticipated the transformations to come in the next decades. The civil rights movement had begun in Montgomery, Alabama, a few years earlier, but it had only had a limited impact on Nashville, chiefly in the form of desegregation of the public schools by one grade per year. Having opened the Divinity School to African American students and offered the hope that more could follow, many in the University might have believed that it needed to do little more. The beginnings of the sit-in movement in February 1960 and the succeeding crisis period that came to be called "the Lawson affair" in the Divinity School and the University demonstrated how naive that belief would have been. Dean J. Robert Nelson was one casualty of that crisis, and his resignation from the faculty was a condition of the final agreement. Despite their magnitude, the events of the Lawson affair proved to be only a beginning in the institution's engagement with southern and national culture on issues of racial justice. Other theological institutions would perhaps learn from Vanderbilt's experience, but none in the country would be unaffected by similar presentations of issues relating to race, religion, and culture over the next four decades.

Other developments followed that altered the face of theological education across the country. The Vietnam War and the national reaction to it, the emergence of the counterculture and its attendant challenges to authority, the women's movement and "second-wave" feminism, claims for gay liberation—these are only a few of the events that made the sixties a pivotal period in American history. Each issue had an impact on virtually every theological institution; in combination, they produced tensions and conflicts. Out of these conflicts often emerged a more energized, more immediately relevant theological education with new subject areas, literatures, courses, and research topics. The Divinity School offers an excellent case study of larger movements in theological education in this country. Specific dimensions of this transformation are explored in the chapters by Howard Harrod on social transformation and theological education, Kim Maphis Early on the activities and influence of women in the Divinity School, and Peter Paris on the African American presence.

The chapters in this section are less attentive to the contributions of individual deans or faculty members than a strictly chronological pattern would be, and thus some additional chronological narrative will help to provide the institutional framework within which the major transformations may be viewed.

After one year with Professor Herman Norton as acting dean, William C. Finch, president of Southwestern University in Texas, became dean. Finch had come to Chancellor Harvie Branscomb's attention through the latter's contacts with Methodist bishops. His brief deanship was clearly a transitional period. The Lawson affair and its aftermath resulted in a drop in enrollment and a demoralized faculty, and some of the contentiousness from the affair remained in the years that followed. At the end of the fall 1964 semester, Finch left the deanship to become president of Emory and Henry College in Virginia.

Finch's many years in Methodist higher education served him well in his effort to establish stronger connections with the Methodist church while at Vanderbilt. One result was the creation of a "Methodist chair," annually funded jointly by the Methodist Board of Higher Education, the Tennessee Conference of the Methodist Church, and the Divinity School. That arrangement was meant to ensure that the School would continue to cultivate its connection with the church; in just a few years, however, the connection was lost. Another of Finch's projects was to conclude the work begun by Dean John Keith Benton in securing support for a chaplaincy position at the University hospital (designed to include half-time teaching in pastoral care at the Divinity School); he also assisted in the creation of the University Chaplaincy, although that was not completed until 1967.

James Sellers, whose field was theology and ethics, succeeded Finch, but he served an even shorter period before returning to the faculty. He was the first of four deans to be chosen from the faculty, a subtle but distinct shift from the previous pattern. The notable event of his deanship was the merger that brought the Oberlin Graduate School of Theology to Vanderbilt. Two professorial titles with modest endowment, six faculty members (one dividing his time between Oberlin and Vanderbilt), and a number of students came to the school in 1966, after Oberlin College decided not to continue its theological school. It was hoped that the connections Oberlin had with its alumni and with congregations in Ohio and related states would enlarge the Divinity School's support and recruitment possibilities. While some of that did develop, much that had been hoped for did not. In a short time the Oberlin students graduated and three of the faculty left for other positions. In recognition of the joining of institutions, however, the Divinity School building took the name "Oberlin Quadrangle."

Walter Harrelson followed Sellers as dean from 1967 to 1975. A specialist in Old Testament studies, Harrelson came to the school in 1960 from the University of Chicago Divinity School and was caught up in the negotiations surrounding the Lawson affair even before he moved to Nashville. Early in his deanship, the School followed a national pattern by making the Master of Divinity (M.Div.) the first theological degree. With the addition of the Oberlin faculty, the expansion of the graduate program in both program areas and numbers of students, and the beginning of a Doctor of Divinity program for practicing ministers and theological school graduates (D.Div., soon changed to D.Min., again following the national pattern), Harrelson led the school to its first genuinely national reputation. He promoted faculty conversations on the possibilities for ecumenical cooperation with other theological schools in the region; one result of these efforts was a joint D.Min. program with the School of Theology at Sewanee, part of the University of the South (with courses held in a summer session on each campus), that started in the mid-1970s and ran for a decade. The first Roman Catholic faculty member, John Donahue, S.J., came in 1973 to teach New Testament studies. In 1974 the Divinity School and the Law School began to offer a dual-degree program of study, where the respective degrees of each school (normally taking three years each) could be earned in five years; its first graduates received their degrees in 1980. A continuing education program for laity, conducted with the support of a number of Nashville churches, also began during these years.

In the late 1960s, as a corollary of the expansive mood, the larger faculty, and the interest to build a broader reputation, the school began to run an annual budget deficit—with the support of the University administration. Student-led protests of the Vietnam War, countercultural experimentation, and the continuing impact of the civil rights movement affected the school in profound ways. Such events created opportunities for public activity and testimony by students and faculty; on more than one occasion in these years, Divinity students helped to keep the demonstrations nonviolent. Occasionally there were difficult choices: while dean, Harrelson once testified as a witness for the defense at a pornography trial, and as a result lost some promised funding for his major research effort to microfilm ancient manuscripts in Ethiopia. The high enrollment during the Vietnam years turned almost as quickly to low enrollment when the war ended, and this too had an impact on the school's budget. Faculty were concerned that large tuition increases would deter potential students from enrolling and put the school in an adverse competitive relationship with denominational seminaries. In this period Harrelson hired the first administrative officer responsible for development and alumni relations, who also became involved in the recruitment of students.

The size of the faculty steadily increased in the 1960s; the 1960–61 catalogue listed sixteen full-time faculty members; a decade later there were twenty-six, including additional faculty members in ethics and pastoral theology. This increase was accompanied by a significant change in personnel; Lou Silberman and Herman Norton were the only persons from the events of 1960 still on the faculty in 1973, and only one of the Oberlin persons who had come in 1966 remained on the faculty by 1972. Yet out of this period of great change emerged another period of stability, as several of the faculty members who came to the school in this era stayed to retirement some thirty years later.

Enrollment patterns in the school since 1960 have reflected larger social transformations in the society as well as developments in theological education. The presence of older and often second-career students was a feature of theological schools across the country from the early 1970s, as was the steady increase in the number of women students. The increase in D.Min. programs across the country meant a reinvigoration of post-M.Div. work; at Vanderbilt this work chiefly accounted for increases in total enrollments in two five-year periods, 1973–78 and 1982–87. When a two-year Master of Theological Studies (M.T.S.) degree was introduced in the late 1980s, enrollments in the program soon helped to balance a decline in numbers of M.Div. students and a corresponding decline in the D.Min. program. The percentage of women in the M.Div. program (now, with the M.T.S. alternative, the one more obviously for students interested in the ministry) passed 40 percent in 1986 and 50 percent in 1989, with percentages staying between 50 and 60 percent since 1992.

Sallie McFague, assistant professor of theology, became the first woman dean of a major theological school in the country with her appointment in 1975. Her initial appointment in the school as a "part-time, full status" faculty member was the first of its kind in the University; the efforts of Dean Harrelson in getting this idea accepted at Vanderbilt opened up new possibilities for spouses (then almost exclusively women) of faculty members. Under McFague's initiative, a committee of faculty and students undertook a major study of the school's curriculum, leading to the institution of a new program in 1981. An increasingly serious financial situation in the school led to the appointment of a full-time development officer and posed some hard decisions with respect to the school's budget. Also during this period, a Davis Cup tennis match held on the campus in 1978 raised the issue of apartheid for the University in a more direct way than most people had anticipated, and the Divinity School became one of the rallying points for opposition to the University's sponsorship. In the aftermath of this event, McFague resigned the deanship and returned to the faculty in 1979.

H. Jackson Forstman, professor of historical theology, succeeded McFague as dean and served for ten years. His primary focus was on the school's external relationships, notably the need to increase the number of supporters among alumni/ae and friends and the need to expand the school's development program. He worked at developing a constituency of support first within Nashville and then across the region (a giving society, *Schola Prophetarum*, was begun in these years) and with the Board of Trust as well as reducing the school's budget deficit. A generous matching challenge from within the University substantially assisted this effort. Early in his tenure as dean, he appointed the school's first full-time admissions officer.

Joseph C. Hough, Jr., served as dean 1990–99. Soon after arriving from the School of Theology at Claremont, where he had been dean and professor of Christian ethics, he introduced a long-range planning process with the faculty involving two years of review and reflection on the school's problems and opportunities. The final report this process produced included a reduction by three persons in the size of the faculty, to be accomplished through retirements. Important work during his deanship also included raising endowment moneys for professorships and scholarships and continuing to reduce the annual budget deficit. The D.Min. program, which had seen declining enrollments, was closed to new admissions in 1993. A new All Faith Chapel was constructed out of a large classroom in the early 1990s and quickly became the primary worship space for the school; the absence of permanent religious symbols enabled this chapel to be used by a wider number of religious communities, in keeping with the increasing diversity represented in the Divinity School and the University.

The end of the century saw a period of major transition in the faculty, through a combination of retirements, replacements, and the establishment of new professorial chairs. A new dean, James Hudnut-Beumler, took office in 2000 and will lead the school into a renewed consideration of the opportunities and challenges that lie before it, as past deans have done. One should not project in advance the contours of those future transformations. We might anticipate, however, that the stated commitments of the school, printed in the catalogue since the early 1970s and expanded as new issues have been engaged (see Appendix F), will continue to provide a framework for any new articulation of the school's mission.

6

The Lawson Affair, 1960:
A Conversation

*With James M. Lawson, Gene L. Davenport, Langdon Gilkey,
Lou H. Silberman, John Compton, and Charles Roos;
Convener, Dale A. Johnson*

O N OCTOBER 2–3, 1998, A CONVERSATION WAS HELD AT VAN-
derbilt Divinity School among persons who participated in what has
come to be called "the Lawson affair" in February–June 1960. This
conversation took place in Tillett Lounge around an imposing wooden table,
one of the pieces of furniture retained in the move from Wesley Hall to the new
Divinity quadrangle in 1960. That table would be mentioned in the course of
the conversation as one of the connecting points between an earlier decision in
1952 and the present day.

"The Lawson affair" became one of the defining moments in the Divinity
School's history. For a few days in June it seemed as though it might even bring
down the Divinity School itself and have serious repercussions for the University as a whole. It was touched off in late February by the activities of James M.
Lawson, an African American divinity student, in his leadership of the sit-
in movement in Nashville, and news of the controversy quickly spread around
the country.

The series of events that followed contained a number of complicating
dimensions: a fledgling civil rights movement attempting a new protest strategy,
a history of racial segregation in the South, differing regional and local perspectives on national priorities, a developing plan by Chancellor Harvie Branscomb
to integrate the University, as well as a variety of governance issues within the
University. It was not only a critical moment for the University and the Divinity

School, but for Nashville and the larger culture as well. How can we best tell such a story within the context of the history of the Divinity School? The only published account of these events is in Paul K. Conkin's history of Vanderbilt University, *Gone with the Ivy* (1985). One Divinity faculty member, Arthur L. Foster, dictated an extended account that was later transcribed. He placed a copy of this document in the University Archives, and Conkin used it in his construction of that particular chapter. Beyond that, however, no other Divinity faculty wrote accounts of their experiences, despite occasional suggestions that some should write what they remembered so that future generations would have material to attempt to understand what had happened. A few conferences have been held over the years, bringing participants in the events together for conversation and reflection on this critical period, but more for the benefit of the attending audience than to create a published set of recollections.

Obviously, this topic warrants a chapter in a volume on the school's history. However complicated the events, we decided not to write a narrative parallel to Conkin's chapter, but rather try to add material to the historical resources and to provide personal reflections by holding a conversation among several participants. We decided that it should be a representative group of individuals, but not so large as to prevent a genuine conversation. By the late 1990s, however, a number of the key participants had died, including James Sellers and Herman Norton of the Divinity faculty; Chancellor Branscomb died in July 1998, at the age of 103. The group as eventually constituted included two people who had been Divinity students at the time: James M. Lawson, the central figure in the story, and Gene L. Davenport, president of the Divinity School's student government in 1959–60; two Divinity faculty members: Lou H. Silberman, who was Hillel Professor of Jewish Literature and Thought, and Langdon Gilkey, professor of theology; and two faculty members from the College of Arts and Science: Charles Roos, then associate professor of physics, and John Compton, then associate professor of philosophy. The volume's editor served as arranger, host, and moderator of the conversation. This chapter is an edited version of that two-day conversation. In the course of the discussion there were a few surprises, as the participants themselves came to learn more about the events in which they had been so deeply involved.

Lou Silberman, Charles Roos, and John Compton retired from Vanderbilt as emeritus professors in the 1980s and 1990s. James Lawson retired in 1999 after a long pastorate at the Holman United Methodist Church, Los Angeles. Gene Davenport is professor of religion at Lambuth College in Jackson, Tennessee. In 1963 Langdon Gilkey accepted an appointment as professor of theology at the Divinity School of the University of Chicago; he returned to Vanderbilt in the fall 1998 semester as the Wilson Visiting Distinguished Professor.

In the summer of 1998 David Halberstam's book, *The Children* (Random House), had been published, a fascinating story of the young people who were centrally involved in the sit-in movement in Nashville. More than one person in our conversation referred to the book for details of the events. Halberstam carried the story up to the present by reporting what happened to these individuals in the years following 1960. Lawson featured prominently in this narrative of the movement, though the issues that arose from his relationship to Vanderbilt University are treated much more briefly. Halberstam was a reporter for the Nashville *Tennessean* in 1960, so he had an early connection to this story. As it happens, he was himself part of the story, as will become apparent in the narrative, reporting on the issues in that crucial two-week period in June.

Lou Silberman began the conversation by recounting an important prologue to the 1960 events.

LOU SILBERMAN: I think that the prologue to what happened in the spring of 1960 is necessary, so I want to go back and talk about what happened in 1952 at a meeting of the faculty of the School of Religion. The only other person who was present at that meeting and who may still be alive is Everett Tilson, and I haven't seen or spoken to him in a great many years. As I look down, I think that this table, if it could speak, could tell us what was going on because this was the table of the faculty room in the late lamented Wesley Hall. [The Divinity School moved from Wesley Hall to its new facilities in the spring of 1960.—Ed.]

I came to Vanderbilt in the fall of 1952, as did John Compton. The first faculty meeting I attended was in October, in the back room, down the back corridor of Wesley Hall. Chancellor Harvie Branscomb presided at that meeting. I had no idea, of course, of what portentous matters were going to happen at that moment. The Chancellor presided, the usual sort of things took place, and then something happened that everyone else seemed to be anticipating. The previous spring, members of the faculty of the School of Religion had sent a memorandum or a petition to the Board of Trust, saying that the faculty could no longer in good conscience allow the school to be segregated.

I think that what lay behind this was something that happened earlier that year at the School of Theology in Sewanee, Tennessee, where a similar demand had been made. I do not know the details, but several of that school's faculty members, including the dean, announced that they were prepared to resign (and they eventually did resign) at the end of the next academic year if the Board of Trustees did not permit the school to admit qualified black students. I think that event made an impact upon the School of Religion faculty at that time; I say, I was not privy to it, but I understand it happened. They asked the Board of Trust to allow them to have black students in the School of Religion, and Harvie Branscomb was there to report that the Board of Trust had granted the request of the faculty to allow black students to be admitted. Nothing else regarding integration was happening in the University. I understand that at the time the Law School was under some kind of pressure from the American Association of Law Schools to do something similar, but their faculty did not do anything, so far as I know. I can remember the tension in that room; many of the faculty members were southerners. I remember particularly a professor of church history, Joseph Batten. Joe was a Virginian, and I saw that man almost in tears muttering, "Thank God, thank God, thank God." I am a far westerner, and I have never been involved in that kind of tension before, but that is what happened in October 1952.

But there was a restriction placed upon us; no public statement was going to be issued by the University, but such news apparently began to move out. The following spring I went to Lane College in Jackson, Tennessee. Lane was a black college; it had a school of theology, and I went under the auspices of the Jewish Chautauqua Society, as I often did in those days. I preached in the chapel, spoke in a class, and then had lunch with the faculty. During the lunch someone turned to me and asked, "If a black student were to apply to the School of Religion at Vanderbilt, do you think that person would be admitted?" I said, "Oh, I cannot make a public statement; but this is what I will say—it is my opinion that if the proper person were to apply to the School of Religion, that application would be given very serious consideration." And what happened? The president of that theological school, Joseph Johnson, who had a doctorate in theology from Iliff School of Theology but did not have a Bachelor of Divinity—lo and behold, Joe Johnson applied, left the presidency, and became minister of a CME church [Colored (later, Christian) Methodist Episcopal—*Ed.*] here in town. He became the first black graduate of Vanderbilt University. After he graduated, he wanted to take a Ph.D., and the faculty (we had not permission on that ground at that high level) said to the administration, Mr. Johnson is a Bachelor of Divinity from Vanderbilt University, and there is no reason in the world why a Bachelor of Divinity from Vanderbilt University cannot be admitted to the Ph.D. program in Vanderbilt University. And he was admitted in 1956.

LANGDON GILKEY: How many more black students were there between 1952 and 1960? Were there any besides yourself [James Lawson] when you came?

GENE DAVENPORT: There were three in 1958, I think.

SILBERMAN: That sounds right. Joe was still here working on his Ph.D. The faculty insisted that all aspects of the university be opened to him, so that whenever he went to Rand Hall for lunch, a member of the faculty went with him to make sure that nothing untoward happened—and nothing untoward ever did happen.

CHARLES ROOS: I came to Vanderbilt because it was the first school in the South to integrate. I am a fifth-generation southerner, from Texas, and I was at Cal Tech. I had meetings with the Cal Tech provost, Bob Backer, who told me that we needed to build up physics in the South. "You can come back if it doesn't work," he said. So I came to Vanderbilt holding a faculty appointment at Cal Tech for the first four years I was here. I stopped on the way and talked with Holmes Richter, dean of the faculty at Rice University. I asked him, "What do you think of Vanderbilt? I don't know much about it." He said, "You've got a good chancellor, a courageous man who is pushing, very forward thinking; he is going to build a good university." So I arrived in a very fortunate position in the spring of 1959 and was immediately accepted personally by Harvie and Margaret Branscomb. Margaret Branscomb and I happened to be distant cousins or something. We had relatives in common named Upthegrove.

When Jim Lawson's problem arose in the spring of 1960, I held the largest scientific grant in the college and the first one in physics. It was a grant of $85,000, which was ten times my salary; it does not sound so big today, but that was big money at the time, my position was very strong.

When I came to Vanderbilt, I heard that the dean of the Divinity School, Bob Nelson, was the clear replacement for Branscomb; he fully expected to be named chancellor.

GILKEY: We didn't know that.

SILBERMAN: There were a lot of things we didn't know.

ROOS: I was introduced to him in 1959; he was the dean of the Divinity School, and he told me that Harvie had been a dean of a divinity school before becoming chancellor.

DALE JOHNSON: Jim Lawson, would you talk about your coming to Nashville and the Divinity School?

JAMES LAWSON: In the spring of 1957, I decided I would leave the Graduate School of Theology at Oberlin and move South so as to get involved specifically in the southern struggle. I had met Martin King on the sixth of February at Oberlin, where he spoke, and told him of a long interest in living in the South in order to see what could be done about segregation from the nonviolent perspective. We hit it off immediately and he said, "Don't wait, come now—we need you now; we do not have anyone with your specific background in nonviolence." So I said that I would come as soon as I could; I prepared then to drop out of school and move South, intending to go to Atlanta and perhaps then to enroll at ITC [Interdenominational Theological Center]. In the meantime, however, somewhere in the fall of 1957, I informed A. J. Muste, a mentor and a friend who was executive director of the Fellowship of Reconciliation [FOR] in New York, that I was going to move South, that I wanted to put to work some of my thoughts and ambitions of the past. He said fine, but then he said, "Don't make any plans until I've talked to you again." That was the way we left it; sometime that fall he called back and said, "What about your becoming the southern secretary of FOR?" I said, "That's wonderful, I'll be glad to do that." So we then prepared for me to come. Part of that preparation was having Glenn Smiley, the field director of FOR, get in touch with me and then our talking about how we would make this transition. It was he who suggested that Nashville was a better site than Atlanta and who also suggested that Vanderbilt would be the place to enroll when I was ready. That is how I left it, and I came to Nashville in January, if I recall, of 1958.

I immediately began a travel schedule with the Fellowship of Reconciliation, moving out of various places of tension and struggle. Then, that winter/spring I made application to transfer into Vanderbilt and was accepted. So I came to Vanderbilt really as a part of a larger decision-making process in terms of my vocation. FOR was thinking in terms of what was the best center to live in and to work from; they had more FOR members here in Nashville than in Atlanta or anyplace else, and they thought that FOR people here would form a good support community for me and for the work that I would do. So I worked for those first eight-and-a-half months full-time with FOR, and then as I enrolled at VDS I continued to work part-time, chiefly in the evening and the weekends. That is how I came to Vanderbilt; for me the work was as critical as the theological school. I relished my time at Oberlin because, having spent time in prison and having spent time in India as a Methodist missionary,[1] I had a lot of questions formed in my own heart and life. Theological school was for me a wonderful adventure and experience—at Oberlin and Vanderbilt as well. But at the same time I was deeply enmeshed in the Little Rock crisis over the desegregation of the schools; I knew all the nine black students there. I was also running in and out of Birmingham, Alabama—a place that we called "Bombingham" in those days—and with every bomb, I was being asked to go into Birmingham in 1958, 1959, and 1960.

I found the Divinity School to be a very fine place; I knew the reputations of any number of the faculty people. I knew a number of them from Methodist student affairs and conferences and camps across the years in the Midwest and in the South. I had friends in the Board of Evangelism and in the Board of Education, both headquartered in Nashville, because I had served with them in different settings in the Methodist Church. So I felt myself very much at home in Nashville. I had been here on a number of occasions for meetings prior to 1958. When I came to Vanderbilt, I had no notions about limitations upon my being who I am or who I was then. That meant that Gene Davenport became a friend, as well as Dick Allison and other guys. We ate together whenever we decided to eat at Vanderbilt University. I loved sports then and wanted to play football and basketball with the Divinity School teams, and I did (I learned later on, of course, that this had some eyebrows lifted). I moved about as a theological student and activist without fear or trepidation of being here, but enjoying the experience and enjoying the study and enjoying also my work in the field.

JOHNSON: Could you describe the organization of these meetings that you were having while you were at the Divinity School?

LAWSON: While I was at the Divinity School, I was doing workshops on non-violence in various places around the South. I did tours into Virginia, into Alabama, into Arkansas, into North Carolina. I did workshops with the then-developing Southern Christian Leadership Conference with Martin Luther King in South Carolina and other places, including Mississippi. I approached Glenn Smiley, my immediate supervisor, with the notion that in this traveling about I wanted to try to organize a struggle in a given place and that I ought to do it in Nashville. He agreed, so my work in Nashville also represented my work for FOR. Kelly Miller Smith, pastor of First Baptist Church, Capitol Hill, had by this time invited me to join the executive committee of the Nashville Christian Leadership Council as a person in nonviolence and strategy. We had workshops in 1958 in Nashville sponsored by Kelly Miller Smith's church. In a couple of workshops in 1959 we took the first step of the nonviolent approach—that is, to settle on an issue, to examine the situation, and to decide where we wanted to focus. We did that in two or three workshops at Bethel AME [African Methodist Episcopal] Church, over on South Street. Out of that we determined that we would desegregate downtown Nashville—that would be our project and our effort. So we proceeded to organize a series of nonviolence workshops. I think they began in September 1959 and ran through October or November; most of these were held at Clark Memorial Methodist Church, where Alexander Anderson was the pastor. He and I had become fast friends by this time, and those workshops were held every Monday evening for about a three-hour period. It was to those workshops that a number of people from the community and a number of students from Fisk University and American Baptist Theological School came: John Lewis, Jim Bevel, Bernard Lafayette, and a number of others, Diane Nash, Paul LaPrad, Marion Barry, Angela Butler, as I recall, and a number of other people from Fisk—they were the two schools mostly represented. In the

Divinity School, as you know, most of us did some work; if we didn't have a congregation, we were on somebody's staff someplace. My work was a little bit different in that I traveled a lot. But I did do the schoolwork basically; I don't think I neglected my studies. I could have been a far better student, but I tried to be a good student without neglecting the work.

JOHNSON: Did you talk to people in the Divinity School community about what you were doing?

LAWSON: I don't remember this. I think people knew that my fieldwork was different.

DAVENPORT: People knew it.

LAWSON: I'm not sure. We must have talked at lunchtime and around the tables. We would take our time with lunch in the cafeteria, and we would visit about lots of things.

DAVENPORT: But it was a natural part of the daily conversation.

LAWSON: Yes, I didn't make something extreme about it.

GILKEY: I know Gordon Kaufman and Jim Sellers knew it, and they thoroughly supported it.

JOHNSON: Gene Davenport, what might you remember hearing about activities that were taking place in evening study groups or of what was coming? Did the student body know about the coming sit-ins?

DAVENPORT: Well, I can't speak for others. There may have been some students who were aware of what was going on, but I was not aware of the specific activities. I think the first really clear picture that we had was when the sit-ins themselves began. The general reaction of the student body was very diverse because there were students from a diversity of cultural and theological backgrounds. There were some students, maybe two or three (Freeman Sleeper especially comes to mind), who participated in the sit-ins. In the Student Cabinet we spent a great deal of time talking about what our reaction should be. It became pretty clear that Jim was going to be in deep trouble with the University, and the simplest way that I can describe what the student government tried to do, rightly or wrongly, was that it basically tried to keep the two issues separated: the downtown issue and Jim's life as a student on campus. This was primarily because we did not want the University to see our defense of Jim as being simply because we were involved in the sit-ins. I don't mean to leave the impression that that was why more students did not participate in the sit-ins, but that was urgent for the Student Cabinet: to try to keep the two issues separate. In the years since then, I have wondered about our actions and rolled them over in my mind, but that is all hindsight. Jim Lawson had every right in the world to participate downtown, and whatever he felt called upon to participate in should not have affected his relation to the University and the Divinity School.

JOHNSON: We may be ready to hear Jim Lawson's narrative about the events of February of 1960, as it led up to his engagement with the University.

LAWSON: I think that one of my errors in that period was that I did not more explicitly talk about the workshops. Freeman Sleeper was critical of me because I had not told him, and he was a good friend. Dick Allison was also. "Why didn't you tell me?" he asked. And a Ph.D. student in church history, Paul Bushnell, was also upset. So I did receive a little bit of static, and I admit that this was going on and I had not talked to any of them about it. I should have openly invited people from Vanderbilt to be a part of the workshops and the preparations; of course, a number of them did join the sit-ins themselves. We had these workshops, as I said, in the fall of 1959, and we did some testing of the places downtown in November, a couple of weeks of experimental testing. This was to allow people to test themselves, but also for us to find out who was responsible for the decision regarding desegregation and to see how the protesters were treated—and, if possible, to talk to a manager or a policy maker in each of the places. I do not remember all of the places that we sent a team to; we sent them in teams of four to six people, but I remember Cain-Sloan's and Harvey's department stores and, I think, two or three of the five-and-ten-cent lunch counters. Five to seven different teams went; we shared our information and our experiences with each other, and then we waited until after Christmas to start back up again—and with exams at Fisk and Vanderbilt, that got delayed some more.

Then on February 1, 1960, the Greensboro, North Carolina students started their sit-ins, and we immediately called meetings among ourselves. To the first meeting some seventy-five students came, and we talked about what we would do and when, and we planned it for, as I remember, February 13; that was the first Saturday that we sat in. Some 250 people sat in, and we had it in five or six places. It went very well; the police were orderly, the managers kept people from congregating without shopping, and the police did the same thing. There were plainclothes detectives, so for those two weeks the demonstrations went on with complete smoothness, well organized and without a hitch. We had observers in the streets. Will Campbell [local representative of the National Council of Churches—*Ed.*] had put together a number of white observers to be present every time we sat in, in case we needed witnesses—so we had that organized. Others of us walked from place to place and kept our eyes on things and also observed. So the workshops went very well, and in the meantime we were continuing our training and our teaching. We were also staying in touch with the pulse of the community and with the official city government, police especially, and we were staying in touch with managers and merchants. We had uncovered by this time a number of friends in the merchant community downtown. We discovered that Harvey's Department Store was owned by a group in Chicago and that this was their second or third store. They were interested in making the changes that could be made, but they did not think they could do it by themselves.

DAVENPORT: I want to pick up on something that Jim Lawson said when he was talking about Will Campbell organizing observers. A half-dozen or so of us on the Student Cabinet did go downtown fairly often as observers. At one point one of us, Wilson Yates, suddenly was in the middle of the demonstration. The demonstrators were walking in a circle, carrying placards, and one of them had left the circle. I do not recall exactly how it happened—whether the demonstrator was arrested, just left the circle, or what, but Wilson wound up carrying the abandoned placard. One of the young toughs on the outside of the circle stepped up, hit Wilson on the back of the head, and knocked him to the ground. The police then arrested Wilson. George Barrett, Wilson's lawyer, asked two or three of us to appear as character witnesses for Wilson at his trial. So one of the roles that some of the students who were not involved in the demonstrations themselves did play was that of observer.

[The largest sit-in to that point occurred on Saturday, February 27, 1960, when eighty-one students were arrested. Their trials began on the following Monday. That day, the Nashville *Tennessean* identified Lawson as a Vanderbilt student and the leading organizer of the demonstrations. On Tuesday, March 1, the *Nashville Banner* in a lead editorial described Lawson as "continuing to advise the element behind him to violate the law. That is the incitation to anarchy."

On Wednesday, March 2, the Executive Committee of the Vanderbilt University Board of Trust was scheduled to meet to consider launching a large capital fund drive. The Divinity School dean, J. Robert Nelson, was summoned to this meeting to participate in the discussion of Lawson's activities downtown, and he presented a statement from Lawson regarding his views on the law and one's right to oppose existing law. At this meeting the Executive Committee determined that Lawson would be given until 9 A.M. the next day to decide whether to withdraw from the University or be expelled.

The Divinity faculty held a meeting with Chancellor Branscomb on

Wednesday afternoon, where it heard the decision of the Executive Committee meeting. Most of the faculty reacted with anger and dismay. The next morning the Chancellor held a closed meeting with Divinity students and faculty, at which he announced that Lawson was no longer a student at the University.—*Ed.*]

SILBERMAN: The first the faculty knew of what was going on was at a brown bag lunch. We heard that Dean Nelson was called to Kirkland Hall to discuss something about Lawson's status. The consensus was that Branscomb was too wise to let the matter go further. We were amazed when we were later told that Lawson was to be dismissed.

DAVENPORT: When we had the meeting with the Chancellor, with most of the students attending, Dean Nelson asked that all of the press leave. He really insisted that they leave. In the meeting several students really pushed Chancellor Branscomb very hard on this whole issue of Jim's expulsion, and it became very clear to all of us that his mind was made up and that there would be no backing down whatsoever.

LAWSON: I sat in the back of the room and heard the exchange.

DAVENPORT: After the meeting, although I do not remember exactly when, was a worship service of confession and repentance for Divinity School students and faculty.

LAWSON: I don't think I was there, but I do remember it because it was after that meeting, around noon, that I learned that a warrant was out for my arrest and we agreed that I would go to First Baptist Church, Capitol Hill, to be arrested.

DAVENPORT: Three or four of us went down there. I remember when you were arrested that some of us followed you out to the vestibule.

[Lawson was arrested on Friday, March 4. A photo of four police sergeants ushering Lawson out of the church appeared on the front page of the Nashville *Tennessean* the next morning; that photo included the sign in front of the church announcing the title of the Rev. Kelly Miller Smith's sermon for Sunday, "Father, Forgive Them." A faculty committee composed of Dean Nelson and Professors Tilson and Kaufman posted bail for Lawson on Friday evening.—*Ed.*]

DAVENPORT: I remember Chief Hosse standing there facing you, Jim, when he arrested you. I asked, "Whatever happened to the idea of the church as sanctuary?" If I recall correctly, Chief Hosse answered something to the effect that the meeting was not a religious meeting, but a political gathering. The story of the arrest, of course, made the afternoon television news.

[In the midst of the issues generated by Lawson's dismissal, the new Divinity quadrangle was dedicated on March 21. In conjunction with this event, an expanded Cole Lectures, with four speakers representing each of the curricular areas of study, took place; the *Tennessean* reported that two of them publicly expressed their opposition to the University's expulsion of Lawson. A substantial number of Divinity School alumni/ae, present for these events, signed a petition to the Chancellor asking for Lawson's reinstatement. The entire occasion provided support for the position of the Divinity faculty as well as the opportunity for more discussion of the issues in the press.—*Ed.*]

GILKEY: It is ironic that the new building appears and was inhabited this same spring. There was a dedication, and Liston Pope from Yale Divinity School was the speaker. He gave, as I remember, a rousing criticism, with Chancellor Branscomb sitting there, of Vanderbilt University, and a rousing statement of support from Yale University and its Divinity School of the stand of the Vanderbilt Divinity School. So this was a very ecstatic, happy occasion for the faculty. We knew of support from around the country, as I am sure Charles Roos did from the sciences. We were in touch with the larger theological world, and we took it for granted that they were supporting us, but it was very nice to have Liston Pope come down and say what he did. Branscomb and he were very old friends, but Branscomb just completely frosted him out after his speech. Liston told us that there were no happy words as they marched back down the aisle. Liston really gave quite an address.

[From mid-March to late May, various Divinity faculty members had conversations with University officials, including Chancellor Branscomb, Vice-Chancellor Purdy, and Robert McGaw, secretary of the University. James Sellers and Lou Silberman were selected by the Divinity faculty to be its representatives in these conversations, by which it was hoped a quiet solution to the issue of Lawson's expulsion might be reached. In the 1998 conversation Silberman indicated that the Divinity faculty in this period did not believe they had much support in the University. Although a number of possibilities were offered, including that Lawson might complete his work in absentia and receive his degree, no agreement was reached. But there were other conversations going on during this period, as the following remarks indicate.—*Ed.*]

ROOS: The first time I was really aware of Jim Lawson was when they pitched him out and said that he was a member of this subversive organization, the Fellowship of Reconciliation. Now that created a problem for me because my mother was at the time the representative to the United Nations for the Fellowship of Reconciliation. I had a complete report on Jim the next day, as my mother checked him out with A. J. Muste, who said that he was a good guy. So I wrote Chancellor Branscomb that next day and simply told him I thought he had made a major mistake. We had many discussions, and I also met many times with Rob Roy Purdy about it. One of the things Branscomb later held against Bob Nelson was that if Jim had simply said for the Executive Committee meeting of March 2, "I respect the Constitution as the supreme law of the land," that would be adequate. But Nelson met with Jim and produced a five-page paper instead. I don't know what Nelson was thinking—Harvie needed an ambiguous statement. There were a number of meetings over this issue. Unlike some of the Divinity faculty, I always had access to Branscomb and Purdy.

JOHNSON: What did you talk to Branscomb and Purdy about in the weeks that followed?

ROOS: That this just had to be settled, that it was not possible to build a major university with this problem. In one sense, I did not care about the Divinity School per se; it was just that you could not write off a major school on an issue like this. It was all one university, and we had to get some resolution to this.

GILKEY: That is what the Divinity faculty kept saying.

JOHNSON: Did you have support from your colleagues? Lou Silberman said earlier that he did not think there was much University support.

ROOS: I did not seek much support. I had enough of a personal relationship with Branscomb that I could talk to him any time I felt like it. Branscomb did point out that I had been the first to complain, but I think he appreciated that I had not made a public statement. I was not going to grandstand this; if it didn't get solved, I was going back to Cal Tech, and that would be the end of it for me.

JOHNSON: John Compton, can you speak to this point from the perspective of the other faculty members?

JOHN COMPTON: There was a group of about thirty college faculty who met regularly through this period—Avery Leiserson, in political science, and others were something of a coordinating group. I have seen a list from that time, which includes my own name and others such as Phil Hallie, from philosophy; Cal

Izard, psychology; Ingram Bloch, physics; and several other colleagues. Across the board, faculty members from various disciplines had indicated collectively that they would write to Branscomb and Purdy, speak to their own department chairs and tell them they were prepared to make a move themselves, if they could, if this were not resolved. How much of that actually got done in detail from person to person and from department to department, I cannot say.

But there was a lot of internal college faculty discussion of this sort that apparently never eventuated in much direct personal support to Jim Lawson or to Divinity faculty members. For my own part, I had my own small window on Harvie Branscomb, an ambiguous one at best; he knew my father, he approved of me, and I spoke and wrote to him on a number of occasions about my concerns. But my chair, Sam Stumpf, was a supporter of Branscomb's through this whole thing. Consequently, Phil Hallie and I together were at odds with our department chair. Most of what I understand the college faculty members to have done was individual and local and stimulated by this discussion. There were then some public announcements, with extensive signatures on them at certain points, although I cannot remember the details.

Roos: There was a lot of internal communication.

Silberman: As far as the events were concerned up until May 1960, that was sort of the end of the matter as far as negotiations between James Sellers and me for the Divinity School and the members of the administration. Langdon can talk about other reactions of the faculty. There was considerable outside interest in our situation; for one thing, early in June the president of Chicago Theological Seminary, Howard Schomer, came down and said that he would hire all of us.

Gilkey: I would like to say that almost all the Divinity faculty with very few exceptions supported our move. I can say that without any question. Phil Hyatt certainly did not, to the surprise of many of us for whom he was a close friend. Otherwise, I think the faculty generally supported us. To my surprise at the end, when we finally said we were going to resign, Herman Norton said, "I'm going with you." Up to that point we had not really known. I want to say also that we were astounded by the response of our students, knowing that most of them came not only from the middle South but from the deep South, and they said to us without any question, if you faculty had not protested, we would have been out of this building. I remember that very clearly. I also remember that when a poll was taken in the College of Arts and Science, the students said by some 70 percent that they wanted to keep segregation. Let's not then be Pollyanna-ish about this, but the Divinity School students were absolutely behind us. I do not know of any exceptions, but there was no question of their support. Now with the faculty, generally, we knew we had friends in the Philosophy Department such as Philip Hallie and John Compton, and we knew about Sam Stumpf's opposing position. We also had friends in the Political Science Department; I was in touch with Avery Leiserson a good deal of the time. We especially had friends in the Drama Department; Joe Wright and Bob Baldwin were with us all the way and were very, very vocal in their support.

COMPTON: They had offices in the Divinity School building.

GILKEY: Nothing was unvocal about Joe Wright. He let his decision be known all the time. I also knew how Charles Roos felt, but I did not know how all the sciences felt. We knew very well how the Medical School felt; one Medical School faculty member, David Rogers, was on the phone with us all the time and, rather interestingly, kept urging us to resign. "Why haven't you guys resigned yet?" he would ask. We just said that we think our institution is terribly important and we do not want to let it go. Harvie Branscomb had told us unequivocally that if we all resigned, he would turn our new building over to the Law School. We did not want that to happen, and that was, I think, the way that the students felt. And we were convinced that the administration would finally understand you cannot run a university on these grounds. That was what Lou kept telling them, that was what we kept telling them.

Have you read David Halberstam's *The Children*? I was interested to see that he almost makes a demon out of James Stahlman, the editor of the *Nashville Banner* and member of the University Board of Trust. I do not know whether that role was there, but if there is anybody with horns in that fracas, Stahlman is the one. It really is amazing when one reads Art Foster's chronological account to see that the *Tennessean* was fairly negative about Jim Lawson's work at the beginning. And it was really very negative—the opinion was that these people were breaking the law, and you don't break the law. That the whole issue will turn into anarchy, and so forth. No statements about the immorality of the law, no qualifications about segregation and so forth—which, of course, anybody with any sense, having lived in India as Jim Lawson had, would know. I would like to remind us of that. The *Tennessean* slowly came around, I think, maybe with the work of David Halberstam and some of the others; John Siegenthaler at the *Tennessean* came around to a quite different position by the spring. At the beginning it was not as loud and blatant as the *Banner*, but it certainly was negative.

DAVENPORT: There was a difference between the editorial position of the *Tennessean* and the reporting of the *Tennessean*. The *Tennessean* was undergoing a transition in its editorial staff at the time, and the switches brought on differences of viewpoint from time to time. With only a few exceptions in the stories, David Halberstam was the only reporter covering the sit-ins for the *Tennessean*, and he has told me that he was given free rein in his reporting. I recall his reporting as being very accurate. In fact, I called David one afternoon and introduced myself as the president of the Student Cabinet at the Divinity School. I heard him catch his breath. Then I told him that I really appreciated the reporting that he had done on the Divinity School, and I heard him exhale. He thanked me and said that he had received quite a few calls of the opposite sentiment.

Of course, the Divinity School became part of the overall Nashville story after Jim Lawson was apparently singled out for attack by certain members of the downtown power structure. Some of our students were demonstrating and some faculty were more involved in various ways than others, but it was the *Banner* zeroing in on Jim and his later expulsion that focused attention on the school itself.

LAWSON: The *Tennessean* even then was one of the two or three best papers in reporting what was going on in the civil rights movement.

GILKEY: That is very helpful to me because I knew David Halberstam and Wally Westfeldt quite well, and I felt their support of everything we were doing. We talked a lot, so I was surprised to see those original editorials. But I think they changed the editorial stance of the *Tennessean* by the end of the spring, and it is very important to have that clear.

COMPTON: Halberstam credits Coleman Harwell, then editor of the *Tennessean*, with being responsive.

ROOS: I might mention one source of potential support that was never known. I never told Harvie that several members of the trustees of the Ford Foundation were also members of the Fellowship of Reconciliation. My mother knew that, but she told me not to use it in the conversations; they could do what they wanted about that. Harvie Branscomb was looking into a loaded gun barrel when he was trying to get the support of the Ford Foundation. That was part of why I knew there was no hope at Vanderbilt if they could not resolve this issue. There was constant talk of whether we were going to get this money from the Ford Foundation, and I was the only one who knew they had lost it because of the trustees.

JOHNSON: Jim, what did you do from your expulsion in March until late May?

LAWSON: I was working full-time for the Fellowship of Reconciliation. I did a number of workshops in that period in various places around the country. I helped to organize the Easter weekend at Raleigh, North Carolina, in April, where we organized the Student Nonviolent Coordinating Committee, and I helped to promote that conference. I worked with the movement in Nashville in various ways and cooperated with the faculty to the best of my abilities.

JOHNSON: Did you keep in touch with student colleagues?

LAWSON: To a certain extent, yes. I stayed in touch with some of the students who were here, but I did not make a lot of visits over to the school during those periods. I went on about my work basically, and that was my approach to it.

JOHNSON: Did you have any sense that this might be resolved in your favor, or were there invitations to go to other institutions?

LAWSON: Yes, there were invitations to go to other universities, but I did not respond to any of them because I wanted to be free to remain in Nashville and return to Vanderbilt if that worked out. So I cooperated with the process here without any reservation in the matter. I do not remember who the faculty people were who stayed in touch with me when they thought something was developing. I think Everett Tilson might have been one, and Gordon Kaufman, perhaps.

GILKEY: Let me just say something about the relation of the faculty to the dean, Bob Nelson, which was barely diplomatic during these months from March to early June. We did not understand him, we did not understand what he had done, we did not understand what he was doing, and he obviously was out of touch with us. When he was asked, I remember him reading a statement to the faculty; he read a statement on Christology, and we did not see that that was relevant. We thought that Christology itself was very important, but not relevant to the political problem we were facing. There came a point when this issue became quite explicit in the minds of many of the faculty, and they were furious with Bob. That was when we decided to re-admit Jim Lawson to the school—we decided that the faculty was going to act without Bob. All our discussions were without Bob, all our decisions were without Bob. As I remember, our decision to re-admit Jim was quite without Bob.

We did it in private meetings. Privately in somebody's house—Gordon's house or Lou's house or wherever. We made the commitment that we would all resign if this was refused. And it was refused, so we met again and reaffirmed our commitment; I remember we said that we must tell the dean about this and we cannot act entirely on our own. So we told the dean about this, and to our consternation he announced to the papers that he was going to resign. So the headlines came out in the *New York Times*, the Chicago paper, the Boston paper, "Dean of Divinity School resigns, and it is thought the faculty may follow him."

Well, the faculty were furious; we were all pretty mad, so we had some trouble from then on negotiating that he would not be fired, negotiating that he would retain his professorship, because there was a great deal of real antipathy at this point. I do not think anybody felt at all badly about whatever happened to Bob because he had gone on the national media circuit as being the hero who had resigned, when actually the faculty had debated a long time whether they were going to bring him in on our resignation or not—and we decided we would.

[From mid-May, discussion of the issues that had been going on since March took a different turn. Key Nashville stores agreed to desegregate their lunch counters, and the charges against Lawson and the student demonstrators were dropped. In the University, despite some prospects that the Lawson case might be resolved, either to reinstate him or re-admit him to the Divinity School for the summer session, Chancellor Branscomb informed the Divinity faculty that there was very little support for such an action in the Board of Trust. Some discussion occurred over whether Dean Nelson would be able to continue in his position, and the faculty received conflicting statements on this matter from the administration. Informal conversations took place in May between some Divinity faculty and Medical School faculty regarding appropriate action to take on the Lawson case. At this point a majority of the Divinity faculty decided not to appeal to the Board of Trust for resolution but to admit Lawson for the summer session and bring the recommendation to the Chancellor.—*Ed.*]

GILKEY: The faculty decided, after Lou Silberman and Jim Sellers had reached the end of their patience and everybody's patience with regard to talking to Vice-Chancellor Purdy, that we would have to bring this to some kind of a head. Graduation was approaching at the end of the term. I do not know where the suggestion came from that we readmit Lawson. That was an action we could take; we did not need any permission to do that admitting, and we would admit him to return to do his degree. I would not say we were quite excited, but we knew this was an act we could take, not just continuing to talk. We all decided that if this was turned down, we were then really going to resign. That was the commitment, and that was where Herman Norton said, "I'll go with you," and as far as I can remember everyone agreed at that point, except Phil Hyatt. So we re-admitted Jim, and then it was refused. I think that Jim cooperated with that re-admission.

LAWSON: Oh, yes—I had application forms. I filled them out as I was told. I don't remember who approached me about it, but faculty people approached me and said that there was some talk that if I would re-apply, the faculty would re-accept me. There was the thought that if Branscomb had this happen, it would give him an out, and then he would let it happen. As though some conversation had been held with him and there was some understanding.

GILKEY: I don't think there was. I think he was adamant all the way through, and the faculty decision was turned down. Whether it was turned down mainly by his office or by the Board, I don't know, but it was turned down. We were notified that the admission had been refused.

[The University Commencement took place on Sunday, May 29. On the following day the Chancellor met with the Divinity School's admissions committee and reported that he had denied the proposal to re-admit Lawson. Anticipating this decision, the faculty members' letters of resignation, effective at the end of the following academic year, had been prepared. Dean Nelson indicated to several faculty members that he would resign as well. This information was conveyed to Chancellor Branscomb at his home on the evening of May 30, and on the following day the story was carried by the Nashville newspapers and the wire services.

A total of nine faculty members signed the letter of resignation (Foster, Gilkey, James Glasse, Kaufman, Lee Keck, Sellers, Silberman, Ronnie Sleeth, and Bard Thompson); they were soon joined by Kendrick Grobel, on leave and out of the country, and Walter Harrelson, who was to join the faculty from the University of Chicago Divinity School in the fall. Two faculty persons with administrative positions, Frank Grisham in the Divinity Library and Norton as Dean of the Disciples Divinity House, agreed in principle with this action. Four other faculty persons did not offer their resignations; one of them, Tilson, had already accepted a position at another institution and thus could not resign.

While the newspapers were full of this story in succeeding days, a number of conversations continued between Divinity faculty members, now including Harrelson, and members of the University administration, in the continuing hope that a resolution could be reached on the Lawson issue short of these faculty resignations. By this time Lawson was in Boston, preparing to enroll in Boston University's School of Theology for the summer session and to receive his degree there. There being no movement in these conversations, the Divinity faculty, on Tuesday, June 7, declined to meet again with the Chancellor or with Harold Vanderbilt, the chair of the Board of Trust. At a called meeting of the University faculty at 1 P.M. that day, the Chancellor announced that negotiations had failed and criticized the Divinity faculty for refusing to continue to talk.—*Ed.*]

GILKEY: Bob Nelson and I went to that faculty meeting. This was when the newspapers and a good many people were saying that we in the Divinity School were rabble-rousers, that we were interested in becoming famous. This is of course the way people who do not like what you are doing are inclined to interpret a thing like that, and we were booed by the faculty. We were hissed when we came in and when we left. We were the representatives of the Divinity School, and the university faculty as a whole was not in favor of our actions.

When we decided to resign, the admission having been refused, I got on the phone with David Rogers in the Medical School and said to him, "We have decided this, and this includes most of the faculty." I said to David, "You have been urging us to resign all the while; we have decided to resign—what are you guys going to do?" I don't think I was rude enough to say "put your money where your mouth is," but that was the general point. Bless his heart, he said, "We will, and we will let you know tomorrow what we do." And of course they did, and in that group there were four or five medical faculty.

SILBERMAN: I think there were seven.

GILKEY: I know, at least, that we were very impressed—a cool $7 million a year for cancer research was involved. They got on the phone to Branscomb and informed him, and moments after that Branscomb was on the phone to Lou saying, "Let's talk." I think that's a very dramatic thing—up to that point, it had been, "We'll turn your building over to the Law School, we aren't doing anything."

SILBERMAN: The minute the medical faculty told Branscomb what they had in mind, it was all going the other way. Harold Vanderbilt had been enormously embarrassed; he did not have a lot to do with the place, but it was nonetheless his place. His grandfather had built it.

GILKEY: I would like to say that we heard that Harold Vanderbilt really did have some role here. There was a story that he was sitting in the Harvard Club in New York, and somebody came up to him and said, "I understand that university with your name is being turned into a southern finishing school." Vanderbilt put down his newspaper and said, "What do you mean?" Then the other man told him our story. I think Vanderbilt was embarrassed and a bit outraged that his name and the name of his family were getting into this kind of trouble, and he was there at meetings showing his support for Harvie. That was something I think that impressed Harvie. Apparently it did not impress the Executive Committee of the Board of Trust. I think we should record that Harold really did help at that point and was very courteous and charming to us.

SILBERMAN: At the end Harold Vanderbilt took me aside and said, "We've got to get this matter settled."

GILKEY: With this Medical School threat, negotiations started. Apparently there came an agreement between Branscomb and ourselves with regard to Lawson's re-admission, and Branscomb said he would get this through the Board. I know we had a big celebration. Bob Baldwin, Joe Wright, and I had a celebration that night; but at the end of the celebration we heard the news that Branscomb had been turned down by the Board. At that point, let me say, the University faculty dramatically shifted sides. They were outraged that the Board had turned down the chief administrator of the University, and they suddenly found us to be something they could tolerate and support. I think that was great and marvelous, but I don't think it should be read back into history.

The physiologist in the Medical School, Rollo Park, from Baltimore, was a wonderful man and one of those who would have resigned. We were sure we could talk the Board of Trust into a different position, so he and I went to three members of the Board of Trust at their homes in Belle Meade. I will never forget that morning. They all regarded me as a communist, needless to say, since this was my reputation in town. But they were very polite, asked us in for a drink and to sit on the front porch—it was hot and we would have a little bourbon. Park did all the talking. He said, "We hope you realize that with this, Vanderbilt ceases to be a major university in America. You will not be able to get an appointment from anybody from MIT or Cal Tech or the University of Chicago or any other place. No one will consider coming here, and you will become a southern finishing school." He said this to all three of them. And all three of them replied, "Well, sir, we'll take the southern finishing school." Park and I went away very, very discouraged.

ROOS: Let's go back to the incidents of June 7, which began the most critical period of this story. We all went to this faculty meeting expecting to have a resolution. I remember just being absolutely shocked; I thought Harold Vanderbilt was there to help make the announcement. Instead, Harvie had brought Mr. Vanderbilt with him to back him up and explain that the Divinity faculty's proposal had been rejected, this issue was settled, and there was to be no further discussion about it.

I don't know how things got organized, but that evening a group of us "hardliners" met in our home; it was near the campus, on Orleans Drive. We had at our house about twenty-one people (I think it ended up being nineteen) who were certainly going to resign. It included almost every holder of research grants in the University: Keith Innes and Tom Martin in chemistry, me in physics, others in microbiology, right down through the sciences. One young French professor also came; we were in the kitchen preparing coffee for the group when he came up to me in a panic. "Charlie," he said, "you've got to stop them, they are going to resign." I said, "I am too, I can't stop them." He was almost in tears; he was in French, it was hard to get a job, and he was concerned about his family. I took him by the arm and I said, "Look, here's the back door; just go to your family. You don't belong here and you know it; you don't need to be here." So he left.

It struck me that I was in a real moral dilemma. I had an appointment at Cal Tech; it was not a big deal to leave Vanderbilt. We had halfway built a house, but professionally I could get out of here. But I realized that this probably would be the end of any significant University growth for probably ten years. To lose the sciences and medicine, it's not something to happen casually. The strong feeling of the faculty members at my house was that they were not interested in debating the merits of Jim Lawson, whether he was a good man or a bad man. A school of the University had resigned. If a school of the University felt there was a problem, the rest of the University also had to feel there was a problem. So it was the predominant feeling that the resignation of the Divinity School faculty made it clear that the rest of us were going to go also. There was some discussion as to mechanisms. Tom Martin wanted me write the resignation letter for the faculty, but I said, "No, I am not going to do that; everybody can write their own. I am not going to take responsibility for a group decision; it is not something to rush people to do."

It was a long, sleepless night. I kept reviewing the arguments that Branscomb and I had exchanged in correspondence. I had spent my hours on Purdy's couch. When morning came [Wednesday, June 8], I suddenly realized that I knew what made Branscomb tick. I had had thirty-three years' experience. He was just like my father. He was a man quite sure of himself, very intelligent, he knew what he was doing. When my father died, he was the economic advisor to half of the productive capacity of the United States. He was a man who was right 95 percent of the time, and he was pure hell when he was wrong. I realized that Jim Lawson, whether he was a good man or bad man, did not really have anything to do with it. Branscomb was concerned about showing that he was in charge, just as Langdon said. I had been wasting my time arguing Jim Lawson's case; this was really about administrative power.

I looked at the morning paper, and there was the key right on the second page: two contrasting photos, one of Branscomb with the faculty and the other of Jim Lawson in Boston. So I told Anne I was going to write a conciliatory note for Chancellor Branscomb to send to the Divinity faculty. I wanted her to take

Margaret Branscomb out of the picture because Margaret was more traditional than Harvie. She might give him a phone call and urge him not to back down. So Anne and our three children spent the day with her and cooked a leg of lamb for lunch.

I went over to the university early and typed a conciliatory note; it did not really say much, but basically said let's talk some more. Then I called up Branscomb. It is sort of surprising when you think about it in retrospect; there I was, a thirty-three-year-old associate professor, and I talked to the Chancellor immediately. He said I could come over right away; Harold Vanderbilt had to catch a ten o'clock plane, and I could have fifteen minutes. I was over there about nine o'clock. I pulled out the *Tennessean* and said, "Gentlemen, the issue is, who is running this University? We need to bring control back to Nashville; look at this page—there's not a smiling face here in Nashville." The photo had Chancellor Branscomb and Mr. Vanderbilt looking glum at the faculty meeting. On the same page the *Tennessean* had a provocative photo showing Jim Lawson with a tremendous smile with two Boston University students. It was not the kind of picture you wanted published at a time of social tension—the *Tennessean* was very ambiguous. I said, "Look at this smile, look who's in charge of this situation; we have got to bring control back to Nashville." That was a new thought. They asked what we should do. I said that we have to buy time, you are about to have an explosion: "I do not know what to do; we have to get some time first, and then we can figure something out." Then I pulled out the note. I said, "Send this to the Divinity faculty and keep talking until this can be resolved." I told them about the twenty people at my house last night. "I am going to leave, not in anger but in despair because I know you cannot build a university with this. Your goals are no longer possible. I came to help you build a university, but I cannot do it with this problem. It is going to be with a great deal of despair and regret, but that is what I am going to have to do."

I knew Branscomb did not want to react to a threat; it was the last thing you wanted to give him. I said, "Why don't you invite Lawson to come over to discuss the situation; that will give you a couple of days while he gets down here." Branscomb said, "Oh, he would just take advantage of us and get a free plane trip." Branscomb then left the room to check on Harold Vanderbilt's timetable. I turned to Vanderbilt and said, "If we can get out of this mess for a couple of plane tickets, it will be the best money this university has ever spent." Vanderbilt nodded. We looked each other in the eye for what seemed like forever, but was about twenty seconds. He gave a little nod, and when Branscomb came back, Vanderbilt said, "Roos and I speak the same language; cancel my trip." Then he took charge of that meeting, and the settlement proposal was negotiated by Vanderbilt, not by Branscomb. It's an important difference. Vanderbilt considered the Board of Trust members James Stahlman and John Sloan as much a part of the University's problem as Jim Lawson. To him it was a ridiculous situation. He did not appreciate that the administration had not been able to solve it; he did not appreciate the Divinity faculty. To him, he was in charge of a university with problems about to explode. The people from *Life* were there, and he didn't like it. He sat there and drove that meeting. We stayed there from 9 A.M. until 4 P.M., the three of us. Vanderbilt was a real master. It was very interesting to watch Harold Vanderbilt in action. Branscomb and I would square off on an issue, and Vanderbilt would blast me with various barbs—I was intransigent, or I was stubborn, I had to think about the good of the university. Then he would propose a settlement that was 95 percent my way and insist that I compromise. It was clearly for Harvie's benefit. He never criticized Harvie, he always criticized me, and then we would go on to another thing. I had the feeling that I was the anvil and he was the hammer. Branscomb was just sort of sitting there, and it was just . . .

GILKEY: Someone else in charge, a little bit bigger?

ROOS: That's right—absolutely. There should never be any doubt as to who took charge—it was Harold Vanderbilt. The moment he came into the picture, the power changed.

The Board did not realize, when they tried later to get Vanderbilt to change, that this was Vanderbilt's agreement. Branscomb was quite annoyed at Jim Lawson and felt that he was ungrateful; he had gone out of the way to make these opportunities, and Lawson had upset his timetable. Vanderbilt said to him, "Harvie, I think you would have done the same thing." Harvie thought about it a little bit, and he said, "You know, I probably would have." But it took Harold Vanderbilt to tell him that. We had an agreement within thirty minutes that Jim was going to come back. My instructions were that anything the Divinity School proposed that had not been publicly turned down would be accepted. Then we got on to Nelson, and Branscomb was very insistent that he wanted to turn back all resignations except Bob Nelson's and keep that one because he wanted it and the issue would be solved. I had to tell him it could not be done. There was no way that the Divinity faculty could accept Nelson's unilateral dismissal like that. It took six hours to finally get that part settled. I heard all about what Nelson had done and had not done. Branscomb did not forgive him for not resigning right away.

SILBERMAN: The Divinity faculty thought the same thing, don't you think? If he had resigned immediately, his stature with the faculty would have increased, he would have been the one to deal with the administration. But the fact that he held on made it more difficult. When Branscomb and Vanderbilt and I talked two days later, Branscomb knew what he was willing to do. One of the things that was important was simply the agreement about Jim's status—what would happen—and second, that after it was all over, Bob Nelson would be permitted to resign his faculty position. That was what Mr. Vanderbilt had worked out.

GILKEY: Are we talking here about resigning as dean or resigning as professor?

SILBERMAN: Just as dean. We had the assurance that they would keep him as a tenured professor; he would not have to resign as professor, but he had to resign as dean.

ROOS: I don't think that the Divinity faculty knew the whole story on June 8. Harold Vanderbilt had instructed me to meet privately with Bob Nelson; I was to inform him the University wanted his immediate resignation as dean and his resignation as professor one year later. Nelson was to be "permitted to resign with dignity" as dean rather than be summarily fired. The Divinity faculty was not informed about the proposed settlement with Nelson. This was to be a private matter between Nelson and the University.

I had to agree that Branscomb as the chief administrative officer had an absolute right to dismiss a dean at any time. What took six hours to get was an agreement that Nelson would delay resigning his professorship for a year. He was expected to ask for a sabbatical and leave the campus. The University would give him full salary for a year, and he would not come back, but would find something else. It took quite a bit of pushing to get even that because Branscomb wanted nothing to do with him. Harold Vanderbilt almost got to a point of exasperation; he did not want to quibble over a year's salary for Nelson. I argued that the University could not afford to damage Nelson professionally, but must give him a chance to go somewhere. He could leave the University, get a year of research, and find a good job. That was to be the basis of the agreement; I felt firmly convinced there was no other alternative. There was no future for Nelson at Vanderbilt, with the Chancellor as dead set against him as he was; that was the best he was going to get. It was not a decision of the Divinity School faculty.

I do not remember whether we had lunch or not. If we did, we had it in the same room. They may have brought in a sandwich, but we did not leave that room for seven hours. Finally, Branscomb got around to the note that I had written earlier; he changed two words in it. That was the note I eventually brought over to the Divinity School to show the faculty that serious negotiation was starting. The faculty did not know that I had written it.

I called to get the Divinity School faculty together, probably about 2 P.M. or so, when it was clear that we were going to get something. There was an AAUP meeting going on, and we were going to schedule our meeting right after that. Vanderbilt wanted to keep tight control over everything. Then the question of whether Branscomb was going to sign this letter came up. I told them I did not think it was necessary as long as it was typed with his royal blue ribbon. There was a particular ribbon that he and only he used, and we all recognized that it came from the Chancellor's office.

So he had the note typed. I was told that I could show it, but I was to keep possession of it. Then I was to report back to him the Divinity School's reaction as soon as I could. Harold Vanderbilt then sat down and spent about thirty minutes going over with me what I could say and what I could not say, just making sure that I knew exactly what the position was. All resignations would be returned, but there would be a separate agreement with Nelson that he would give his resignation in a year; he would be permitted or encouraged to go on leave with full pay.

I remember coming over and delivering my message, taking Nelson aside and telling him the bad news. I was completely shocked because I did not realize that there was a split between Nelson and the faculty.

I felt under the circumstance it was a fair decision. When you have got the administration set against you, you might as well look for another job. Nelson had been given a year to do it, and he was free to go any place he wanted to for that time. That was as good as we were going to negotiate. Frankly, Harold Vanderbilt had a certain amount of contempt for his Nashville Board of Trust members. They were not his peers. He was not going to be that influenced by what Jimmy Stahlman thought. Stahlman was publishing a nothing newspaper in Vanderbilt's view. He was always gentlemanly, but he made his feelings pretty clear to me. Branscomb was scared of Stahlman, there is no question of that. In defense of Branscomb, it is not a question of his administrative ability; he just did not feel he had the power to buck Stahlman. He was trapped; he had seen the collapse of all that he had worked to achieve; he did not see any way out until Harold Vanderbilt began to use his power and show that there was another side to this issue. When I came over to the Divinity School, I was carrying a note given by direction of the Chairman of the Board of Trust.

I think that my part at that point consisted mostly of getting a nap on the couch while the Divinity faculty discussed the consequences of it. Maybe we should turn this next section over to Lou or Langdon because I was strictly the messenger at that point.

GILKEY: I am very interested to hear the account of how that message of acceptance of our position was itself generated because I did not have any idea about that at all. We understood that some of the Medical School faculty had tendered their resignations, but we did not know about the other scientists. This was not part of our consciousness as a group. There may have been a lot more support in the University, but as far as we were concerned, it was silent. We were not aware of it. But we were aware of what some of the Medical School had done, we were aware that this had changed Harvie Branscomb's mind, we were aware that Mr. Vanderbilt was there urging Harvie in a certain direction. We heard that there was a relatively satisfactory solution to the dean's problem, and we were prepared to withdraw our resignations. And then the Board turned us down.

ROOS: We need to point out that it was the Divinity faculty that came up with the idea that Jim would simply be allowed to complete the semester in which he was registered. He would take the exams and courses that he had started, and no further action was needed. The Divinity School could then claim that the student had completed the semester in which he had paid his tuition and received his degree. The other people could say, well, he did not come back to class. But the idea of completing the semester in which Jim was registered met the requirement that I had been given that it had to be something that had not previously been turned down by the Chancellor. It turned out that it was acceptable, so I called Branscomb's home. I had been told as soon as I had a report, I should come over and discuss it. Harvie said Harold Vanderbilt had already gone to bed. I think it had taken three or four hours that evening; could we meet the next morning at 7 A.M. at his house? He did not want a meeting on the campus, as there were too many reporters present. I told him that the Divinity faculty had selected Lou Silberman as its representative.

COMPTON: It was not strictly a re-admission in that case. That was part of the point.

ROOS: It was as if the expulsion had never happened. Harold Vanderbilt made it very clear that anything the Divinity School faculty wanted to do to get him prepared for his final exams, they certainly could do. But there was one condition associated with that, which was that Lawson was not to come back as a graduate student while Harvie Branscomb was Chancellor. He could get his B.D. degree; and after Branscomb retired, whatever Lawson wanted to do was up to him. That was all part of the agreement.

SILBERMAN: That interim period is not really very clear in my mind except I knew that I would have to appear at the Chancellor's house, at least to indicate the Divinity faculty's wishes in the matter, and be ready to accept the position that had been worked out previously. Mr. Vanderbilt was very gracious about the matter. I came back then and told the faculty what had happened. Of course,

Bob Nelson was not at that meeting of the faculty; the faculty existed and functioned completely without him.

ROOS: At that meeting at the Chancellor's house on Thursday morning [June 9], it was John Stambaugh who was very unsupportive of any solution. He was vice-chancellor for Business Affairs, and he made some comments about what faculty had to do and not do. Then Lou made a speech that was one of the greatest discussions of the rights and obligations of faculty that I have ever heard. I was not familiar with the eloquence of this man, and I am sorry it was not recorded, but I would like Lou to tell us what he said. It was a wonderful speech, and when he finished there was not another word from Stambaugh the whole day.

SILBERMAN: I talked about what a university is. I guess I still have a very old-fashioned idea of what that is. I went to UCLA and to Berkeley, graduating from Berkeley in 1934. Berkeley taught me what a university is all about. It was full of people with worldwide reputations who were perfectly willing to teach students. I guess I got imprinted there. If you belong to a university, you belong to one of the great creations of Western civilization—at least I thought so. That is what I told John Stambaugh.

I think that the whole thing at Vanderbilt came together at that moment, as the term has been used before: were we going to be a university, which was what Harvie Branscomb wanted, or would we remain, as it were, a southern finishing school? As I said before, the real die was cast around this table in 1952, when a bunch of ordinary and simple (I don't say that in a bad sense) people made up their mind to challenge the ethos of Vanderbilt University. When that decision was made as we sat around this table, the die was cast—this was going to be a university and not a southern finishing school. These people didn't know, I didn't know, that they were revolutionaries.

GILKEY: It is very important to start there.

ROOS: After Lou had taken Stambaugh out, there was effectively no further discussion. Purdy was quite happy to do whatever Chancellor Branscomb wanted. By this time it was clear that Harold Vanderbilt was calling all the shots.

SILBERMAN: Harold Vanderbilt called me out, and we went out to the anteroom. He told me his response to what we had said, and that was the way it was going to be. There were no votes or discussion or anything; Mr. Vanderbilt said this is the way it is. I came back to the campus to give the report.

ROOS: The question was what each of us was going to do. Lou was going to go back to the Divinity School faculty. I was going to go teach my class. But Harold Vanderbilt said, "No, you're not. You get somebody to teach your classes, and you stay with the Divinity School; I'm going to stay with the Chancellor until we get this settled." Then I carried a couple of notes back and forth about Dean Nelson's resignation. This was a further negotiation that I think probably did not concern the rest of the Divinity faculty. Then I was told to be ready to meet with the Board of Trust that afternoon [Thursday, June 9] about four. So I went home to get a suit on.

Before we went into the Board of Trust meeting, Harvie told me I had done a great service for the University and asked if I wanted to be dean of the Divinity School. This was sort of a joke. I declined, and then he offered it to Lou. I said, "Well, I think I would be the only physicist without any training in theology to be a divinity school dean." Lou said he would be the only Jewish head of a Christian divinity school. Both of us seemed to have things that kept us from being qualified.

I addressed the Board, but I have to admit that I was not very effective. I had been two days without sleep, and the question was asked, what would I do if the proposal was rejected? I said I did not know; I thought this was a hard-fought compromise and that it was in the best interest of the University. We needed to close this matter out. I was excused, and I thought the thing was done, and so I was shocked to get a call that evening that the Board had turned it down. I went over to Bob Nelson's house to discuss the matter. There was the Divinity faculty, Rob Roy Purdy and Bob McGaw from the administration, and Wally Westfeldt and David Halberstam from the *Tennessean*. A number of the Divinity faculty were claiming this was just a typical Branscomb trick—Nelson particularly was claiming that. I said I was not going to comment until I had talked to Chancellor Branscomb, but he had left town. The *Tennessean* was able to track him down in Williamsburg, Virginia.

When they got the Chancellor on the phone, I went back and got the call. He told me that he had tried, but the Board had turned it down. I did not know whether he had really tried or not; I knew that Vanderbilt had been pushing the settlement, but I was not sure how hard Branscomb was pushing it. So I was first a little angry—I thought I had been lied to. Then as I was walking from the phone back to the room, it occurred to me that I was going to write the headlines. It really did not make any difference whether Branscomb was telling me the truth or not, I was going to accept him at his word. I was able to talk about the conflict between Branscomb and Vanderbilt and the rest of the Board. I said I had just talked to Chancellor Branscomb, and he told me that he had tried, but that the rest of the Board refused to accept the compromise that he and Vanderbilt had worked out. Purdy and Bob McGaw could make no comment because they had not talked to the Chancellor—and the dispute between Harold Vanderbilt and the Board was the morning headline.

The next morning [Friday, June 10] we met, a group of various radicals. I really went three days without sleep, wondering what our next steps were going to be. There was a lot of discussion as to what should be done, and various people had ideas. Keith Innes said, "Charlie, tell us what you want, you will get it." So I said I wanted a petition supporting Chancellor Branscomb in his fight with the Board of Trust. I figured that all the faculty who had been afraid to challenge Chancellor Branscomb now had to sign that, and of course the others who were in favor of Lawson also could sign it. So that petition was gathered on Friday. Tom Martin called up excitedly that evening to tell me that more than 160 had signed and said I should come over and celebrate. I said, "Tom, I'm going to sleep, I have not slept in three days."

Of course, that was Saturday's headline. Branscomb was concerned that he was going to lose Harold Vanderbilt on the Board because this now was a challenge to Vanderbilt himself. Branscomb was looking at Vanderbilt giving a lot of money, and he was very proud of the fact that he had got the Vanderbilt family back interested in the University.

So we got a solution when Branscomb decided on Monday, June 13, after all, that he had authority as Chancellor to admit a student back and that he would do it. I think this made the Board happy because they frankly had the reaction that Branscomb had created the problem in the first place. They had done what he had asked initially, then they were asked to reverse themselves— why did they throw the student out in the first place? If it was an administrative problem, then they did not have to take any action. Also, it was clear to the Board that if they objected, they were going to lose both Branscomb and Vanderbilt.

That sort of calmed things down, but it was not as satisfactory as it should have been. I talked with Purdy afterward, and he asked me if I was satisfied; I said, "Well, it could have been nicer." He asked, "Are you planning any other action?" I said no. "Well," he said, "we can handle the rest of the campus." Although this did not help at the time, Branscomb and I became close friends over time. He began to appreciate that he and the University had survived. Vanderbilt had protected him; he was really trapped until Vanderbilt came in with both feet. I felt I had a very privileged position to see just how effective Harold Vanderbilt could be. Branscomb did not have the power, I think, to reverse the decision. Branscomb knew he had made a mistake; he as much as admitted to me the week after Jim was dismissed. But I think he felt trapped by what he could do. After Branscomb fully integrated the University in 1962, he came over and joined me for coffee at the Rand cafeteria and said, "I paid you back."

LAWSON: During much of this time I was really out of it. I knew little of this, and you have now informed me in ways that I did not know. It was deliberate on my part to be outside of the Vanderbilt scene. I worked in the movement, as I said, and to me the movement was the main story. I was delighted later on to learn that as a consequence, the University did make certain that a student had to be given a fair hearing. I held no ill will toward Branscomb as a consequence of my expulsion—primarily, of course, because of the nonviolent Christian understanding. You take positions for change that you think are correct, right, and compassionate, and you expect to pay the price. I did not anticipate being expelled from Vanderbilt, but when it did happen, against my will and wish, nevertheless, I went on with my life.

GILKEY: After all this, the issue for us was, if Jim does not come back, what do we do with our resignations? Lou and I, and I guess Jim Sellers, decided that you can't raise the ante in the middle of the game. Jim has a perfect right to stay at Boston University if he wants to. What we have got to do is get him so that he can come back if he wants. The fact that he did not come back was not our business. I must say the rest of the country thought, "Oh, he didn't come back; they have given in." But I think we were absolutely right to do that. You can't say, "we demand his re-admission," and then if he says, "I do not choose to do this," you simply continue with your plan to leave. We talked about that (Lou Silberman, Jim Sellers, Gordon Kaufman, and I) and made a very definite decision at that point. But it was hard to convince the rest of the faculty; they were ready to flee, they really were.

SILBERMAN: We talk about the Chancellor and his particular role, but it was one that you can call almost a tragic role. To go back to where I began in 1952, it is quite clear that Harvie Branscomb—whatever the Board of Trust wanted in this matter of admitting black students to the Divinity School—had forced them to do it. They did not do it of their own free will. Certainly he and Dean Benton had plotted this very, very carefully.

You must remember that he came to Vanderbilt from Duke, where he was dean of the Divinity School. I think he was determined to raise the level of the School of Religion in Vanderbilt to that of national importance. The very fact that he was anxious to establish a chair in Jewish studies is one indication; the other is the role he played in the integration of the school. I am sure he was behind the move. Thus the events of the spring of 1960 seemed to him to endanger his hopes.

I had an admiration for him, I have to say. It was a man like Harvie Branscomb who made it possible to have Jewish studies at Vanderbilt when, outside of Harvard, Columbia, and Duke, there were no professors of Jewish studies in the United States. It was important for him to do that. I don't equate that, however, with admitting blacks to a southern university.

GILKEY: He was a courageous man on the right path. It was a real tragedy for him.

LAWSON: I am sure it was, in my mind, too.

GILKEY: And he admitted this in the end.

LAWSON: Yes, he did.

DAVENPORT: I want to offer a footnote to the events of the faculty resigning and then taking back the resignations. When the faculty resigned, I wrote a letter to Leonard Beach, the dean of the Graduate School, saying I would not be coming back in the fall as a graduate student. Later, my wife and I were at the Nashville airport, getting ready to leave for Israel, when I saw in the newspaper that things had been worked out and that the Divinity School faculty would be returning. From the airport, I called Dean Beach to see if I could still get into graduate school. He laughed and said, "Of course." I had been accepted at Harvard and put on the waiting list at Yale, but I wanted to study at Vanderbilt. When I got to Israel, I discovered that G. Ernest Wright and Lawrence Toombs were there (that was while Wright was working on the digs at Shechem). Well, we worked out a deal. They wanted to know what had been going on at Vanderbilt; I wanted a tour of Shechem. So one evening we sat and talked about Vanderbilt. I remember distinctly Wright's response to the faculty coming back was that their names would be mud, as he put it, throughout the theological world. At that moment I thought, I am glad I decided not to go to Harvard and that I won't be studying with you.

GILKEY: Well, the names were not quite mud, actually, but it was ambiguous.

SILBERMAN: There was always in my mind an ambiguity. While it was created as a perfect world, something happened.

COMPTON: I think ambiguity *is* the word. I found myself using it early on for the way in which many of us college faculty members felt. Not all, perhaps not even a majority, as there still was in those days a much more conservative faculty than there is now. There was a desire to support the Divinity faculty, a deep regret of Branscomb's actions, but also a sense of being in the middle of a situation that we had no serious control over, and at once hoping it would go away and not wanting to be called to any ultimate action, like resignation—living in a kind of ambiguous hope. Finally, when the resolution came, there was great relief.

GILKEY: I think *ambiguity* is a very good word here. Reading Art Foster's account, I realized that we did not always make the right decisions by any means; there were a couple of points where we were wrong. But I do wish to record my feelings that our decision, when re-admission had been granted to Jim Lawson and he would not come back, our decision to withdraw our resignations, for which we were criticized, was not ambiguous at all. That was the right thing to do. That is one of the few things where we did do the right thing. We debated it, I think Lou and I and probably Gordon Kaufman. We were a minority. We finally talked the rest of the divinity faculty into withdrawing their resignations. That was a very, very, long and tense discussion, and I think we did the right thing.

LAWSON: I think Gordon Kaufman conveyed the decision to me, did he not?

GILKEY: We called Jim on the phone, and Jim said that this was the right thing to do.

SILBERMAN: One of the saddest things to come out of this (I have to say this because he is such a dear friend of mine) had to do with Everett Tilson. From the time that I came to Vanderbilt in 1952 until this happened, Everett and I were very good friends. But Everett was out of it because he had resigned the previous fall to go to the Methodist Theological School in Delaware, Ohio. He was constantly torn within himself because he really could not take part; there was nothing he could do that would in any way affect his future. He never forgave me, by the way; he never spoke to me again.

JOHNSON: He never forgave you for what?

SILBERMAN: For having been involved, and having decided to stay.

GILKEY: I think Lou is right; I think he was tortured by the fact that he could not resign. He could not take an action, and he was very disgusted with us for even considering staying. From the very beginning in any discussion that we had, he was not part of it because he thought we all ought to be out of there right away. We talked about the value of the school to the region and about other points, but he was pretty adamant.

JOHNSON: Having considered the immediate events of the spring of 1960, we should now turn to some reflections and consideration of some of the implications from and continuing associations with those events.

DAVENPORT: I would like to make an observation with regard to things that were said earlier. Two or three times we said that there was a lot of ambiguity; and I agree. But I think that whereas our actions were ambiguous, the issue itself was not ambiguous. Granted my unreformed neo-orthodox view that all actions are ambiguous, I think that in this whole matter Jim Lawson is the one person who comes out as the one right on target. I think that ought to be said.

LAWSON: It should be said, it seems to me, that when a crisis comes, all kinds of things happen. In the midst of a crisis a focus has to be developed, as George Houser, a pioneer in both the Fellowship of Reconciliation and the Congress of Racial Equality, taught me years ago: In the midst of a crisis you must make your peace, you must come to terms with your life, and you make your peace and must live through the crisis out of that peace. When it is a conflict like the one in 1960, where we had the city on the one side, a determined movement on the other side, and the University—that has explosive qualities that none of us could have predicted or understood. So it was trial by experiment, by error, for all of us.

One of the things I have reflected upon is that I feel very strongly that Harvie Branscomb made a major error in his life. It was in contradiction to his books, his own temperament, and his whole work. I felt that even back then because I had read his book on Jesus years before; I knew the name very well and was pleased that he was the chancellor of the University. He made an error in judgment; he obviously did not have enough people around him to help him get through in a fashion that could have reduced the tension in the University. My own major reflection as I look back upon it is that we have to accept the man as he was, as we have to accept ourselves because in the situations we get, we all make errors. But our whole work is not dependent upon some error; our life reputation is not dependent on mistakes we make, in my judgment.

JOHNSON: How were the issues discussed among the faculty? Even beyond the immediate issues, what substance did different people bring to the question?

COMPTON: Among the College faculty who discussed these things, there was considerable support for Sam Stumpf's view that legal procedures and the gradual process of legally instituted change was the way to go. Nonviolent protest was too risky and perhaps also risked crossing the line of an ethical responsibility to law and order. A certain number of faculty definitely agreed with Harvie Branscomb in that position. Many faculty did not, of course. I had no doubt that the University, through Mr. Branscomb, had made a terrible mistake, precisely on procedural grounds. Nothing else being considered, to have unilaterally expelled a student from one of our schools without the consultation of the faculty was absolutely impossible. Never mind the larger issues. This was a very strong conviction. But for me, and many of those with whom I talked, the focus was mainly downtown on the demonstrations and the hope that they would succeed.

Still, the way Jim's case had been mishandled on campus did provoke a sea change in Vanderbilt's policy regarding student activities. The whole legal basis for expelling Jim was that he was "a discipline problem," and he was initially brought under the no-panty-raid legislation, which said you cannot participate in activities that lead to public disorder like those folks who entered women's dormitories. It was absurd.

ROOS: Actually, it was worse than that. This was an undergraduate regulation, and for either the Divinity School or the Graduate School it did not apply. I think the Beach Report may have been almost concurrent with these other things. Harvie clearly wanted to lock the door so that this kind of situation would not happen again.

COMPTON: Yes. Already in March 1960, Branscomb had appointed a University-wide committee to propose a revision of student disciplinary policy. It was chaired by Leonard Beach, dean of the Graduate School, and included faculty members from medicine, law, the College, and Bard Thompson from the Divinity School. This committee reported on June 1, proposing a full hearing procedure for any student accused of misconduct. It would begin within the student's school and be followed, if necessary, by appeal to a University Committee of Appeals before any disciplinary action would be taken. The process took account of a student's right, on and off the campus, to communicate freely "by speech or action what is believed to be the truth" and explicitly acknowledged the special circumstance in which a student might find him or herself in possible jeopardy before the civil law "for the sake of conscience." The report was later adopted and is still, so far as I know, part of student disciplinary policy. Clearly, as Charles Roos said, Mr. Branscomb wanted to prevent the kind of precipitous action he had found himself taking in Jim's case.

ROOS: I have to say that on June 8 I watched Harvie first start out extremely angry with Jim Lawson for upsetting his timetable. Then when Harold Vanderbilt popped the question to him, "Wouldn't you have done the same thing in his position?" Branscomb stopped and thought for a long moment and said yes, and the whole thing changed. He did not appreciate Jim, but he admitted that that is what he would have done. He could not really fight Jim's return any more.

LAWSON: Throughout the years from that time, I was prepared to visit with Harvie Branscomb, and I let that be known. Bob McGaw tried to work with me in the late sixties and early seventies; at least he called me about it, and I said I was perfectly willing. So in 1996, when Dean Joe Hough approached me about the possibility, when Dorothy and I were here, of my having a visit with Harvie Branscomb, I eagerly said yes. We had a very pleasant visit in his home. I felt no animosity in the man, and I had none toward him when we visited this time. I think for both of us it was a closing of the chapter, a closing of the door on an event that had been a monumental event for both of us and for the University.

ROOS: I had never really felt free, when Branscomb was alive, to emphasize the role of Harold Vanderbilt because I thought in some sense this detracted from the solution Branscomb was pushed into.[2] But in fairness to Branscomb, he felt he had no options; his behavior was that of a deeply distressed person who did not see any way out of the trap he was in. He felt he could not appear to be backing down from the Board's position, but he knew he made a mistake. I also know that in time Margaret softened her views, and, of course, we all changed. I think we have to give Branscomb considerable credit; the Civil Rights Act of 1964 gave the cowards the courage of the crowd. Branscomb was first; this was the first university in the South, a private university, to integrate; this was not something being done in 1952. There were lawsuits about public universities, but this was a private university! And as he had very grudgingly got the support from the Board, Branscomb was not free to charge ahead; he had to work within constraints that some of us liberals did not think should be there. But he was well aware of them, as has been shown. He gets a compromise, and the Board, the locals, throw it out.

LAWSON: And Duke and Emory by this time had not even talked about integration. They were out of it.

ROOS: All of them were out of it—Tulane, too.

SILBERMAN: I think what happened at Sewanee influenced the faculty and influenced Branscomb. It is clear that Branscomb was the moving spirit behind integration at Vanderbilt. Not that the faculty would not have felt deeply about it, but whether they would have been ready to act or not, I don't know, because I was not a member of the faculty at that time. But I think that Branscomb and John Keith Benton decided that was how it was going to go; I think Dean Benton was involved.

GILKEY: When I came to Vanderbilt in 1954, this was the first thing said when they approached me and Roger Shinn. We came together. The first thing they said was, we have integrated, the first place integrated in the South. We said we would not otherwise have considered it.

ROOS: This was also important in physics. Why would I leave Cal Tech to come to Vanderbilt?

SILBERMAN: This was the place where something was going to happen.

GILKEY: You could live a decent life here in an integrated situation—which many people would not have thought was possible.

SILBERMAN: May we turn the discussion at the moment beyond what we have been talking about? What were the continued repercussions in the Divinity

School and in the University at large? We were not entirely forgiven. Herman Norton became acting dean, and then a new dean was appointed. Mr. Finch was appointed without very much consultation with us; and though Bill Finch was a very nice man, we treated him absolutely dreadfully, piled up sin upon sin. I think that the faculty were a bunch of intellectual snobs in one way or another. That was part, I think, of the result of it; they were going to keep an eye on us.

COMPTON: One of the aftermaths that occurred in the fall of 1961, involving Divinity faculty members and many others, was *Founders Capers*. It developed out of the need to pick up the pieces of a really fractured faculty across the University—we had experienced a great sense of disappointment and frustration; relief, yes, but anxiety as well. The dean of men, Sam Babbitt, his wife Natalie, and Ronnie Sleeth's wife Natalie composed a musical, the theme of which was the faculty of Anonymous University trying to find its founder. They wrote the script and cast it with members of the faculty from the entire University. The Medical School made up the football team. There was a Faculty Wives' Club and a cheerleading squad, all faculty and faculty wives. Langdon Gilkey was a detective, Ronnie Sleeth was the campus security, Tom Martin was the star football player, Phil Hallie was the football coach, and I was the chancellor, Caesar Brainstorm. Joe Wright directed, and Bob Baldwin helped build the set. People from the Law School, Divinity School, and Medical School, as well as college faculty, were all involved. It was a marvelous, unifying, and sort of releasing event. Mr. Branscomb was deeply nervous about the whole show. He did not indicate until the very last minute that he would even come. Bob Baldwin's story is that Branscomb secretly availed himself of a script to find out what it was before he would come. And on opening night, there he appeared. He sat right behind my wife, who actually heard him laugh!

The message I retain from all of this was that we as a faculty needed a lot of therapy of various sorts. And that play was part of it.

SILBERMAN: In terms of connections between this issue in the University and the larger issue in the society, we should mention the coming into existence of the Nashville Community Relations Conference. I think it was probably based initially at the Belmont Methodist Church, where John Rustin was the pastor. A very large group of people came together there; it was formed before 1960, and it had a continuing life for a long period of time. Its impact in the beginning, I think, was not great, but it got people involved. After the events of 1960, I think more people were involved, and it began to play a more significant role. The influence of the group continued, and a sea change was taking place here in Nashville. It did not mean that everybody was suddenly converted or anything like that, but the temper of the community began to shift, and more people who may have stood on the sidelines were involved in the program.

I got more and more involved in it on several levels. I had been the chairman of the Community Relations Committee of the Jewish Community Center Council, and then I got involved in Nashville Community Relations Conference and ultimately became president of it. Then, if you will recall, there was a change in the governmental structure of Davidson County, where the county and the city formed one government. Soon after that President Lyndon Johnson's Office of Economic Opportunity was created, and Nashville wanted to get some of the money that flowed into the communities that had organizations. So the Metropolitan Action Committee was created; I moved into that and got into a lot of trouble for being sassy, but this was part of the continuing repercussion in the Nashville community. Jim Lawson's group, in a sense, started this kind of revolution. What happened in the Divinity School played a role, and the community was aware of it. We have to be thankful to David Halberstam and Wallace Westfeldt, for they played a role in telling the story in the *Tennessean*. I think that it was Vanderbilt University and in a sense the Divinity faculty of Vanderbilt University that, I won't say made the change ultimately, because a lot of other things intervened, but at least prepared this community for greater events.

ROOS: I might add another little incident that took place in 1962. Dave Kotelchuck worked for me in my research group, and he achieved prominence by being hit on the head with an axe handle while he was attempting to help integrate the Campus Grille across the street. This made a front-page picture story in papers all over the United States. Some of the Board of Trust members were fussing, asking what is a Vanderbilt professor doing out there protesting on private property. Harvie Branscomb asked me privately whether Dave was all right, and I said, "Yes, I think he is recovering from a nasty head wound, but he is doing much better." He said, "Well, just tell him I was concerned. I didn't want to talk to him because I might scare him to death if I asked him directly." There certainly was no suggestion from Harvie that David should call anything off, except he might better protect himself a little bit and not get hit on the head again.

LAWSON: The Nashville movement did, of course, affect the entire movement in the country and in the South. Martin King called our movement the model movement up to that time. Eventually, any number of us served the Southern Christian Leadership Conference staff, including C. T. Vivian, Diane Nash, Jim Bevel, and Bernard Lafayette. I became director of nonviolent education for the SCLC. We of course became very influential with the Student Nonviolent Coordinating Committee, which later on many white liberals picked up as being the vanguard of the movement, so our movement had a large effect upon Nashville and far beyond. The Nashville people, for the most part, led the way, insisting that peace was a primary issue, that the Cold War was a primary issue. Our colonialism in places like Vietnam (before it was very well known in the U.S.) and our relationships and policies in Angola and Mozambique were particularly important to me in the early 1960s. Jim Bevel, Bernard Lafayette, and Diane Nash in particular became identified with the larger struggle for social justice and for peace here in the United States. We greatly influenced Martin King in that respect. He was very much convinced of the nonviolent perspective and early on had a deep sense of his own integrity in the relationship between nonviolence and other issues in the world; but as the overwhelming spokesperson for African Americans by 1965, he had much more at stake as to the question of when he could publicly express some of his feelings about Vietnam. So the Nashville scene perhaps more than any single scene, with the possible exception of Montgomery in 1955–56, became in many ways the most significant movement in terms of its ongoing effect across the country.

COMPTON: I think my experience was that of many who lived through the period from 1960 to 1963—seeing the development of the South and having come through the process to positions critical of various governmental, cultural, and social institutions. That made it much more natural, even though it took a great deal of further thought, self-doubt, and external events, but it made it much more natural to take positions when the Vietnam protests came around. And bit by bit, I think I felt and I think many of my colleagues felt that through that period, through the late 1960s and then on into the beginnings of the environmental movement, the feminist movement, and so on, we were on a kind of continuous development toward a very different set of attitudes toward our wider culture, our government and legal practices and politics than we grew up with. It was really the transformation of a whole generation of attitudes; this is not big news, but it certainly transformed the way in which one did one's work as a teacher. Teaching in the university from 1960 on through maybe 1975 was the most exciting period, the most productive period of my teaching life. I felt this way, as did many of my colleagues, because you were not in the position of having to initiate questions, queries, and concerns, trying to persuade students that they should give thought to the conduct of their lives or to the meaning of their beliefs. You did not have to push people into issues, instead you had to be there to respond to the concerns that kept being heaped upon you. And the whole educational process became one of learning from one's students as much as teaching them—looking outward toward the significance of what you are doing as a teacher for the preparation of these young people who are going into a very different situation in life from your own background. Teaching in that period was wrapped up in changes of consciousness—ethical consciousness, political consciousness. Teaching in that setting was a terribly stimulating and challenging business and, I think, the best education I ever took part in.

Institutionally, it was important, too. It was during that period, for example, that the University Chaplaincy was begun. I had a certain amount to do with that, and Harvie Branscomb created it—if we want to come back to him and his leadership. Here is a university without church connections since 1914, and, despite its predominant Protestant culture, it had been a studiously independent institution for fifty years; along comes Branscomb and says we need to have a university chapel. What? In the middle of a secular, independent, institution? He set up a committee to develop an account of what the chaplaincy would be, and one of the main things he had in mind was the model of Duke University that he had known. The chapel there had a preacher to the university in a nondenominational context. Branscomb thought that preaching in such a context would really bring quality thought to religious issues and engage the Vanderbilt community in discussion of these important matters. Sam Stumpf was chair of the search committee that hired Beverly Asbury, then college pastor at the College of Wooster, as our first chaplain. I was the chairman of the first University Committee on Religious Affairs and helped Bev fashion the organization for the Office of University Ministry. He filled the pulpit in Benton Chapel between 1967 and 1975 and filled that chapel during the period of the late civil rights movement and the Vietnam War. The incredible social struggles around us and the internal debates and tensions on the campus made Benton Chapel and the University Chaplaincy a terribly important resource, a support for ethical reflection and conversation. Often in the arena of contending parties and debates, Bev made himself *persona non grata* to many people—as he should have. He was a strong, liberating voice.

Although the Benton Chapel program and the Chaplaincy changed a great deal in later years, Branscomb's invention, the University Ministry, continues to challenge the university community through programs such as the Holocaust and Martin Luther King lecture series.

Roos: Harvie Branscomb retired in 1962, and I think he lost practically a semester on his program, with the problems of the Divinity School and Lawson. On the other hand, I think it made him more determined than ever to push this program. Harold Vanderbilt had pushed him beyond where his local Board wanted him to go, and he had won; this gave Branscomb more courage to proceed. I think before he was so afraid of what James Stahlman and John Sloan were going to do that he had to seek their approval. Now he effectively had been lifted beyond that. I think that Harold Vanderbilt provided much stronger support afterward than he did before. Prior to 1960 he was passive and his contact limited with the university that inherited his name. They made him chairman of the Board of Trust, and he showed up for a meeting or two. But afterward he took a much more active role and questioned, I am sure, Harvie on what he was doing and when he was going to move forward. While the Lawson incident might have had the effect of temporarily slowing things down, I think it ultimately speeded it up.

GILKEY: I have been thinking since we have been talking about the kinds of arguments one ran into in the community in 1960 that dominated this situation. One of them raises questions of the utility of the Constitution. The other raises questions of the prevalence or existence of a moral dimension beyond the law. To me the Constitution is an Enlightenment document. It had legal provisions, to be sure, but fundamental to it were the ideals of liberty and equality and so on. I won't say the pursuit of happiness, but nevertheless liberty and equality were what this Constitution was about. Therefore, wherever in the country there was not anything like liberty and equality, then the Constitution, whatever its legal provisions, demanded that this be put in in order for us to be living under the Constitution. I was very interested, in coming to Nashville in the 1950s (and I do not mean I would not run into this in Evanston, Illinois, or any other place), that the Constitution here was understood to be a document concerning states' rights—that it was, to put it into philosophical language, a positivist document that had no general natural law or rational, ethical ideas behind it; it specified powers. I would urge that this interpretation of the Constitution was very prevalent throughout the South at that point.

About that time I read a marvelous book, W. J. Cash's *The Mind of the South*, which some of you may know. I found it tremendously interesting to learn that the Enlightenment had certainly been basic to Virginia, but then had disappeared under the plantation economy. I realized that there was a real difference here. Now this was not a difference that really was between North and South, but there was a little bit of a difference, generally speaking. The liberals of the South, of whom there were many, shared my idea of the Constitution. They were in very radical disagreement with many of the people that they dealt with, and this has continued in our political life, all the way down the line. I suggest that this is one of the two fundamental intellectual, ethical, and spiritual issues lying back of these events of 1960.

The other one is the relation between law and morals. Probably the even more familiar argument that we all ran into, and we have the newspaper editorials that said it, was that you cannot upset THE LAW. It is well for us to remember something here, that there is a false lure of democracy, of the democratic process, and many people I talked with would fall for that false lure—namely, we have the democratic process, and the way to do it is to let that process go along, not interfere with it. I think that was the issue being confronted here, that many of the people really wanted to get somewhere, but you had to use the normal legal processes, and so forth, which is, it seems to me, a fatuously optimistic view of human society. What was lacking here was the biblical relation between law and moral obligation—in which laws could be unjust laws, could be immoral laws. Under those conditions I would call on that prophetic tradition, which all of us who have been involved in theological education have done, but which is there also in aspects in the history of our country. At certain times one has to broach for a higher law, one has to broach the law—the law does not express the ultimate moral position and never will. We have tended in America to be lured by the goddess of process. But the tradition, which is also part of our national heritage—that there is an obligation that transcends the law—was very much a part of what Jim Lawson and his colleagues were doing and leading us toward. That tradition is apt to be discarded, forgotten, or evaporated in the American experience because we are so sure that our processes are the ones that will reach the goal.

Now, I see a series of events beginning with what the people in the civil rights movement were doing, but moving on into Vietnam and beyond, that really challenged that view—and that seemed to be much more realistic. I am a child of Reinhold Niebuhr's *Moral Man and Immoral Society*, which argues that where the law has become an instrument of oppression or an instrument of injustice, it must be challenged. And one must be prepared to take the consequences. In all those cases, I would say that that is the equivalent of the prophetic denunciation of even a righteous people. That was the prophetic movement.

I think that behind what we are talking about, there are these issues. A national debate was going on—it is legal, it is constitutional, it is also moral and personal—about what the Constitution really means. I think you could have got the whole Board of Trust to say that they believed thoroughly in the Constitution. But if you had asked them what they meant by that, it would have been a very different story. This issue was one, of course, that Gandhi raised and that nonviolent protests raised, and which had appeared, let us remember, among the pacifists in the First World War—and they were all sent to jail unequivocally. This is the issue of what is your "moral right" or "obligation" to protest against and become non-involved in the law that you think is immoral. I think that remains an issue, but we are inclined to the lure of democratic process; we should realize that we could get ourselves very quickly into very serious moral trouble through the democratic process.

ROOS: On the question of the Constitution, I do not put much faith in the will of the majority. I think the majority cause always ought to be able to defend itself. The real issue is the protection of the minorities.

GILKEY: Absolutely. That is the point of the Constitution. And that is relatively unknown in the community.

LAWSON: And it remains unknown in the nation. One of the other effects of the Nashville struggle itself was that the sit-in movement became, in one way, the first nationwide movement for change. I think the Nashville scene had a lot to do with that. Because my picture went around the country for this expulsion, for example, in almost every university in the country—maybe not so much in the southern white universities, but almost every college and university in the country—there were support efforts for the sit-in campaign. These support efforts were not simply romantic. They also led people to check around and see what their university was doing in relation to race and discrimination. From Harvard, Yale, UC-Berkeley, and all over the country, we began to get phone calls from groups and from individual students who were talking about what they wanted to do. And they located the issue in their own scene, not just in the southern scene.

I have never forgotten that Harvard international students could not get decent housing off campus. One of the projects of the groups up there immediately was to demand that the university put certain housing with landlords off-limits to Harvard University people and to students if they did not have a non-discriminatory clause. I have never forgotten that episode later on in 1966.

SILBERMAN: Let me suggest that we cannot live in the past. Thirty-eight years ago is a very long time. The world turns, and the world turns, and the question still remains. We have seen—there is no doubt—that we had an impact. What happened here in Nashville were important changes that cannot be undone. But there are all kinds of new problems, all kinds of new questions that face us in our society. The lessons that we have learned and what we may have taught, no one hears any longer. And there are unforeseen consequences—the very things that were done in the sit-ins and the like to protect and to open up things are being used today by people for quite contrary reasons. I have for a number of years preached on the Holy Days, not in the main synagogue of the congregation to which I belong, but in the chapel where there are more elderly people who like a more traditional service for a synagogue. When I preached the other day, I commented on something that one of my colleagues had said—he had never noticed before how interested the newspapers were in the ideas of sin and forgiveness. The media was suddenly caught up in a great interest in sin and forgiveness. But the newspapers are no longer very much interested in sin and forgiveness a week or two later. We were involved in 1960 in sin and forgiveness in a much more important and a much deeper sense than all the vulgarity that is in our newspapers of record. When I feel as badly as I do occasionally, I turn to the New Testament. I turn to the last book of the New Testament, the Apocalypse of John, the book of Revelation, and I am comforted to know exactly what is going to happen—I am waiting for the seventh seal [see Revelation 5–8—*Ed.*]. We should be grateful for what we have done, and we can only pray that there will be some people who tomorrow and tomorrow and tomorrow will take their stand and dig in their heels and be ready to suffer the way that Jim Lawson suffered and to undergo the agonies that some of us underwent because they believe.

OTHERS AT THE TABLE: Amen. Amen.

ROOS: Now you can see why poor Stambaugh did not have a chance.

I was with Harvie Branscomb the day before he died. I am one of the six he asked to be ushers at the funeral. He has got to be completely at peace with this whole issue. I think he was scared and did not see a way out, and that was his problem. I realized, after arguing morals and so forth, Harvie knew that this was not the issue. He just did not see how to do it. I have come to be quite an admirer of the man. I think we sit in his monument; he gave us all a hard time, but we gave him a hard time. I think he appreciated the fact that the University had advanced in some sense—just as Branscomb was an autocrat with respect to the Board, he also protected the University from the Board. Part of the after-effects of this event was that other aspects of the University have gotten stronger—faculty governance, for example—so that people like Stahlman were no longer in control. We have to remember that it was an incredible feat that Harvie pulled off, in the face of the Board he had to work with.

LAWSON: It would have been a shame for the course of the University to have been halted for an indefinite period of time. To emerge from being a southern finishing school to become a strong and viable university, that certainly was the course that it had to take.

ROOS: When we pass the statue of Harold Vanderbilt on the Library lawn, we should realize that he is the one who held the university together. It was Harold Vanderbilt who took control of the situation on that June 8.

GILKEY: I just wish that some public word about Harold Vanderbilt's role in this could be given because I do not think that ever has been heard. I think he should be congratulated and celebrated in some appropriate way. That was a very creative role. The Divinity faculty suspected it, but we did not know. We had a picture of him standing behind and pushing Harvie, but we did not realize how the conversation and the movement of the whole thing developed under Harold Vanderbilt's leadership.

COMPTON: You may remember, it was 1961 or 1962, a sculptor had for some time been at work on a statue of Harold Vanderbilt. It was finally completed and unveiled, I think, in the fall of 1962, certainly by 1963, and he unveiled it himself. It stands on the Library lawn. The rumors going around before it had been unveiled were that he would be pictured holding the steering wheel of a yacht (he had been involved in the America's Cup races) or that he would be pictured holding a deck of cards (he invented the game of contract bridge). Coming back to the serious point, he was actually pictured holding a gavel. This is our very point—here was the chairman of the Board, and he was in charge.

GILKEY: He was quite a guy—those three possibilities are not something everybody could have.

JOHNSON: I cannot tell you how grateful I am to all of you for your participation in this event. It has truly been powerful to hear your stories and your reflections on this important event in our history. The Divinity School and the University are in your debt. Thank you very much.

Addendum: The Meeting between Branscomb and Lawson

Joseph C. Hough, Jr.

In the preceding conversation, James Lawson mentions a meeting with Harvie Branscomb. It occurred on October 24, 1996, prior to Lawson's being honored the next day as the first Vanderbilt Divinity School Distinguished Alumnus. The following is an account of the events that led to that meeting and what transpired there.

Shortly after I came to Vanderbilt in 1990, I was introduced to Harvie and Margaret Branscomb, the former chancellor of Vanderbilt University and his wife. During the next six months, I visited with them several times, and when my wife joined me in Nashville the next August, we became rather frequent visitors to the Branscomb home.

Harvie Branscomb became one of our most loyal and valued friends. He was very supportive of the Divinity School and followed with great interest our progress in long-range planning and development. As our friendship deepened, he began to share with me some of his reflections on his own career at Vanderbilt, his high points and his low points. The one matter that seemed to trouble him most was his decision to expel James Lawson. He said that he put himself into a very difficult position by deferring to his Board of Trust in what he later saw to be an administrative decision. At least one member of his board, James Stahlman, the editor of the *Nashville Banner*, virtually demanded Lawson's expulsion. Branscomb never denied his own responsibility for his decision, but it was clear in several of our conversations that he now thought his decision was wrong both politically and morally.

During these conversations I told Harvie that James Lawson was a friend of mine for whom I had great respect, and I shared with him some of the many occasions on which Lawson had given significant national and regional leadership to the churches and the wider society in the cause of justice and reconciliation. In late 1994, Harvie asked if I would be willing to arrange a meeting with Jim, and I readily agreed. As I pursued the matter, both indicated that they had made attempts to arrange a meeting, but for a variety of reasons they had not spoken directly since Lawson was expelled from the Divinity School.

In the spring of 1995, the Alumni/ae Council of the Divinity School suggested that we inaugurate a Distinguished Service Award for the alumnus or alumna who made outstanding contributions to church and/or society. James Lawson was the unanimous choice to receive the first award. I personally visited Harvie to inform him of the decision of the Council before the announcement was made public. His response was very positive. He had arranged for someone to read to him the materials I had given him on Lawson, and he was impressed with his record. He then asked if I thought that it would be possible to arrange a meeting between him and Lawson when he came to receive the award. I called Jim, and he immediately agreed to the proposal. Harvie asked that only he, Jim, and I be present for the meeting and that there be no prior public announcement of it.

On the appointed date, James Lawson and I met with Harvie Branscomb in his home. It was one of the most moving moments I have experienced in many years. Harvie congratulated Jim on his many outstanding achievements and asked about his current ministry. I do not remember the exact words, but I am clear about the substance of what happened next. After a few moments of conversation, Harvie said something like this: "Dr. Lawson, I want you to know that I now regret the decision I made in 1960, and I think it was a mistake. I want you to know that, and I should like your forgiveness for any harm that came to you as a result of that decision." Lawson responded with words along these lines: "Dr. Branscomb, I have long ago forgiven you for any wrong I felt was done, and I have never thought ill of you nor have I held any malice toward you since that time. I never thought you were anything less than a Christian man who was trying to do the right thing in a very difficult situation." There was more conversation for a while, and then we left, both men wishing each other well.

The next day, Harvie came to the luncheon honoring Jim and Dorothy and sat at the table with them. It was a wonderful symbol of a new reality for both of these outstanding men, and it was a high moment in the history of Vanderbilt Divinity School and its University.

7

Social Transformation and Theological Education at Vanderbilt since 1960

Howard L. Harrod

The fundamental shifts in cultural values and social organizations that erupted in the 1960s reshaped the life of Vanderbilt Divinity School, and the responses of the faculty and staff to these critical events played an active role in how that reshaping occurred. In this chapter I focus on the ways in which the Divinity School responded to changes in the social world stimulated by movements for justice, peace, and liberation that began with the civil rights movement. I describe these experiences, events, and institutional structures from the point of view of one who participated in them.[1]

I do not claim that Vanderbilt Divinity School was a special case, since other universities, divinity schools, and seminaries across the country struggled in their own ways with events that formed the context of the 1960s. What I offer is a detailed analysis of how the faculty and students in one institution interacted around particular curricular, institutional, and social issues that arose, often in painful ways, in the internal life of the school. My broader purpose is to show that these interactions were not simply responses to internal institutional matters, but rather were influenced in fundamental ways by what was happening in the wider society.[2]

Taking up the Divinity School as a case study may illuminate the experience and memories of those in other institutions who were seeking to shape their own interpretations of and responses to the challenges of the social movements that affected us all. For example, after 1960 the civil rights movement was increasingly informed by the highly charged vision of a beloved community of multiracial peace and justice articulated by Martin Luther King, Jr. This vision of a new world breaking into and through old, unjust, worn, and destructive social structures promised to make all things new. The experience of many, especially on university campuses, was invigorated by the anticipation that the promises embodied in this vision were being fulfilled. An entire generation of students, not all of whom were full participants, was affected by the sensibilities projected by the civil rights movement, as well as the War on Poverty, and the resistance that arose to the war in Vietnam.[3]

Such changes cannot simply be understood as the one-way effect of external causes on the school. Rather, the social transformations that the Divinity School endured during the 1960s and beyond were the outcome of a complex social process in which the school played an active part. Understanding the matter from this perspective opens a way of viewing social change as involving a variety of factors interacting with one another, as compared with a monocausal model of social change. A monocausal model might, for example, attribute primary significance to a social movement, such as a student protest, making this factor the fundamental agent of change. By contrast, the more multidimensional interactions explored in this chapter involve responses and counter-responses of students, faculty, and staff to a number of events. These responses and counter-responses did not represent perfectly coherent perspectives but rather took the form of conflicts of interpretation, both within groups and between groups. These conflicts of interpretation, furthermore, focused upon matters that were central to the interests of theological schools, their faculties, and students. Struggles of interpretation revolved around fundamental understandings of religiously based cultural values, such as justice, peace, reconciliation, and the good society. These moral dimensions of the struggle were intertwined with theological understandings of the nature of divine activity in relation to movements for economic and racial justice; more recently, these understandings have been extended to include liberation of the natural world. Anthropological understandings accompanying these discussions often portrayed human beings as faulted and violent, but at the same time offered hope that what was envisioned by King and others was actually powerfully breaking through seemingly intractable human conditions.

Institutional practices and norms and their legitimating ideologies proceed out of deeply hidden layers of social life. In the case of the Divinity School, one of these realities was an ethos formed by faculty members who were present at the beginning of the 1960s. These faculty members shared a particular generational experience.[4] Most of them had undergraduate degrees that reflected an older "pre-theological" course of study. Some had majored in philosophy, some in one of the humanities, and some in a concentration called "letters," the latter of which usually required a distribution of courses in the humanities such as English, history, and philosophy. This preparation led rather directly to study in a seminary or divinity school, and a degree from a seminary or divinity school directly supported work toward a Ph.D. in religion.

This rather coherent, step-by-step educational process from the under-graduate level through seminary or divinity school to the Ph.D. degree was complemented by another pattern. Many Divinity School faculty during this generation had been ordained, and many of them had at one time or another served as congregational ministers. After entering into an academic career, these faculty members tended to maintain an active relationship with their denomina-tions, preaching regularly and lecturing in various settings in churches. The professional role of teacher was often associated, in the same person, with the role of pastoral ministry. This fusion affected the way in which students per-ceived their theological education, as the coherence they saw between the two roles represented by the faculty helped ease tensions between the "practical" and the "academic" dimensions of the curriculum. At Vanderbilt, however, these tensions became structural as the Graduate Department of Religion became larger and more important in the life of the school from the mid-1960s on.

These generational patterns gave rise to an ethos that both responded to and was shaped by the social movements that arose in the 1960s. One may typify this ethos in two ways. First, it was an embodiment of classical liberalism—specifically, the values of freedom, equality, justice, and the dignity of persons—grounded in various interpretations of the philosophical and religious traditions of the West. The shape these values took at Vanderbilt was fundamentally Prot-estant, refracted more specifically through the traditions of mainline denomina-tions heavily represented in both the faculty and student body. Most numerous were Methodists, Disciples of Christ, and Presbyterians. The ethos was also refracted through the experience of a group of faculty who gradually replaced those who had experienced the early stages of the civil rights movement in Nashville and lived through the agonies of the Lawson affair. Some of them, such as J. Philip Hyatt, Herman Norton, Lou Silberman, and James Sellers, bridged the two eras. Several new faculty members arrived at Vanderbilt during the 1960s who not only shared a version of the older liberal ethos but were socialized in the same graduate program during roughly the same time period.[5] The faculty did not universally share the ethos I am describing, but it is fair to say that this was the dominant perspective that characterized the institutional life of the school from 1960 well into the 1990s.

Second, this ethos was characterized by what might be called the "critical principle," which meant that all knowledge mediated from the past—including biblical sources and religious traditions—must be subjected to critical thought. No assertion or description could be grounded in ecclesiastical authority or a particular doctrine of biblical revelation. The commitments to the values of classical liberalism were partly justified on the basis of critical discourse and were mediated in a larger consensus shared by the faculty. This larger consensus was not fully subjected to the "critical principle" until it was challenged by the events of the 1960s, particularly represented in the attitudes and behaviors of the students. It continued to be challenged as the sociological composition of the school changed during the 1970s and 1980s. Nevertheless, a generally shared version of the liberal ethos was a symbolic horizon that often enabled the institution to be creative in shaping responses to the civil rights movement, the War on Poverty, the Vietnam War, and countercultural attitudes among students. This ethos has increasingly been challenged in more recent decades by greater diversity in the student body in terms of gender, race, and sexual orientation.[6]

In addition to the values of classical liberalism mediated through mainline denominations, their religious traditions, and the notion of critical thinking, a vision of the church as a locus for social change leading toward peace, justice, and the liberation of all of life predominated. This vision may have been rooted in memories of the Social Gospel, but it also found support in the example of African American churches, many of which were highly visible institutional loci of the civil rights movement. In the early years of the sit-in movement, for example, protesters were trained in the ideology and techniques of nonviolence. As the movement gathered strength and visibility, the pulpits and meeting halls in many black churches became places where goals and strategies for social change were discussed and developed.

In theological schools like Vanderbilt, the notion that the church could be an agent of social change was one of several competing ideas at the dawn of the 1960s. The tradition of individualistic piety that emphasized the necessity of transforming internal life in order to effect changes in the social world was very strong in southern Protestant churches, and this ethos was—and continues to be—represented in the experience of some students in the school. By contrast, the ideology of the counterculture, represented by Students for a Democratic Society, the Berkeley free speech movement, and the protest against the Vietnam War, produced in the minds of some students the sensibility that major institutions in the society, including the churches, were complicit in the destruction, continued racism, and violence that seemed to characterize the majority culture. This sensibility gave rise to an increasingly strident anti-institutionalism that deeply affected patterns of theological education as well as social relations between students and faculty.

The Vietnam War brought with it some of the largest enrollments of students, many of whom were seeking deferments from the draft.[7] The popular assertion that so-called liberal theological schools like Vanderbilt were havens for unpatriotic "draft-dodgers" contained only a partial truth. Certainly, some male students who came to the school during this period were seeking to avoid the draft and participation in a war that had not been successfully legitimated at the symbolic level of the national society and had not been declared by the Congress. As a consequence, the student body included a group of largely middle-class, often very privileged young white men whose consciousness was not dominated by deeply held notions of patriotism and whose motivation to resist the war was fueled by highly charged discussions in university contexts, both formal and informal. "Hell no, we won't go" was a popular cry that concealed a variety of motivations, some fueled more by fear than by idealistic visions of a peaceful world. But many of the students who came to Vanderbilt interpreted their opposition to the war and their support for the civil rights movement in the light of religious and moral traditions they had learned in the churches.

Since this chapter offers an analysis of social transformations and their effect on theological education, it is appropriate to subject some specific structures, such as the curriculum, to a more extended analysis.[8] The broadest function of the curriculum in any school is to socialize persons, to enculturate them into the values, languages, interpretations, and visions of the past and present that characterize a particular group or society. The erection of educational structures and procedures to accomplish the transmission of traditions is partly a conscious function of the intentions of those who are responsible for their construction and maintenance. This process also operates at deeper, less visible levels of institutional life, and it sometimes has unintended consequences that are beyond the purview of and perhaps even in tension with the purposes of the individuals who are engaged in the construction of the curriculum.

The process of socialization, like social change, is interactive rather than unidirectional. It involves structures of transmission (intentional and unintentional), an authority structure (grades and the control of the certification process), the complex responses of those who are subjects of the process (students), and the further responses of those responsible for managing the process (faculty).[9] Some of the changes in the curriculum of Vanderbilt Divinity School since the 1960s and 1970s can be interpreted as complex responses to the significance of wider social movements. A 1967 faculty retreat during which matters of the curriculum were discussed illustrates this point. Before 1960, the curriculum was structured according to the model of a traditional "core" of requirements in biblical, historical, theological, and practical studies. A few electives allowed students to pursue their own interests; but the dominant model was projected in the core, and the authority structure of the school—its grading system and degree-granting powers—was focused on maintaining this transmission process.

At the 1967 faculty retreat at Paris Landing State Park, the curriculum committee presented a report that included recommendations for modifying the core curriculum.[10] These modifications included the formation of a new field called "Studies in Religion and Culture," which was envisioned as an area that would include not only the social sciences (sociology, anthropology, psychology) but also religion and literature, religion and art, social ethics, theology of culture, and history of religions. It was intended to promote interdisciplinary work and more extensive interaction with colleagues in the university. The committee proposed that the core structure be modified by reconceiving the required introductory courses and by introducing a system of distributional requirements. The required courses were to be more than simply "surveys" of the several fields; they should be opportunities for students to be introduced to the possibilities that biblical studies, church history, theology, and practical studies held for creative ministry. In addition to the courses representing the traditional four-fold division were two new required courses, Introduction to Theological Education and Introduction to Ministry. The committee also recommended that the advisory system be strengthened to provide an adequate consultative structure for planning student programs. According to this plan, advisers were to have greater authority to approve student programs and were responsible for seeing that the program fit the student's vocational goals.

During the discussion of this report, it became apparent that a number of faculty members were dissatisfied with the way the curriculum was structured. Although not as vast a social process as Thomas Kuhn described, a curricular "paradigm shift" was about to occur.[11] This paradigm shift seems to have been motivated in part by the sense that there were internal contradictions that had rendered the idea of a core curriculum—even one creatively reconceived—irrelevant to the emerging cultural situation. More mundane motivations such as fatigue and boredom connected with teaching several required classes year after year certainly played a role. But some of the faculty motivation rested upon an increasing awareness of what was happening in the social world beyond the confines of the culture represented by the school.

For example, between 1960 and 1967 the civil rights movement had matured and Martin Luther King, Jr., had begun to engage more intractable problems such as housing and employment, especially in northern cities. He also expanded his vision to include world peace, which meant that the movement began a critique of the ongoing Vietnam War. King's vision of a multiracial, integrated society was challenged during this period not only by Malcolm X but also by the more broadly based Black Power movement. In addition, the student counterculture became symbolically powerful and increasingly strident (and sometimes violent) during this period, and its effects were felt to one degree or another on university campuses across the nation.

Beginning in 1961, a series of national and international events deepened tensions in the national culture. The years 1961 and 1962, for example, saw the erection of the Berlin Wall, the Bay of Pigs disaster, and the Cuban missile crisis—all clearly indicating that the Cold War was at a very high level of intensity. The country was plunged into conflict and collective agony when President John F. Kennedy was assassinated in Dallas in 1963. In 1965 President Lyndon Johnson sent the first U.S. ground troops to Vietnam, and in June of that year he increased the troop strength from 65,000 to 130,000. During this same year the communist government in China announced its support of the Viet Cong (a year before the Chinese detonated their first nuclear weapon). In July 1967, the Viet Cong mounted a surprise attack on the U.S. air base at Da Nang, killing and wounding American troops and destroying twenty-five aircraft. By the end of this year, the number of U.S. troops in Vietnam had risen to 480,000.[12] Clearly, the period leading up to the faculty retreat was highly charged, filled with intense conflicts at all levels in the society—political, economic, racial, generational, and international.[13] The outcome of that retreat was affected by these events. After receiving the committee's recommendations, the faculty constituted itself as a committee of the whole and proceeded to create six new committees to continue the curricular review. Two results of this work are particularly relevant: additional recommendations concerning field structure and recommendations concerning required courses.

The committee on field structure recommended to the faculty a fundamental set of changes: the existing discipline-based curricular structure was to be abandoned, and courses were to be listed according to a flexible and presumably changeable notion of "fields of study." Further, it recommended that there should be no prerequisites attached to these courses. Students were to build a coherent and vocationally relevant program of study with the help of an even more elaborately conceived advisory structure. These recommendations were adopted by the faculty substantially as proposed. The idea of creating a new field called "Studies in Religion and Culture" was abandoned.[14]

The committee on introductory courses recommended that a new course entitled "Introduction to Theological Education" be required of all entering M.Div. students. The course was conceived in terms of two parallel yet interacting tracks, one historical and one problem-centered. It was to be staffed by a faculty team, would include student discussion groups, and was to be the *only* required course at the introductory level. After some development of the original proposal, the faculty passed this recommendation substantially as described.

The actions of these two committees illustrate well the cultural values at work in the wider social world. The faculty showed its impatience with old, presumably irrelevant, curricular structures, and the wider cultural struggles certainly suggested a move toward a less structured, more experimental, and freer curricular arrangement. Some of the most powerful energies of the counterculture were explicitly focused upon the liberation of the individual from an outmoded as well as corrupt past. Convictions that the young could take charge of their own actions and construct a new and more just society certainly stimulated the move toward vesting greater responsibility for the formation of student programs in the students themselves. As it turned out, the way Introduction to Theological Education was taught during the first year illustrates these themes even more specifically.[15]

The specific content for the two tracks of the course, the historical dimensions and the problems to be studied, were to be determined by the teaching staff. Track One was to have two units, one on the self and society and the other on institutions and changing society. One initial projection of the course included two components not articulated in the Paris Landing retreat documents: "the Plunge" and the "Listening Post."

The Plunge was designed to challenge the students' understandings of identity and social location by exposing them to Nashville's urban environment without any traditional support systems. During a two-day experience they were to take only $2.50, no extra clothing, a comb and toothbrush (they were allowed to take a social security card or a draft card—if they had not burned it). Students were advised to learn how to "make it" under such conditions from people they met on the street. They were to find out from the denizens of the urban community where they might get a meal, find a place to stay for the night, or perhaps a place to pick up a few dollars working at a menial job. Students were also encouraged to undergo this experience alone, avoiding contact if possible with other divinity students. After experiencing the Plunge, students were assigned to Listening Posts in institutional locations in Nashville at which, with limited time commitments (2–4 hours per week) but over the course of a full semester, they would by their presence associate with people whose experiences and situations presumably were very different from their own.[16] The Listening Post was envisioned as a way of beginning theological education through immersion in the ambiguities and concreteness of people's lives, with the idea that this was where the fundamental data for theological reflection could be found. Encountering this data would lead students to discover that the traditional disciplines of theological education have direct relevance for the pain and ambiguity of life. "In short," the teaching staff argued, "through sensitive involvement in the human situation we hope that you [the students] will begin to seek both the wisdom of the tradition and the best contemporary insights available for developing professional competence."[17]

Two additional pedagogical assumptions lay behind the Listening Posts. The first was that previous academic training had assimilated students into a world disconnected from the concreteness of life, a world of typifications that had become closed to experiences arising from radically different social locations. The Listening Post forced students into a condition of ambiguity, with the hope that previously formed cultural patterns would be broken open. Once this relatively safe world was de-centered, the student's theological and ethical imagination would be stimulated, providing the ground for formulating more fitting public policies. "Those who have had the experience of relating to the poor and the black in our society are more likely to develop creative social policy than those who are isolated from the problem both socially and physically."[18]

Both the Plunge and the Listening Posts were attempts to relocate the educational process, to undermine the power of the core curriculum and constitute material for reflection in the realm of experience. This relocation, it was argued, would motivate students to turn toward the broader biblical, historical, and theological traditions in order to find elements that were relevant for understanding the experiences that flowed from the Plunge and exposure to the urban environment through the Listening Posts. The requirement that students attend small group sessions ensured that they would engage in a process of reflection on their experiences. In addition, students were granted considerable authority to use these experiences in shaping their own programs of study, even though the faculty intended to strengthen the function of the advisory system at the same time.[19]

The vision of the qualities that would characterize graduates of the new program was often unclear, but it included at least the following elements: they should be open to experiences of those vastly different from themselves, especially those who were marginalized by the majority culture; they should be sensitive to aspects of the religious heritage mediated by the churches that could move both society and the churches toward greater social justice and peace; and they should be "self-starters," able critically to analyze the tradition, choose for themselves how to interpret it, and develop their own constructive views (which were to be embodied in each student's Senior Project). According to these expectations, graduates of the school were to become "change agents" who addressed problems of peace and justice for their time.

These changes in the curriculum represented some faculty responses to the wider culture. It is likely, however, that particular students or groups of students were more deeply affected by the changes in the social world than were the faculty. Students shared a different generational position and were thus exposed to forces, such as the draft, in a more direct way than the faculty. Differences in generational position within the faculty might have played a role in this process as well. However one assesses these matters, what the faculty did at Paris Landing was to dispense with the traditional core curriculum, reflecting in its own institutional life the winds of change blowing through the wider culture that were powerfully embodied by the students who came to the school.

Before the first semester of Introduction to Theological Education ended, however, questions were raised concerning its structure and its fundamental purposes. Gradually, these questions extended to the structure of the curriculum as such. This free curriculum (more negatively known as a "cafeteria-style" arrangement) evoked discomfort in some faculty members. For example, an internal paper, "Theological Education at Vanderbilt" (1969), argued that the faculty should take greater responsibility for the curriculum and, more specifically, provide structure in the form of distributional requirements. The so-called free curriculum gradually gave way to the more intentionally structured curriculum organized around the image of "minister as theologian."[20]

Student evaluations of Introduction to Theological Education expressed concerns about what they experienced as a lack of structure and viewed as the mediocre character of the plenary sessions—which often included lectures by faculty members addressing aspects in the "historical track" of the course.[21] Staff evaluations also probed what were viewed as problematic aspects of the course. For example, the Paris Landing curricular revolution had placed an enormous burden on the student to take responsibility for his or her own education. This was a rather direct, though perhaps not fully conscious, response on the part of the faculty to what was being asserted by countercultural attitudes toward education. Influenced by Paulo Freire's critique of the "banking model" of education, entailing the passive reception of knowledge mediated by an authority figure (teacher), students asserted that they were responsible for their own education.[22] By contrast, staff evaluations began to question whether students had sufficient intellectual skills or maturity to take on this burden. The teaching staff began to consider whether students might be aided by a more coherent reading list and by increased contact with the teacher, whose role it was to engage the student in the educational process.[23]

The Paris Landing curriculum and its aftermath can be understood as a struggle on the part of the faculty to respond to the cultural situation as filtered through their own experience. Confusion about how to engage in theological education was evident in both student and faculty responses. This unsettled institutional situation continued through the mid-1970s and began to diminish with the approach of the 1980s. Not only had the Vietnam War ended, but the extremes of the Weathermen as well as the spectacle of Patty Hearst and the Symbionese Liberation Army had created a cultural backlash that made more visible in the nation the values and norms that probably had represented the majority in the society all along. The visibility and influence of the counter-culture faded, and a sense of social stability and relative calm emerged.

As the society moved toward greater cultural coherence and order, so did the curriculum at the Divinity School. Despite the apparent calm, however, this curricular order concealed forces at work in both the culture and in the school. Some of these forces became the now familiar "identity politics" that has continued to characterize present cultural experience. With the emergence of a critical mass of African American students, frustrations and anger arose around what was identified as continuing racism in the school. A coalition was formed between two student groups, the Black Seminarians and the Office of Women's Concerns. In the discourse during this period, issues of race and gender were joined, and a sense of solidarity in the experiences of oppression among African American men and women and white women emerged. As the tensions mounted between 1986 and 1988, another group in the school joined this increasingly powerful coalition. Gay and lesbian students, who had become a growing presence, began to define what was perceived as widespread discrimination and insensitivity as part of a larger pattern that included not only race and gender but also sexual orientation.

In the fall of 1986 these gathering energies erupted in a painful manner that surprised and finally chastened the faculty, leading to a number of changes in procedures and curriculum. The occasion for this eruption is less important in retrospect than the sensibilities that fueled it. The flash point had been reached, and only a spark was needed to start the social conflagration. The spark occurred during a visit by a white Methodist minister from South Africa. His informal comments about education in South Africa were perceived by some students to be racist.[24] South Africa had come to symbolize deep attitudes that were believed to infect the social world, not only in that country but elsewhere as well. The discrimination and violence toward blacks in South Africa were viewed as part of a larger world pattern. According to this diagnosis of the situation, students were able to locate what they interpreted as multiple oppressions surrounding race, gender, and sexual orientation lurking in the institutional procedures, the classes, and the wider institutional structure of the Divinity School. Perhaps most painfully, some students identified these destructive forces not only in systemic forms but also in the personalities and behaviors of specific faculty members.

Several factors may be identified which in the heat of the conflict could not be clearly understood. The most obvious factor at the time was the presence of strong student leaders, persons who were highly focused, angry, and possessed of considerable leadership skills. These student leaders also had the benefit of institutional structures that had fully legitimate standing in the school. The Office of Women's Concerns and the Black Seminarians were natural arenas from which to mount the sort of student protest that occurred.[25] When the students reacted to the remarks by the visiting minister from South Africa, their first move was to demand that he be "dis-invited" to preach at the school's weekly worship service. Students asserted that allowing him to preach was tantamount to legitimating what he was alleged to have said. They demanded that instead of a preaching context, he be asked to appear at a forum to respond to student questions about his attitudes toward education and the South African government. The dean did not accept this demand, and a compromise was worked out that involved shortening the worship service and leaving time at the end for dialogue—in effect, attaching a forum at the end of the worship service. As it turned out, the worship service went longer than planned, and there was insufficient time for the kind of dialogue that was needed.

In the months following this event, meetings were held (both large and small), apologies demanded, and new demands made. Clearly, there was resistance to the student demands; what was unclear to the students were the reasons for this resistance. One factor had to do with the shared experience and memory of the faculty. There were the obvious matters of civility, courtesy, and a commitment to free speech and "open forum" that operated on the surface and conditioned the response to the student demand concerning "dis-inviting" the minister. But deeper confusions were evoked when student frustration and anger focused not only on the ethos of the school but also on individual members of the faculty. Charges of racism and discrimination created a kind of "cognitive dissonance" in the faculty that challenged their identity and called into question the memory of a shared past.

A core group of the faculty had been together since the late 1960s and had worked together for some twenty years by the time the events of 1986 occurred. This group had inherited the memory of "the Lawson affair"; they had lived through the tumultuous times of the civil rights movement, the counterculture, and the Vietnam War, and they viewed their positions on these matters as expressions of a deep commitment to social justice, peace, and opposition to discrimination of any sort. These faculty members remembered protesting against what were viewed as racist practices of the Vanderbilt food service. During the late 1960s the practice of the food service had been to place whites in positions of authority, such as at the cash register, while blacks were relegated to the food line and the kitchen area. The faculty demanded that a black woman be trained to run the cash register, which they believed would begin to constitute a new pattern of relations in this critical area. This effort succeeded, and a black woman assumed a position that had been held only by whites. The Divinity School refectory food line was closed by 1986, and those who had joined the faculty most recently, as well as the student protesters, had no memory of that earlier event.

The faculty also had memories of participating in a protest against discriminatory practices in a restaurant near the campus, demonstrating in a town southwest of Nashville over issues of racism in voter registration, and marching in protest when the University hosted a Davis Cup tennis match with South Africa in 1978.[26] These memories and the commitments they reflected had become part of the identity of a significant number of faculty members, although these shared sensibilities remained largely taken for granted. The challenges presented by black students, women, and gays and lesbians threatened this level of faculty consensus and identity, bringing painfully to the surface matters that had previously been unexamined. Part of what was perceived as resistance by the faculty surely must have had to do with the hesitation and confusion that emerged when this shared identity was challenged.

Students also could not have known the efforts of search committees to seek out qualified women and minority applicants for any faculty position. Search committees were given their mandates by the dean, and positions were recommended to the dean by the Personnel and Policy Committee. These discussions often ended with the conclusion that if a woman or a minority person, particularly an African American, could not be appointed, the search would continue. The commitment of the faculty in this respect is indisputable, but the public often had little knowledge of the process. Likewise, the commitment of the faculty to increase the number of women on the faculty was little known in the student body. Students, of course, graduate, so traditions in the student body are difficult to maintain.[27]

While this identity was shared by those who had developed it over a twenty-year period, it was not shared by faculty who had been more recently appointed; and it was certainly not shared by the students involved in the protest. Some faculty who were appointed during the 1980s were influenced by intellectual currents such as liberation theologies, postmodernism, deconstruction, and the emergence of postcolonial discourse. Some of these newer faculty members were African Americans, women, and other minorities who identified themselves with student sensibilities concerning oppression. Many of the older faculty still identified with theological and political liberalism and its message of social justice for all people. They were also probably still committed to some version of Martin Luther King, Jr.'s vision of an *integrated*, multiracial society.

The leaders of the student protest were mature individuals who had been influenced by the civil rights movement but who had also experienced the frustrations of the continuing effects of racism and sexism in the wider society.[28] They had experienced the era of affirmative action, but they had also experienced a period during which the rising affluence and materialism of the larger culture had not extended to many minorities, and during which many of the legislative and judicial gains of the civil rights movement were eroding. The 1980s were dominated by the policies and symbolic legitimations that ran counter to the aspirations of many in the Divinity School, both students and faculty. Under the leadership of Ronald Reagan, the nation moved toward the right, purporting to recover the values dear to the dominant middle class: work, fair return for effort, and a wholesome family life. The Religious Right took up these themes as well, developing a complex of ideas under the rubric of "family values." Tax policies increasingly favored the more well-off in the society, and minorities felt themselves slipping from the high symbolic ground that had been theirs during the 1960s and 1970s. Anger and frustration had become common experiences for the poor, women, African Americans, and gays and lesbians. These energies were focused in the events at the school in 1986 and reflected the sense that oppression was pervasive in all quarters of the society and was expressed in continuing racism, classism, patriarchy, and homophobia.

Those who participated in the student protests did not share the vision of a multiracial, integrated society still held by many of the faculty. Their views were more separatist in nature, reflective of the "identity politics" of the 1980s. Their discourse was controlled by the emerging notion of "multiculturalism." Through the politics of exclusion, for example, these students and faculty argued that groups with deep and legitimate cultures had been marginalized by the dominant society. Their perspectives, literatures, values, and aspirations had been suppressed. It was therefore necessary to bring to the center of attention those previously suppressed perspectives and make them central to the educational experience of the Divinity School. As the older notion of integration was displaced by the idea of multiculturalism, the vision of the student leaders was aimed directly at the ethos, procedures, and curriculum of the school.

The events of 1986–88 represent an ironic situation in which the formerly "younger faculty" who represented the liberal ethos and had participated in the struggles of the sixties and seventies found themselves typified as conservative—even racist, sexist, and homophobic. The earlier history that was sedimented in the experience of the faculty was not necessarily communicated to the student body. The students of this period represented a different generational experience, and it was natural, in retrospect, that this experience would be projected on the faculty and the curriculum; it was also natural that the liberalism of the now older faculty members would be challenged and that they would respond with confusion, dismay, and defensiveness.

As a consequence of the continuing pressure by the students and the residual capacities of the faculty to respond, modifications in the curriculum and procedures of the school were made that embodied at least part of the student agenda. That agenda was developed as a consequence of a number of social processes that followed the first protests in 1986. A seminar on racism convened by Professor Wallace Charles Smith in the spring semester of 1987 prepared a set of policy recommendations addressing the curriculum, the composition of the faculty, and policies with respect to black students.[29] Concerning the curriculum, it proposed that: (1) the foundation curriculum should contain black (including womanist) perspectives as essential components; (2) all students should be required to take one course each in black theology, liberation theology, comparative religion, and womanist/feminist theology; (3) courses in black theology, black liberation ethics, the black Christian tradition, womanist/feminist theology, and liberation theology should be regularly available in the curriculum; (4) to assure that foundation courses have all of these elements, implementation should not depend solely on the individual faculty members who teach the courses.

Concerning the faculty and teaching procedures, it recommended that minimum target percentages be set for faculty composition (25 percent people of color and 40 percent women, with 30 percent of the latter being women of color). It proposed further that faculty participate in an annual seminar on racism, that course evaluation forms include questions about the degree to which black and womanist perspectives have appeared in the courses, and that these evaluation forms be summarized and published each semester.

Regarding students and student services, the document proposed minimum target percentages within the student body of 20 percent black students and 10 percent international students. It urged that financial aid for black and international students be increased substantially, in part to enhance recruitment of students from lower economic backgrounds. It sought the appointment of a black writing tutor and a black chaplain or dean of black affairs (the latter could, for an interim period of no more than one year, be combined with the position of the director of the Kelly Miller Smith Institute on the Black Church). Finally, a standing committee to monitor racism and to function as a grievance committee should be immediately appointed, and a majority of this committee should be people of color.

These recommendations were clearly radical and sweeping, and the students viewed the faculty responses as unclear, hesitant, and even obstructionist. Thus the anger, frustration, and organizational activities of student groups continued to mount, and voices demanding change were increasingly strident. During the fall semester of 1987, forums were held and memos exchanged between faculty and students. None of these activities produced any solution from the students' point of view, and by the spring semester student leaders perceived that the environment had become even more poisoned. An open meeting, announced as a "Forum on Backlash," was held in February, where student grievances were aired, including a number of issues not mentioned in the document produced by the seminar on racism.

At this highly charged meeting, frustrations were expressed about University policies that seemed to make groups like the Black Seminarians have less legitimacy than other student organizations. Suspicions were raised about the relations between student officers and members of the Divinity School administration. Anger was expressed concerning teaching methods and what was perceived to be a pervasive pattern of racism in grading practices. In a follow-up memo a few days later, student leaders argued for an expansion of the items in the previous discussions to include such matters as the public posting of minutes of all faculty committees, opening up the budget process of the school, discontinuing the practice of giving hand-written student evaluations to professors before they had been typed, adding a statement in the catalogue concerning opposition to homophobia, and including sexual orientation in the school's anti-discrimination policy.

While student anger and frustration continued, and while faculty members were charged with obstructing the process, the energies of the student protest were directed at a whole range of policy issues. At the same time, the faculty perceived themselves to be members of a community where actions were *deliberate* and were performed within structures created for this purpose. Some of these structures in the University were controlled by traditional procedural rules, and some had legal dimensions as well. In the Divinity School, deliberation occurred in informal faculty discussions and formal faculty meetings, but when issues were grave or involved problematic features, they were referred to "appropriate committees." These rather arcane processes must have seemed to students, caught in the heat of a righteous social movement, to be excessively obstructionist, which probably deepened their frustration and anger.

Examples of how the faculty responded within the formal and informal structures available for decision-making illustrate not only their attitudes toward student demands but also why the student frustrations probably could not have been addressed successfully—at least from the students' point of view. The demand that faculty be *required* to attend a workshop on racism did not sit well with some individuals. Tenured university professors are typically resistant to being required to do anything, especially when demands come from students.[30] Some faculty suspected that such a workshop might take the form of an "encounter group," which was something in which they did not wish to participate. Furthermore, the person the students had suggested to be the workshop leader did not receive the support of several faculty members; in a memo to the dean, one faculty member suggested another individual, but wondered at the same time about the purpose of such workshops should they continue to be held.

The faculty response to the student demands took the form of an open letter addressing specific issues. It specified both a timeline when particular issues would be addressed and the appropriate forum, person, or committee to deal with the matter. The faculty specifically committed itself to insuring anonymity in student evaluation forms, designing a more appropriate grievance process in the school, and creating more opportunities for faculty–student dialogue. It further affirmed its intent to invite C. T. Vivian, a prominent civil rights leader, to the school for a consultation. This would replace the two-day workshop requested by the students. The faculty also agreed to devote a number of faculty sessions to a discussion of racism, sexism, and homophobia.

Two additional matters were sent by the faculty to the Personnel and Policy Committee for deliberation. One had to do with student demands regarding the curriculum. Some of the student demands were later sent by this committee to other standing committees for study, but others were more problematic: "Some suggestions . . . do pose exceedingly difficult issues which must be considered carefully and charitably among us. *The Divinity School is not an autonomous body that can fully determine its own policy, but exists as a part of the University*."[31] This statement is an example of something that was probably not entirely understood or appreciated by the students at the time. The second issue for the Personnel and Policy Committee had to do with the idea of appointing a committee on racism. The faculty also requested this committee to seek a meeting with black students as soon as possible in order to clarify and begin to resolve their mutual difficulties. This seemingly innocent and, certainly from the faculty's perspective, appropriate move evoked a storm of anger from the Black Seminarians. In good revolutionary fashion, they saw this move as an attempt to co-opt the movement and defuse the power of the coalition that had developed among black students, women, gays, and lesbians in the school. Their words are instructive: "We view it [the suggestion to meet with the Personnel and Policy Committee] as a tactic to circumvent our leadership. Be it . . . known that we reject such a move. Our elected co-convenors have full authority to represent our voice as a people in solidarity. We also denounce the faculty's effort to split the coalition created to address the issues of racism, sexism, and homophobia in this community. Be it . . . known that we stand in solidarity with all of the oppressed."[32]

The tone of the memos exchanged among the faculty during this period expressed disbelief that racism could be as explicit and virulent as the students had charged. It was not difficult to appreciate that sexism and homophobia had to be addressed, but the history of the school on the issue of race and the participation of the faculty in that history made them hesitant to accept the students' direct charges concerning racism. Faculty members were painfully experiencing the reality of a confrontational situation in the light of the memory of the 1960s and 1970s, when the relationship between students and faculty seemed more of an alliance. Some faculty acknowledged, however, that "residual racism" was a continuing problem. But from the students' perspective, the hesitation and apparent resistance served only to provide further evidence of their hypothesis that the disease of racism was present and its symptoms pervasive in the school.

As the 1980s came to a close, the tensions between students and faculty began to subside. All of the issues had not been addressed, but there was clear evidence that some of the faculty responses had become institutionalized—although not in the way that had been demanded by the students. The faculty did make a good faith effort to attend to a variety of perspectives (heretofore neglected, according to the students) in the foundation curriculum. Some existing courses were identified and new courses developed to address the issues of race, gender, and sexual orientation. These courses, together with courses in world religions, formed three "clusters," and students were required to include one from each set in their programs of study in the Divinity School. For a few years a new required foundation course, Religion in American Life, was taught. The faculty had anticipated that this course would address a number of student concerns, and in a certain limited sense it did. In the end, however, there was a problem with staffing the course, and it was dropped from the curriculum.[33]

A large part of the difficulty during the 1980s lay in the view that the purpose of theological education (and the task of the faculty who engage it) was to provide the historical and critical background for interpretation and formation for ministry. That is, the faculty resisted and has continued to resist pressures toward domination of the ethos of the school by a single perspective or approach—even to the problems of racism, sexism, classism, and homophobia. At the same time, the shared liberal ethos supported attitudes that were usually sympathetic to attempts to move toward solutions to these social problems. For the most part the faculty continued to represent the broader symbolic heritage of the churches as resources that are essential to the transformation of the society without becoming ideologically monolithic. Such pressures are not absent from the faculty, but thus far a more pluralistic, historically grounded, and theologically open perspective has been normative.

It is appropriate to conclude with the observation that the "Commitments" section of the Divinity School catalogue contains affirmations about the elimination of racism, sexism, homophobia, and other forms of discrimination. This section, which first appeared in the 1971–72 catalogue, represents the residue of the ethos that has been forged over the last forty years. The dialectical conflicts between students and faculty attempting to respond to their cultural situation were essential to this formation. The language of the statements evokes a vision of a world where human flourishing is supported and where the promises so evident in the symbolic heritage of the Christian faith can be more fully embodied. It is abundantly evident that these commitments attract students to the Divinity School. It is also abundantly evident that the students who come to the school find that there are differences between the moral telos envisioned there and the broken reality of any human community, including a divinity school.

The "Commitments" stand, however, at the beginning of a new millennium as a telos that hopefully will continue to guide the school and inform the dispositions of its members as they move into the future. It will be a future shaped by new faculty and new students. What the character of the Divinity School will be depends on how the ethos is transformed by internal changes to the school and by what will certainly be the continuing transformations in the social world that will require faithful and critical response. Only time will tell whether those responses will be continuous with the shared ethos that was developed over the last forty years or whether, in a new creative surge, a different ethos will be born.

8

Women's Work

Kim Maphis Early

HERE HAVE ALWAYS BEEN WOMEN AT THE DIVINITY SCHOOL. From the earliest days, when Myrta Woodson Wattles served as manager and dietician in Wesley Hall, to the 1990s when the number of women students surpassed that of men, women have been central to the operation of the institution. Their contributions in those early days—cooking, laundering, copying notes, sweeping, taking dictation, preparing for meetings—are as numerous as more recently chronicled accomplishments. Their crucial tasks of registering students for classes, keeping the deans organized, and overseeing the Divinity Library made possible the work of generations of faculty members, administrators, and students. It is the purpose of this chapter to remember many women: the often untitled and unheralded women who contributed the balance of their professional lives in service to the school, as well as the pioneering women who first appeared on the faculty, in the student body, and in administrative roles.

While significant figures and achievements appear in each of the four decades that are the proper subject of this chapter (1960–1999), the 1970s constitute the time of greatest activity and advancement of the status of women within the Divinity School community. Throughout this forty-year period, the school was more often preoccupied with the questions of race. But the attempts to overcome a history of regional racial injustice gave way for a moment in the 1970s to the primacy of the concerns and demands of women. During this decade, led primarily by women students, the framework for policies, curricular offerings, and representation of women was set in place. Through organization and confrontation, these women provoked remarkable institutional change, challenging the very structures of academic discourse in the Divinity School.

The Setting

In the 1970s the Divinity School, like many other institutions, found itself the inheritor of an earlier generation of women activists. The first half of the twentieth century laid the groundwork for the gains of the 1970s. Sallie McFague describes the twentieth-century feminist movement in the United States as having occurred in four stages: the period of attempting "to succeed in a man's world on a man's terms" (1920s–1960s), the period of feminist redefinition and activism (1970s), the critique of white feminism (1980s), and the shift to understanding gender as a socially constructed phenomenon (1990s).[1] The first part of this chapter uses this periodization as a framework to describe the situation and achievements of women at the Divinity School and consider the place of women in ministry and the academy.

Stage 1: "Just Like Men, Only Women," 1920s–1960s

The reformers of the 1920s, primarily suffragettes, not only secured the right for women to vote, but also founded many women's colleges. These colleges, in sharp contrast to the more traditional finishing schools for women, were rigorous and demanding and had lofty academic and professional goals for their students. They gave birth to many of the political, social, and educational leaders of this stage of American feminism.

The women educated in these schools or affected by the ethos of this educational movement were surrounded by accomplished and ambitious women. The outcomes were perhaps predictable. In McFague's words, "women were trained to be surrogate males, just like men, only women." The products of this style of education often advanced professionally or academically, but just as often were the only women in their disciplines or professions.

Vanderbilt's enrollment of women students came surprisingly early. Kate Lupton was awarded a master of arts degree in 1879, just six years after the founding of the University, but she did not march in the commencement, nor was her name listed in the program's roster of graduates. There were always a few women in classes, especially the daughters of professors, and women were formally registered as degree-seeking students when granted official admission to the University in 1885. In 1887, women gained the opportunity to be considered equally with men in the admission process, and by 1912 women had claimed the Founder's Medal for highest academic honors for four successive years. In 1926 the new Medical School welcomed Katherine Dodd to the faculty as instructor in pediatrics at the same salary as male faculty members; the school admitted women students the same year.[2]

Only a few women appear on the registration rolls during the years of the Biblical Department. The first to graduate was Mamie Bays, from Arkansas, who completed the English theological course in 1895. Sometimes women were admitted for coursework alongside their spouses who were also students. The first to receive a ministerial/professional degree (B.D.), however, was Susie C. Kachelhoffer from South Africa in 1930, who later served in the field of religious education in her home country. Another female graduate, Inez Keener Johnson, received a "diploma of graduation" in 1931. Altogether, seven women graduated from the School of Religion through 1945, three of whom graduated in the same class with their husbands—Alma Barham in 1936, Amy Fowler in 1940, and Veneta Whitmer in 1942. H. Louise Panigot, who received a B.D. in 1940 (and was awarded the Founder's Medal), later earned a Ph.D. in religion at Vanderbilt and served on the faculty of Huntingdon College in Montgomery, Alabama. In general, denominational seminaries preceded interdenominational schools in awarding degrees to women. The Methodist institutions, Boston University School of Theology and Garrett Biblical Institute, did so in 1878 and 1887, respectively. In 1889 Hartford Seminary began the first efforts to recruit women to theological degree programs. A woman graduated from Union Theological Seminary in New York in 1901. Although other schools opened admission to women, those accepted were restricted to programs for religious education rather than professional programs for ministry. At Yale Divinity School, the first woman to graduate with a B.D. completed her degree in 1934. Harvard Divinity School did not admit women to the B.D. degree program until 1955. Women were not admitted to the University of Chicago's Divinity School until 1960.[3]

Throughout the 1950s and 1960s, Vanderbilt Divinity School's occasional student journal, *Prospectus*, made only infrequent reference to women. When women are mentioned, it is seldom in recognition of educational or professional accomplishments. An issue from the 1957–58 academic year even went so far as to offer fashion advice. The invitation to the annual winter banquet came with the following addendum: "Since some of the girls are curious as to what to wear, wear what you'd wear to church on Sunday." But by 1959, *Prospectus* featured a first-year student, Jo McCall. When the interviewer elicited her professional goal as a youth and student worker, he received no response to his rejoinder, "Is a girl called to do something like this?" The editor did, however, go on to rate McCall's cooking as "treMENdous."[4] That same year, Eunice B. Goodall was highlighted in the paper as "one of the few but charming women students of the Vanderbilt Divinity School." Goodall was taking coursework in preparation for mission work in the Congo with her husband, a surgical resident, and their three children. Sponsored by the Christian Missionary Society (Disciples of Christ), she was involved in this work until she died in a plane crash in 1968. A memorial scholarship fund for Disciples students at the school bears her name.

While faculty minutes display no concern about the recruitment or support of women until much later, someone in the administrative office was apparently curious enough about the phenomenon to keep statistics on the number of women applicants, admits, and enrollees. In an entering class of thirty, there might be four women, but for every two women accepted, three withdrew their applications. Other internal documents reflect the culture's language and attitudes about women. Announcements about parties, architectural plans for the new chapel, and recommendations for student housing refer to men only, occasionally extending hospitality to students' wives.

During the remainder of the 1960s, concerns regarding race relations swamped intermittent intentions to seek gains for women. Foreshadowing the developments of the 1970s, Dean James Sellers proposed in 1965 to establish a specific committee of faculty and students to investigate student life. Problems to be examined included "the different problems of male and female students."[5] Yet women could only have viewed such attention to their concerns as infrequent and short-lived. A cartoon appearing in *Prospectus* as late as 1968 suggests that women were not taken seriously at the school. The drawing depicts a buxom blonde in a strapless black cocktail mini-dress offering coffee to two males seated in Benton Chapel's pews, as a male preacher looks on. On sighting the woman, one of the males declares, "Chapel attendance will be better this year!"[6]

Occasionally a woman struck back in print. Harriet Stewart responded in 1963 to a *Prospectus* announcement that the theme song of the Divinity School men might be "standing on the corner watching all the girls go by." In an article dripping with sarcasm, she observed,

> Some men are Enlightened. If the divinity dame will always say, "I think I want to go into Wesley Foundation work," she will receive a tender smile—truly she is a good fellow! Every male student director needs a female assistant these days, and sometimes at a women's college, a woman alone might suffice. Of late, there is prestige here, ladies. . . .
>
> While we carry out our plot, the men adapt to our presence. By

selective inattention we all become "one of the boys," accepted, consulted, admired, etc. If we cannot seem to be placed into the category of "one of the boys," there is always one other method. Since obviously any woman in seminary is looking for a divinity helpmate, one of them (divines) will be chosen to marry-her-off, thereby obscuring any sinister intentions she might have.

Carry on. We shall overcome.[7]

Not to be left out or left behind, the wives of Divinity students began to organize. "Divinity Dames" was formed to include wives of new professional and graduate students, faculty members, and administrators, as well as new women students. Professors spoke at regular evening meetings of the group, and the group elected officers and recruited a faculty member's wife to serve as an adviser. The organization solicited lecturers to introduce various disciplinary fields in theological education, held discussion groups on the works of particular theologians, took field trips to community organizations of social concern, and held social events for the entire school.

The school's understanding of and appreciation for women students and women in ministry was enhanced by its merger with Oberlin Graduate School of Theology in 1966. Church history professor Richard Wolf, who came to Vanderbilt in the merger, later commented on the role of Oberlin in the history of theological education for women: "From the very beginning, [Oberlin founder John. J.] Shipherd and his crew were going to . . . give an equal education to women, and they also had a place for people of color. . . . Women were admitted to Oberlin for an equal education—equal education, not equal participation in the social life. But there were always women, always women. They were always part of the whole; they were not a special group."[8] Antoinette Brown, a theological student at Oberlin 1847–50, became the first woman in the United States ordained to the Protestant ministry. Later generations of Oberlin theology students were encouraged by staff members Gertrude Jacob, who served for fifty years as registrar and voluntary archivist, and Emma Frank, librarian.[9]

Throughout this period, the most prominent women at Vanderbilt's School of Religion and Divinity School were staff members. The school's first secretary was hired in 1920. Elisabeth Cooke (changed by marriage to Abernathy) earned her B.A. at Vanderbilt in 1917 and worked for more than forty years at the school. Known affectionately to students as "Mrs. Ab," she worked in a variety of capacities, assisting the dean and registering students. Grace Teague worked in the Divinity Library 1936–72. Students in 1953 chose to feature Mrs. Syd Oliver in a *Prospectus* profile, describing her as "really the power behind the dean." The dean's secretary had the reputation as "one of the friendliest persons connected with the school."[10]

A second wave of women employees whose tenure as staff members spanned several deans began with the hiring of Annette MacBean in 1965. MacBean served as assistant to the dean for twenty-seven years, supervising staff and monitoring the budget. Following MacBean in 1966 was Bettye R. Ford, secretary of the Graduate Department of Religion, along with Rose Mitchell, Divinity School registrar. In 1967 the school hired a recent graduate of its B.D. program, Dorothy Ruth Parks, as circulation supervisor of the library. A former Methodist missionary, Parks had first studied at the school during a sabbatical from her term of service in Malaysia. During a second appointment to the Philippines, she was evacuated due to illness and, following her recovery, returned to the school to complete her degree. In 1998 she retired, having served over the course of her thirty-one-year career as public services librarian, reference librarian, director, collections librarian, and associate director, before moving to part-time work in 1994.

While these staff members were a visible part of the administrative structure of the school and were widely known among students, there were no women in the ranks of the faculty. At the close of this period the school made its first offer to a woman to join the faculty in a full-time position. In 1969, Leila Foster, having completed a Ph.D. at Garrett-Northwestern, was invited to join the faculty in pastoral theology and counseling. A former attorney, Foster was also a psychotherapist. She declined the offer in order to concentrate on private practice. It would be eight more years before another offer of full-time faculty employment was extended to a woman.

For the few women students who had moved beyond the academy and into the life of ministry, the discouraging situation in the churches mirrored the larger culture. Congregationalists and Disciples of Christ ordained women as early as the nineteenth century, while the United Presbyterian Church delayed until 1956 and the Presbyterian Church in the United States until 1964. Veneta Whitmer was ordained after receiving B.A. and M.A. degrees at Phillips University. When she and her husband graduated from Vanderbilt's School of Religion, they served for fifteen years as missionaries in the Belgian Congo supported by the Disciples of Christ Mission Board. After her husband died in 1969, Whitmer took short-term and interim ministry positions in Kansas and in states bordering it. Reflecting on her career in 1973, she wrote,

> Joe and I worked well together and all was well, for he was the minister and I the assistant. Now that I am alone, circumstances are, of course, much different. Churches are not prepared to accept a woman and I

can well understand. Until women are more commonly employed, a woman must find her ministry in places of need and in churches which are willing to accept her.[11]

Marietta Mansfield may have been the first woman to graduate from the professional program at Vanderbilt (1961) and then become an ordained minister. The only woman in her graduating class, she was the first woman in the Louisville Conference of the United Methodist Church; later she became president of the American Association of Women Ministers. Mansfield, however, was a rarity. Donna Scott, who first began seminary in the 1960s, recalled her initial interviews with her bishop at that time. When he told her that "over my dead body would a woman become a priest in this diocese," he echoed the sentiments of many church officials.[12] (Scott received her degree in 1985 and has served as an Episcopal priest in Nashville.)

Stage 2: Empowerment and Organization, 1970s

Forsaking the pattern of surrogate maleness, women in the 1970s began to consider themselves as distinct from men, and consequently the goal of becoming "just like men" faded. Women began to forge identities with other women in formal and informal associations. Consideration of how women differ from men became the overriding topic of conversation, research, and writing. Within this stage, a separatist feminist strain developed, advocating for women to isolate themselves from the relationships and institutions constructed and ruled by men. "A sense of possibility and of resistance from the culture makes you fight harder," McFague commented. Women at the Divinity School embraced this shift in the feminist movement in varying degrees, meeting regularly and without men present to explore common experiences. During this phase, sometimes referred to as the "essentialist" period, women told stories of discrimination and sought agreement on the peculiar shared qualities of "women's experience."

Women argued that the same attention should be given to sexism as had been given earlier to the problem of racism. In a *Prospectus* article appearing in 1970, Ann Denham remarked,

The Divinity School, of course, employs no women professors. Whatever the reasons and difficulties are, all students, and particularly the women, are disadvantaged. If the school is to engage the problem of community discrimination it can hardly do so from a position of segregation. . . . A good example of acceptance of local bias is the invitation to participate in the Roman Catholic Clergy Study Day which went out to all faculty and students at VDS—unless you happened to be a female. The notice stated—for all to see—that the real session, social hour, and dinner was for males only. That the rules for the affair were not set by the divinity school is granted. But VDS distributed the notice to all boxes. No one thought about it or was concerned. Yet to issue a "whites only" invitation would be unthinkable. And there would be strong debate as to the integrity of attending.[13]

The enrollment of women students climbed dramatically through this decade, increasing from 8 to 28 percent over the ten-year period (see Figure 8.1). An alumni newsletter reported that of the fifteen new M.A. students accepting admission for the fall of 1972, more than half were women. The same issue noted that in 1971–72, thirty-two women were enrolled (a 50 percent increase over the previous year), with twenty-one in the Divinity School and eleven in the Graduate Department of Religion. International women students, as well as women from under-represented racial and ethnic minorities, increased their ranks within the student body. African American women gained visibility in governing organizations, as well. In a five-year projection (1971–76) presented to the provost, Dean Walter Harrelson indicated how the school's interests in increasing the enrollment of women had led to a new item for its catalogue statement of commitments. That statement read,

> [The school] is committed to enrolling a larger number of women students in all degree programs, in the conviction that women have a larger place in the ministry and in teaching than they now enjoy and that their presence and contributions strengthen and enrich the life and work of the School. This commitment entails a readiness to eliminate any form of discriminatory treatment of women that may be present in the School.[14]

By 1971, the school's financial aid policies began in some small measure to address the differing economic realities of women. By reducing the required estimated financial contribution of women students to $1,000 (as compared with $1,500 for single men), the school hoped to address the problem of lower wages for women. The word "spouse" appeared in financial aid review sheets rather than "wives," suggesting the awareness that women could be married students too. Allowance for a thirty-dollar-per-week babysitting expense was also made, increasing the amount for which need-based aid would be awarded.[15]

But in 1970 there were no courses specific to women. Students took the

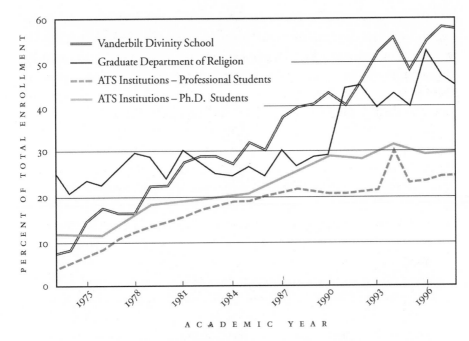

Figure 8.I. The Enrollment of Women: Vanderbilt and National Statistics

initiative developing courses and eventually staffing them as well. Mary Aquin O'Neill, RSM, a doctoral student in theology, offered the first course in 1971 and continued teaching it for two years before turning it over to two other graduate students. Students frequently presented proposals to the faculty for courses such as "Implications for the Ministry of Changing Sexual Ideas," but few were offered, and when offered they were taught by graduate students or adjunct faculty.

In a move that resulted in a powerful focal point for women, a position was added to student government offices in 1972 to represent the concerns of women. Through this representative, women students began to voice their positions and suggestions through official channels and to put them in writing for the public record. From this addition to the Student Cabinet, representation grew to the point of establishing an Office of Women's Concerns in 1974. Initially intended as a resource for curricular development and a library for materials related to women, the work of the Office expanded, making it the hub of feminist activism within the Divinity School. By the close of the decade, the Office of Women's Concerns had overseen the first women's studies lecture series at the Divinity School and in the University. It also instigated efforts to adopt a statement and later a policy guide for the use of inclusive language in the classroom and public discourse at the Divinity School.

Women students were leading in other realms as well. In 1972 Ann Updegraff became the first woman elected president of the student body. In that same year, the Divinity Dames no longer appeared in the school's listing of official organizations. Wives, active since the 1960s in attempting to make a place for themselves as their husbands pursued theological education, found their organization pushed to the sidelines, perhaps, by the gains of women students. An article by Updegraff, "Women in the Church," published soon after becoming student government president, surveyed the situation of women by reviewing images of women in scripture, praising the unrecognized service of women in church, and criticizing the seminary experience, all in three pages:

> A woman in divinity school or seminary finds that her professors and peers in general attempt to perceive her according to the traditional images. . . . If she is not out for a husband (the temptress image), then she is innocently, sweetly naïve and out of touch with the real world (the passive image). . . . Her peers do not know how to approach her as friend, but they are afraid of any contact that would affirm her as a woman. Professors either ignore her completely or put her on the spot with contemporary jargon (Why don't we ask our liberated woman?).

Soon an entire issue of *Prospectus* was devoted to "Women in the Divinity School." Most interesting, perhaps, were the comments of men, interviewed as to their opinions about the presence of women in the school. These ranged from "doesn't matter, don't care" to "absolutely necessary." Throughout the articles, the greatest identified need of women was for their concerns to be integrated more directly into the curriculum.[16]

This need was addressed in some measure by the course "Introduction to Theological Education," required of all first-year divinity students. In 1973 the faculty expressed its intention to use this course to survey the American religious experience, with special attention to the black church and women's topics, in an attempt to keep the issues of race and gender integrated within the required curriculum. Rather than moving coursework about and for women to a separate curricular track, it affirmed the incorporation of women's issues as subject matter in all courses. In this way it was hoped that all students, regardless of level of interest or commitment, would be exposed to materials related to women in religion.

Curricular advances, however, did not produce similar advances in attracting women faculty. A 1971 report on hiring goals did not specifically mention gender as an important consideration for faculty appointments. The faculty meeting where it was discussed noted this omission, but the dean thought that language in the report concerning oppression of all "minority groups" made such a reference unnecessary.[17] In 1972, Sallie TeSelle (after 1978, Sallie McFague) was appointed to a part-time faculty position, but her presence on the faculty, while encouraging to students, did not inaugurate great advances for women. The regularization of her teaching position, though part-time, came after several years of negotiation by students for increased responsibility and visibility within the faculty for women.

As faculty appointments continued to be offered to men, questions were raised as to the availability of qualified women candidates. By the spring of the following year, the situation was considered serious enough for the school's policy committee to approve the addition of a task force on women as a new committee of the faculty.[18] Through 1975, however, students in the Graduate Department of Religion taught the bulk of coursework focusing on women offered in the Divinity School.

This marginal position within the academic life of the school would soon change. In 1975, McFague was named dean, immediately bringing the spotlight to women at Vanderbilt and McFague in particular. As she has noted, "You cannot imagine the unimaginable. There has to be some kind of visualization of it or embodiment of it. This is why it was important in those years that I was a dean. Women saw a woman doing it. This is why increasing the numbers of women in all aspects of the school's life was so important." McFague became the first woman to head an accredited theological school in North America. Enrollment of women students surged during her tenure. McFague would lead the school to realize a long-held goal, the hiring of a woman to a full-time faculty appointment.

Peggy Way was appointed in 1977 to a position in pastoral theology. This was not Way's first time being the first full-time woman on a theological school faculty. Earlier she had been that at the University of Chicago Divinity School, the first of two women at the Jesuit School of Theology in Chicago, and the first woman faculty member in a field other than Christian education at McCormick Theological Seminary. Way confessed that she "would not have been nearly as open to coming to Vanderbilt had Sallie not been dean, because all the other schools on whose faculties I have served had male deans, and I decided the last time I was on a faculty that I wouldn't join another faculty in which I was the only woman. As a woman, I have always been in oversupply for the number of places that wanted me!"[19]

This decade witnessed the arrival of women faculty members not only to the Divinity School, but also to its peer schools in theological education. Margaret Farley became the first full-time woman faculty member at Yale Divinity School in 1971. The University of Chicago Divinity School appointed its first woman to a tenure-track position in the early 1970s and its second in 1975. The first woman to hold a permanent appointment at Harvard Divinity School was Margaret Miles (in 1978), who later became dean of the Graduate Theological Union. Women in the American Academy of Religion and Society of Biblical Literature formed formal caucuses or interest groups in the early 1970s, and the Association of Theological Schools began keeping statistics on numbers of women students and faculty members in 1972.

Way was not shocked at the delay in hiring women to full-time positions. "It simply wasn't done! There was no pressure in most schools, and little awareness."[20] Within days of her arrival, she had made her mark at Vanderbilt. Necessitated by a mobility impairment, Way's office was located on the ground floor, unlike other faculty and staff offices. Always the most heavily traveled, that floor also contained classrooms, a student common room, and student government offices. Her door almost always open, Way's office became the gathering place for women and men. Faculty as well as students counted on her generosity as mentor and counselor.

Also in 1977, the University's first major Affirmative Action report occasioned a serious review by the Divinity School faculty. Intense discussions in the faculty centered on the effect the report should have on the school's hiring decisions. Dean McFague presented an analysis of data regarding the availability of women for faculty positions. The data could be interpreted to suggest that the school should make hiring women a priority, but one professor contended that it should be just as high a priority to hire blacks. Race was again vying with gender for attention. A potential church history appointment in 1978 highlighted these difficulties, as faculty deliberated on the questions, "What weight should affirmative action have in future deliberations? And which group should have priority in appointments, African Americans or women?"[21] As a "stop gap measure," Mary Lynn Ogletree was appointed to a part-time position as lecturer in Church and Ministries in 1978. Again, in 1979, the search for an ethics faculty member concluded with no women among the final candidates.

One of the ironies at the Divinity School is that while there were few faculty appointments of women, some of the most visible and energetic supporters of women were male faculty members. Dale Johnson, professor of church history, was among the first faculty members to focus scholarly attention and teaching on women in religion. In 1980, he began working with women students to develop a course in church history concentrating on works by and about women in England and America over a two-hundred-year period. The materials studied were in many cases unpublished, and it was not unusual for Johnson to appear in class with just-printed computer paper readouts. "As fast as he could get material, he would put it in your hands," said class participant Margaret

(Peg) Leonard-Martin. "We found ourselves arguing about writings that no one had seen or studied in years. It was history in the making about history in the making."[22]

Johnson's experience with the class had ramifications beyond the subject matter. In an article published in *Prospectus*, he argued that studying the contributions of women might help to provide a better historical understanding from which to consider contemporary issues in the church and academy. He cited his course, "Women in Religion in England and America, 1700–1920," as an example of how the recovery of the work of women in an earlier time is neither an easy nor an unbiased process. "But one of the functions of historical study is to make clear at what points and to what extent you will not be content with the legacy of the past. To face demons of the past may not eliminate them, but it can be one way of asserting your power over them and helping others to be freed from captivity to them."[23]

Along with the school's progress in enrolling women, appointing a woman dean, and welcoming its first full-time woman faculty member, the number of women staff members was also growing. The academic year 1977–78 welcomed Doris Hall to the Divinity School as assistant to Kelly Miller Smith in the Black Church Relations office, one of the first two African American staff members. "I was not aware that Edwina Smith [secretary and later Divinity School registrar] and I would be the only African American women on the staff when I was hired," she says. "I don't think it would have mattered if I had known. I became more aware of our absence at Vanderbilt when I attended staff orientation, or enrichment classes and staff council meetings. The only African American employees [in these situations] were grounds crews and service workers. I believe that I was a welcome presence here because I was expected." Hall later moved to the Office of Admissions and Student Services. A few months after Hall's hiring, Aline Patte began her work at the Divinity School, first as faculty secretary and, two years later, as registrar. She also served for several years as adviser to the Office of Women's Concerns.[24]

Beyond the Divinity School, strategies were developed for increasing representation of women at all levels of University life. There were still quotas for women students in the College of Arts and Science (one-third of total enrollment) as the 1970s opened. Women were not allowed to work alongside spouses in the same departments, and only one member of a couple could have tenure. In 1971 the role of women in the University was taken up briefly by the Faculty Senate, which debated cases of employment of two members of the same family in the same department. The University also voted that year to phase out the enrollment quotas for women. The University's first women's studies course was offered in 1972. In 1973, the Senate discussed maternity leave policies for the first time, and three women were added to the Board of Trust in 1974. "Women's Emphasis Week" was celebrated in the fall of 1975 with a library exhibit, a campus-wide survey, panels of women representing different fields, worship, films, and a lecture.

In 1977 the Commission to Study the Status of Women at Vanderbilt, appointed by Chancellor Alexander Heard, issued a report after four years of work. Its contents were to remain a mystery until early 1978, however, when the report was made public under pressure from faculty and students. The Senate requested that the chancellor respond to all recommendations in the report by the close of the spring semester and voted to approve the creation of a Women's Center on campus.[25] In November the University established this Center, with Nancy Ransom as its part-time director.

The activism of Divinity students affected others on the Vanderbilt campus. Susan Ford Wiltshire, professor of classics, recalled her conversion to feminism in a 1983 article. "I trace that back to a conversation about a dozen years ago with a student at Vanderbilt Divinity School named Pamela Owens, who was the first feminist I ever knew. At our house at dinner one night, she was talking about feminism, and my husband put his arm around me and said with pride, 'Well, I married a liberated woman.' I was very proud of that, too, until I heard her say, 'Just because you work doesn't make you a feminist.' I think Ashley and I both count that as a turning point for us in redefining our roles, redefining mutuality."[26]

Off campus, women in religious communities were sharing similar stories of change, led by many of the first ordained women. The Lutheran Church in America and the American Lutheran Church began to ordain women in 1970, with the Episcopal Church following, officially, in 1976 (after twelve were ordained without full approval of the denomination in 1974). From Hebrew Union, the theological school for the Reform Movement in Judaism, women students began to be ordained to the rabbinate in 1972.

While prospects for women in these traditions improved over the decade, other groups were slower. As Jo Clare Wilson commented when selected as coordinator of the Office of Women's Concerns in 1976, "The real issues are not those in the seminary. Women at VDS are comfortable and are encouraged and supported. We feel good about going into ministry but that good feeling and support are often in conflict with the real situation in the parish. Women need to be made aware, in seminary, of the problems they will encounter when seeking placement in the parish. . . . [I]t may be a long haul for women in the ministry but with the good start we have, we must keep moving."[27]

Helen Lee Turner, ordained as one of the first twenty-five women in the Southern Baptist Convention in May 1975, reports that there were no jobs in the church for her at that time, so she reluctantly returned to the Divinity School to pursue a second professional degree. Glenda Webb wrote on the challenges of being a woman minister in a team ministry with her husband in Elkton, Kentucky. "First be clear in your own mind as to who you are and what you see your role to be. Everyone with whom you come in contact will have a different conception of what you as a minister are supposed to be and of how you are supposed to look, to act and to fulfill your duties. Without a sure footing within your own being, you will be tossed upon the sea of utter confusion and your ministry will be worth nothing. . . . [B]ecause I have come to see and feel myself to be a minister, members of our congregation now introduce me to friends as their 'preacher.' "[28]

At the Divinity School, as in the church and the larger culture, this feminist movement was predominantly made up of and led by white women. In spite of its lack of broader representation of women outside the white majority, women could only view the 1970s as a period of incredible accomplishment. The decade ended with an official student government office to represent women, a statement in the catalogue expressing the school's commitment to their rightful place in ministry and the academy, the adoption of an inclusive language initiative, a woman in its chief administrative position, the first full-time woman faculty appointment, a lecture series, a voice in curricular reform, and work on the larger campus. Because of very powerful constituencies of women, the school approached the 1980s with a unique curricular design in which the representation of women was expected in every course rather than contained within a women's studies track. McFague calls this period "ground setting," although many graduates characterize it as earth-shattering. Vanderbilt's progress on women's issues within the larger context of the University, theological education, and ministry was very early and very strong.

Stage 3: Fractured Feminism, 1980s

Fueled in part by Audre Lorde's critique of the feminist movement as insensitive to differences of race and sexual orientation, the myth of feminist unity against the male oppressor exploded in the 1980s. As women students, pastors, and scholars began to deny that there was one nature for all women, a variety of forms of feminist thought related to race, class, and culture of origin emerged for consideration. This concern for contextualization led to women becoming the subjects of research and to questioning how women differ among themselves. As more women and more different kinds of women made their way onto faculties and into student bodies, challenges to pedagogical styles, methods of evaluation, and curricular offerings preoccupied campus discourse. Schools were forced to adapt with new styles of teaching, as well as greater representation of various constituencies in course topics and required readings. Religious institutions and professional organizations either welcomed women into the ministry or tried to block their way.

Although numbers alone do not tell the story, they do convey the rapidity with which the educational and religious scene shifted. The numbers of women in accredited theological schools in the United States rose from 1,077 to 6,108 between 1972 and 1987, while the number of male students pursuing M.Div. degrees dropped from 22,031 to 21,251 in the same period.[29] As the numbers of women at the Divinity School continued to increase, so did the diversity of the women. The sense of common purpose among the women in the student body gave way to competing claims of differing groups of women and the inclusion of men in the debate. Evangelical women made appeals for theological tolerance. An increasing number of women attended school alongside spouses or brought babies to classes. Accustomed to Roman Catholic women in religious orders in the graduate program, the predominantly Protestant school witnessed the arrival of Catholic lay women in its ministerial programs. Second-career students enrolled in greater numbers, returning to school after work in education, social work, public relations, and child-rearing.

The first African American woman M.Div. graduate in the school, Lillian Wynn, received her degree in 1980, followed soon by Catherine Clark Kirk in 1981 and Pamela Yates in 1983. In 1985, Marcia Riggs, an African American Ph.D. student in theological ethics, posed the problem of African American women at the Divinity School for the readers of *Prospectus* by describing her own journey through college, divinity school, and graduate school as a black woman. With no role models since her high school days, Riggs was forced to conclude that while black men and white women had advanced in the wake of the civil rights and feminist movement, black women had been isolated and left behind.[30]

The first Divinity School feminist retreat for men and women was held in February 1983, designed to foster dialogue between men and women. Unthinkable during the more separatist days of the 1970s, men now asked that they be included in the dialogue. An occasional man's name showed up on the roster of the Office of Women's Concerns Steering Committee or the Antoinette Brown Lecture Committee, as well.

A survey conducted by the Office of Women's Concerns in 1983 illustrates the varied professional goals of women that the Office was expected to honor and address in planning and programming. Of fifty-one responses, eleven hoped to secure jobs in college or graduate level teaching, twelve hoped to be ordained for parish ministry, eight sought various forms of chaplaincy work, eight identified themselves as preparing for "alternative ministries," two were pursuing religious education within the church, two envisioned a life doing research and writing on religion, and eight checked the "other" box—to include joint law/divinity students and hospital management.

Another constituency mobilized and sought formal recognition within the women's community in 1984. Six students began meeting to form a gay-lesbian caucus that year, and in 1987 the school moved to adopt a statement for its catalogue committing itself "to confronting the homophobia that prevails throughout much of the church and society." Compared to the struggle of African Americans and women for recognition and representation, the approval of a statement on sexual orientation by the faculty and the establishment of a student advocacy group, GABLE (Office of Gay, Lesbian, and Bisexual Concerns), was swift and without rancor. Coursework was quickly added to the curriculum as well.

Alumnae of the school were ordained in greater numbers and moved into positions in parish ministry with increasing frequency during this decade. A study of graduates from the years 1977–87 confirmed, however, that "fewer women than men who desire to serve in the local church actually find employment there. Even as more women have moved into the parish . . . , [their] longevity . . . is poor. Problems not only appear at an entry level, where women experience appointments to isolated and dying parishes and difficult relationships with senior ministers, but also when they attempt to move, perhaps to a solo pastorate."[31] For Ph.D. graduates, the situation was better. In what had previously been a closed job market, alumnae of the Graduate Department of Religion now found themselves in demand as many undergraduate religion departments were replacing retiring faculty.

Four women were also added to the Divinity School faculty during this period. Following her resignation as dean, McFague returned to the faculty as a full-time member in theology, and in 1981 Mary Ann Tolbert, a former visiting professor, returned as assistant professor of New Testament. During the spring of 1982, McFague wrote about minority and women's concerns as part of the school's self-study in preparation for an accreditation review. Analyzing data from surveys of students, faculty, and staff, and gathering information from public meetings, McFague concluded that "it seems evident that the matters of greatest concern to both minority and women students focus on the *faculty*—both hiring more minority and women faculty and educating the present ones to be more sensitive to and knowledgeable about black and feminist issues so that these matters become an intrinsic part of the regular curriculum."[32] In 1983, Jean Porter was appointed to the faculty in the area of ethics, and later that same year Elisabeth Schüssler Fiorenza became the first solo woman Cole Lecturer. Joretta Marshall, an alumna of the school, joined the faculty in pastoral theology in 1989, replacing Peggy Way.

In 1987, Renita Weems joined the faculty in Hebrew Bible, the first African American woman to hold a full-time faculty position at the school. Although other staff and faculty members report that there was much discussion and excitement attending Weems's appointment, she does not recall this peculiar milestone being celebrated at the time. "I wonder now if it was a 'gender thing,'" Weems reflects. "By that I mean, I wonder whether the fact that the school had African American men on the faculty made my presence as an African American woman seem less than extraordinary. Hiring me helped the school to continue its commitment to an African American presence on the faculty, plain and simple." Weems reports that she has experienced racism at Vanderbilt, but it is difficult for her to separate these experiences from prejudice based on gender:

> I have come to realize that part of the problem is that for many non-black students I am the first African American female teacher they have ever had in their lives. While I am known in some certain circles to be downright witty and have a great sense of humor when I lecture, it seems that no matter what I do at Vanderbilt, overall my African American female presence here is perceived as intimidating and unapproachable. But I've learned that what is perceived in men as proof of their being 'serious' and 'knowledgeable' is perceived as 'intimidating' and 'put offish' in women. What is forgiven and tolerated in male faculty generally is unforgivable and intolerable in female faculty. Women faculty are expected to have open arms and open doors. Men faculty are permitted to keep both shut.[33]

In 1985, the M.Div. Studies Committee presented a set of recommendations for the incorporation in all foundation courses of an emphasis or focus on women, women's issues, and women's concerns. The proposal was endorsed following a discussion on the different ways in which this could be accomplished.[34] By 1989, although women's issues were addressed with increasing regularity in all foundation courses, more concentrated opportunities for study were recommended to the faculty. "Cluster requirements" were adopted, mandating that all M.Div. students complete as least one course in feminist and sexuality studies, world religions or interreligious dialogue, and African American and race studies.

In recognition of the gains and importance of women on the faculty of the Divinity School, the E. Rhodes and Leona B. Carpenter Foundation endowed a chair in 1989 to honor the contributions of women in Christian ministry and theological scholarship and education. The first incumbent was Sallie McFague, in recognition of the historic place she held both at Vanderbilt and in theological education.

In the University during this period, women from the Divinity School continued to organize on behalf of women's issues. Catherine Snow and Gay Welch, two of the founding steering committee members of Women's Equity At Vanderbilt (WEAV), were alumnae of the Divinity School and Graduate Department of Religion. The organization was formed to try to reverse the denial of tenure to an English professor, Elizabeth Langland, in 1981; it became a rallying point for women across the University.[35] In response to the public furor attending the process, President Emmett Fields appointed a committee to study the status of women and minorities at Vanderbilt, chaired by the Divinity School's Peter J. Paris. This committee made its report in the fall of 1981, citing the necessity of hiring faculty members from under-represented groups and recommending the expansion of curricular offerings to include materials and course topics for these same minorities. The provost responded with additional faculty hiring funds to help attract the best-qualified women and African American candidates to Vanderbilt.[36]

Langland's court case resulted in the realignment of campus coalitions, as the University's action on tenure cases involving race were made public. Overnight, supporters of the advancement of racial minorities were polarized against those championing gender equality. Eventually the case was decided in Vanderbilt's favor. Despite the sense of loss over that case, WEAV had a lasting positive impact on the campus. It succeeded in rallying significant alumnae involvement in issues over the status of women faculty, staff, and students, and in propelling the University toward more concrete action to advance the recruitment and retention of women staff and faculty members.

By 1986, when the Women's Center published a pamphlet entitled "Women's Places," women at Vanderbilt comprised 73 percent of the staff, 47 percent of the students, and 20 percent of the faculty. In spite of this, only two undergraduate core courses and three electives in women's studies were listed. The pamphlet recommended that students interested in additional courses in the subject consider taking ones offered by the Divinity School and the George Peabody College for Teachers (soon to become a part of Vanderbilt).

What had seemed impossible in the 1960s was an established pattern in the 1980s. Women accounted for more than 40 percent of enrollment in the Divinity School and nearly 30 percent of that of the Graduate Department of Religion. The decade closed with two more women being appointed to the faculty. The student body was splintered, perhaps unavoidably so. African American women directed the Office of Women's Concerns and the Vanderbilt chapter of the Black Seminarians. International women students hosted forums to educate Americans about the plight of women in other countries and to question the consumerism of the American economy. But women were more than ever before in almost every facet of the school's life.

Stage 4: Redefining the Enemy, 1990s

The 1990s saw exciting new possibilities and challenging new problems. The gains of women in the larger culture made possible new types of friendships between men and women, along with the realization that in some ways men and women may share similar characteristics and experiences. Interdisciplinary studies expanded the definition of gender beyond the biological determinism of prior theories, moving many in the academy to study gender as a socially constructed reality. With gender understood as influenced by social location and societal norms, it became impossible for women to characterize all men as oppressors.

At the same time, this decade saw a backlash as women, after decades of gains, encountered the "glass ceiling" of limited professional advancement and political rhetoric demonizing women working outside the home. Women were often characterized as being divided into only two groups: "the mommy track" vs. career women, ignoring the broad range of women's life situations. "The first generation [of feminists] made choices not to have children or not to have a career," said McFague, while later generations, having gained entry to the academy and professional life, attempted to do both. In the 1990s, many women grappled with the dawning realization that they could not be "superwomen," "trying to manage both career and family in a society that is not family friendly. Given the fact that the biological window is very, very small for childbearing, women have just those years. Those are the very same years you prepare yourself for your career or pursue your education." The tension in the workplace and in the larger culture made some environments inhospitable to women.

The impact of this was felt among the women attending the Divinity School as well as graduates seeking employment. The decade of retirements, when it had been predicted that women would pour into religious leadership and academic advancement, was nearly over, and the statistics revealed a surprising phenomenon, explored in a 1998 study.

> The low proportion of clergy women in the general population is likely to surprise many people. They see the rising numbers of women enrolled in seminaries, the dramatic increases in the number of women

being ordained, the greater visibility of women clergy in the churches, and the majority of lay women in the pews and they conclude that we are moving toward a time when male clergy will be in the minority. Our findings suggest that this time remains quite distant, for two reasons: first, while the numbers of women in the ministerial profession have been rising, they have risen more slowly than have the number of women in other professions; second, while the rate of female ordination is increasing, it is not increasing as quickly as it once did.[37]

Women also found themselves primarily as associate pastors, unable to move into solo or senior pastorates. In 1992, for instance, John P. Marcum reported that the majority of female pastors in the Presbyterian Church USA were associates, while the majority of males were solo or senior pastors.[38]

A similar situation exists for women in the academy. While tremendous gains have been made, women still constitute less than 20 percent of all faculty members in theological schools. The Divinity School's recent history reflects this reality. Although three new women faculty members were added in the 1990s, the school also witnessed the departure of three women. From 1993 to 1998, the average annual faculty compensation in the United States increased 21.14 percent for women and only 18.46 percent for men, but women's compensation was still $8,000 below the national average.[39]

McFague sees this issue as a challenge for theological education as new faculty members are appointed. The search for replacements in senior positions restricted to particular areas of scholarly expertise "restricts the pool so dramatically as to exclude women. I believe that we have less affirmative action now than we did. It's being chewed away, sort of frayed at the corners. We were serious when we stated back in one of our five-year plans that there was to be parity on the faculty, and we're a long way from that. Our faculty should be half women."

Peggy Way also views employment as a continuing problem. "We're still dealing with the problems both ministers and first-year teachers face because of the inability of some males to work with female associates, and the problems of placing older and divorced women. 'What is partnership, especially when the junior partner is a woman?' 'What is the nature of authority?' These are the old questions that we're still asking."

While significant gains at the Divinity School were made and solidified in the 1980s, faculty appointments and staff advancement provided impetus for continued progress during the 1990s. At the request of the school's policy committee, the Office of Women's Concerns Policy Guidelines Committee drafted a "Statement on the Status of Women at Vanderbilt Divinity School and Graduate Department of Religion." Approved by the faculty in March 1990, the document proposed goals for the school: to seek to fill faculty vacancies with women of various backgrounds toward a goal of at least 50 percent female faculty; to continue to develop curricular, library, and faculty support for studies related to womanist/feminist perspectives; to create a positive learning and administrative environment through support of the recruitment and education of women together with attention to the placement of and financial assistance for women students; to compensate support staff through fair wages and benefits; and to seek to fill administrative vacancies with women through extraordinary recruitment and training opportunities.

In the midst of some discouraging statistics, there was good news as well. No longer required to justify their existence in theological school or to spend already limited energy outside the classroom organizing around women's demands, women students were more free to pursue their scholarly interests and to make connections with an already established and growing body of feminist scholarship. New feminist literature, produced throughout the world, presented feminist interpretations on a variety of topics. Senior projects by women students of the Divinity School exemplified the abilities of students to make these connections across disciplines; "Feminist Theology and Women with Disabilities" and "The Relation of Animal Rights to Feminism and Gender Analysis" are only two examples of such work.

The school also had the delight of welcoming a second generation of women students. Gay Albers graduated from Vanderbilt thirty-eight years after her mother, Martha Albers, completed a degree in the Graduate Department of Religion in 1955. Tamara Lewis, the 1998–99 Kelly Miller Smith Scholar, is the daughter of Bettye Lewis, who received her degree a decade earlier. In reporting on this second-generation phenomenon in theological schools, journalist Gustav Niebuhr recorded some heartening statistics in 1999. In the Episcopal Church, women make up nearly one in seven of its clergy; in the Evangelical Lutheran Church in America, they are one in six. Women now make up one-third of Jewish Theological Seminary's student body. Since 1972, 29 percent of those ordained for the Reform rabbinate have been women, and this has risen to 45 percent in the past decade. Women represent 51 percent of the ordained clergy in the Unitarian Universalist Association, up from less than 3 percent in 1968. But a survey of female clergy members in fifteen denominations found that women were still paid less on average than men, even when the levels of education and experience were similar.[40]

The early 1990s also occasioned construction projects to address the reality of a majority of women within the Divinity School student body. A "Bathroom Protest Petition" enlisted support for changes in the toileting facilities of the

Divinity quadrangle. The petition was accompanied by a fact sheet describing the lack of available stalls and a threat that absence of a response would be met by a modified version of a sit-in. Under the humorous banner, "Potty Parity," the Divinity School undertook the reassignment and remodeling of bathroom facilities.

Continuing the trend toward greater diversity among women in the student body, first witnessed in the 1980s, the 1990s welcomed more international students from a wider range of countries such as Germany, Yugoslavia, China, Korea, Kenya, and South Africa. The school also enrolled the first Jewish women in its professional programs. In 1992, the number of women students surpassed that of men, a trend continuing through the decade; the same phenomenon occurred in the Graduate Department of Religion in the 1995–96 academic year.

In 1993, Renita Weems made history once again. Her daughter, Savannah Nia, was born in January, making her mother the first full-time faculty member to give birth while holding a position as a professor at the Divinity School.

Perhaps the most significant development in the Divinity School during the 1990s was the establishment of the Carpenter Program in Religion, Gender, and Sexuality. Made possible in 1995 through a gift from the E. Rhodes and Leona B. Carpenter Foundation, the Carpenter Program exemplified the "new look" of gender studies. Designed to foster conversation between and among religious institutions and the academy, the Carpenter Program's focus moved beyond the study solely of women. Programs included workshops on sexual violence and recovery from child sexual abuse, a panel discussion of the black church and homosexuality, visiting lecturers for classes and public presentations, work with local pastoral counselors, and co-sponsorship of the annual meeting of the American Men's Studies Association. The president of the Carpenter Foundation, Ann Day, spoke of the impetus for such a program: "I believe that more and more thoughtful religious people are tired of huddling in pale light when it comes to real life questions about gender and sexuality. Not only are many of the religious answers to the questions insufficient, but the questions themselves are often inadequate to move dialogue and understanding forward."[41]

Within two years, the Carpenter Program began to offer a certificate in Religion, Gender, and Sexuality Studies as a complement to the graduate and professional degree programs offered at the Divinity School. Students accepted into the certificate program completed courses in textual interpretation, theology and ethics, contemporary practice, and a project related to community issues surrounding the complexity of religion, gender, and sexuality. Plans are underway to expand the certificate program to admit students from other departments of the University, including undergraduates. Amy-Jill Levine, Car-

penter Professor of New Testament Studies and director of the Program in
Religion, Gender and Sexuality, reports that

> the Program—through its website, mailings, events at Vanderbilt, and
> publicity generated when I or our certificate students do external
> speaking—has generated enormous interest. We receive numerous
> calls, letters, and especially e-mails with an enormous range of ques-
> tions: from students interested in enrolling in the Divinity School,
> to parents asking if their gay children are going to hell, to women
> seeking a supportive worship community to help them escape or re-
> cover from domestic violence, to questions from the general public as
> well as from the media about divorce, adultery, women's 'submission' in
> marriage, whether the deity is male, and whether circumcision should
> be outlawed.[42]

The Carpenter Program, in the words of McFague, moves Vanderbilt "into the
premier position to address these issues of gender and sexuality."

Snapshots

Placed within the wider context of the feminist movement, the larger University, and the rise of women in the ministry and academy, the characters and
events represented in the struggle of women at the Divinity School carry deep
meaning for participants and observers. Several stories of these women, organizations, and events represent in microcosm the wider changes experienced by
the school since 1960.

The Student / Teacher

Mary Aquin O'Neill, RSM, grew up in a southern Protestant milieu. She
attended single-sex schools, entered the Sisters of Mercy (a Catholic religious
congregation) at seventeen, and completed a B.A. in French at her religious
community's college for women. Convinced that ecumenism was the future of
Christian theology and determined to find a place and a way "to defend the
truth of the imagination," she came to Vanderbilt's Graduate Department of
Religion in 1970 to study systematic theology.[43]

The first social invitation she received was to join the Divinity Wives Club.
This put her in an awkward situation—she was a student, not the wife of a
student. Reflecting on such experiences she now says, "Since Catholic sisters
are sometimes considered married to God," she enjoyed the irony. "There was

no ill will or malice; faculty and students alike were a bit bewildered, for I was something of an 'exotic' in their world."

Describing her feminism as "inchoate at that time," O'Neill assumed that there would be women on the faculty. Upon her realization that there were none, and few in the student body, she found that it was "all so new and I was so scared, but I wasn't going to leave. There were sexist jokes like there always are and ruffled feathers when we [women students] found our voice and pointed out their mistakes. The dominant discourse used 'man' so familiarly." As the only woman in her theology class, "I would raise my hand and literally no one would call on me; everybody was too busy smoking their pipes to notice me."

This experience of invisibility and the peculiarity of being a nun made a response to the situation complicated. Her consciousness had been shaped in a woman's world, "so I didn't react in the ways women who have worked in relation to men do." Then she met Pamela Owens, a graduate of the College of Arts and Science at Vanderbilt and a Divinity student. To O'Neill's mind, Owens was the organizer at the Divinity School, the person who gathered the women and formulated plans for action. Owens's persistent question, "Why can't we have a course in women's theology?" was born of what O'Neill describes as the "uncomfortable feeling that there was something wrong with us. We felt ourselves to be somehow invisible, and often like second-class citizens, second-class students. For about a semester each of us carried that around in her heart, and then we began to talk to one another. From that we discovered that (1) we were not alone, and (2) there were changes that should be made in the institution—our own attitudes and those of others needed to be changed."[44]

Owens and O'Neill approached Sallie McFague to teach a course on feminist theology. At the time, she declined, telling the students that she felt unprepared, whether by virtue of not having worked closely with the material or out of the vulnerable position of having a part-time faculty position. Owens then turned to O'Neill and said, "You've taught before. You can teach it." In retrospect, O'Neill is amazed that she so readily and easily accepted. "Sometimes the confidence of other people pulls forth from you things you would never dare alone. Besides, I love to teach. So I accepted the challenge." Together, Owens and O'Neill proposed the course to Dean Harrelson, who was open to the idea and took the proposal to the faculty. The course and instructor approved, O'Neill began teaching in 1971, and two years later opened the course to the Nashville community. Remuneration for teaching the course became her scholarship for two years.

The title of the course, "Woman in the Family of Man," now appears jarring, but went unnoted at the time. The course offered an opportunity for women to "tie together our discomforting experiences and our rich experiences with a religious tradition. Preparation for class was exciting, even though the materials we had on hand were in pretty primitive condition. I was working primarily with xeroxes from periodicals; there wasn't a body of published works on women's theology at the time." The course increased in popularity and eventually two sections were offered. McFague sat in on the course during its first year, but other professors never appeared, either as interested observers or as monitors. "They just let me do it. People got credit for it and I got paid for it. It was nothing short of miraculous."

The course's popularity did not cement it within the regular curricular offerings of the full-time faculty. It was handed on to another set of graduate students each year for several years. O'Neill suspects that "nobody wanted to spend the time getting up to speed to teach it—at worst because it was not considered 'real' theology, or at best because no one was interested to develop it as a specialty."

Sometimes the growth in consciousness came in the form of an unflattering assessment. Once, when the priest who was to say the weekly Mass for Catholic students did not arrive, O'Neill suggested that the congregation do the readings, sing the hymns, and say the prayers. Instead, they walked out. One of her classmates remarked, "You Catholics can't even pray without a priest." Shocking as the statement was to her at the time, the observation has remained with her. She now brings this awareness to her work, from participation in bilateral dialogues to the founding of a theological center for women. She sees her work as "encouraging women attempting to integrate table hospitality, prayer, and study and to claim an active role in shaping inherited faith traditions for a future of life and equality for all." In 1981, O'Neill received her Ph.D. in theology, with her research concentrating on imagination in the thought of Paul Ricoeur.

Thinking back on her experience of teaching the course, O'Neill observes that higher education as it has been traditionally conceived presents problems for students. "The interests of the individual faculty member have dominated. With huge societal issues such as racial and sexual equality, however, it is not sufficient to hire an 'expert' who will be responsible to teach in the area. Concern for and some knowledge about how such issues affect theology as a whole need to be shared by the entire faculty."

Yet, in O'Neill's estimation, the Divinity School and Graduate Department of Religion seemed to be on the cutting edge of the feminist movement in higher education, ahead of other departments and other theological schools. "Apart from contact with Susan Wiltshire, and one invitation to appear at a symposium at the Law School, the activity and ferment in the Divinity School was pretty isolated. My peers at other theological schools did not report anything like the progress we felt we were making at Vanderbilt."

Following a career in higher education, O'Neill now serves as director of the Mount Saint Agnes Theological Center for Women in Baltimore, which is co-sponsored by the regional communities of the Baltimore and St. Louis Sisters of Mercy. "We have here a safe place for women of faith to gather and sort through religious traditions. We're based in a home to honor the place where women have passed on the faith and wrestled with questions of faith on the frontline and to make a place where women feel most comfortable." The work of the center has spread to New Orleans and Birmingham and through its website receives contacts from around the world.

The Dean

Perhaps no other woman in the history of the Divinity School deserves and receives more attention than Sallie McFague. First as a teacher, later as dean, then as the holder of the first endowed chair to honor women at the school, McFague witnessed, participated in, and presided over the most dramatic period of women's progress in the academy and church.

A *magna cum laude* Phi Beta Kappa graduate of Smith College in 1955, McFague completed her B.D. and Ph.D. degrees at Yale, the latter in contemporary and systematic theology. "I had those four wonderful years at Smith with such great self-esteem, but what naïveté! At Yale the visiting Episcopal bishop not only barred me from meetings attended by other Episcopal students (male ones), but from dinner as well!" When she arrived in Nashville in 1969, she came not as a teacher, but as the editor of *Soundings*, an interdisciplinary scholarly journal. She describes this work as "a lifesaver" while she was at home taking care of young children and prospects for teaching jobs were bleak. She was introduced to administrators at Scarritt College and Fisk University, but neither had openings for her. The 1970s began auspiciously with her appointment at Vanderbilt as a lecturer in theology. McFague was to teach one course, "as needed." The Divinity School would never be the same.

McFague recalls that, on the advice of her mentor from her undergraduate days at Smith, she requested that she be named as a part-time, tenure-track lecturer. It took a year to approve this rank of faculty employment in the Faculty Senate. "Vanderbilt was just doing what other institutions at that time were doing, using women who were geographically limited because of marriage and finding it economically beneficial to employ them without commitments."

Women students had written to the dean in 1972 in support of the appointment of a woman as a full-time professor and had endorsed McFague for the position. By the 1972–73 academic year, her position was regularized as a part-time assistant professor for a three-year term, with service counting toward tenure. In support of this change in status, Dean Harrelson remarked that McFague "is regarded by colleagues here and throughout the nation as a most able scholar; she is an outstanding teacher; her work with women students as counselor, guide and role model has been particularly important." But the appointment was not met with unanimous approval by the faculty. Although there was considerable emphasis on the importance of having a woman on the faculty and on the danger of alienating women students (as well as some men) should McFague not be given regular faculty status, there was also some concern that the faculty needed teachers for other courses, especially New Testament and church management. Convinced by Harrelson that the possibilities of making an appointment of a woman in either of these areas having the training, talent, and national standing of McFague "appear almost non-existent," the faculty agreed to the appointment.[45]

McFague's work and visibility in the community expanded rapidly. In December 1974, the faculty received a recommendation that she be promoted to associate professor with tenure, although still at part-time status. At the very same meeting, the faculty heard that McFague, along with two other Vanderbilt Divinity faculty members and three outside candidates, were being considered for the position of dean. (Harrelson had previously announced his intention to return to the faculty.)

McFague decided to withdraw her name from consideration. Before she could do this, however, Chancellor Heard called to request that she remain a candidate. McFague muses, "I suppose because of affirmative action they needed a woman as a major administrator." In the ensuing days, McFague met once with the assembled school's faculty, "the only time I've ever been interviewed for a job," and with Harrelson. In what would prove invaluable advice, Harrelson recommended that, if selected as dean, McFague ask that her contract stipulate a return to the faculty as a full-time member at the end of her deanship.

On July 1, 1975, McFague became dean. At the age of forty-one, she had catapulted from editor of a journal and part-time faculty member to dean, the first woman to hold this office at a major theological school in North America. "It is a risky but exciting time to be dean of a divinity school and particularly of a school such as Vanderbilt's," McFague declared at the time. "Fortunately, the risk is less and the excitement greater than is true, I believe, at many other divinity schools . . . because Vanderbilt Divinity School is somewhat different from many other divinity schools in maintaining a balance between professional and graduate education." Cognizant of the historic nature of her appointment, she continued,

> Vanderbilt Divinity School has a tradition of commitment to minorities and to women. The number of women has risen in the school

dramatically in the last five years and my appointment, I think, can be seen as an indication of Vanderbilt's concern to further the status of women. Like most universities, Vanderbilt has a low percentage of women in top faculty and administrative posts and while the university has made impressive progress in appointing women to lower ranks, it has, in a tight job market, had difficulty making higher-level faculty and administrative appointments. I see my appointment as "one small step for womankind" at Vanderbilt, though I do not see the position as a platform for women's concerns. My first concern and loyalty is to the well-being of the Divinity School, though I see that well-being as closely associated with the advancement of women and minorities since I believe any institution which does not concern itself with the just advancement of these people will not itself prosper.[46]

McFague's deanship brought both welcomed and unwelcomed attention to her and to the school. Her second book, *Speaking in Parables: A Study in Metaphor and Theology*, was published just prior to her appointment, and she found herself suddenly in demand as a speaker. This resulted in some curious invitations. She was named as one of thirteen "Legendary Ladies" to be honored at a college in the South, an event covered in *People* magazine. The honorees were met at the college by female greeters in full "Old South" dress and escorted by men in tuxedos. The guests included everyone from Congresswoman Lindy Boggs, the African American head of the Girl Scouts, and a medical physicist, to a dress designer, a discotheque owner, and the cosmetics industry executive Esteé Lauder. McFague shakes her head at the memory: "A caricature of southern womanhood honoring people who had achieved something as women—it was a strange phenomenon."

Her work with faculty members, however, was more rewarding. She related to the faculty in a collegial way, feeling herself more "a facilitator than the typical model of a dean." The school was in the infancy of forming a fund-raising program and had received a grant from the Lilly Endowment to explore faculty development and curricular revision. It was a time of productivity and cooperation among the faculty, and McFague said she "enjoyed immensely the work I was given to do."

A political crisis precipitated McFague's resignation as dean. In March 1978, the Divinity School faculty prepared a petition to the chancellor protesting the University's agreement to host a Davis Cup tennis match with South Africa. McFague spoke out strongly in support of the faculty petition and was photographed checking on protestors during their picketing. The photograph was carried over the national wire services, and her support for the protestors was interpreted as a challenge to the University administration. After the appearance of the photograph, she felt more and more isolated by the upper administration of the University; fearing that the Divinity School would suffer from these strained relationships, she decided to resign and return to full-time teaching. After she announced her resignation, the faculty issued a statement acknowledging the ways in which her leadership had brought her the recognition denied her as a part-time faculty member: "We also wish publicly to acknowledge her enduring contributions to our school and to theological education in North America. During her tenure as dean and through her writings and public addresses, she has emerged as an intellectual leader among those engaged in professional education for ministry."[47]

Her writing and teaching flourished in the coming years. In 1988, the American Academy of Religion honored McFague for her book *Models of God*. The following year she was named the Harvie Branscomb Distinguished Professor in the University. A second book award, from the Midwest Independent Publishers Association for Best Religious Book, was bestowed upon *The Body of God* (1993). Her profile also expanded internationally as she appeared on Bill Moyers's PBS documentary *Spirit and Nature* and addressed the World Council of Churches in France and the Vatican Observatory Conference on Science, Philosophy and Theology in Rome.

In 1989 McFague became the first incumbent of the E. Rhodes and Leona B. Carpenter Chair at the Divinity School, honoring the contributions of women. Of this historic gift, Ann Day, United Church of Christ minister and president of the foundation, said, it is "a lighthouse, a source of illumination and hope, one that will explore and expand the wisdom that God's daughters have brought to Christian faith. Sallie is the first keeper of that light."[48]

Yet McFague has never strictly categorized her scholarship or her presence in the community as being primarily about or solely for women. "I have never particularly wanted to be known as a feminist theologian. I am a theologian who is a woman, and I have been deeply influenced by the feminist vision which is an alternative to the patriarchal pattern. I believe that the feminist theological vision of the world is superior to the patriarchal one, and so when I teach constructive Christian theology, I like everyone in the school to be exposed to this feminist vision. I think it is healthier, and better for Christian faith."

Nonetheless, McFague's influence on women students, in particular, has been profound. Cynthia A. Jarvis, in describing her experience as a woman at Vanderbilt in the early 1970s, offered a tribute in 1983:

> Sallie McFague, more than any other person, was for us, and that reality grounds every other observation one would make about Vanderbilt and women in ministry at that time. She was mother, sister, mentor, critic,

counselor and more. . . . She was the voice who mediated God's call to one who did not believe she could ever be called to do or be much of anything in the life of the church, and I suspect she was that voice for many more than me. Her ministry with us and to us incarnated the possibility of ministry for us. So it is that every time I find myself saying that my theology is "radically incarnational," I have Sallie in my mind's eye. And because of who Sallie was for us, I believe we left Vanderbilt with a deep commitment about who we had to be for the women coming after us. There were doors to be opened, stories to be told, tears to be caught, and because it had been done with us, we were strengthened to do it with those yet to come.[49]

The Office of Women's Concerns

In the early 1970s, the Divinity School experimented with a variety of forms of representation for women within its organizational structure. Initially, an informal women's caucus provided a continuing structure to deal with issues of the women's movement as they related to the school. This informal group gave way to a faculty-appointed task force, which, as one of its major accomplishments, coordinated the first Antoinette Brown Lecture in 1974. Later that year, the position of Women's Coordinator was approved. In 1975, Ann Day was appointed Coordinator for Women's Studies, with responsibilities for distributing bibliographic materials and other texts related to women. A year later the activity was called the Office of Women's Concerns, and the task force was dissolved.

An early questionnaire distributed by the Office revealed the diversity of the views of both women and men on women's liberation. One man commented that he saw it as "a movement of frustrated women who refuse to do the things they're supposed to do!" An equally disparaging remark came from a woman: "I see it as a group of poor misfits unable to fulfill a role of wife, mother, and working woman, a group of 'sour grapes' because they are unable to receive the love of a man, to love a man, or to respect others for their way of life." Others offered such recommendations as "it would be helpful for teachers to take 5–10 minutes to seriously deal with the issue if, for example, a theologian is critical of women." The coordinators of the Office had a complex task to accomplish if all these voices were to be addressed.

The coordinator of the Office, along with a steering committee and faculty adviser, provided a center for the support of women and a central administrative structure for activities related to women. At regular potluck dinners they formed friendships and developed strategies for change within the educational institu-

tion. Bewildered at first by women-only events, men were jokingly mocked by
women as being victims of "potluck envy."

The Office also served as a link with other student constituency groups.
Margaret (Peg) Leonard-Martin, coordinator of the Office during the 1979–80
academic year, remembers in particular her relationship with Ralph Tucker, the
president of the Student Cabinet and convener of the Black Seminarians: "He
helped me to understand the racist construction of much of the feminist movement. We tried to form an alliance between the Office of Women's Concerns
and the Black Seminarians to do cooperative forums for the whole community.
No one was exempt from the discussion. I learned so much from Ralph and
from his wife Linda." Tracey (DeVol) Robinson-Harris, Leonard-Martin's successor, was able to use her administrative skills to solidify the gains of the 1970s
with an increased visibility for the Office in public life in both the school and the
University, an increased budget, and additional research materials by and about
women. As an experiment in different forms of leadership, the Office of Wom-
en's Concerns by-laws were changed to allow for a coordinating team.

In the late 1980s, questions regarding diversity of programming occupied
the steering committee. Was the Office supportive of the needs of women with
children or more inclined to value service to the academy over service to the
church? How was it to cooperate in funding programs with other student advocacy groups such as the Evangelical Student Association and the Black Seminarians? How should it address the increasing numbers of African American
women in the student body? These questions set the agenda for the Office's
work in the 1990s.

The Antoinette Brown Lecture

One of the unique and continuing legacies of the women's activism at
Vanderbilt during the 1970s is the Antoinette Brown Lecture. It honors the first
woman to be ordained (by Congregationalists in 1853) in the United States,
Antoinette Brown, and it represents an important strand of the Divinity School's
Oberlin legacy. The lecture was made possible initially through a gift from
Sylvia Sanders Kelley, an alumna of the College of Arts and Science, and was
designed to "bring to the school distinguished women theologians to speak on a
variety of concerns for women in ministry." In a conversation with Dean Harrelson, Kelley proposed a conference sponsored by the Divinity School to address issues of leadership for women. It was Harrelson's counterproposal to
Kelley that "the best way to influence society was to support the emerging
feminist religious scholarship. He asked me if I would be interested in funding a
lecture series to introduce feminist scholars to Vanderbilt Divinity School."[50]

Beverly Harrison of Union Theological Seminary in New York became the first Antoinette Brown Lecturer in 1974.

The lecture became a rallying point for the women in the Divinity School and Graduate Department of Religion and the centerpiece of the earliest "Women's Week" observances of the University. The Antoinette Brown Steering Committee eventually became the most visible and active group within the Office of Women's Concerns, designing and producing publicity materials, offering educational and social events in conjunction with the lectures, and hosting the lecturers. With the initial funding no longer adequate, an endowment campaign in the 1990s to raise $100,000 to support the Lecture was successful, in large measure due to the commitment of alumnae whose involvement in the earliest lectures remained an important fixture of their experiences at Vanderbilt.

Inclusive Language

A review of the faculty minutes, committee minutes, student newspapers, and other early documents of the Divinity School confirms in language the absence of women in the minds of the speakers and writers. Seldom are women mentioned at all; when mentioned, it is most often as "wives." Even when the presence of women students is acknowledged, the language of public discourse assumes that men are the recipients of its educational efforts and the holders of faculty positions. The generic "man/men" or "mankind" is used throughout even the most passionate documents in support of civil rights for underrepresented minorities.

But by the 1970s, shifts in thinking about the appropriate use of gender-specific language had begun. As the decade progressed, the debate about language intensified, reaching full flower in 1978. In an article in *Prospectus*, graduate student Martha Reineke outlined the argument for the careful use of gender-specific language:

> My own concern with language is relatively recent. It is not surprising given the history of philosophy that as an undergraduate I considered I was studying "a man's world" as an "observer." The questions of my inclusion in the language of this world did not occur to me. At Vanderbilt, a changing awareness of my commitment to a particular understanding of the world has made this distance impossible. . . . I find it impossible to remain a mere "observer" of "a man's world." It is my world now and I am pained and angered by my invisibility in its language.[51]

Another graduate student, Elouise Renich Fraser, later described this experience this way:

> I forget when the light dawned fully. It happened sometime during
> graduate school. I remember the pain of waking up day after day realiz-
> ing I had spent most of my life reading books written by men. Most
> were white men, but emotionally it didn't matter what color they were
> or where they came from. What mattered was that my reading life, like
> my life generally, had been ruled by men's voices. . . . Now it seemed the
> male authors of all the books I had read had come to life. They were
> joining all these other men in my life, a deep and confident chorus
> of male opinion and interpretation. The library stacks didn't feel as
> friendly as they had before.[52]

Nadia Lahutsky experienced her conversion in a more positive way. Arriving at Vanderbilt in 1973 from Hiram College, where "feminists were equated
with socialists," Lahutsky's philosophical and theological sensitivity to language
evolved, primarily due to the guidance of more senior students such as Linda
Tober, Ann Updegraff, Mary Kelly, and Mary Aquin O'Neill. Lahutsky reports
that there was no open confrontation in the classroom on the topic of inclusive
language, but much discussion. In a course entitled "Christian Faith and Ministry," she heard Sallie McFague change the pronoun "he" to "she," and at another
time in McFague's religious autobiography class, the personal stories of other
women students opened Lahutsky to the ways in which language could be
exclusive. Still, according to Lahutsky, "The primary vehicle for instruction
about inclusive language was the informal but regular potluck dinners hosted by
the Office of Women's Concerns."[53]

In 1978–79, the Office of Women's Concerns began working on a statement for the school arguing for the use of inclusive language. Lahutsky,
Reineke, and Fraser began as a working group, later expanding to a committee
to include other students and faculty members. As chair of the committee,
Lahutsky recalled that at the time, the opposition to inclusive language was not
organized, "but people were raising justifiable concerns. There were attacks on
particular words, for example, 'chairman.'" Some evangelical students found
inclusive language to be an addition to the list of grievances that they had with
what was perceived as the liberal ethos of the school; some African American
students, for whom inclusion in the school and representation in the curriculum
were more pressing issues, did not see inclusive language as vital to their ministerial education.

Leonard-Martin described the years 1974–80 as an "explosion, profoundly revolutionary. There wasn't a place in the building from the refectory to the restroom to the classroom where people weren't talking, arguing, or crying about the issue of inclusive language." Regarding the creation and adoption of inclusive-language guidelines, she observed that "everybody took it *so* seriously. Every single faculty member was trying to understand and to experiment in their own ways with this new reality." Crucial to the success of these efforts was the fact that the school was small enough that no one could hide. "The relationship-building that went on in our small groups was phenomenal. You were growing up and falling down in front of people who were your friends." When individuals regressed into patterns of exclusive language, faculty and students were quick to remind them that there were inclusive forms of expression.

In March 1979, the Working Group on Language presented a letter regarding a "Statement on Sex-Inclusive Language" to the faculty for discussion. Some faculty members voiced concern regarding academic freedom and reiterated some student opposition based on religious conviction. The document was referred to the Personnel and Policy Committee for more study prior to a decision by the faculty. In August, "Toward a More Inclusive Language for VDS/GDR" was published. This five-page document gave a brief historical background of the concern that generated its writing and the intention of its writers. Sections followed with suggestions for alternatives for language about humans, God, work with biblical translations, and worship. The document also listed resources and encouraged continuing discussion on the subject.

By the beginning of the next academic year, the school's commitments, as published in the annual catalogue, reflected the faculty's growing consensus on the adoption of inclusive language. Retaining the statement previously adopted opposing sexism, the paragraph went on to declare the school's intention "to eliminate all forms of discrimination in attitudes, practices, and language. The school regards its use of sex-inclusive language as an expression of its opposition to sexism."[54] A review of theological school catalogues suggests that the Divinity School was the first to adopt such a statement for its publications. At its retreat that fall, the faculty took up the topic and its ramifications for scriptural translation, liturgical rubrics, hymn singing, and classroom discussion and assignments. Strategies for action to educate and encourage students in the use of inclusive language included recommendations that a document be made available to students and faculty each year outlining the acceptable conventions of language use, and that forums be scheduled for discussion of the issue.

The matter was never fully resolved to everyone's satisfaction. Articles in *Prospectus* over the next two years continued to debate the necessity and appropriateness of inclusive language, and in the fall of 1984 an entire issue was devoted to the topic. Given the internal debate, it is ironic that in September 1984, the University Senate announced that it had chosen the statement appearing in the Divinity School catalogue as its model for a Senate statement regarding inclusive language.

Conclusion

As with any successful movement resulting in the upheaval of established social and religious patterns, the entry of women into the life of theological education at Vanderbilt Divinity School is a remarkable story of hard-fought accomplishments and continuing challenges. Given its historical situation in a predominantly white southern university, the school's record of student enrollment, institutional leadership, curricular representation, and support for inclusive language is especially impressive.

In spite of the failure to bring the percentage of women on the faculty up to that of the student body, the lack of women in upper level administrative posts, and the decline in the number of women of color on the staff, the school rightly is known as a progressive environment for women. Women graduates of the Divinity School have made significant contributions in many arenas. A legacy of involvement in social service has resulted in the founding of several community organizations, and women graduates have assumed both local and national leadership as directors of such organizations. Churches of several denominations have hired alumnae as their first women pastors, and some of these women now hold regional or denomination-wide administrative positions. Innovators in cross-disciplinary studies and in bi-vocational ministries, women have also stretched curricular and professional boundaries by combining theology and social work, education, public policy, nursing, and law. Throughout the nation, alumnae of the Graduate Department of Religion teach in more than sixty colleges, universities, and theological institutions.

The current absence of a sense of urgency or unified purpose in pursuing gains for women at the school is perhaps inevitable. It is impossible to recover the energy invested in the advancement of women at a time when many gains have already been achieved and the goals of women are as diverse as the women themselves. It is also the case that with the Carpenter Program in Religion, Gender and Sexuality, the school's attention has been turned to a wider range of people and issues. In reflecting on her time at Vanderbilt, Peggy Way observes, "The focus on gender at the time was a luxury, just as the current focus on gay/lesbian issues is a luxury. Some issues are more important than gender and sexuality, like what is the mission of a school or the church? What is the role of university-based divinity schools? What are the critical research questions? What is the future of a Ph.D. program, given the shifts of religious life in the culture?" Even more urgent, perhaps, are the questions of global trends and world religions. "Are the cultures going to be able to live together or kill each other? There are women in India who don't have water. Personal issues are not as important as water."

9

The African American Presence in the Divinity School

Peter J. Paris

ROM THE END OF RECONSTRUCTION (1877) THROUGH THE EARLY 1960s, racial segregation and discrimination were rooted firmly in the laws of the southern states and universally practiced throughout the region. More than anything else, the superordinate/subordinate division of the races characterized the so-called southern way of life. Prior to the early 1960s, there had been virtually no public criticism of that tradition, and few whites could even dream of its actual demise. Within the safe havens of the black community, especially the churches, a number of courageous, prophetic voices arose that dared to think about an alternative societal arrangement where racial equality would be the law of the land.

During the Second World War some of those voices openly defied the so-called Jim Crow tradition. James Farmer represented one of the first such efforts when he founded the Congress of Racial Equality (CORE) in Chicago in 1942. Inspired by the nonviolent resistance movement of Mahatma Gandhi, Farmer's courageous endeavors to desegregate interstate bus travel in the South in 1947 failed; CORE had to wait another decade and a half for the necessary conditions to arise to support its aims of dismantling racial segregation. In the meantime, significant preludes to the pending racial crisis in the South were observable. Some of the most notable of these included the limited desegregation of the armed services during World War II; President Harry Truman's Fair Employment Practices Act in 1948; Jackie Robinson's becoming the first African American major league baseball player in 1947; Ralph Bunche's receiving the Nobel Peace Prize in 1950 for arranging a Middle East armistice; and Thurgood Marshall's successful legal challenge to the "separate but equal" doctrine established in *Plessy v. Ferguson* (1896), which culminated in the *Brown v. Board of Education* decision in 1954.

These events, along with numerous less public occurrences, signaled the steady development of cracks in the social order. Although all of them occurred outside the South, they were destined, nevertheless, to have a ripple effect on the social mores and customs of the old South. Clearly, any radical change would involve a major struggle, though its exact form was not yet known.

On the social level, the universality of racial segregation in the South was evident in dual systems of churches, schools, colleges, and universities. While whites were welcomed in the black institutions, blacks could be present in white institutions only as subordinate workers and never as social equals. On the political level, various methods were used to prevent blacks from registering to vote. In the judicial system all the judges and juries were white; in interracial disputes, few, if any, verdicts were ever rendered in favor of black plaintiffs. In the business sector, blacks could shop in the white stores but were often treated very discourteously. Since eating together implied social equality, blacks could not eat in restaurants or at the lunch counters in the department stores where they were allowed to shop. Train and bus stations had racially separate waiting rooms, bathrooms, and water fountains. Every other dimension of social life was structured similarly, including schools, colleges, hospitals, churches, and social and recreational facilities.

This was the racial context in which Vanderbilt's School of Religion existed up to the 1950s. Apart from the few persons in menial jobs, Vanderbilt's environs, including its School of Religion, were strictly off-limits to blacks throughout the first half of the twentieth century. Long acknowledged as one of the most liberal theological institutions in the South, the school had gained that reputation largely through its faculty's embrace of historical criticism as a legitimate method for biblical study.

Beyond affirming historical criticism, the School of Religion embraced an even wider liberal spirit. In his study of university divinity schools, Conrad Cherry notes the broad importance of this development:

> From his own modernist perspective, [Harry Emerson] Fosdick certainly had discerned the implications of a potent movement that was shaking the foundations of American Protestantism. The higher criticism of the Bible, the Darwinian theory of evolution, toleration of diverse religious beliefs, concern for the unity of the Christian church

and for the capacity of a unified church to heal the wounds of the world—all of these modernist Protestant advances decreed that the fundamentalists should not be allowed to win the minds and hearts of the people and thus turn American religion back toward an antediluvian dogmatism. The leaders of the divinity schools agreed.[1]

If these are marks of theological liberalism, there is much evidence to support the claim that Vanderbilt's School of Religion merited its reputation of being a liberal theological school. Its interdenominational faculty had studied at many of the leading universities in the world.

Through the years 1875–1925, many liberal seminaries created a space for teaching the implications of Christianity for the social order. Positions were created in sociology or social ethics for that purpose, since both fields at that time were devoted to the promotion of social welfare and social reform. Cherry claims that the divinity schools in the West and the South did not offer as many courses or programs in social ethics due to a lack of financial resources; but some did, and Vanderbilt was among them, led chiefly by the work of Alva Taylor. Although it is well known that the Social Gospel leaders in northern cities paid little attention to the problem of racial segregation, those in the South could not undertake social analysis while turning a blind eye to its pervasive presence.[2] None of the Social Gospel endeavors, however, equaled those of the post–civil rights period of the early 1970s and beyond. They were merely precursors of the civil rights movement that gained full expression in the 1955 year-long Montgomery bus boycott that catapulted Martin Luther King, Jr., to worldwide acclaim.

Racial Desegregation in the School of Religion

The cautious efforts of the Social Gospel advocates in both their teaching and charitable works were rooted in an optimistic view of social institutions and a naïve belief in rational persuasion as a method for social change. This is clearly seen in the way the School of Religion effected the admission of its first black student in 1953. Prior to that time, Vanderbilt University actively supported the status quo with respect to its admission policies. It appears that Chancellor Harvie Branscomb decided to begin quietly and cautiously desegregating the school. As with several divinity schools in southern universities, Vanderbilt's desegregation process was initiated from within the institution and from the top down. Thus, in June 1952, Branscomb asked Dean John Keith Benton to investigate the practices of theological schools in the South concerning the admission of black students to their degree programs.

Benton submitted his report to the chancellor the following September. It contained data on thirteen of the fifteen white theological institutions in the South. After stating that he had not received any word from the Episcopal Theological Seminary in Virginia or the Lutheran Seminary in South Carolina, Benton presented the information received from the other schools. (In the report, he consistently used the lowercase for the word "Negro"; he may or may not have been aware of the importance of this for blacks.). He noted first that most permitted interracial meetings in seminary buildings when sponsored by the school (Duke in North Carolina and Brite Divinity School in Texas did not); ten also permitted interracial meetings sponsored by outside groups, but two of these (Columbia in Atlanta and Austin Presbyterian in Texas) specified that the sponsoring group must be acceptable to the administration. He then reported that ten institutions admitted blacks as regular students, but in general the enrollment was restricted to candidates from the denomination to which the school belonged (Phillips in Oklahoma and Union Presbyterian in Virginia had no blacks enrolled, but their regulations did permit such enrollment). The Methodist divinity schools at Duke and Emory did not admit black students.

The report also addressed the variations in the practices of the ten schools that admitted blacks as regular students. In all ten, blacks were taught in classes with white students and were able to graduate and receive the regular seminary degree. In eight seminaries (not Columbia or Brite), they were allowed to eat with other students in seminary dining rooms; in six schools (not Brite, Columbia, Austin, or Southwestern), they were allowed to live in regular university or seminary dormitories. Finally, in five of the institutions, blacks were accorded the same educational and social privileges as white students without discrimination; these included The College of the Bible in Lexington, Louisville Presbyterian, Southern Baptist in Louisville, Phillips, and Perkins at Southern Methodist University. At Perkins, he added, blacks were accorded full social privileges in the seminary but not in the university as a whole. The data provided in this report indicate that in the early 1950s the freestanding seminaries of the South were much more accessible to African American students than were the divinity schools attached to southern universities.[3]

Two days after sending his report, Benton sent a letter to Branscomb containing a resolution that had been adopted at the School of Religion faculty meeting the day before: "We, the Faculty of the Vanderbilt University School of Religion, record our conviction (1) that the practices of the School of Religion should in all possible respects be in accord with the gospel which it is our responsibility to interpret; and (2) that if the practices of the School are to be in accord with this Christian gospel the fellowship and instruction of the School should be open to qualified students without reference to their race or color."[4]

At the October meeting of the Board of Trust, arrangements for the opening of the University Center had been completed. This was a collaborative venture involving George Peabody College, Scarritt College, and Vanderbilt that, among other things, permitted student enrollment in courses at any of the three institutions. A question before the Board was whether two Negro students at Scarritt could take courses at the Vanderbilt School of Religion. The Board voted to grant such permission. The press release by Chancellor Branscomb stated the following rationale: "We felt that this was right both because of the values of the Scarritt–School of Religion relationship, and on its merits. The School of Religion studies and teaches the Christian Gospel. Christianity is not the sole or private possession of any one race or nation, as every missionary movement since the dispersal of the first apostles to the far corners of the earth has witnessed. We were not willing in this simple issue to vote against that principle."[5]

Concerning Vanderbilt's admission of the first black student to a degree program, the Board of Trust adopted the following resolution on May 1, 1953:

> The School of Religion at Vanderbilt University has received the application of Rev. Joseph A. Johnson for admission to the School of Religion. Mr. Johnson is the president of and a teacher in Phillips School of Theology, a seminary of the Colored Methodist Episcopal Church located in Jackson, Tennessee. He is a person of maturity and character and is academically qualified for admission. He has been accepted by institutions outside this region, but for valid reasons, he desires to study in his own state and closer to the institution for which he is administratively responsible.
>
> The Board of Trust does not believe that Vanderbilt University should admit Negro students to courses of study which are already available to them in this vicinity in institutions of strong resources and established reputations, and with which we have always cooperated. No negro [*sic*] graduate or accredited school in the field of religion, however, exists in this city or state. We recognize that Christianity is not the exclusive possession of any one nation or race.
>
> In accordance with these principles the Board of Trust has voted to admit this applicant.[6]

Days before Johnson became a student in the fall of 1953, Benton wrote to Malcolm P. Calhoun of the Board of Church Extension of the Presbyterian Church in the United States, stating that "he will be accorded all the privileges that are normally extended each student, but will probably not eat his meals in the University dining room or live in one of the university buildings. Negro students are not admitted to any other division of Vanderbilt University at the present time."[7] Thus, unlike the admission of white students, Johnson's admission carried certain limitations. Because of his race, he was not granted all the privileges afforded other University students. The compromise arrangements were that he would receive equal treatment in the School of Religion and could eat in the University dining facility. Even so, faculty members accompanied Johnson at meals lest someone should insult him. Since Johnson was married and had a family, and since he pastored a Nashville congregation, the issue of integrated living arrangements in the school or University was never tested. David Halberstam maintains that there was a gentleman's agreement with the school's dean that blacks would "be invisible men, not seen and not heard, if at all possible, outside of the classroom."[8] After successfully completing his B.D. degree in 1954, Johnson was admitted to the Ph.D. program in New Testament, where he completed a dissertation on "Christology and Atonement in the Fourth Gospel" and received his degree in 1958. Approximately two decades later the Black Students Association at Vanderbilt named its campus center the Bishop Joseph A. Johnson Black Cultural Center as a tribute to his courageous spirit.[9]

Johnson's admission took place so quietly that it could hardly be called a public act, since no one outside the School of Religion was affected by it. The lack of any wider publicity about the event limited its significance to the private sphere of the school itself. In fact, most of the University and virtually everyone in the city knew nothing about the event until long after Johnson had graduated. Clearly, his admission constituted no significant systemic change in race relations either at the University or in the city at large. The school's compromising posture of requesting the University's permission to desegregate its own space while not pressing it to universalize the principle of racial inclusion throughout its domain failed to prepare the University for the trauma it would confront a few years later when James Lawson, one of the principal architects of the civil rights movement, was admitted to the school. Lawson clearly understood that racial justice was a wholistic principle and that its indivisibility disallowed the kind of compromise that the school had embraced when it admitted Joseph Johnson. By contrast, Lawson could not separate his thought and practice at the school from his commitment to the larger goal of dismantling racial segregation everywhere. His position was summarized later by Martin Luther King, Jr.'s phrase, "Injustice anywhere is a threat to justice everywhere."

Kelly Miller Smith: Premier Civil Rights Leader in Nashville

Two of the principal leaders in the Nashville sit-in movement, James Lawson and Kelly Miller Smith, will always be linked with the story of racial desegregation at the Divinity School. In 1958 Lawson was admitted to the school's B.D. program as a transfer student from the Oberlin Graduate School of Theology. Lawson was an extraordinary person in every respect. In addition to being an excellent student and athlete, he came to Nashville with a clear focus. As a theology student at Oberlin he met Martin Luther King, Jr., who invited him to join the movement in the South as a teacher of nonviolent resistance. Clearly, this courageous, well-experienced intellectual, deeply committed to the method and goals of the civil rights struggle, would not be easily corralled by any implicit "gentleman's agreement" concerning the covert practices that had characterized Vanderbilt's system of desegregation.

It was in the basement of Kelly Miller Smith's First Baptist Church on Eighth Avenue that Lawson held weekly workshops on nonviolence. Commentators on the Nashville story of racial desegregation have long noted that Smith, pastor of this prominent black church, merits major credit for the process of racial transition in Nashville. His leadership was thoroughly redemptive for the entire city.

Smith was an eloquent orator with rare intellect and astounding persuasive powers. From the time he assumed his pastorate in 1951, he was involved in every activity aimed at challenging racial segregation and effecting racial justice. As president of the local chapter of the National Association for the Advancement of Colored People (NAACP) three years after his arrival in Nashville, and immediately following the Supreme Court ruling in *Brown v. Board of Education*, he joined with twelve other black parents in filing suit in U.S. District Court against the Nashville Board of Education. Later, as one of the architects of the Nashville Plan for the Desegregation of the Public Schools, he led his six-year-old daughter Joy by the hand to become the first black student in her school. Smith was a charter member of the Nashville Urban League, a founding member of the Southern Christian Leadership Conference, and a close friend and colleague of King. He also served as president and founder of the Nashville Christian Leadership Council. As a part-time homiletics professor at Nashville's American Baptist College and the pastor to many of the administrators and faculty members of the four black colleges and universities in Nashville, Smith clearly enjoyed the confidence of Nashville's black elite.

Permitting Lawson to hold workshops on nonviolent protest in his church won Smith the enduring confidence of the students involved in the movement. Soon the church would become the staging ground for the Nashville sit-in movement, which in turn became a significant microcosm of the civil rights movement in the South. Smith's personal attributes of grace, warmth, dignity, and diplomacy commanded the respect of the ruling white elites in the city as well as the entire black community. During the Nashville sit-in crisis, he was the only person in the city who could be an effective intermediary between the two communities. He received special support from two new colleagues in this period. In 1957, soon after arriving as the official representative of the National Council of Churches, the Rev. Will Campbell, who like Smith was born and reared in Mississippi, became the first white person to join First Baptist Church. Campbell's many public acts of defiance against racial segregation endeared him to both Smith and the black community of Nashville. Similarly, Walter Harrelson of the Divinity School faculty joined First Baptist in the early 1960s as its second white member. Unwittingly, perhaps, that act prepared the way for the next step in the Divinity School's gradual pilgrimage toward desegregation.

By the late 1960s, Vanderbilt had desegregated its undergraduate student body and all of its schools. The next obvious step was the recruitment of students and the development of supportive programs. Each school devised its own approaches to those matters. Once again, the Divinity School led the way. In June 1969, following various conversations with Smith, Harrelson, then dean of the school, wrote him a letter of appointment as lecturer in Church and Ministries and assistant dean. It was to be a one-third-time appointment for supervising the recruitment of black students and teaching one course in the spring semester. The proposed salary was $6,000. Harrelson's letter made no mention of benefits or program budget (fringe benefits being only available to persons with at least half-time appointments), but it did promise secretarial support. Thereafter, until his death in 1984, Smith's appointment was renewed annually. Due to his inadequate salary from his church, Smith became very much dependent on the financial package that Vanderbilt offered him. Toward the end of each academic year, he endured considerable anxiety as he waited patiently to receive the dean's letter of reappointment. For reasons that were never clear to this writer, Smith never took any initiative in negotiating the terms of his appointment. Rather, he simply waited uneasily for the annual letter. While the dean may not have entertained any doubts about his reappointment, Smith could never be sure until he had received the actual letter; he was doubtless unaware that administrative appointments were routinely renewed on an annual basis. A less stressful arrangement for him would have been a three- or five-year renewable appointment. By 1972, Smith's appointment contained fringe benefits and a designated expense account.

As noted previously, prior to Smith's appointment Vanderbilt University had been a most inhospitable place for African Americans. Some doubted that it could ever change its racist image. Left to its own devices, it probably would not have been able to do so. On the one hand, Smith's appointment was a stroke of genius on Harrelson's part. On the other hand, it was the clearest sign of the school's minimalist commitment to institutional change. Smith's unique status in the Nashville community, his charisma, and his capacity to affirm all peoples were ideal attributes for the task at hand. He soon developed a program of enrichment and reconciliation for all concerned. Accordingly, he used most of his program budget to support one or two annual conferences on various subjects pertaining to the black church. Over the years he brought to the campus most of the leading black theological scholars of the day and many of black America's greatest preachers. While the themes of the conferences changed from year to year, their format remained the same. Smith regularly planned for part of the conferences to be held on Vanderbilt's campus and part in a black church. In other words, the strategy aimed to bring the black churches (clergy and laity) to the campus and to take Divinity students and faculty into the black community. At first each was an alien experience for the other, but over time each would become more comfortable with visiting the other's domain. Gradually the unfriendly ghosts of the past receded, and, once again, Kelly Miller Smith had been the effective intermediary. Concerning one 1973 conference on "Black Religious Leadership and the Needs of the Black Community," Smith wrote what came to typify all subsequent conferences he sponsored:

> The conference was one of many sponsored or co-sponsored by the Divinity School of Vanderbilt which are designed to address the needs of the black community in a realistic and practical way. They have all dealt with crucially important topics and all have held sessions both on the campus and in the black community in the facilities of the black church. The reason for this is an attempt to span the yawning chasm between the Divinity School and the black community.
>
> It goes without saying that divinity schools and other parts of predominantly white universities have not been overly zealous in addressing the specific needs of the black community. This has been one of the glaring omissions of the past. These conferences do not adequately remedy that situation, but they render an important service.[10]

Smith's greatest joy in his years at Vanderbilt came from those conferences. Unfortunately, few whites in the Divinity School fully understood or appreciated the import of his work for the life and mission of the school. Consequently, the school failed to celebrate Smith's program in a manner appropriate to its real merit. The conferences not only united theological thought and Christian ministry, but also reconciled blacks and whites in theological education and beyond. There soon developed a faithful core of conferees both from within and without the Divinity School. Further, Smith reached out to the few black faculty in other parts of the university for leadership in his conferences, providing opportunities for them to associate with the wider Nashville community. He was also an active participant in the nascent Vanderbilt Association of Black Faculty and Administrators, which met regularly as a support group.

Beyond his many and varied activities in the Nashville community, Smith brought distinction to Vanderbilt on various other fronts. Among the numerous honors he received during his lifetime, the most relevant to his work at the Divinity School included Howard University's Distinguished Alumni Award, the 1979 Humanitarian Award from the National Conference of Christians and Jews, and his inclusion in *Ebony Magazine*'s list of America's "Ten Most Outstanding Preachers." He was a founding member and later president of the National Conference of Black Churchmen and a member of the Faith and Order Commission of the World Council of Churches. In 1983 he delivered the Lyman Beecher Lectures at Yale University, later published as *Social Crisis Preaching* by Mercer University Press. Unfortunately, the first copy of the book arrived in Nashville on the day of his death. It had been sent to Will Campbell, who brought it to this writer, who, several months earlier, had helped Smith prepare the book for publication.

Smith's appointment marked the first stage in the Divinity School's process of developing a racially integrated faculty and administration. Since he served at the privilege of the dean, and since the dean did little to interpret the importance of his position for the school and the larger university, Harrelson's successor, Sallie TeSelle (later McFague), assumed office with little appreciation for Smith's program. In that first year she called him into her office for a conference and raised serious questions about his program. Smith was offended at having been asked for such an accounting, and he constructed a long response over the next few days in which he addressed the several issues. The first had to do with the cost of an observance in memory of Martin Luther King, Jr., for the Nashville community, one part of which involved a service in the Divinity School's Benton Chapel. How would the expenses for a nationally known speaker be covered? Smith believed that the dean had directed him to use the balance in his budget for this purpose. He was certainly willing to do that; however, he believed it would be important for the school if the dean contributed to the cost, "making it clear that the total school is supportive of this important event rather than relegating it solely to Black Church Relations sponsorship."

Other topics dealt more directly with the Black Church Relations program. Smith explained that this program had developed out of the peculiar history and special needs of African Americans; the conferences were frequently held by design in the black church in order to foster a relationship between the churches and the school. He noted that "the Divinity School has not always projected a positive image in the Black community, nor has it always been willing to discover what it could learn from that community"; this was part of what he had tried to change. But he was concerned that white faculty and students had shown little interest in recent years in his programs, and he thought that the school should attend to this matter.

To the concern expressed over the small number of students in his classes, Smith noted that the number of black students in the school was itself small, but pointedly reminded the dean that very few white students had shown any interest "in that which pertains to Black people and the Black Religious Experience." He thought that faculty advisers and administrators could assist in reminding students of the courses he offered, and he contended that the entire school and not just his program should take responsibility for making theological education meaningful for black students.

He took great exception to the suggestion that the program in Black Church Relations could or should take the work of the school's Women's Task Force as a model. The differences between these respective concerns stemmed not only from centuries of racial segregation and the cultural traditions of African Americans, he contended, but also from the specific agencies and institutions within the black community that have important histories in dealing with issues of oppression. In addition, virtually all fields of scholarly research, including religion, have contributed to the dehumanization of blacks "through neglect, misunderstanding, and destructive intent."

After calling for a larger role for administrative dialogue within the school, Smith concluded by warning of the results of curtailing his modest program and budget:

> This would be a tragic retreat from the position which this school was finally attaining among Black religious leaders and nonleaders. . . . A retrenchment would give aid and comfort to those who have contended all along that the school should not have opened its arms quite so wide and it confirms the position of those who never thought it was genuine in the first place. Retrenchment would suggest that the work of Black Church Relations is expendable and is therefore to fall victim of the well known dictum that Black persons and causes must be the last hired and first fired. The day that this is done will be a day of infamy.[11]

Although the dean did not send a written reply to Smith's apologia for his program and work, she did support those activities and no retrenchment was contemplated. Still, issues that Smith had discussed remained unresolved in the school a decade later.

The accolades that Vanderbilt failed to grant Smith during his lifetime were bestowed posthumously as living memorials to the legacy he had left. Foremost among these was the inauguration of the Kelly Miller Smith Institute on the Black Church, followed by the official opening of the Kelly Miller Smith Research Collection[12] in the Jean and Alexander Heard Library on April 25, 1985. At long last, the University had begun to make solid institutional commitments in its transition from the mere formality of racial desegregation to a substantive program of racial integration.

At the inaugural event for the Kelly Miller Smith Institute, the official program included former and present deans of the Divinity School (Walter Harrelson and Jack Forstman), former and present chancellors of the University (Harvie Branscomb, Alexander Heard, and Joe B. Wyatt), and a host of local, regional, and national figures in theological education.[13] After acknowledging his fifteen years of service as assistant dean and faculty member, as well as his work in planning conferences on the black church that "brought together the Black Church and the local community as partners with the Divinity School and the University in the analysis and pursuit of critical issues threatening the quality of our common life," the program declared,

> The Divinity School wishes to perpetuate those conferences by establishing The Kelly Miller Smith Institute on the Black Church as a living memorial to one who meant so much to us all. The Institute will carry on the work of the conferences, thus maintaining the ties between Church and University that Kelly developed so well. It will also be seeking to do a number of additional things when funds and staff are available. Hopefully, certain forms of research might be initiated and/or sponsored by the Institute. The Institute would assist as well in the recruiting of scholars and clergy for the Black Church and for other institutions of the society, national and international. To these ends funds will be sought from friends, alumni/ae, churches and corporations to endow the Institute.

At the site of his memorial, Kelly Miller Smith's dream for Vanderbilt, Nashville, and the nation was realized for a brief moment, when the power elite in the city and the University joined together in celebrating the life and mission of the black churches and launching an endowment for the perpetuation of their teaching and study at Vanderbilt, which itself was barely two decades removed from segregation.

Black Faculty and Students

During the years 1972–85, Vanderbilt Divinity School had two black faculty members: Kelly Miller Smith (1969–84) and Peter J. Paris (1972–85). During that period black students ranged between 4.8 percent and 10.7 percent of the total student enrollment. Paris was the first African American at Vanderbilt to gain tenure and rise through the ranks from instructor to professor.

Since 1987 the Divinity School has had the following full-time black faculty members: Walter Fluker in ethics (1987–91), Eugene Sutton in homiletics (1992–95), Renita J. Weems (1987–) in Hebrew Bible, and Victor Anderson (1992–) in ethics. Weems and Anderson came out of doctoral programs (the former at Princeton Theological Seminary, the latter at Princeton University) and were promoted in due course to the rank of associate professor with tenure. In this same period, the school employed Wallace Charles Smith, successor to Kelly Miller Smith as pastor of First Baptist Church, Capitol Hill, as a part-time faculty member in homiletics and the practice of ministry (1987–91). The appointment of Louis Baldwin to the Department of Religious Studies in 1984 and his steady rise to the rank of professor has brought considerable value to the Divinity School through his teaching, research, publications, mentorship, and collegiality. During this same period the enrollment of black students varied between 13.9 percent and 19.5 percent of the total student body; the number of African American women students doubled in the 1990s. Such statistics demonstrate a clear correlation between the number of black students enrolled and the number of full-time black faculty and administrators at the school. As will be seen, the constant monitoring of the racial situation by black students, faculty, and staff has been a necessary condition for the preservation of racial justice at the Divinity School.

The Davis Cup Crisis

In 1978, the Divinity School joined a broad coalition of forces for the purpose of persuading the University to rescind the decision of its Athletic Committee to host a Davis Cup tennis competition between the United States and South Africa. This group believed that hosting this event would damage race relations both in the University and in Nashville itself. The issue coincided with the mounting pressure throughout the country to persuade American institutions to support economic and social sanctions against South Africa for its policy of apartheid. In its ongoing concern for racial justice at Vanderbilt, the Divinity School faculty believed that by rescinding the invitation, the University could send to the nation and the world a powerful message on the issue of race. Accordingly, on January 28, 1978, it took the initiative by unanimously adopting a motion to request a meeting with University officers. The motion declared:

> In view of the South African government's apartheid policy, its repression and disenfranchisement of all non-whites, its continuing brutality toward non-whites, its refusal to respond to internal and external requests for a broadened franchise and guarantees of human rights, and

evidence that the South African government will use the visit of its Davis Cup team to Nashville for political propaganda, we believe that Vanderbilt University, in permitting the use of the Memorial Gymnasium for the final round of the Davis Cup competition, has allowed itself to be exploited for a partisan political purpose in a matter which will draw national and international attention. Therefore, the faculty of the Divinity School protests the use of the Memorial Gymnasium by the South African tennis team on March 17–19, 1978, and requests that the University reconsider the question and rescind its previous action.[14]

For the next six weeks, the University was embroiled in a major crisis over this issue. Repeated meetings with the chancellor and president failed to persuade them to change their minds. They persisted in their position that the University was an open forum, that the Davis Cup match represented such a forum, and that hosting it did not imply Vanderbilt's support of apartheid or its devaluation of human rights. They held their position in the face of daily demonstrations around the administration building as well as letters of protest from various individuals and groups within the faculty. Letters were also received from civil and religious groups in the city and across the nation. On the day of the match, the NAACP in alliance with several other organizations held a mass demonstration that included a march to the University and past the site of the match, for a rally in nearby Centennial Park. In a letter to "Friends of the Divinity School," Dean McFague, a strong supporter of the protests, stated her own position on the matter. She noted that those who objected to the University's hosting of the Davis Cup match did not see themselves as adversaries of the University but rather acted in the hope of helping prevent what they believed to be a mistake. She then pointed out how the principle of the open forum—"a cherished principle of all universities and one which we also heartily support"—stood here in conflict with another principle important to all universities, namely that of commitment to human rights, which those who objected to the event thought should have taken priority. Focusing her attention on the ongoing issue, she concluded: "I still believe it is a mistake to host the match, but participation in the protest at this point no longer addresses that issue. Rather, all those opposed to apartheid in South Africa as well as to racism in this country now have an opportunity through the protest to express their opposition. I believe, and I am sure all of my colleagues would agree, that the University's image as a supporter of human rights will continue to be one of its major strengths."[15]

For the second time in two decades, the Divinity School was at the center of a major issue pertaining to racial matters on its campus. At long last, the Divinity

School had gone public on the issue of race, leveling a major challenge to the practical wisdom of Vanderbilt's central administrators. In many subtle ways, the school suffered considerably from the accusation that it had embarrassed the University. Soon thereafter McFague resigned her position as dean, and the school would not regain its good relationship with the University authorities for several years.

A New Racial Crisis

A major issue emerged in the school in the fall of 1986, sparked by comments made by a visiting white minister from South Africa that black students and others considered to be both racist and sexist. In November the Black Seminarians and Black Graduate Students presented a so-called "Black Manifesto," which initiated discussions concerning the need for systemic change in both the Divinity School and the Graduate Department of Religion. Throughout that academic year students convened a series of open forums "to encourage the widest possible participation and dialogue in thinking through creative alternatives to the existing systems which perpetuate racism, sexism, homophobia and an authoritarian, classist model of education."[16]

Throughout the 1987–88 academic year a general malaise permeated the Divinity School, occasioned by issues that had surfaced at an open forum, including allegations that an inordinate number of black students had received grades of C in two foundation courses in church history and accusations that faculty and teaching assistants were both ignorant of and insensitive to the black religious experience. In an open letter to the school, Gary Martin, the co-convener of the Black Seminarians, drew attention to an incident in which two white male students verbally attacked two black women whom he thought had been honestly expressing their opinions. He was disturbed mainly because neither the dean nor the faculty did anything to restore order. He doubted that this would have been the case had two black males verbally attacked two white women in a similar way. Accordingly, he claimed that the school's desire for ecumenism and inclusivity could not be achieved in a context where such ignorance regarding black history was so widespread among the faculty, administrators, and students. He called for the addition to the core curriculum of a course on the Black Church as well as a course on Women in the Church.[17]

Six student leaders reiterated these sentiments a few days later in a more sweeping proposal to the administration and faculty, which, among other things, called for a radical modification in the foundation curriculum to include black, womanist/feminist and lesbian/gay perspectives "as authentic, legitimate and essential components" of those courses. One outcome of the crisis was "A

Document on Racism at Vanderbilt Divinity School and the Graduate Department of Religion," prepared by members of the Seminar on Racism in the spring of 1987. Its preamble was written by faculty members Baldwin, Fluker, and Weems. Wallace Charles Smith coordinated the effort and compiled and edited the final report. The preamble and introduction provided an excellent analysis of the persistence of racism in all predominantly white American institutions, including the Divinity School. The basic value of the document lay in the theological and ethical rationale it provided as justification for the demands of that latest proposal.

Near the end of the spring semester 1988, students and faculty met face to face in a good-faith effort to resolve their differences. This marked major progress over the war of memos that had characterized the dispute throughout the year. The religion editor of the *Tennessean* caught the spirit of the meeting in an article titled "Meeting Eases VU Divinity School Tension."

> "What took place today was a genuine conversation that can be viewed as a beginning," said Jack Forstman, Divinity School dean. "Give and take was becoming impossible. The faculty was looking for a way to open discussion, and students made it possible."
>
> The faculty agreed to establish a grievance committee, invite student input into school budget, publish summaries of committee meeting minutes and consider hiring a black chaplain. They also agreed to meet with civil rights veteran C. T. Vivian tomorrow in a two-hour "consultation" and cleared the way for allowing Vivian to hold a two-day workshop on racism.[18]

A statement issued by the faculty in late March had helped to ease tensions and the mistrust by students of faculty and administration. The faculty acknowledged its failure to communicate and committed itself to address community and curricular issues over the coming weeks and months. One priority was the development of a "document on racism" that could be used, as the document on inclusive language had been, as a stated goal for the community.

The events that culminated in this faculty statement, as difficult as they were for the Divinity School community, did signify the coming of age of the African American community in the school. Three decades before, the school had quietly admitted its first black student. At that time, the only consideration at stake was the formal act of racial desegregation. It would appear that those at the helm of that enterprise viewed the admission of a black student as an end in itself. No one could imagine that in the not-too-distant future, more than 10 percent of the student body would be African American. Nor could anyone have imagined a time when African American students would be demanding systemic change in the curricular offerings, faculty pedagogy, and academic methodologies in order to relate the mission of the school more adequately to the African American religious experience. The articulation of such demands in the mid-eighties clearly revealed the growing maturity of the African American community at the Divinity School. Rather than bemoaning the conflicts that surfaced in the open forums and elsewhere during that year, all should rejoice and celebrate those nascent attempts to reshape the school to embrace the new traditions embodied by those who were once viewed as racial pariahs both at Vanderbilt and throughout the region.

Signs of a New Day

The appointment of two full-time, tenure-track African American faculty members in 1987, the 1990 appointment of Samuel D. Procter as Anne Potter Wilson Visiting Professor at the Divinity School, and the participation of James H. Cone as the 1995–96 Cole Lecturer signaled a distinct change in the school's understanding; it acknowledged that serious engagement with racial integration implied a corresponding institutional commitment at multiple levels of administrative and faculty action. Even more programmatically significant was the 1988 appointment of Forrest Harris, who had studied with both Kelly Miller Smith and Peter Paris, as the first director of the Kelly Miller Smith Institute on the Black Church. One of his first acts was to sponsor a conference on "The Religious Thought of Kelly Miller Smith," at which Paris gave two lectures.[19] Harris has also held positions as dean for Student Life, dean of African American Church Studies, and assistant professor of the Practice of Ministry. The several additions to his title are indicative of administrative efforts to deal with several issues at the same time.

Over the years Harris's efforts have been instrumental in causing the Institute to flourish. The establishment over the course of its first decade of an endowment to secure its future was a notable achievement. The work of the Institute has brought together the black church community and black educational institutions in partnership with the Divinity School to study and research issues important to the practice of faith and ministry in the black church, the single most important institution in the African American community.

As a center for research and praxis on issues of theology and ministry in the black church tradition, the Institute has focused on (1) the education of clergy and laity for leadership in ministry; (2) the promotion of dialogue between African American theologians and church leaders; (3) the development of research materials on the history of black religion in America, leadership in black churches, and black church theology; and (4) the development of educational programs to enrich the ministerial praxis in the black church. Some examples of each area of work will illustrate the range of activity. The Institute provides opportunities to work with the black church community by sponsoring study forums, clergy and laity study conferences, and retreats for the purpose of examining the critical social ministry needs of the African American community. Most significant among such events was the national dialogue on the question "What Does It Mean to Be Black and Christian?" This exploration involved several thousand participants at a number of sites across the nation over a two-year period and resulted in two publications.[20]

One prominent research focus of the Institute has been the legacy of black religious leadership. Under this general rubric, the Institute's primary interest has been to investigate how ethical and moral discourse emerging out of the African American religious traditions, including womanist ethics, affects the development of faith, leadership, and culture. A corollary of this activity is the goal of developing a comprehensive research archive on black religious leaders.

Although Harris accepted the presidency of American Baptist College in 1999, he continued his association with the Divinity School as director of the Institute. This joint relationship is important because American Baptist College has sent students to the Divinity School since the 1960s. Many of the school's most distinguished African American graduates are alumni/ae of the American Baptist College, and several of the latter's most distinguished alumni/ae were major leaders in the Nashville civil rights struggle (notably Congressman John Lewis, James Bevel, and Bernard Lafayette). Harris's appointment to both schools seals a significant cooperative mission.

Although the Divinity School may not yet have reached its zenith in the sphere of racial justice, its historic pilgrimage is light years beyond where it was at its beginning, or even fifty years ago. Through conflict, struggle, and accomplishment, it has led the University while itself struggling to be faithful to its basic commitments. The transformations have been significant, but continued attention to the issues involved in dealing with race in the University, the region, and the nation is necessary if these accomplishments are to be sustained and to become foundations for the future.

Benton Chapel, March 21, 1960,
following the dedication of the new
Divinity School quadrangle.

*Photo by Howard Cooper; Photographic Archives,
Vanderbilt University*

Benton Chapel interior.

James M. Lawson, focus of the crisis in the
University in the spring of 1960, on one of his visits
to the campus in the 1980s.

Photo courtesy of Vanderbilt University
Alumni Publications Archives

Divinity students in front of
Kirkland Hall protesting the expulsion of
James Lawson, March 1960.

Photo by Gerald Holly

Statue of Harold S. Vanderbilt, president of the
Board of Trust during the critical events of spring 1960;
he was instrumental in resolving the crisis.

Photo by Neal Brake

Lou H. Silberman, Hillel Professor of Jewish Literature and Thought, 1952–80.

Photo by John Halliburton

Rabbi Sol Bernards of B'nai B'rith leads a seminar
for the Summer Institute on Judaism for college, university,
and seminary faculty, early 1970s.

Photographic Archives, Vanderbilt University

"Three Deans." Former dean Walter Harrelson with
new dean Sallie McFague on the occasion of her installation,
1975 (portrait of former dean Tillett looks on).

(Photo by Gerald Holly)

Kelly Miller Smith speaks in Benton Chapel
during Commentary 1981 (program in connection
with the Cole Lectures).

(Photo by Clay Kinchen Smith)

Herman A. Norton,
professor of church history and dean of
Disciples Divinity House, 1951–86.

*Photo courtesy of Vanderbilt University
Alumni Publications Archives*

"Noah's Ark" faculty skit,
written by Sallie McFague and performed at the
Divinity School spring gala, 1980. Pictured are
Ted Brown (development) as a squirrel, Howard Harrod
(social ethics) as a buffalo, Peter Paris (ethics and society) as a
penguin, and Dean Jack Forstman as Noah.

Photo courtesy of Vanderbilt University
Alumni Publications Archives

PART IV
Studies

National, regional, and institutional contexts shape the character and mission of a school, but education is what it does. The four chapters in this section illustrate several dimensions of the complex reality that is theological education at an interdenominational, university-related divinity school. The combination of themes may be distinctive of Vanderbilt, but any theological school can identify with one or more of them. In addition, Vanderbilt's history is representative of both developments and tensions that have taken place in the field of theological studies in the past century.

Edward Farley's consideration of the history of the basic course of study for the ministry frames curricular developments in relation to enduring value conflicts that have occurred at most of the theological schools and seminaries of America. His chapter suggests that the structure of a theological institution as reflected in the curriculum is a product of the faculty's fundamental theological commitments. Those commitments are affected by changing issues, faculty transition, and the claims and interests of generations of students. Curricular shifts are thus the results of negotiation and interpretation; they reflect theological commitments, but do so imperfectly, and the content of one structure often continues in some form in successive shifts.

One of the realities considered by both Farley and Eugene TeSelle is the emergence and consolidation of separate fields of study within the larger category of theology. These fields are encouraged by the modern research university and reinforced by guild associations, professional journals, academic publishing, and the like. They have provided the framework for graduate study in religion as well as for theological education, despite questions regarding the extent to which field-specific interests should drive curricular patterns. This has been made more complex by the development in the last quarter of the twentieth century of a religious studies approach that has challenged perceived hegemony on the part of theological studies. Such conversation and debate has occurred in theological institutions as well as the public and private colleges and universities where the religious studies approach first emerged.

The development of Jewish studies at Vanderbilt in the second half of the twentieth century, considered by Peter Haas, is an important instance of how the university context assisted the work of the Divinity School by enlarging its vision and enabling Judaism to be studied for itself and not merely as background to Christianity. This course of study has had a substantial impact on succeeding generations of divinity and graduate students, shaping personal theologies as well as greater understanding of Jewish-Christian history and contemporary relationships.

Anthony Dunnavant's discussion of the role of the Christian Church (Disciples of Christ) in Vanderbilt's ministerial and graduate programs shows more than the significance of denominational relationships to the school. It suggests that theological education involves denominational support, congregational involvement, experiences of community for students, and faculty leadership within denominations. Engagement with its southern constituency was important for the Disciples, and the Disciples brought much-needed denominational visibility to the Divinity School in one of its more vulnerable periods. For the Disciples students, as Dunnavant makes clear, theological education was a combination of serious academic study and the formation that occurred in the community of the Disciples House, the congregational settings of worship and field education, and the particularities of the southern and university setting.

Tracking the Course of Study
in the Divinity School

Edward Farley

THE SUBJECT OF THIS CHAPTER IS WHAT THE VANDERBILT DIVIN-
ity School was brought into existence to do, namely, to provide a specific course of study for the education of ministers and other religious
leaders.[1] This topic may sound dry as dust, calling to mind forgotten catalogues,
lists of courses, and moldy struggles over "theological encyclopedia." Yet, determining the course of study is the most important thing a faculty, staff, and
student leadership can do. If a specific course is ill-conceived or irrelevant or a
specific faculty member is pedagogically challenged, students can still experience a fruitful and even life-changing education. But if the course of study itself
is badly flawed, if it simply perpetuates idiosyncratic interests of the faculty, if it is
over-weighted toward a particular "cause," or if it omits crucial matters (e.g.,
practical theology, the experience of women or African Americans), the students will be ill-prepared for exercising religious leadership.

The issues that affect decisions about the course of study, whether by their
presence or absence, are not simply "academic." Whole branches of Christendom have gone at each other by way of word, courtroom, and even sword and
cannon over what the Christian faith is. The outcomes of these struggles over
confessions, ordination, science, methods, spirituality, and politics are embodied in the education of priests and ministers. These struggles continue, if not
between the branches and denominations of Christendom, then within denominations and inside schools as they attempt to listen to (or ignore) the voices

of oppressed groups, the texts of the past, the discoveries of the sciences, and the rigors of critical scholarship. This is to say, decisions about the directions of a course of study have to do, finally, with the concrete life of the students and the situation of whatever institution they will serve. If the problems associated with the long-term invisibility of African Americans and women have no place in the course of study, students will likely perpetuate that in their ministry. If the course of study contains no critical engagement with the texts and beliefs of the religious tradition, the student as minister may be of little assistance to those in the parish who find that tradition puzzling, embarrassing, or irrelevant. This is why a lot of heat and passion, even mutual recrimination, attends large-scale curriculum revisions. The course of study may be dry, but it is surely not unimportant.

Conflicts of Loyalties

In the next section, I review six major curricular shifts in the Vanderbilt Divinity School's history. In this section, I discuss some of the basic conflicts underlying the debates over curriculum changes. In almost every case, the change of graduation requirements or of the course of study attempted to resolve a conflict of basic values or loyalties. To understand what was going on in these shifts calls for an awareness of the way the very idea of a divinity school creates an environment structured by inescapable tensions and value conflicts.[2]

A divinity school is a post-college, degree-granting school for the preparation of clergy and other religious leaders that is located in a university. In most cases, it also includes or has close relations with a doctoral program in which most of the school's faculty participates. Because the course of study takes place in the setting of a university committed to the canons of open scholarship and research, a divinity school first of all carries out its teaching in and through a commitment to open inquiry and appropriate methods of scholarship. Even if a divinity school understands its primary mission to be the education of ministers, its commitment to scholarship guides its pedagogy. The primacy of scholarly study and inquiry sets up enduring and, in principle, irresolvable tensions in the self-understanding, policies, and course of study. These tensions are not simply logical incompatibilities that pose a problem to be solved. The idea of critical scholarship is not a logical antithesis to liberating praxis or personal piety. Rather, these tensions reside in the realms of personal and institutional value, importance, and loyalty. They evoke responses of emphasis and de-emphasis more than logical resolutions.

Four fundamental areas of value conflict have been at work throughout the history of Vanderbilt Divinity School. In each of them, the school's fundamental commitment to ongoing, open, and rigorous scholarship has been one pole of the tension. This scholarly ideal has come into conflict with four other values: a confessional religious tradition, formative education (*paideia*, piety, spirituality), professional education, and world-changing praxis. These conflicts or tensions have had many locations and have shown themselves in a variety of ways: in conflicts between segments of the faculty, between faculty and students, between the school as a whole and its denominational constituencies. They have shown themselves in disputes over fields, faculty hiring, curricular structures, graduation requirements, and pedagogies. All four tensions are intrinsic to the life of the Divinity School and as such, some version of each has been present at Vanderbilt from the time of its founding. These conflicts, then, cannot be eliminated so much as negotiated, with a certain value—for instance, professional practice—being prominent at one time and less important at another.

The Tension between the Scholarly Ideal and the Confessional Tradition

The very act of founding a school such as the Biblical Department brought about tensions between the "scholarly ideal" and the confessional tradition of a Christian denomination, loyalty to which was fostered by the University's aim to educate Methodist clergy. Although the first members of its faculty seemed unsympathetic to continental historical scholarship, the Department gradually moved in a more liberal direction. When T. H. Huxley, a leading Darwinist of the day, lectured in Nashville in 1876, the dean of the Biblical Department introduced him. By 1900, Dean Wilbur Fisk Tillett had embraced historical criticism and was open to Darwin and the notion of the evolution of species. (The University's openness to Darwinism soon drew fire from the church.) A social liberalism was manifest in faculty member Thomas Carter's book on Wesley (1905), in which he appealed for moving the curricula of Methodist seminaries away from their "long-reigning conservatism." And in 1905–6 Dean Tillett broadened his course offerings from traditional confessional studies to one that included philosophy of religion and current theology. [3]

What started as a slight broadening of conventional forms of theological education and the (Methodist) confessional tradition in the first quarter-century of the school became a self-conscious commitment to new forms of scholarship after the break with the church in 1914. The new aim was a religious scholarship and approach to teaching ministers that was "nondenominational" and ecumenical. One of the earliest members of the Biblical Department, Henry Beach Carré, used Dibelius, Boussett, and others to reconstruct a historical Paul. In the 1920s Tillett's systematic theology marked a major departure from the tradition of orthodox theology. The tradition of historical scholarship, social liberalism, and openness to the sciences continued in the 1930s and 1940s in Umphrey Lee and Robert Hawkins. Also in the 1930s Dean O. E. Brown, who had been at

Vanderbilt since 1892, spoke of his teaching of Darwin and evolution as important to church historiography.[4] John Keith Benton, dean from 1939 to 1956,
brought to the school the whole movement of modern psychology, having
written a dissertation at Edinburgh on "modern psychological theories of religion." Tillett appears to have been the primary shaper of this growing liberal
tradition of the School of Religion. His leadership displayed an early and growing commitment to the scholarly ideal. This is not to say the Divinity School
was "modernist" in the "Chicago School" sense of the term, with a primary
focus on method and the study of religion. Even with the new focus on "religion in general," its emphasis was always the great truths and agreements among
major Christian traditions. Thus, the way the scholarly ideal appeared in the
school was as a Christian "liberalism," in the sense of a concern to communicate
basic Christian truths to the contemporary world.[5]

The conflict between the scholarly ideal and the confessional tradition appears in at least three forms in the history of the school. From 1875 to 1914, the
tension was between what comes with academic life (ancient languages, objec-
tivity, examinations, scholarship) and a denomination deeply suspicious of these
as necessary preparation for ministry.[6] The second form of conflict (after 1914)
was between the critical, objective aims of the scholarly ideal and commitment
to the truth and importance of a particular religious faith, Christianity, a tension
that continues to this day. The third form appears throughout the history of the
school, but it has yet to engender serious conceptual struggle or institutional
conflict. This is the tension between valuing the study of "religion in general,"
world religions, and religion outside a framework of any particular religious
heritage or advocacy, and valuing a specific historical faith (Christianity) that
comes with the education of Protestant ministers. In this case the scholarly ideal
comes to mean commitment to general religious scholarship, and the confessional side comes to mean any privileging of specific religious faiths. The study
of world religions found its way into American seminaries and divinity schools
under the rationale of the Christian world mission.[7] The study of religions was
important in the curriculum of the Divinity School from 1914 on. In the late
1940s, four hours in that area were required for the B.D. degree, the rationale
being the importance of the knowledge of religions to the field of missions. The
field of comparative religions was taught by faculty appointed to the school
(George Mayhew, Winston King) until it was transplanted to the new Department of Religious Studies in the College in 1968. Since that time, the study of
religions has been available to students but not as an intrinsic part of the school's
own faculty and course offerings.

From the 1970s to the present, this third form of tension took on the
language of the differing approaches of "religious studies" and "theological
studies." "Religious studies" names not only the study of religions but a way of

approaching that study outside any specific religious framework and outside any and all advocacy and assessment. According to George Lindbeck, during the 1970s and 1980s, the divinity schools gradually shifted away from theological studies to religious studies.[8] The result was that some divinity faculty located themselves primarily in religious studies and others in theological studies. These self-identifications are extremely difficult to interpret due to the muddiness of such concepts as advocacy and non-advocacy—"meaning-mongers" and "describers" as Ray L. Hart calls them[9]—and also due to the multiple meanings of the terms *religion* and *theology*. The tension is real, however, and bodes future changes in the way divinity schools conceive their degrees and programs of study.

The Tension between the Scholarly Ideal and Student Formation

The earliest and most fundamental meaning of education is some sort of human formation. Clark Gilpin has reminded us that the term *seminary* means etymologically the cultivation of seedlings.[10] David Kelsey uses the labels "Athens" and "Berlin" to describe two quite different types or models of theological education: "Athens" refers to the process of "culturing" or forming, and "Berlin" to scholarly ideal (represented in the German word *Wissenschaft*).[11] While Kelsey uses this distinction to study a debate over theological education in the last two decades, it is applicable to the history of the education of ministers in the United States since the very first seminaries. Those seminaries presupposed that exposure to the biblical texts and the great truths of the Christian faith would form or nurture young ministers. At the same time, the seminaries became more and more committed to scholarly inquiries whose primary aim was to assemble evidences, clarify, and understand, not form. As Kelsey notes, American theological education is located between these two ideals. Vanderbilt Divinity School is no exception. It gradually and inexorably developed in the direction of "Berlin," thus opening itself to English and German scholarship and eventually investing much of its energy in a sizable graduate program.

At the same time, "Athens" has always been central to its self-understanding and aims. "Athens" as the symbol of the power of the educational process to form or shape the student has worn many faces in the school's history. The earliest version of formation was that of Christian piety, the civilized and moral behavior congregations would expect from their leaders. Later interpretations included psychological wholeness, spirituality, and the *paideia* aspect of "the minister as theologian." The most recent version of formation urges a community and classroom ethos that forms inclinations toward solidarity with oppressed groups and actions that would transform society. In this version of "Athens," a proper pedagogy incorporates awareness of and opposition to discriminations and oppression. Deep commitments to these types of formation have prompted some to question the value and perhaps even the possibility of the scholarly ideal. Deep commitment to the scholarly ideal has led others to include in the process of formation the rigors of inquiry and evidence.

The Tension between the Scholarly Ideal and Professional Training

Virtually all theological institutions resolve the tension between scholarship and professional training toward one side or the other. Prior to the twentieth century, that group of studies pertaining to a minister's congregational responsibilities (preaching, polity, church administration, the "cure of souls") had a subordinate presence in theological education.[12] Prior to the seminary era in this country, the field of practical theology was almost identical with preaching and scripture reading. But when the Biblical Department was founded, practical theology—which consisted of homiletics, church polity, and "pastoral charge" (plus vocal music)—was one of the four areas to be taught, and one of the first three professors (John C. Granbery) was appointed to teach these subjects. Over the decades, the school's commitments to both scholarship and professional training intensified. The school applied the highest standards of scholarship to its professional and graduate programs, its faculty, and their research and pedagogy. At the same time, the practical field added both regular and adjunct faculty and utilized the adjacent schools, Scarritt College and Peabody College, for music and education.

With these increased commitments came conflicts over very deep values. Given a limited budget, how does a school adequately cover by way of faculty expertise the fields of its Ph.D. program and all of the subjects needed by active religious professionals? Should the school hire faculty members who are leading scholars in their fields but have little interest in ministry and its professional challenges? Should the school hire faculty to teach in practical theology areas who have little interest or ability in being "scholars"? How does the scholarly ideal figure in practical theology courses, and how can courses and seminars that embody a faculty member's ongoing research help students prepare for the activities of ministry? Throughout much of its history, the Divinity School has struggled with these questions, ever attempting to do justice to the demands of both critical scholarship and the needs of clergy education.

The Tension between the Scholarly Ideal and Social Praxis

Recent decades have seen an extensive literature on the education of clergy. Judged strictly on the basis of that literature, the primary issue would appear to be the conflict between "Athens" and "Berlin," or student formation and scholarly pursuits.[13] Judged by what actually took place in those decades, another set of issues is much more prominent: social justice, the struggles of oppressed minorities and women, and ethnic and religious pluralism. The civil rights struggles of the 1960s, the feminist movement, and the cause of gay and lesbian rights introduced radical changes in the seminaries. Hence, the most visible social change in the school was a new demography, a new population of faculty and students: African Americans, women, ethnic minorities, students from developing nations, gays and lesbians. Measured by curriculum, pedagogy, and the organization of fields, clergy education at the beginning of the new millennium may not look very different from a generation ago. On the other hand, the make-up of the student population and the faculty suggests something close to a revolution. Concern for social justice in the seminaries was not, to be sure, an invention of the 1960s. Protestant seminaries fully participated in the great watershed period of American religion, 1880 to 1920. One of the powerful movements of that era was the Social Gospel.[14] Accordingly, courses in sociology and applied Christianity began to appear in schools' offerings in the early 1900s. However, the Social Gospel fervor was not to last, declining, according to Conrad Cherry, by the 1930s. When H. Richard Niebuhr and others studied North American theological education in the 1950s, they concluded that ethics and social studies received "minimal attention" in most of the schools.[15]

It should be apparent why the scholarly ideal and social praxis are conflicting values in a theological school. Both rest on passions and evoke deep commitments: the one to discovery, knowledge, understanding, clarity, and intellectual honesty; the other to the alleviation of the sufferings that come with systemic oppression, moral indifference, and various kinds of racism. The one asks how a school can be a school without a determined and uncompromising pursuit of the scholarly ideal. The other asks how any institution is justified that does not try to change the world for the better, starting with itself and its own policies. These two commitments set the terms for ongoing debate over the aims, priorities, curriculum contents, faculty structure, and pedagogy of the school. While the population of American theological institutions has diversified, there does not seem to be as yet even a tentative consensus about how the scholarly ideal and social praxis merge in a vision of theological education.

While the four conflicts outlined above are intrinsic to the structure of divinity schools, they can evoke a range of responses. Each of these interpretive attempts to negotiate the conflicts shows how the two sides are related, as well as how the conflicts themselves are part of the larger agenda of theological education. In other words, the negotiation and interpretation of these tensions requires constructing a coherent philosophy (or theology) of clergy education, a task yet to be taken up by the majority of theological schools.

Shifting Curricula

One strand of a school's history is its ever-renewed attempts to frame an adequate course of study. The term *course of study* gathers up several dimensions: graduation requirements, symbols of successful completion (degrees, certificates), the ratio of required to elective courses, faculty specialties, and pedagogies (what actually happens between teacher and student). *Curriculum* names the school's course offerings taught by regular or part-time faculty members. *Encyclopedia* (as in "theological encyclopedia") refers to the way the courses are organized into areas or fields such as practical theology, ethics, or world religions, plus the rationale for such organization.[16]

The Divinity School's changing encyclopedia or way of organizing its fields is displayed through its past catalogues. Yet, a school's catalogues present only the fixed façade of its field organization. New types of studies, pedagogies, methods, and specialties may already be at work in the classroom, thus blurring old lines between fields and creating new areas that are not expressed in the catalogue. New and dynamic fields and ways of thinking about them may be at work in the school even when the catalogue organization of fields suggests that nothing new is afoot. Further, the organization of fields will be an expression of the set of negotiations that took place between the value conflicts built into the school. The terms *field* and *discipline* are not without ambiguities. The typical meaning is a scholarly specialty, thus a unity of subject matter, methods, technical language, and relatively clear boundaries. A rarer pedagogical meaning is that of an "area of study" in the students' course of study.

We should not be surprised to learn that a history of a school's course of study is a very entangled affair. At work in that history are the school's larger vision of its task and its basic commitments as they are polarized into conflicting values. Also at work are the primary values that determine what actually is included in the course of study: for instance, whether women's studies, field education, or history of religions are important enough to be listed as areas of study. Furthermore, any such history must record the major changes or shifts in graduation requirements, curriculum, and field organization. Easiest to spot are the shifts that are brought about in self-conscious, planned curriculum revisions. Harder to track are the small, momentary yet important changes that occur as the school responds to various events and trends in its cultural and scholastic environment.

In the case of Vanderbilt Divinity School, there are several identifiable shifts of curriculum and field organization. Needless to say, the further back one goes in the school's history, the less access there is to what prompted the change and the more dependent one has to be on catalogue records. In more recent cases—the "minister as theologian" curriculum, for instance—the long process of planning, debate, and construction is fully documented. Two things tend to happen in these shifts. First, the shift is an expression of an attempt to negotiate one or more of the basic conflicts or tensions. Second, its outcome tends to persist throughout later shifts. In other words, the shifts are usually not temporary changes that eventually become passé and are left behind, but rather are cumulative, semi-permanent accomplishments. In this sense, what the shifts accomplished remains with us and we are their beneficiaries.

The Biblical Department developed from a certificate-granting institution with no academic admission requirements (a letter from a student's Conference sufficed) and a wide range of student preparation to a theological school on the model of the best of the seminaries. Its first decade, in other words, saw it becoming a theological *school* in the full sense of the word. In the face of serious resistance in the Methodist Episcopal Church, South (MECS), and even in the Board of Trust, and under the leadership of Bishop Holland N. McTyeire, Chancellor James H. Kirkland, and Dean Tillett, the Biblical Department was soon able to require two years of college work for admission to its regular program, distinguish between different courses of study, and offer a Bachelor of Sacred Theology (from 1882, replaced in 1886 by the Bachelor of Divinity). The Department began with three professors (New Testament exegesis, systematic theology, and practical theology) with a planned fourth area, Hebrew and Old Testament exegesis.[17]

Broadening Purpose and Scope

After the turn of the century, several historical forces at work on the American religious scene pressed the school to revise its course of study. The Social Gospel's influence was clearly behind a new field, Applied Christianity, and such courses as "The Social Teachings of Jesus." In addition, Oratory and Expression (which later became Public Speaking and Debate) was offered as a new field. In 1903–4 the Correspondence Course, a long-time mainstay of the education of Methodist ministers, found its headquarters at Vanderbilt. In 1904–5 the Biblical Department underwent its first major curriculum change, which represented a broader understanding of its work. The school's "purpose and scope" was now preparation of students not just for the pastorate but for "missions, Sunday School work, and city evangelization." "Major" courses (four hours per week per term) and "minor" courses (two hours) were introduced, an anticipa-

tion of the core courses of the future. More important, the hitherto fully required curriculum was replaced by one permitting about one-third electives.
Nine areas of study (called "schools") were listed, including Biblical Theology
and English Exegesis, Practical Sociology, and Religious Education. The faculty had grown to five professors, plus adjuncts and instructors. Reflecting the
broadening—one might say liberalizing—of the course of study were the dramatic changes in Dean Tillett's offerings in systematic theology. In 1905–6 he
offered, in addition to the survey of doctrines, courses in "Christian Ethics,"
"Philosophy of Religion," "Theology of the Poets," and "Current Theology."
Shortly thereafter he added "Philosophy of Christian History."

A Nondenominational School of Religion

The second curriculum shift followed on the most important event of the
school's early history, the separation of the University from the oversight of the
MECS. After the break, both Kirkland and Tillett worked hard to retain in the
University a school for the education of Protestant ministers. This set the difficult task of surviving as the one university-related, nondenominational theological school in the South. As to the course of study, the break continued the
broadening tendencies already at work after the turn of the century. The new
name, the School of Religion, sounded the new direction. The new catalogue
statement announced a broadened, transdenominational, but Christian course
of study that shifted from a confessional Methodist orientation to a new set of
aims. "Religion in general" and "religion and ethics" rather than "theology"
was its focus. Further, in addition to preparing students for traditional Christian ministries, it would educate them for leadership in social service.[18] But the
course of study did not change dramatically. The primary change was the addition of a new department, Comparative Religion and Missions, with courses
in ancient religions, Hinduism, Buddhism, Islam, and Confucianism.[19] Curricular changes continued throughout the following decade. Dominating this
second shift was the tension between the broad commitments of the scholarly
ideal and the particular needs, agendas, and traditions of a specific Protestant
denomination.

Toward a New Nomenclature

The period between 1914 and 1940 saw few major changes in the course of
study. Throughout most of this period, only a handful of students actually
graduated each year with the B.D. degree, and until the 1930s the size of the
faculty remained at five or six professors, plus associates or lecturers. Neither

practical theology nor practical sociology (formerly "applied Christianity") had chairs in the faculty. One development of the 1920s was a curriculum in religious education. A professor was hired in the field who also taught sociology. The number of fields decreased from twelve in 1930–31 to seven in 1935–36. This change resulted from a reorganization that placed fields under other fields, rather than a fundamental rethinking of the fields themselves.

In the opening years of the 1940s, however, a rethinking of fields and curriculum did occur. Two features stand out. First, the criteria for identifying fields were primarily pedagogical rather than by specialty identities. Second, the new organization constituted a break from the standard four-fold division of theological disciplines. Three of the five fields were standard: Bible, Christian Historical Development, and Religions of Mankind. A fourth, called "The Religious Interpretation of the World and Man," included the subfields Philosophy of Religion, Psychology of Religion, Christian Theology, Christian Ethics, and Social Thought. The underlying motif of all of these subfields was "interpretation" or constructive thinking. They were thought of not so much as disciplines isolated from each other as different aspects of a common enterprise. The fifth field, "The Work of the Church at Home and Abroad," gathered up missions, religious education, practical theology, and ecumenics. In 1942 a sixth, "The Church and Community," was not so much a gathering of fields as of institutions. It was a way of listing course offerings at Scarritt, Peabody, and the Graduate School of Vanderbilt in sociology, anthropology, folk arts, and other areas. These changes of the early 1940s enriched the curriculum, especially at the point of such extra-theological subjects as culture, world religions, and types of world interpretation.

The new nomenclature did not last long. By 1944 the curriculum had returned to the standard four fields plus sociology, and in what now appears to be a regressive move, comparative religions was placed under historical studies. Thus, after almost seventy-five years, the school returned to the four-fold organization of fields in place at the time of its founding. After World War II, an ever-larger percentage of required courses appeared in the course of study.[20]

Practical Theology Comes of Age

The fourth curricular shift in the school's history was not so much the result of a deliberate curriculum revision as of one of the most important grants ever made to the school. In the memorandum to the Sealantic Fund (prepared, it seems, by Divinity faculty), Chancellor Harvie Branscomb pointed out that its grant (eventually announced to be $2.9 million in 1955) would turn the Divinity School into "a school of national significance and broad regional influence."[21] The proposal contained a variety of items, but emphasized the needs for a new building and an enlarged faculty, especially in the area of practical theology. A decade after the Sealantic gift, a new Divinity quadrangle had been built, the faculty had doubled in size, and the practical theology area had undergone a major rejuvenation.

At the time of the school's founding, practical theology was restricted to homiletics, polity, and pastoral care, although it also offered public speaking and debate, vocal music, and religious education. But early on the school lost its professor of practical theology so that through most of its early history (until 1956), these subjects were taught by other members of the faculty, by local clergy, and by Scarritt (music) and Peabody (education).[22] The appeal to the Sealantic Fund asked for three professors in practical theology: homiletics, church administration, and pastoral counseling. Thus, in the late 1950s the first professors of practical theology since the early days of the school joined the faculty: James Glasse in church administration and fieldwork (1956), Ronald Sleeth in homiletics (1957), and Arthur Foster in pastoral counseling (1959). These initial appointments began the school's continuing commitment to the practical theology areas as disciplines in the fullest sense of the word. The results were many: the creation of field work (later, field education), doctoral programs in pastoral psychology and homiletics, the Doctor of Ministry degree, and the development of joint degree programs with other schools.[23]

With the Sealantic grant and the new status of practical theology, the Divinity School moved into a period in which the tension between its commitments to the scholarly ideal and professional education intensified. The creation of the practical faculty coincided with the creation and infancy of the new graduate program. In the broader setting of theological education in the United States, both pastoral theology and homiletics were on their way to becoming academic fields, with their own Ph.D. programs, technical literature, and field-wide language. At the same time, the mainline denominations were discovering psychology, and "the minister as professional" was about to enter theological education as its dominant unifying model. Such developments set the stage for faculty members to identify themselves with one side or the other of an academic or practical polarity. Additionally, broader social and political developments, including the Vietnam War, student protests, civil rights, and the anti-authority subcultures of the 1960s, were about to erupt, setting the stage for the school's next curriculum shift.

Paris Landing and After

Even before the 1957 publication of the study of theological education by H. Richard Niebuhr, Daniel Day Williams, and James M. Gustafson, North

American seminaries experimented with curricular change. [24] These curricula of the 1950s exemplify the post–World War II trend toward a largely required curriculum that peaked at the end of the decade.[25] In the 1960s seminaries began to reduce the number of required courses. By 1966–67 only 54 of the 90 total hours for graduation were specifically required at Vanderbilt Divinity School. At this time, two movements were on a collision course. In the larger culture, the student protests were increasingly radicalized.[26] In addition to debates over and protests against the Vietnam War, the most passionate issue for students was that of institutional authority. A broad discreditation of the adult culture and its institutions, plus a kind of aesthetic narcissism in the youth culture, mobilized a determined revolt against hierarchical determinations of degree requirements, specified courses, and grades. In the midst of all of this, the Divinity faculty in 1965 set a committee to work to revise the curriculum. After two years of meetings, the committee brought its new curriculum to the faculty meeting at Tennessee's Paris Landing State Park in April 1967.

The committee's document was thoughtful and inventive, but, all in all, it was more a continuation than a break with the mood of the 1950s.[27] The major ideas and aims of the new curriculum were solid ("profound excellence," acquaintance with the work of all five areas, "theological work as holistic," minimizing of field lines), and ten years later they might have been accepted. However, in 1967 the faculty would have little of it. At Paris Landing the ethos of the 1960s and concern for a basic core of requirements collided. The faculty responded in two stages. In the first (at Paris Landing), it rejected the proposed required curriculum but adopted a few items that became valuable curriculum additions: A Doctor of Divinity degree program was begun, and a Senior Seminar was retained from the committee's proposals as the place where the student integrated "academic instruction" and "professional practice."[28] In the second, at a retreat in 1970–71 at Montgomery Bell State Park, the faculty adopted a largely laissez-faire curriculum that was typical of many seminaries at the time.

This curriculum was not utterly lacking of requirements.[29] But the key phrase in the catalogue noted that "each student is encouraged to plan his own program." While all four conflicts or tensions built into the life of the Divinity School were present, two of them are especially prominent in the curriculum shift of 1970–71. The first is the tension between the scholarly ideal and student formation. The formation issue dominated the ethos of the 1960s. At first sight that would not seem to be the case, since students were protesting this very issue—the presumption of educational institutions that they had the right and the ability to form students in ways that they chose. Yet the non-authoritarian alternative remained an issue of formation, the assumption being that students mature (are formed) best in a non-authoritarian and laissez-faire course of study. According to this approach, formation takes place by way of the withdrawal of authority, and by bestowing on the students the freedom to determine their own course of study.

As to the second conflict, the 1970s began the era of "the minister as professional" in North American theological education, one that to a certain degree still continues.[30] This model gradually entered the school as the result of the new commitment to practical theology and field education that began with the Sealantic grant. By 1966–67, the practical theology faculty included six professors plus a number of adjunct appointments. In this same period the school first made a concerted effort to appoint minorities and women to the faculty. In the 1970s, the mood of the general culture, and thus the seminaries, began to move away from laissez-faire pedagogy to an increased willingness to determine the direction of student formation. In addition, serious questions began to be raised about the model of the minister as professional. By the late 1970s these changes of mood prompted the Divinity School to reexamine the prevailing presuppositions of theological education. The result was the sixth major shift in the course of study in the school's history.

"The Minister as Theologian"

Five years after the school dropped most of its required core curriculum, it had become clear that its course of study was not adequately preparing students for leadership in the religious or secular worlds. Yet the faculty had little enthusiasm for another curriculum revision. When the Lilly Endowment offered Dean Sallie McFague a small discretionary fund in 1976, she proposed to use it for faculty development. That meant specifically the opportunity for the faculty to come together in workshops, weekend retreats, and seminars on such basic problems as the relation between the Bible and ethics, theology and ministry, and the problems and possibilities of theological education. In 1977 a Curriculum and Theological Education (CTE) committee was created to assist the school in an extensive examination of these issues. Thus followed five years of committee meetings, student forums, on- or off-campus retreats, faculty seminars, and a national conference on theological education.[31] The result was the course of study announced in the catalogue of 1980–81. However one assesses the details of this new curriculum, the process of arriving at it was a remarkable event in the history of the school, virtually a model for what it takes for a faculty to develop and implement a major shift in the course of study. It confirmed what everyone suspected, that mutual intellectual engagement between faculty members on issues outside of each one's specialty and area of teaching comes only with determined commitment to time-consuming, collegial labor. Only such cooperative intellectual work could have drawn the faculty beyond the level of obtaining curriculum change by mere political negotiation.[32]

Looming over the whole inquiry and explicitly addressed by the CTE Committee were the tensions between the scholarly ideal and professional education, and between the scholarly ideal and student formation. As to the first tension, the faculty was dissatisfied with a theory/practice way of thinking that emptied the practical, professional, and functional side of the course of study of scholarly commitments and isolated theology, ethics, Bible, and church history into mere "theory." With respect to the second tension, it sensed that separated fields, with their technical language and methods, left students without any single interpretive way of existing as religious leaders. Students were thus trapped in the situation of having to bridge a number of theoretical methods to the situations of ministry. The new course of study found expression in the phrase "minister as theologian." The notion of "theology" and "theologian" in the phrase cut in both negative and positive directions. Negatively, it described the religious leader as one who had the resources to oppose and transcend secularist, bureaucratic, ideological, moralistic, and privatistic forms of religion. Positively, it claimed that, however "professional" a minister was, what made that person a minister was the ability to bring interpretive insights into every ministerial, churchly, and social activity. Accordingly, a *theological* education was first of all a forming of that ability, and all the teaching areas of the school should play a part in this forming. Furthermore, the CTE Committee proposed that three crucial but always intertwined educational "moments" were necessary to this formation: *representation*, in which the student engages the content and heritage of Christianity; *appropriation*, the grasp and interpretation of that faith in contemporary and critical modes of understanding; and *incorporation*, the embodiment of that faith in social organization and human activity. These three moments together specify what the term "minister as theologian" actually means. Further, not only should the total set of courses, foundational or elective, contribute to these moments; each area of study and the courses offered should embody in some way all three moments. Thus, for instance, preaching, pastoral counseling, or education call for interpretive acts in which all three moments converge. They are not, in other words, simply fields of "application."

The course of study itself was a departure from most other seminary curriculums in three respects. First, it proposed that all the courses in the Foundational Curriculum (Bible, history, Christian theology, etc.) function not simply as an introduction to a scholarly discipline but as a resource and beginning of theological formation, defined by the three moments. All should play a part in moving the student toward critical, theological interpretation. With this in mind, new introductory courses were added and traditional ones were revised. Second, it proposed a way for students to plan and experience coherence in the elective part of their course of study. The CTE Committee proposed a way for each student to plan, with a faculty adviser, a coherent pattern of elective studies called the Program Focus. Here the student takes responsibility for her or his own post-foundational education. While spontaneous interests unrelated to an overall rationale were not ruled out, the Program Focus idea emphasized discovering a route through the elective curriculum that correlated with the student's deepest personal and professional interests. The planning itself was meant to be an educational experience, bestowing on the student's program a certain unity and even an accumulating interpretive or hermeneutic competence. The Program Focus thus retained elements of the 1960s laissez-faire curriculum and the old idea of a major, now redefined as a coherent pattern of elective studies. Third, the faculty decided to replace the old organization of fields with a pattern whose main aim was to assist the student in thinking about his or her Program Focus. These six areas were called Tools and Methods (including languages), Formative Periods and Literatures, the Historical Course of Christianity (including thematic histories), Constructive Interpretation, the Contemporary Religious Situation, and the Dimensions and Tasks of Christian Ministry.[33] While the curriculum of 1980–81 has undergone changes over the years, both the extended process that brought it about and the determination to frame an educational experience that forms students by way of a unifying interpretive ability may be the enduring legacy of the "minister as theologian" era.

Intensified Commitments to Praxis and Pluralism

A comparison of the Divinity School's faculty and course offerings of 1985–86 to those of 1999–2000 reveals one dramatic change. In 1985–86 the faculty included four women and one Hispanic male, but no African Americans. Three courses on themes of gender and women and two courses on African American themes were listed, each of the latter taught by Lewis Baldwin of the Department of Religious Studies. In 1999–2000 the faculty included six women, three African Americans, and one Hispanic, plus African American and women adjunct professors. Two courses were offered on issues relating to homosexuality, ten courses on subjects of women and gender, eleven on the black church and the black experience, most of them in a new curricular area, the Black Church; and the Carpenter Program in Religion, Gender, and Sexuality had been established. Thus, in thirteen years, issues pertaining to women, minorities, and gays and lesbians had come to occupy an important place in the school's course of study. This change was not brought about by a single curriculum revision. It took place gradually as the school became increasingly committed to and successful at attracting minority and women faculty whose presence added new resources and dimensions to the curriculum and the life of the school. However, a two-year period of student protest (1986–88) was the primary motivator in pressing the school to intensify its commitments to gender and minority issues.

Vanderbilt Divinity School has had a long history of involvement with social justice matters.[34] Faculty were involved in the Social Gospel and issues of racial discrimination in the early history of the school. In the fall of 1960, following the Lawson affair, the faculty adopted a report that declared an intention to recruit African American students, hold conferences on such subjects as "race relations," take up the task of "engaging in criticism of the culture," and be a prophetic voice in the University.[35] In the spring of 1978, many of the students and faculty as well as the dean of the school protested the University's decision to host a Davis Cup tennis match at Vanderbilt in which apartheid South Africa participated. Throughout most of the school's history, the conflicts and issues were invariably between the school and its external environment: the general culture, the city of Nashville, the University. In 1986–88 the conflict was internal, and the curriculum was only one among many points of the controversy. One result of that engagement, if not a new curricular structure, was at least a new dimension to the curriculum, and with that a renewed alertness to racial, gender, and gay and lesbian issues.

Conclusion

The story of Vanderbilt's course of study is one of abandonments, accumulations, and new commitments. Abandoned were the denominational ethos and orthodoxies of the early years and the exclusion of women and minorities that was standard in the first half of the twentieth century. Early on the school became committed to a transdenominational and liberal theological education of ministers. Through the twentieth century, the school made permanent commitments to critical scholarship, the importance of practical theology, social justice and praxis, and religious pluralism. Religious faiths other than Christianity still remain marginal to the course of study, and the place of the arts, present in the first decades of the school's history, is not currently an issue. Although "religious studies" is the primary self-understanding of the undergraduate Department of Religious Studies and certain Divinity School faculty members, its relation to the "theological studies" of the Divinity School has yet to be articulated. The global setting of theological education is beginning to be discussed, and global and social issues of world change continue to surface. There is, in other words, a kind of hidden fermentation of issues that will no doubt come to the surface in the school's future determinations of its course of study.

Graduate Studies in Religion

Eugene TeSelle

T HE ROLE OF GRADUATE STUDIES AT VANDERBILT UNIVERSITY HAS been affected by the contrasting visions that were present from the founding of the University. Some wanted a theological school that would train an educated ministry for the Methodist Episcopal Church, South (MECS). Other visionaries wanted a church-sponsored university that would rival those of the Northeast, and some of these believed theological education was a subordinate concern. The founding of Vanderbilt as the "Central University" of the southern Methodists resulted from a coalition of the two groups.[1]

Tensions between regional and national frames of reference were probably fated from the beginning. Nashville has always been a point of transition between South and North. Cornelius Vanderbilt's gift was given with the hope that it would "contribute . . . to strengthening the ties that should exist between all geographical sections of our common country."[2] Vanderbilt has thought of itself in national terms from the beginning, especially where research and graduate studies are concerned; in turn Vanderbilt often has played the role of "token southerner" or "honorary Yankee," one of the few southern schools that the northern universities considered to be part of their own group.

It is probably fortunate that these varying aspirations have been efficacious in the subsequent history of the University, causing repeated identity crises that were painful but also stimulating and ultimately beneficial. Especially when it comes to graduate studies, the University has been constantly influenced by wider currents in the intellectual world and in society. At the same time it has had to respond to these in its own place, with its own resources, and, inevitably, under the pressures of the moment.

The first and most notorious crisis centered on Alexander Winchell, a professor of geology who championed the theory of evolution and specifically the existence of human beings before Adam. Because of Methodist opposition, his appointment was not renewed and the position was abolished in 1878. Several years later an anonymous southerner wrote to *The Nation*, commenting that "Vanderbilt University . . . which ere this should have been a Cornell or an Ann Arbor, is now not much more than a large theological seminary, where the free discussion of scientific truth will not be tolerated." The correspondent went on to call the MECS, the largest and most influential denomination in the region, "the bulwark which opposes all liberalizing tendencies of our Southern denominations."[3] Despite the negative image associated with the Winchell affair, Vanderbilt continued to be listed with Cornell and the University of Michigan, Harvard and Yale, as one of a small group of leading universities in the country.[4]

Vanderbilt's chancellors tried to make the University less "sectarian" to broaden its faculty, student body, and funding base. The link with the MECS was purposefully limited to the Biblical Department. Chancellor Kirkland, aware of the difficulties posed by the sectarian status of Vanderbilt when he sought Carnegie funding for the Medical School and tried to persuade the George Peabody School for Teachers to move near Vanderbilt, worked carefully to diminish denominational ties. The court decision in 1914 siding with the University was widely regarded as a victory for higher education and academic freedom.[5]

Graduate study and the Ph.D. degree came to the United States based on the German model, precociously at Yale in 1861 and more normatively (that is, setting the precedent for many other universities) in 1876 at Johns Hopkins University. The latter was founded about the same time as Vanderbilt and was its only rival in the South for endowment and income, but it quickly outpaced Vanderbilt in academic achievement. The first Ph.D. degrees at Vanderbilt were given in 1879, in Greek and chemistry, followed by several other fields, not including religion.[6] The M.A. was awarded by the Academic Department, later the College of Arts and Science; students in the School of Religion could pursue the M.A. jointly with their studies for the ministry.

For several decades the most distinguished Vanderbilt faculty members were two specialists in ancient philology, who published the Vanderbilt Oriental Series (nine volumes, 1899–1918). J. H. Stevenson, professor of Hebrew and Old Testament, an expert in Assyrian and Babylonian cuneiform texts, often was attacked by southern Methodists for his approach to the Bible. Herbert

Cushing Tolman, professor of Greek, was a product of Berlin, an expert not only in Greek but also in Sanskrit and Old Persian, on which he published a number of studies. He led the movement to organize the Alpha of Tennessee chapter of Phi Beta Kappa in 1901, and his program was the only one to which new Ph.D. students were admitted during Vanderbilt's time of troubles.[7]

A fire in Kirkland Hall in 1905 that destroyed the library, as well as the break with the MECS jeopardizing financial support, led to the suspension of Ph.D. programs in 1918. Master of Arts programs continued to be offered, however, and during the 1920s Ph.D. programs were slowly revived, with a formal announcement in 1927.[8] Graduate study in religion lagged far behind because of the financial difficulties of the School of Religion during the 1920s and 1930s.

Early Years of the Graduate Department of Religion

John Keith Benton became dean of the School of Religion in 1939; he led it out of financial difficulties, enlarged the student body, and enhanced its role in the American Association of Theological Schools. Under his leadership a Department of Religion was established in the Graduate School in 1942, including seven faculty members and offering the M.A. in three programs (Biblical Studies, Historical Studies, and Philosophical and Theological Studies). The understanding of the faculty was that "all of our work, except the practical courses, were recognized as being of graduate quality," and that "there is no essential difference between the programs and courses offered for the Divinity degree, and the so-called Graduate degrees."[9] The M.A. involved one year of study beyond the B.D. (Bachelor of Divinity), or two years of study beyond the B.A. degree.

In 1946, just before Chancellor Harvie Branscomb arrived, the Department of Religion was authorized to offer the Ph.D. degree in Biblical Studies alone. The faculty was augmented by two members of the School of Theology in the University of the South at Sewanee, ninety miles southeast of Nashville, James Fleming in Old Testament and Robert M. Grant in New Testament. Benton pointed out that "no other Southern institution except Duke University is offering work leading to the doctorate; since Vanderbilt occupies a central position in this region, the Ph.D. program, though limited to Biblical Literature, will serve a great need in preparing teachers in the field of Religion and in stimulating and attracting scholars to this center."[10] Duke was the natural model, the regional school with which Vanderbilt inevitably compared itself. Emory University and Southern Methodist University were more clearly denominational, with bishops on their boards, while Duke, though related to the Methodist Church, did not have the same provisions for church control.

In 1950 the Department was permitted to offer the Ph.D. in Theological Studies, and a Ph.D. in Historical Studies was approved in 1955–56.[11] Although students in Biblical Studies could minor either within the department or outside it, those in Theological Studies were expected to minor in Philosophy, and those in Historical Studies in History. The Philosophy Department had been separated from the Department of Psychology and Philosophy in 1950; after an uncertain start, leadership was supplied by Samuel Stumpf, John Compton, and Philip Hallie. Members of the History Department who were especially helpful included Paul Hardacre in the Tudor and Stuart periods, Dayton Phillips in medieval studies, and Henry Swint in American intellectual history.

The Academic Study of Religion: National Trends

Graduate study in religion began at Vanderbilt, as at most institutions, as a continuation and extension of the study of Christianity that was conducted in theological schools. This never meant, however, that it lacked "critical distance"; increasingly it came to involve historical and philological study of all religious traditions, the use of comparative methods, and the application of psychological and sociological approaches to religious phenomena. Yale Divinity School was called the School of Religion between 1914 and 1920; Vanderbilt, whose denominational ties had just been severed, followed suit. Chancellor Kirkland stated this new understanding at the climax of his address during the semicentennial observance of the founding of Vanderbilt in 1925: "The answer to the episode at Dayton [the "Scopes trial"] is the building of new laboratories on the Vanderbilt campus for the teaching of science. The remedy for a narrow sectarianism and a belligerent fundamentalism is the establishment on this campus of a School of Religion illustrating in its methods and in its organization the strength of a common faith and the glory of a universal worship."[12]

The character of the academic study of religion was shaped by several professional societies that functioned both for peer review of scholars' work and as "reference groups" for their sense of identity. The Society of Biblical Literature and Exegesis had been organized in 1880, and it remained the chief scholarly group in the field.[13] In 1908 the Conference of Biblical Instructors (renamed in 1922 the National Association of Biblical Instructors) was organized to deal with pedagogical issues in colleges and secondary schools. Its very existence reflected three related changes in the study of religion. Undergraduate study of Hebrew and Greek at Harvard and Yale had steadily declined during the nineteenth century; research-oriented chairs of Semitic languages and literatures were established at major universities, in several cases involving Jewish scholars; and courses in "Biblical Literature" or "English Bible" began to be offered at the college level—first at Yale, then at Bryn Mawr College, Smith College, and Wellesley College, reflecting a pan-Protestant interest in the Bible beyond all differences of denominations.[14] Although predominantly male and Protestant, both organizations included women and Jews among their members and leaders.

In 1922 Charles Foster Kent organized the Council of Schools of Religion to encourage the "schools of religion" that were beginning to be associated with midwestern state universities, clearly differentiated from college chaplaincies and student religious organizations. Before long the Council saw the need to recruit outstanding students to undertake graduate study in the field, and in 1923 nine "fellows" were selected. In 1924 the Council was reorganized as the National Council on Religion in Higher Education, broadening its concerns to all institutions of higher education. To be elected a fellow was an indication not only of intellectual accomplishment but also of a broad perspective on religion, especially as understood from the standpoint of the northern tier of universities. Placement activities became a major emphasis, and college deans or presidents often turned to the Council for recommendations.[15]

Vanderbilt's graduate department was one of the ten founding members of the Council on Graduate Studies in Religion (CGSR) in 1947, formed at the invitation of the American Council of Learned Societies. It was made up of those schools that offered a Ph.D. in religion and whose admissions and programs were controlled by graduate schools rather than theological institutions. Its purposes were to determine the functions of graduate study in religion in light of current vocational needs, to formulate standards of instruction, and to guide and stimulate research.[16] In 1950 the CGSR underwent a brief identity crisis. Some felt that "its functions had been taken over, at least in part, by the Committee on the History of Religions of the American Council of Learned Societies"; so the Council decided to continue its existence "in a state of suspended animation." Within a few months there was agreement that the Council should be continued, because it had a task that the Committee on the History of Religions could not perform.[17] In 1952 it began publishing an annual list of dissertations in religion. It continues to meet annually to discuss the nature of Ph.D. programs in religion, standards, and statistical information. Although the Council makes no claim to be an accrediting agency, it does formulate expectations for member institutions, and admission to its ranks is a sign of status.

Development and Growth, 1950s and 1960s

The 1950s were years of promise in the world of theological education. Harvard's Divinity School was revitalized after 1956. Scholarship programs for doctoral study were made available by the Rockefeller Foundation and the Lilly Endowment. At Vanderbilt, plans were developing for a new Divinity School building, for an increase in the size of the Divinity (and, hence, graduate) faculty, and for increasing the school's visibility beyond the region. In 1957 Acting Dean Hyatt wrote to Chancellor Branscomb about a conversation with the Jesuit scholar Gustave Weigel, suggesting the appointment of a Roman Catholic to the faculty and listing a number of possible candidates.[18] Although nothing came of this, and the first appointment of a Roman Catholic to the faculty did not occur until 1973, it showed an enhanced ecumenical consciousness in the school.

The "Lawson affair" was at its height during the dedication of the new Divinity School quadrangle on March 21, 1960, preceded by a major conference on theological education. It was a defining moment for graduate studies, not only in religion but also in the University as a whole. When most Divinity School faculty members submitted their resignations, its graduate program, rated among the best in the country, was clearly in jeopardy. When other faculty members—including distinguished and highly mobile researchers in the sciences and the Medical School—also signed statements in support and threatened to resign, the stature of research throughout the Graduate School and its national image were at stake.[19]

In the aftermath of the "Lawson affair," the American Association of Theological Schools sent an investigating team and placed the Divinity School on probation for one year while it determined whether the school's high standing would be maintained. In October 1960, probably in connection with this investigation, the faculty prepared "The Purpose of the Divinity School." Although the document authors began with the education of ministers and took note of the school's relation to the churches in the South, they devoted considerable space to "Our Place in the University," acknowledging that "it is this very relationship to the University which enables us to profess religion with freedom in an atmosphere of scholarly, critical inquiry." The most concrete form of engagement with the University, it said, is the graduate program, qualifying students as college teachers, just as the University had long been doing in other fields. The document concluded with the observation, heard throughout the life of the Graduate Department of Religion (GDR), that "the Ph.D. program enhances the intellectual character of the B.D. program, as long as it is carried out on a modest level, while the B.D. program helps to prevent the Ph.D. program from becoming abstract, intellectual dilettantism, unrelated to the concrete religious life of the churches."[20]

The decade of the 1960s, when the baby boomers entered college, was a period of growth in student enrollments, job opportunities, and interest in graduate study. The nature of the field was also shifting as the "critical study of religion" gained new institutional force. The faculty of the graduate program at Vanderbilt expanded significantly during the second half of the decade, and both the faculty and the nature of the programs reflected these new nationwide developments.

In many state universities the long-standing interest in making religion the subject of academic instruction and research continued and intensified. Several organizational strategies had been tried. The safest, avoiding both First Amendment difficulties and conflict among denominations, was to give academic credit for courses offered by an independently funded "school of religion" or "chairs" in particular religions. Some state schools, however, were already trying other patterns: departments of religion, courses in religion within the department of philosophy, or interdepartmental "programs" in religion.[21]

Legal uncertainties were resolved with the Supreme Court's *Abingdon v. Schempp* decision in 1963, legitimating the study of religion at all levels of public education "when presented objectively as part of a secular program of education."[22] Although the First Amendment and various federal laws for aid to education kept state-supported institutions—and in fact *all* institutions that received federal funds—from "teaching religion" or "training ministers of religion," they were able to "teach *about* religion." In state universities it was necessary, then, to develop a clearly nonsectarian approach, examining religion as a human phenomenon and bracketing ultimate questions of meaning, truth, and value. The tag phrase for this approach soon came to be "religious studies" (as contrasted with "theology" or "theological studies"). On this basis most of the "schools of religion" were soon incorporated into the universities as departments like all the others. Potential employment for Ph.D.s thus expanded well beyond the traditional constituencies of private undergraduate colleges, theological seminaries, and university divinity schools.

The *Journal of the Society for the Scientific Study of Religion* first appeared in 1961.[23] In 1963 the National Association of Biblical Instructors voted to reorganize itself as the American Academy of Religion (AAR). This involved a major change of identity in at least three respects: its focus shifted from pedagogical to research interests, it sought to include all scholars and teachers whose concerns were centered upon religion, and the organization became a major voice for the "academic study of religion."[24] Its annual conference, after 1970 conducted jointly with the Society of Biblical Literature (SBL), became an increasingly important venue for scholarly presentations, discussions of academic policy and politics, and placement interviews.[25] For a time the Society for the Scientific Study of Religion met with the AAR/SBL, but in the mid-1970s it withdrew and has since held its own annual conferences. The tension evident since the late nineteenth century continues: some insist that the study of religion be "objective" or "scientific" or "critical," whereas others feel that it is sufficient for it to be pluralistic in scope and free from control by religious organizations.

An example of this tension occurred when Yale's undergraduate Department of Religious Studies, established in 1947, was expanded in 1963 to include the graduate program. The Department was instantly set in contrast with the Divinity School, although there were many joint appointments, and other faculty members of the Divinity School participated by invitation in the graduate work of the Department. At Duke the graduate program had always been administered by an executive council distinct from the Divinity School and more closely related to the undergraduate Department of Religion.[26]

In the churches, the spirit of ecumenism affected both Protestants and Catholics. Denominational seminaries became less insistent upon denominational identity or ministerial experience when they hired faculty members; because many members of their faculty had come through the major graduate programs, these schools began to look more and more like the faculties of departments of religious studies in colleges and universities. The Ph.D. degree came to be the "common coin" of scholarship in the field of religion, and denominational schools like Notre Dame and Princeton Theological Seminary began to award the Ph.D. as their highest degree in 1966 and 1973, respectively.[27]

Because of all these factors, the traditional student pattern of moving through the B.D. or Master of Divinity (M.Div.) program before entering M.A./ Ph.D. study began to decline. It had always been possible at Vanderbilt to go directly from the B.A. into a two-year M.A. program and then into the Ph.D. program, but there was a noticeable acceleration of this pattern after 1960 in most graduate schools. Although it happened more slowly at Vanderbilt than at other institutions, there were some side effects in this development: a tendency to specialize in one area too soon, and a tendency to separate the interests of those in the graduate program from those in the Divinity School even in the study of the same subjects.

The College of Arts and Science Gets a Department

Starting in 1949 the University's professors of Jewish Literature and Thought, first Samuel Sandmel and then Lou Silberman, held primary appointments in the Graduate School's Department of Religion. In the catalogues of the School of Religion they were listed along with several others as "members of the Graduate School offering courses in the School of Religion." It was about this time that courses in religion also began to be offered in the College. At first these courses, taught primarily by George Mayhew and by Sandmel and then Silberman, were offered in the Division of Humanities and described as offering "general courses . . . which do not pertain to the work of any specific department." College courses in religion began to be listed separately in 1953–54. A "program" in religion (without a major) was begun in 1956–57 under the direction of a faculty committee chaired by Dean Ewing Shahan.

In 1964 Winston L. King joined Silberman and Richard Mead in teaching courses in the College, and they requested the College faculty to transform the Committee on Course Instruction in Religion to a full-fledged Department of Religion that could offer a "concentration" or major in the field. The Educational Policy Committee of the College brought a proposal before the Faculty Council and then to the full faculty. All those who were involved knew that there would be dissension. There were self-proclaimed "Voltaireans" who felt that religion had no place in a university, and high Anglicans who were convinced that only the churches were competent to teach religion.[28] Some were afraid of evangelism in the classroom; others were convinced that another department would mean less money for existing departments. The minutes of the faculty meeting, although they do not reflect all of these views, record a heated debate.[29]

A motion to refer the proposal to the Council for further consideration was supported by Avery Leiserson, who argued that (1) "religion is best taught as part of philosophy, history, psychology and political science" (the latter being his field); (2) in the study of religion "the emphasis is too much on content and lacks an analytic approach"; and (3) with some ingenuity a better way could be found to instruct students in religion. King in reply noted that religion is an important aspect of human culture and that the study of religion uses "an objective approach," not "advocacy." Silberman, too, emphasized the scholarly approach, pointing out that religion is generally considered to be an academic discipline. Charles Scott of the Philosophy Department noted "the distinction between the study of and the confession of religion" and said that in all reputable departments the approach is academic. The motion to refer was defeated by a vote of 28 to 45. Taking the advocates at their word, Leiserson moved that the name be changed to the Department of Religious Studies. The recommendation as amended was finally approved by a 48-to-24 vote.

Silberman and King already held joint appointments in the Divinity School and the Graduate Department; but neither Richard Mead, chair of the department, nor Charles Hambrick, newly arrived to teach in the History of Religions, held positions in both departments. The matter was resolved in 1969 with a unanimous vote by the GDR "that those faculty members of the College Department of Religious Studies at the rank of Assistant Professor or above who are engaged in teaching and research in areas of the discipline of religion in which graduate study is currently offered by the Graduate Department of Religion shall be invited to become members of the Graduate Department of Religion."[30]

Diversification of Programs

In the late 1960s the GDR, with its enlarged faculty resources, carried out a major restructuring of graduate programs. The programs had included Biblical Studies, Historical Studies (including History of Religions), and Theological Studies (including Psychology of Religion and Ethics). In 1968 separate Ph.D. programs in History of Christian Thought and in Ethics, together with an M.A. program in Non-Western Religions, were added. At the same time the course listings in the catalogue were rearranged according to a "religious studies" model, with three broad areas (Linguistic and Methodological, History and Literature, and Analysis and Interpretation) providing the framework for the several programs of study. Because students had difficulties understanding the classification and locating courses, and because the faculty themselves had not embraced the new arrangement, the catalogue from 1984–85 reverted to a listing of the programs of study (at the same time substituting "Hebrew Bible" for the Christian term "Old Testament").

From its inception the GDR had emphasized the traditional "academic" disciplines, but later it moved into the more "practical" aspects of theology and religious studies in two areas. In 1973 a Ph.D. program in Religion and Personality was approved, requiring study in psychological theory, in a particular religious tradition, and clinical experience. The program thus prepared graduates for work in academic, religious, or clinical settings. A Ph.D. program in Homiletics was approved in 1987, a major feature of which was the requirement of "collateral work" (twenty-four hours) in another program in the GDR (the equivalent of a major) as well as twenty-four hours in homiletics. Each of these programs, in other words, was always supported by work in the more traditional "academic" fields and could not be accused of being "merely practical." The Homiletics program was suspended a decade later because of diminished faculty resources, but the rationale continues to be affirmed by the department.

A program in History and Critical Theories of Religion (quickly termed HACTOR) was inaugurated in 1993, accomplishing something that had been contemplated for several decades. A 1976 study of the GDR found that its ranking had not changed, but found "one major gap," work in the history or phenomenology of religion that would better prepare graduates for teaching in college or university settings. It was always clear that Vanderbilt was not in a position to compete with established programs in Buddhist, Hindu, or Islamic

Studies.[31] The HACTOR program focuses its attention upon and expects students to deal with (a) critical theories of religion, (b) interdisciplinary methods based on these theories, and (c) actual religious beliefs and practices in specific cultural contexts, past and present (including an "experiential" or "field work" component). Faculty members are based primarily in the Department of Religious Studies, but the program also draws upon faculty members in anthropology, philosophy, and sociology, as well as upon several Divinity faculty members who also teach in other programs in the GDR. The new program has functioned as both a major and a minor area, broadening the context in which Christianity and Judaism are studied.

Decades of Questioning

The years since 1970 have seen many evaluations, reviews, and self-studies in the field of religion.[32] The vogue for evaluation was stimulated by the unprecedented expansion of almost all programs of study during the 1960s, by the interest in black studies and women's studies and world religions, and by financial stringencies in institutions that had expanded their faculties to meet the boom in enrollment and later found themselves faced with static budgets and diminished opportunities for faculty renewal. In addition, there has been increasing and sometimes frenzied interest in rankings, both of individual programs and of colleges and universities. When rankings are at stake and there is competition for scarce funds, evaluations are not carried out from sheer intellectual curiosity; the very existence of a program can be at stake. The Divinity School and the GDR have repeatedly been ranked among the top five to ten programs nationwide, and within the University this has helped to ward off criticisms based on finances or distrust of the academic study of religion.

The academic job market, vigorous during the 1960s because the baby boomers were in college, declined sharply after 1970. At the same time the increase in Ph.D. programs and the number of students in them produced a surplus of Ph.D.s.[33] The situation did not change for the next thirty years. Graduate students have been responsible for most of the recent increase in membership in the AAR and SBL. The joint Graduate Student Caucus of the two organizations became increasingly active in the 1990s, calling attention to issues such as teaching assistantships, the job market, and temporary employment in academe, and calling for a code of conduct covering all these matters.[34]

GDR faculty addressed the shrinking of the job market in religion in a number of ways. Prospective students and admittees were cautioned about the decreased availability of jobs. The faculty also tried to identify prospective students who would not be affected by the standard job market (for example, those with employment opportunities in their religious group, international students, or those interested in a career as scholar-ministers). Although there was hesitancy about continuing to produce Ph.D.s for an overloaded job market, it was balanced by reluctance to deny admission to students who, understanding the risks, were motivated to do graduate study in religion, willing to live with the uncertainties of the situation, and ready to compete on the job market. As the crisis continued there were national conferences on "alternative vocations for humanists" and extensive discussions in periodicals.[35]

The operation of the job market also changed drastically in the early 1970s. Referrals had been made primarily through what some called "the old boy network." Now the aspirations of the 1960s came to fruition with an emphasis upon opportunities for women and racial minorities. The women's caucus, organized at the 1971 meeting of the AAR,[36] insisted upon open advertisement of all positions. The AAR Committee on the Status of Women in the Profession prepared a "survival manual" for women, but useful to men, too, on the job search, getting started, review and tenure, professional development, and issues like maternity and child care, sexual harassment, and romantic relationships.[37]

The Era of Evaluation

The GDR has been studied repeatedly since 1970. Beyond the accumulation and evaluation of statistical data, one constant theme has been taxonomic, locating the department on the conceptual chart of graduate studies in religion. Vanderbilt's is one of a small group of programs within private, nondenominational universities that have a divinity school. Harvard, Yale, and University of Chicago are the only clear parallels, although there are "cousins" of several different kinds. Union Seminary in New York and the Graduate Theological Union in Berkeley, with links to a private university and one or more freestanding theological seminaries, have some parallels. Then there are universities with denominational ties that have gained stature as research universities, namely, Duke University, Emory University, Southern Methodist University, the University of Notre Dame, and Catholic University. One freestanding denominational school, Princeton Theological Seminary, has achieved eminence in doctoral studies. Several university departments of religious studies have also achieved excellence at the graduate level, including the University of Pennsylvania, Brown University, Indiana University, and the University of Virginia.

Even within the small group of schools in private research universities, the GDR has a unique structure. Some graduate programs are built upon a divinity program (for example, Chicago); others are combined with undergraduate departments of religious studies and are not directly related to divinity schools (e.g., Yale, Duke). At Vanderbilt the graduate department includes faculty members from both the undergraduate Department of Religious Studies and the Divinity School, combining both "religious studies" and "theological studies" approaches and avoiding a binary opposition between them. Although persons both inside and outside Vanderbilt University often regard this structure as overly complex, it does reflect the actual character of the field as a whole, which irreducibly involves undergraduate, professional, and graduate education. The Vanderbilt setting tends to increase tensions between students in the ministerial and the graduate programs; members of each group are often inclined to feel that the institution and individual faculty members pay too much attention to the other. The response of the faculty, and of most students upon further reflection, is that it is beneficial to have both interests being expressed within the same setting, often within the same classroom.

In 1969 the "Welch study" looked at sixty-nine Ph.D. programs in religion in the United States and Canada and divided them into seven groups, based on age, experience, and reputation. The top group, called "older and established programs of the first rank," included (in alphabetical order) Chicago, Columbia, Duke, Harvard, Princeton Seminary, Union Seminary in New York, Vanderbilt, and Yale. The ratings were made not only on the basis of objective indices (library resources, selectivity, financial support), faculty resources, and quality, but also on the general academic quality of graduate programs rated in the 1969 Roose-Andersen Report.[38]

Soon afterward a special study of university-related theological education was initiated under the direction of George Lindbeck. Although the focus of the study was ministerial education, it also took an interest in graduate study and had clear implications for it; in hindsight it is clear that Lindbeck identified trends that have become more salient in recent decades. The principles of selection were a university relationship, involvement with Ph.D. as well as M.Div. work, and lack of a denominational label, in other words, an "ecumenical" orientation. Schools included were Chicago, Harvard, the Graduate Theological Union in Berkeley, Notre Dame, Union–Columbia, Vanderbilt, and Yale. Institutionally these settings, Lindbeck said, are "free to sponsor theological education in as many religious traditions as they wish"; there are no creedal or religious tests for faculty members and students, and the institutions emphasize freedom of thought and research. This did not mean that they were religiously neutral or indifferent. Lindbeck emphasized that their approach was neither "occupational" preparation for ministry nor what was being called the "religious studies" approach; their emphasis was on learning to "think theologically."[39]

Lindbeck took note of the way traditionally "liberal Protestant" institutions had broadened their field of vision, but suggested that they tended to "universalize" this liberal Protestant outlook. Anticipating the "post-modern" and "post-liberal" mood of the 1980s, which he helped to define, Lindbeck suggested that a "homogenizing ecumenism" might contribute to "alienation from specific religious communities." His call, then, was for work that would be "unashamedly academic, unmistakably particularistic and, in this post-Protestant and increasingly post-Christian era of American religious history, genuinely pluralistic whenever this is feasible." Hence Lindbeck identified the task of these schools to be to encourage "particularism"—by which he meant initiation into and intimate understanding of "as many different traditions as can be responsibly handled in a given university center"—but in a pluralistic context.[40]

Awareness of pluralism reached well beyond Christianity, of course. Programs in Jewish studies were being started in Ivy League universities as an explicit alternative to the Christian (usually liberal Protestant) flavor of most departments of religious studies.[41] There also has been a growth of programs in Islamic studies, Buddhist studies, and now, ironically, Christian studies, legitimating the study of the dominant European and American religious tradition by analogy with the study of other religions.[42]

Restructuring for the Future

The 1990s have seen a series of reviews and self-studies, all of them raising basic questions about future directions for the department. Several recurrent themes can be identified. Because of its history and the character of its region, Vanderbilt's constituency has continued to be primarily Christian and Protestant. Yet it was already known in the 1950s as one of very few Protestant institutions with a Jewish faculty member. Roman Catholics, African Americans, Hispanic Americans, and third world theologians have become members of the permanent or visiting faculty, and there is a continuing sense of the need to pay more attention to these traditions.

At the same time, in terms of its programs of study Vanderbilt has always been aware that it cannot do everything; sooner or later the response is always a variant on the theme "we must continue to do what we already do well." The external review committee in 1997 concluded that "the most promising route for future development of the Graduate Department of Religion is to sustain its historic strengths in Christian theology and biblical studies but to recontextualize these programs in the broader conversation about religion that is occurring in the arts and sciences at many universities."[43]

There seem to be good reasons to continue but broaden Vanderbilt's historic patterns. First, although GDR students may come from any region and any country, they are most typically from the Midwest and the Southeast, often from church-related colleges and theological seminaries. In many cases students move from less-selective to more-selective institutions, looking for "a more liberal, critical, and pluralistic graduate program." Second, Vanderbilt's approach seems appropriate to the job market, because its graduates are employed chiefly in private colleges or universities, followed by theological seminaries and by state colleges or universities; ministry, academic administration, social service, and religious publishing are also strongly represented. Analysis of advertisements for teaching positions indicates that most appointments have a discernible disciplinary base, that often a second and third competency in religious studies (not in other departments) is expected, and that a surprising number seek a confessional or denominational connection.[44]

Two issues of size and character of programs have continued to engage the GDR faculty as well as the faculties of many graduate programs in religion across the country for more than two decades. The visiting committee in 1997, although acknowledging the GDR's high reputation and ranking, perceived the number of students to be "excessively large." The number actually receiving the Ph.D. has remained quite consistent, about twelve each academic year; the rest of the entering classes of about twenty either drop out at some stage or remain "in the pipeline," finished with courses and working on dissertations but not yet receiving the degree. This stretching out of the program has been the result of two major factors: the need to supplement income and the lack of teaching positions in the job market.

The two issues are complexly interrelated. Responding to pressures of the job market may at the same time be seen as a threat to programs that faculty members consider vital to the study of religion. Reductions in the number of new students in turn limit availability of course offerings (the "critical mass" issue) and restrict the number of persons who could assist in the teaching program of the department or school. Reducing the number of programs of study, with the hope of making them more permeable to one another, creates another set of concerns, including the guild identifications of faculty members (in other words, the fields to which they attach themselves) and prospects for graduates in the job market itself.

A decrease in the number of programs was recommended in the 1975 review. This came with the suggestion that it might create a stronger sense of unity across the department and allow for a reduction in the student population.[45] The GDR still faces the same issues; they were identified by the visiting committees in 1991 and again in 1997, and they appear in program changes in other institutions. The graduate programs in religion at Duke and Chicago, for example, established three basic programs—but then found it necessary to create subdivisions in these programs.

During the 1997–98 academic year the GDR faculty discussed four so-called clusters—Biblical Studies, Historical Studies, Theological and Philosophical Studies, and Religion and Culture. The list is similar, of course, to the department's programs prior to 1968, with the addition of the HACTOR program, the need for which was already clear at that time. In the end, the faculty decided to continue the existing programs, on the grounds that they reflect the traditionally defined fields with their peer groups of scholars.

Any institution with graduate programs faces a dilemma when it contemplates downsizing of any sort. Both the Divinity School and the Department of Religious Studies need a range of faculty competencies to carry out their respective programs of instruction. Many faculty members are attracted to Vanderbilt because it conducts graduate programs. Even students in the undergraduate or professional schools often seek out a research university as the context of their study. If a smaller population of students is to be contemplated, it is likely to involve a change in teaching methods, perhaps a shift from seminars toward tutorials and modules and individually supervised research.

Preparation of Graduate Students for Careers as Teachers

During the 1997 annual meeting of the CGSR, an informal poll indicated that about half of the approximately thirty Ph.D. programs represented in the CGSR had some form of training for graduate students. There was general agreement that both teaching experience and some form of training in pedagogy were becoming increasingly important in the job market. The GDR undertook such training in a formal way starting with the 1995–96 academic year, aided by grants from the Wabash Center for Teaching and Learning in Theology and Religion.

During the fall semester of their first year, all Ph.D. students enroll in a Colloquium on the Study of Religion, where faculty members from different programs discuss methods, issues, and subject matter in their own disciplines, with the general purpose of acquainting students with the range of the field and facilitating interdisciplinary discussion among both faculty members and students. During the spring semester these same students enroll in a Seminar on the Teaching of Religion, where topics range from educational and psychological theory to issues of context (class, race, institutional setting, genre), classroom methods, and preparation of a "teaching portfolio." Aided by the University's

Center for Teaching and the Master Teaching Fellow in Religion (an appointment given to a senior Ph.D. student each year), students are better prepared to
serve as teaching assistants and to seek positions in academe.

The Nature of the Study of Religion

An era of domination by Protestant scholars, institutions, and ideas has
ended, and greater pluralism—religious, cultural, and institutional—is emerging, without a clear and coherent rationale for any new and dominant paradigm.
College and theological school administrators often express discontent at the
preparation that graduate programs have given to their graduates—narrow specialization and an accompanying lack of understanding of the field as a whole,
emphasis on texts and the cognitive content of religious traditions at the expense
of attention to religious life and practice, and inadequate attention to the various
"publics" that scholars of religion seek to serve.[46]

Because of the different institutional settings in which graduates will teach,
discussions of the field often use the admittedly facile contrast between the "religious studies" model, which emphasizes critical methods (historical, comparative, social scientific, and the like), and the "theological studies" model, which
engages the truth claims and ethical norms of a particular religious tradition.
Clearly there will continue to be a demand for scholars of both types. Theological seminaries and church-related colleges will need scholars and teachers who
understand the relationships among various disciplines in "theological studies"
terms and can prepare students for ministry. At the same time there will be state
universities, liberal arts colleges, and graduate programs that, for a variety of
reasons, must deal with religion in the nonsectarian or nonconfessional way that
is usually called the "religious studies" approach.

When we closely examine the "religious studies" approach, it turns out to
involve three basic clusters of methods. One is the historical study of texts and
traditions, beliefs and practices. A second is the analysis of religious beliefs and
practices with the aid of the "human sciences," including anthropology, sociology, psychology, and comparative or philosophical methods. An unavoidable
third cluster is the consideration of questions of meaning, truth, and value, not
from the perspective of any single religious tradition, to be sure, but still with
sympathy for religious beliefs, in an analytic and comparative fashion. This
might be called the "religious studies" version of theology and ethics, for any
study of religion must inevitably include "great religious thinkers" in its scope.

Because of its heritage, its intellectual commitments, and its institutional
base in both the College and the Divinity School, the GDR has wanted to affirm
all these approaches. As Peter Hodgson put it in the 1996 self-study, "We are

searching for a new educational paradigm that does not yet have a name, one that is at once religious and theological, critical and engaged, interdisciplinary and focused." Reflecting on the place of the GDR in the University, Hodgson said,

> The question might be raised why a university such as Vanderbilt should support the study of religion at either the undergraduate or the graduate level. Our brief answer [is] . . . that religion pervades most dimensions of human experience and demands attention in its own terms as well as those of other disciplines. If the religious dimension is ignored, a primary resource is lost for generating cultural values and responsible human behavior, as well as for informing public debate on pressing subjects such as violence, family values, and environmental issues. Especially in times of deep cultural transition such as our own, society faces the challenge of attending to normative traditions of the past and revisioning them for the present and future.[47]

As the GDR moves into a new century, it experiences the same tensions that have been present since the founding of the University, probably with even greater intensity. If few agreed answers have been found to the questions just mentioned, one reason may be that the faculty continues to be responsive to the many conflicting tendencies in the world of scholarship, including the "guild mentality" at its worst as well as its best. Another may be the conflicting demands placed upon the faculty by the University, which expects excellence both in specialized scholarship and in the education of an increasingly diverse student population. But another reason is the department's commitment to greater cooperation across programs without compromising the integrity of the various disciplines. Because of this the faculty seems willing to bring the tensions into the midst of its programs of study without premature resolution, in the confidence that they will be fruitful for individual scholars and for the ongoing life of the Graduate Department of Religion.

Jewish Studies at Vanderbilt

Peter J. Haas

JEWISH STUDIES AT VANDERBILT UNIVERSITY FORMALLY BEGAN IN 1949, when Samuel Sandmel arrived to become the first instructor of Judaica at the University. The appointment of Sandmel was the result of a vision that the new chancellor, Harvie Branscomb, brought with him from Duke University. Branscomb sought to bring to theological education a new understanding of Judaism as a living religious tradition. In many ways, then, the story of Jewish studies at Vanderbilt has to be seen in light of the new and unprecedented appointment in Jewish studies made in 1943 by Branscomb at Duke University.

Duke was in many ways an ideal institution for innovation in religious and theological study. Founded in 1924, Duke quickly gained national recognition, finding a place alongside, or even in front of, other more traditional universities in the South. Despite its national recognition, however, Duke was still enough of a southern school to require courses in religion. By 1942, Branscomb had decided that such courses should address not only Christianity, but Judaism as well. Trained in the New Testament, Branscomb was especially aware of the importance of Judaism in the formation of Christianity. He therefore set out to establish a program that would introduce his students to the living reality of the Jewish religion.

Toward this end, Branscomb began his campaign by approaching the local Jewish community in Durham for funds. With some financial backing in hand, he then set out to search for a suitable candidate for such an unprecedented professorship. The appointee was expected to be both a person who could present Judaism to the students through teaching and scholarship, and also, in Branscomb's words, "someone thoroughly representative of the religious spirit of Judaism."[1] Although rabbinic ordination was not an explicit requirement, it is significant that the first nominee for the position, Theodor Gaster, was ultimately turned down when he announced that he was an agnostic. The professorship went eventually to Judah Goldin.[2] It was this early experience in reconceptualizing and establishing a chair in Jewish studies that Branscomb brought with him when he became Chancellor of Vanderbilt University in 1946.

These developments begun at Duke and continued at Vanderbilt need to be understood in the larger context of the development of the American Jewish community and the emergence of Jewish intellectual life on American university campuses in the first half of the twentieth century. The Jewish community had remained small and highly assimilated throughout most of the nineteenth century. It was only in the 1880s that large numbers of traditionally observant Eastern European Jews streamed to America and re-created on American soil a reflection of the vibrant Jewish religious and cultural life that had developed in Europe. This wave of immigration, which lasted until about 1920, increased the Jewish population of the United States from barely a quarter of a million to some three million. Although this massive immigrant population remained largely isolated and ghettoized, this was not true of their children and grandchildren. The second and third generation moved out of the Yiddish-speaking ghettoes and in ever increasing numbers went to colleges and professional schools. By the late 1930s and early 1940s, these American-born Jews had made their way into American society and brought their deep Jewish identities with them into American public life. Not surprisingly, as this generation of Jews grew, prospered, and matured, so did the presence of Judaism as a religious and cultural entity grow and mature on the American university scene. These sociological developments, along with the horrors of the Nazi Holocaust and the increasing prominence of Zionism, worked together to generate new popular and theological interest in Judaism as a living religious and cultural force, not just a religion that died two millennia before.

These trends coincided with the maturation of Jewish studies in American universities. The first university positions in Judaism appeared in America only at the end of the nineteenth century, made possible because of a number of developments within the university world itself. Perhaps of greatest significance was the secularization of American academia. Most institutions of higher education had been founded by religious denominations and still considered the teaching of Christianity and the training of Christian clergy to be their primary missions. Although many taught Hebrew and Old Testament as part of their ministerial training, none really taught Judaism as such. But as universities broke from denominational affiliation, they gained the opportunity to include in their curricula sympathetic treatments of religious traditions other than Christianity. The study of Judaism benefited in particular because of certain developments within Protestant scholarship that led to a growing appreciation of the history of Christianity and especially of the importance of the Jewish background of much of the New Testament and the early church. Added to the arrival of masses of Jews, among them Jewish scholars trained in European universities, these trends led by the turn of the century to the creation of positions dedicated specifically to Jewish studies in several major universities.

The earliest such chair appeared at Cornell, which hired Felix Adler, unsuccessful heir apparent to his father's pulpit at Temple Emanuel in New York, in 1874 to teach Hebrew and Oriental Literature. This position lasted only about three years, however. But other universities soon followed Cornell's lead, with more permanent results. Positions in Semitic studies were established in the late 1880s by the University of Pennsylvania, Columbia University, the University of California, and the University of Chicago, all of which hired prominent rabbis to teach. Harvard and Johns Hopkins also had positions in Semitics, although these were not originally staffed by Jews.[3] In all events, by the 1940s, when Branscomb began to think about the nature of Jewish studies at Duke, only six positions existed in the country, all of them with a philological rather than a theological or "religious" focus. It was this paradigm that Branscomb proposed to challenge.

Branscomb's conception of a different mode of Jewish studies for the Duke appointment apparently grew out of a number of factors that had taken shape by the 1940s: the racial war of the Nazis in Europe, the increasing number of Jewish students attending university, and the publication of George Foot Moore's *Judaism in the First Centuries of the Christian Era,*[4] which argued that Judaism had been systematically distorted and misrepresented by Protestant scholarship. The exact ways in which these affected Branscomb are hard to determine, but it is clear that by 1943 Branscomb had convinced the faculty to establish a position in Jewish studies that was unprecedented. It would be designed to teach Judaism as a living and vibrant religion, not merely a fossil worthy of historical dissection. It is of course for precisely this reason that Gaster's announcement of his agnosticism doomed his chances for the position. Branscomb had in mind not only a scholar but also a person who could serve as a credible advocate and spokesperson for Judaism as a living religious tradition.

These events at Duke set the stage for Branscomb's activities with regard to Jewish studies when he arrived on the Vanderbilt campus in 1946. Vanderbilt, like Duke, seemed to offer fertile ground for Branscomb's revolutionary vision. The university had a long history of religious and theological education, with special concern for the education of ministers. Despite the break with the church, Vanderbilt continued to be, like Duke, an institution where religion was an important academic concern. Thus, in 1949, the faculty accepted Branscomb's arguments for having Jewish studies in the university. The position was to be in the Graduate School with courses listed both in the College of Arts and Science and the School of Religion, an arrangement that would remain in place for the next thirty years. Branscomb then turned to funding. Having succeeded in securing a three-year grant from the Carnegie Foundation to support at least part of the salary, he proceeded to search for an appropriate occupant.[5]

Samuel Sandmel was an ideal reflection of Branscomb's interest in having both a university-trained scholar and an "advocate" of modern Judaism. He was a Reform rabbi, having received ordination from Hebrew Union College (HUC) in Cincinnati in 1937. After a brief stint in the congregational rabbinate, Sandmel took positions as Hillel director, first at the University of North Carolina and then at Duke. It was in this latter capacity that Branscomb first came to know Sandmel. But the relationship at Duke was short-lived; in 1942, Sandmel left Duke to serve as a Jewish chaplain in the Navy. After the end of World War II, Sandmel attended Yale, where he earned a Ph.D. in New Testament studies under Erwin Goodenough in 1949. It was just as he was completing his work at Yale that Branscomb began looking for a promising young scholar to fill the new position at Vanderbilt. The young Hillel director-turned Ph.D. came immediately to mind because he combined the scholarship and the religious commitment that Branscomb liked. In short order, Branscomb convinced Sandmel to come to Vanderbilt as associate professor of Jewish Literature and Thought. So in 1949, Sandmel began his tenure at Vanderbilt, teaching a course on the History and Institutions of Judaism. He went on to develop courses in Judaism in the New Testament Period, Hellenistic Judaism, and Post-Biblical Hebrew.

Vanderbilt's commitment to Jewish studies was reflected also by developments in its library. Already before Branscomb's appointment as chancellor, the local community had begun to support the acquisition of books of Jewish interest. Sarah Lowenstein Teitelbaum provided funding in 1944 for the University to purchase the library of the recently deceased scholar of early Judaism, Ismar Elbogen. Elbogen had taught Jewish history at the renowned Hochschule für die Wissenschaft des Judenthums in Berlin until the Nazis came to power in 1933. He then moved to the United States, where he taught at the Jewish Theological Seminary in New York until his death in 1943. His professional library contained more than two thousand books. In bringing the library of this eminent Jewish scholar to Nashville, Vanderbilt signaled its seriousness about

Jewish studies. The deep commitment on the part of the library to building up a Judaica collection is nicely illustrated by a statement made at the time of the purchase by Frederick Kuhlman, then director of the Joint University Libraries:

> I need not tell you how important it is that there should be intensive open-minded study of the problem of the Jew, for if reason, truth, and justice are to prevail in the treatment of the Jews the world over, then we must combat ignorance, misrepresentation, and hate with education and enlightenment based upon the truth and upon goodwill. . . . New centers of Jewish learning are urgently needed. America must become one of the sanctuaries of Jewish scholarship to give the proper perspective for the Jews and the values for which [Elbogen's] best leadership has stood.[6]

The Elbogen collection was only the beginning. In 1951, Sandmel helped procure for the library a collection of some 160 books on the first-century Jewish philosopher Philo from the personal library collection of Howard Lehman Goodhart. This addition to the library seemed to indicate that Vanderbilt was committed to making Jewish studies a major presence in the intellectual life of the campus.

As it turned out, Sandmel remained at Vanderbilt only three years. In 1952 he joined the faculty of his alma mater, HUC. During his short tenure, however, he earned Jewish studies a solid place on campus and worked to develop the budding Judaica collection in the library. Upon Sandmel's departure, Branscomb turned to Lou Hackett Silberman, a colleague of Sandmel, to fill the position. Silberman seemed a logical choice as successor because he and Sandmel had many characteristics in common. In fact, the two had shared some time together at HUC in Cincinnati. Silberman received ordination and earned his Bachelor of Hebrew Letters degree in 1939, two years after Sandmel. After his ordination, Silberman stayed on at HUC for several more years, receiving Master and Doctor of Hebrew Letters degrees in 1941 and 1943, respectively. From there Silberman, like Sandmel, began his career as a pulpit rabbi, working with congregations in Dallas and Omaha. Like Sandmel, Silberman combined both scholarly training and active leadership in the Jewish community. He was thus an obvious choice for the position as Branscomb had conceived it.

Silberman took over Sandmel's position in the Vanderbilt Graduate School in 1952. He continued Sandmel's practice of teaching courses in Judaism in the New Testament period and in post-biblical Hebrew. He also began to offer courses for undergraduates, although these were only available for elective credit because no major in Jewish studies, or even religious studies, yet existed. Among his undergraduate courses were History of the Jewish People, The Literature of Judaism, and Jewish Religious Thought. He also began teaching a course in Psalms for the School of Religion and later developed courses in the newly discovered Dead Sea Scrolls. As with Sandmel's work, his courses, both in terms of content and in terms of listing, were grouped in the biblical area. This dovetailed nicely with the predominant Divinity School paradigm of the time that Judaism was an "Old Testament" religion. It comes as no surprise, then, that Jewish studies at Vanderbilt continued to focus on the period around the time of the emergence of early Christianity. But Silberman was also keenly interested in Jewish-Christian dialogue and did much to foster such encounters at the Divinity School.

Funding continued to be a problem for the position, because the original Carnegie grant ran out after three years. Because the Nashville Jewish community was relatively small, little support could be expected to come from it. So Branscomb looked for outside sources of funding and succeeded in persuading the B'nai B'rith Hillel Foundation to provide at least partial support. In consequence, when Silberman was promoted in 1955, he was given the title Hillel Professor of Jewish Literature and Thought on the Graduate School faculty. Silberman became officially part of the Divinity School faculty in 1964, although he had had an office in the school and had been at least informally acknowledged as a member of the faculty from the time of his appointment.

Funding from the Hillel Foundation remained fairly constant until the mid-1960s, when it began a steady decline. Over the next decade, the College of Arts and Science gradually assumed a greater and greater proportion of the cost of the position. When budgetary constraints at Hillel finally forced the agency to terminate all financial support for the position in 1976, the University turned to the Nashville Jewish community. Realizing the importance of Jewish studies at Vanderbilt for the community at large, the Jewish Federation of Nashville and Middle Tennessee rose to the challenge and began to make regular annual contributions to the "Hillel Chair." At this same time, the Federation also began to provide partial support for an instructor in Modern Hebrew. These contributions lasted, with some fluctuations, until 1991. Beginning in 1992, only one Federation allocation was made for Jewish studies at Vanderbilt, to be split between the professorship and the Hebrew program, as the University saw fit. In practice, funding for the professorship was assumed entirely by the College, while Modern Hebrew, with its often very modest enrollments, was funded on a more or less equal basis by the College and the Federation allocation.

A number of important developments occurred during Silberman's long tenure at Vanderbilt. Most significantly, the library's Judaica collection grew impressively. Shortly after the purchase of the Elbogen library, family and friends of Lee J. Lowenthal, a member of the Board of Trust, established a book fund to purchase Judaica materials. The main force behind the establishment of this fund was a relative, Mary Jane Werthan, who would later become the first woman member of the Board of Trust. The mandate of the fund was to purchase books published since 1914, especially with materials dealing with the crisis of Jewish life in Europe during the 1930s and 1940s. The fund was used to provide books for the Judaica collection until 1960, when it was exhausted.

The end of the Lowenthal fund did not mean the end of significant acquisitions in Judaica, however. The collection received a tremendous boost in 1968 with the purchase of the private library of Arno Poebel. Although this was not a Judaica collection itself, it did contain a number of books relevant to the Judaica collection, strengthening in particular the library's holdings in Semitic language and archaeology. By 1971, Vanderbilt was able to boast that its Judaica collection numbered more than 6,300 volumes, making it one of the most significant in the Southeast.

Other changes were afoot as well. In 1967, Silberman and others succeeded in establishing an undergraduate Department of Religious Studies. From that point on he held appointments in both the College of Arts and Science and the Divinity School. This also opened the possibility for Jewish studies to be offered as part of a religious studies major, and eventually as a minor or major in its own right. At roughly the same time, the Divinity School and B'nai B'rith reached an agreement to hold an annual Graduate Summer Institute on Judaism on campus. It brought to campus some thirty college, university, and seminary professors in theology and religious studies, plus teaching faculty, for a ten-day intensive learning experience. Silberman contributed each year a course on Rabbinic Judaism. The Institute was first held in 1969 and continued annually through 1979.

In the late 1970s two further developments occurred. The first was the creation of the Holocaust Lecture Series in 1978. The prime mover in establishing this series was the University Chaplain, Beverly Asbury. Drawing on both University and community support, it soon became the longest running university-based series of its kind. Over the years, it brought to the campus such scholars and lecturers as Elie Wiesel, Christopher Browning, Jan Karski, and Telford Taylor, thus bringing the Holocaust and its theological implications into the public conversation of the University and the Divinity School. This was accompanied in 1979 by the first course in the Holocaust, developed by Silberman.

Central to the study of Judaism, of course, is the study of the Hebrew language. The study of Biblical Hebrew had been part of the School of Religion from the very beginning. But the Hebrew language continued to be used and to develop even after the Bible was completed. As we have already seen, Sandmel introduced almost immediately upon his arrival at Vanderbilt a course in post-biblical Hebrew, meaning the Hebrew of classical Jewish texts such as the Mishnah, Talmud, and Midrash. Modern spoken Hebrew, however, remained beyond the horizon of Vanderbilt's interests until after the undergraduate department was established and a new constituency for Jewish studies began to form. The earliest course in Modern Hebrew was offered in 1974–75 under the auspices of the Department of Spanish and Portuguese, which was already offering instruction in Arabic. The next year, coincident with the beginning of partial Federation funding, Modern Hebrew became a separate listing. Aviva Dekel, a native Israeli living in Nashville, was hired at adjunct level to teach both beginning and intermediate Modern Hebrew. Upon her departure in 1985, the course was taken over by Miriam Halachmi, another native Hebrew speaker living in Nashville, who also served as educational director of the Conservative West End Synagogue. Although these courses were open to Divinity and graduate students, enrollment figures show that very few such students at first had an interest in the language. This changed in the early 1990s as Modern Hebrew became more and more of a significant research language in such fields as biblical studies and Ancient Near East history. Enrollments remained low enough, however, for the College to make continuation of instruction contingent on partial funding from the outside.

These modest developments in Jewish studies at Vanderbilt were occurring during a time of considerable growth of Jewish studies in other American universities. It will be recalled that in 1949, when Sandmel came, Vanderbilt was one of fewer than a dozen universities that offered any courses in Jewish studies, and nearly the only one that taught Judaism as a living religious tradition. But by the late 1970s, the Association for Jewish Studies counted more than 350 college and university faculty members teaching in a variety of institutions from large public universities to small liberal arts colleges, some 124 of whom had already achieved the status of tenured faculty members in the field.[7] Even more remarkable, by this time several universities had separate full departments or programs in Jewish studies. Scholarly journals devoted specifically to the subject were appearing in ever larger numbers, and Jewish studies sessions were becoming regular features of scholarly associations such as the American Academy of Religion and the Society for the Scientific Study of Religion. The trends visible already in the early 1970s continued over the next two decades. By 1999, significant Jewish studies programs with large and varied faculty existed in more than fifty major universities, including several in the Southeast such as Duke, Emory University, University of Virginia, University of Florida, and Tulane University. Even the University of Tennessee established chairs in Jewish studies in Knoxville, Chattanooga, and Memphis. By the mid-1990s four national Jewish studies organizations existed and nearly two dozen major scholarly journals were being published. Jewish studies programs have become a significant and productive presence on the American university scene.

Unfortunately, Vanderbilt failed to keep pace. The position in Jewish studies remained split between the Divinity School and the undergraduate College of Arts and Science, thus restricting the number of courses that could be offered in each school. Although library resources had grown considerably, the actual course offerings in Jewish studies had changed little since Sandmel's days. Only near the end of Silberman's career were efforts made to raise money to fund a dedicated chair in Jewish studies.

With Silberman's retirement in 1980, Peter J. Haas was appointed to a three-year position in the College of Arts and Science to bridge the gap until money for the fully endowed chair was raised. Like his predecessors, Haas was an ordainee in the Reform rabbinate from HUC in Cincinnati, and in fact had studied early Judaism there under Sandmel. After ordination, Haas, like Sandmel before him, became a military chaplain, serving in the U.S. Army for three years. Following military duty, Haas earned his Ph.D. in History of Religions at Brown University as a student of Jacob Neusner. Haas's appointment marked a change in the pattern of Jewish studies at Vanderbilt in that his position was located completely in the College of Arts and Science. He taught one graduate seminar a year for the Graduate Department of Religion and cross-listed other courses to make them available to graduate and divinity students. Graduate seminars included courses in Judaism in New Testament Times, Dead Sea Scrolls, and various courses in Rabbinic literature, thus carrying forward the pattern established by Sandmel and Silberman. Other courses, offered mainly at the undergraduate level, included Introduction to Judaism, Jewish Ethics, and The Holocaust.

As it turned out, money for the full endowment did not materialize within the time allotted, although a significant gift had been made. Haas's three-year appointment eventually stretched into four years and then seven years, at which point it became a tenure-track position. Jewish studies thus became a regular part of the offerings of the Department of Religious Studies. Meanwhile, efforts continued to raise money for Jewish studies and to complete the endowment for a full chair. The process was still incomplete when Haas left the position in December 1999 to take up the Abba Hillel Silver chair at Case Western Reserve University.

Developments in the library continued apace. A significant gift was made in 1988 by the Raymond Zimmerman Family Fund in memory of his parents Harry and Mary Zimmerman. This gift enabled the library to expand the Judaica collection in a number of areas. The collection was further enhanced in 1991 with the purchase of the Nahum Glatzer library, acquired with money provided by the University. Besides books in Midrash and modern Jewish history and thought, the purchase brought to Vanderbilt a number of Nahum Glatzer's private collections, including part of the correspondence between Franz Rosenzweig and Martin Buber that became the basis for Rosenzweig's *The Star of Redemption*.[8] Together these developments allowed the library to continue its claim to have one of the most significant Judaica collections in the Southeast.

Several other developments from the 1980s seemed to move Vanderbilt toward a more mature program in Jewish studies. In 1969, Randall Falk, senior rabbi of the then only Reform Jewish congregation in Nashville, completed his Doctor of Divinity degree at the Divinity School. His thesis was entitled "The Philosophy of Martin Buber on Jewish-Christian Relations, and Its Relevance for the Contemporary American Community." In 1986–87 Falk began to be listed in the Divinity School catalogue as lecturer in Jewish Studies. He first was involved in a team-taught course with Walter Harrelson, Jews and Christians: Historical Perspectives and Contemporary Concerns; another followed, also with Harrelson and, later, with Dean Joe Hough, on Jews and Christians: In Pursuit of Social Justice. Soon he was teaching an additional course each year for the school on a specifically Jewish theme, including Torah, The Religious and Institutional History of the Jewish People, and Twentieth-Century Jewish Thought. Falk's involvement in the school was supported by a regular grant from the Jewish Chautauqua Society. Between Rabbi Falk and Professor Haas, Divinity students had regular offerings in Jewish studies.

Further enrichment came in 1994, when Amy-Jill Levine was appointed to the Divinity faculty. Although her field was New Testament rather than Jewish studies, her presence provided a powerful Jewish voice in the school and the Graduate Department of Religion. As head of the Carpenter Program in Religion, Gender, and Sexuality, she has brought a number of academicians, including Jewish scholars, to campus for lectures and colloquia. At the same time, her husband, Jay Geller, was offered an appointment as lecturer in the undergraduate Department of Religious Studies, where he offered courses in the Holocaust and in nineteenth-century thought and anti-Semitism. His courses thus supplemented the Judaic courses already being offered.

These appointments had an impact on the undergraduate college as well. Along with two professors of Judeo-Arabic thought located in the Philosophy Department, Idit Dobbs-Weinstein and Lenn Goodman, there was now a sufficient density of undergraduate courses in Jewish studies to make possible the creation of an undergraduate minor in Jewish studies. In addition, the creation of the program in the History and Critical Theories of Religion (HACTOR) in the Graduate Department of Religion gave a context within which graduate work in Jewish studies might take place. Besides offering new possibilities for graduate study, these two initiatives provided a framework within which it became possible for the first time to conceive of working toward the formation of a full undergraduate program, with a major, in Jewish studies.

A significant initiative to enrich Jewish studies in the Divinity School came to fruition in 1997 with the reception of a major gift allowing for the establishment of the Mary Jane Werthan Professorship of Jewish Studies. After a lengthy national search, Jack Sasson was named as the first occupant of the chair, to begin teaching in the fall of 1999. Since Sasson's area is Ancient Near East history, his affiliation was with the field of Hebrew Bible. His appointment dovetailed nicely with a growing relationship taking shape between the Divinity School and the Megiddo archeological dig in Israel. This relationship had its beginning in 1997 when a number of graduate students took part in a dig at Megiddo and returned to Vanderbilt determined to recruit other students for further digs. A very enthusiastic group participated in the dig in the summer of 1998, and a second group went over, this time to Jaffa, in 1999. Both groups received subsidies from a generous gift made by Rabbi Falk and his wife Edna. As a result of the demonstrated interest in archaeology, Vanderbilt in 1999 signed on as a formal member of the Megiddo Expedition Consortium. These excursions, of course, also exposed the students to the vibrant Jewish life of the modern state of Israel.

It has been more than fifty years since Chancellor Branscomb's vision for a modern approach to Jewish studies at Vanderbilt brought its first Judaica scholar, Samuel Sandmel, to campus. Since then Jewish studies has had a significant presence in the Divinity School and the graduate program, a presence now significantly enhanced by new faculty appointments and a highly developed library collection. Branscomb could not but be proud of the legacy he left to Vanderbilt.

13

Educating Disciples

Anthony L. Dunnavant

ALTHOUGH METHODISTS ESTABLISHED VANDERBILT UNIVERSITY, and even after the break with the church in 1914 continued to make up the majority of students in the School of Religion and Divinity School communities, the Christian Church (Disciples of Christ) came to represent a strong presence as well—through its Disciples House, scholarship resources for students, and faculty members. Additionally, its graduates since the early days of the School of Religion, first from the ministerial program and later from the graduate program, have made significant contributions to the denomination and to their own educational institutions.

Early Disciples Theological Education

The Christian Church (Disciples of Christ) is one branch of the religious reform movement that arose in the United States in the early nineteenth century and was given primary leadership by Barton Stone and Thomas and Alexander Campbell. Because these Stone-Campbell traditions[1] were born with a strong impulse to effect a thoroughgoing reformation in Christian faith and practice, their approaches to theological education developed against the backdrop of their particular ideology of reform. Indeed, the constellation of values that combined to constitute the distinctive reform ideology of the Stone-Campbell traditions shaped the Disciples' outlook on theological education in a number of ways. The Disciples' self-understanding as a reformation movement carried with it the assumption that theological education as previously practiced in the historic churches was part and parcel of the corrupted old-world church. That is, existing theological education was seen as mired in human traditions rather than faithful to God, supportive of oppressive clerical hierarchies rather than of faithful church leadership, tied to "sectarian" theological systems rather than to the apostolic norm, divisive rather than unitive, antithetical to evangelism, and thus in tension with God's eschatological purpose. The Disciples' sense that the United States in its early national period was a radically new providential context for reform meant that they could envision breaking with traditional patterns of theological education in favor of new forms congruent with their values and, thus, contrary to the practices of the historic churches.

During the early period of the Disciples' history the congregation itself was the primary locus of theological formation. Alexander Campbell understood the "standing and immutable" order of Christian ministry to be composed of bishops/elders (he saw this as the same office), deacons, and evangelists.[2] The bishop/elder was the primary teacher, shepherd, overseer, and "leader" in the local church, and the deacon was the church's "servant" under the bishops' guidance. Of the formation of bishops, Campbell wrote:

> When the bishop rests from his labors, the church, of which he had the oversight, by his labors, and by the opportunity afforded all the members of exercising their faculties of communication and inquiry in the public assembly, finds within itself others educated and qualified to be appointed to the same good work. The church of the living God is thus independent of theological schools and colleges for its existence, enlargement, comfort, and perfection; for it is itself put in possession of all the means of education and accomplishments, if these means be widely used.[3]

For the professional formation of the movement's itinerant evangelists, an early approach was that of the informal mentor/apprenticeship combined with the occasional preachers' "workshop." The historical figure who best illustrates this is the evangelist Walter Scott. After receiving his university education at Edinburgh, Scott came to the United States, affiliated with the Campbell movement in the 1820s, and entered a mentor-colleague relationship with Thomas Campbell. After 1827, Scott turned from itinerant preaching to providing leadership to short-term schools for preachers. These "workshops" became another expression of the mentoring model that offered an approach to ministerial formation outside of formal theological colleges or seminaries.[4] Thus, in the founding generation of the Stone-Campbell traditions, the informal educational norm or model for church leaders consisted of the academy for basic "literary" education, the congregation for education in the faith for both elders and deacons, and mentoring by colleagues for evangelists.

A new era for higher education in the Stone-Campbell movement began with the founding of Bacon College in 1836. Prior to that time, a dozen or so academies or "preparatory" schools had been founded by leaders of the movement. An offshoot of the Baptists' Georgetown [Kentucky] College, the Collegiate Institute and School of Civil Engineers opened under the leadership of civil engineering professor Thornton Johnson. The next year it was renamed for Francis Bacon as a reflection of the Campbellian admiration of British empiricism. Another institution, Bethany College, was founded by Alexander Campbell, chartered by the Virginia legislature in 1840, and opened in the village of Bethany in Brooke County in 1841. The charter stated the purpose of the college as "the instruction of youth in the various branches of science and literature, the useful arts, agriculture, and the learned and foreign languages." It also contained an article stipulating "nothing herein contained shall be so construed as at any time to authorize the establishment of a Theological Professorship in the said College." This article was long regarded as a reflection of Campbell's own sensibilities as to the dangers of specialized theological schools and his preference for the congregation as the locus of ministerial formation. An 1855 attempt to amend the charter and clear the way to establish a department particularly focused on ministerial education failed. This did not mean, however, that Bethany College did not train ministers. Quite the contrary was the case.[5]

The core leadership of the Stone-Campbell movement as it moved into its second generation was largely trained at Bethany. The educational philosophy, however, was that "those persons who would be serving the church in the role of evangelist, preacher, or pastor would submit themselves to the same studies as those in lay roles."[6] At least preachers and lay leaders would receive their education at the same institution with the same underlying curricular philosophy. This approach to ministerial education has been termed the "undifferentiated" model. It consisted of a "broad liberal arts background with a considerable amount of Biblical instruction thrown in."[7] The undifferentiated model was consistent with the movement's anticlerical reform tenet and with the example of its most influential leaders. The fact that Alexander Campbell himself was a farmer, publisher, postmaster, and college president, as well as a local elder/bishop and itinerant evangelist, underlay Bethany's model of "undifferentiated" Christian community leadership. The importance of the Bethany model for a generation after the college's founding was, in part, that it continued to embody

Campbell's own anticlerical ideal, yet also favored the idea of a "standing and immutable order of ministry." Further, it sustained Bethany's status as the intellectual capital of the movement and placed its stamp upon those who would move beyond it.

The attempt to amend Bethany's charter in 1855 and the fact that a "prescribed course of instruction" for ministerial students was already in place by that year indicate that the Stone-Campbell movement was outgrowing the undifferentiated model of ministerial preparation.[8] A clearly "differentiated" model for theological education within a specialized institution came into the movement's history in 1865. That development occurred within the evolution of Bacon College, which relocated to Harrodsburg in 1839, suffered financial collapse in 1850, was rechartered as Kentucky University in 1858, and relocated again in 1865, this time to Lexington, due to a major fire. Two years later, Kentucky University was operating with four specialized colleges: the College of Science, Literature and Arts; the College of Law; the Agricultural and Mechanical College; and the College of the Bible.[9]

With the opening of the College of the Bible, the Stone-Campbell movement had its first differentiated theological institution. Its curriculum was primarily an undergraduate program for ministerial training, although provision was made from the beginning for graduate study for those who already held degrees. The first faculty members had been trained at Bethany. Therefore, the College of the Bible continued the presuppositions of the Disciples' reformation in terms of basic content. What was new was that the existence of the school as a specialized institution clearly expressed a felt need for theological education beyond the liberal arts, even beyond Bethany's version of the liberal arts.

"The College of the Bible idea" was most fully developed by John William McGarvey, who had studied at Bethany and entered the ministry but soon realized he had "insufficient knowledge of the Scriptures, insufficient general knowledge, and insufficient experience in public speaking." Because McGarvey became the dominant personality at the College of the Bible from 1865 until 1911, these perceived insufficiencies set the trajectory for the new institution. Its educational model called for focused, differentiated, ministerial preparation in biblical studies, "in consecration to the work of the ministry and mastery of the skills of a good pastor," and in the liberal arts. Although it was not distinctively a graduate seminary, it was from the outset distinctively a theological school.[10] Hence, the College of the Bible departed from Bethany's undifferentiated approach to theological education and, to a significant degree, shifted the intellectual center of the Stone-Campbell movement southward to central Kentucky. What remained largely unchanged from the earlier approach to ministerial training were doctrinal content and the fact that such training was, at least in part, undergraduate. Both of these elements would recede with the emergence of a third model.

This next model for ministerial preparation among the heirs of the Campbells and Stone began at the University of Chicago, which was founded in 1892. Its Divinity School, following the outlook of President William Rainey Harper, would champion an "emphasis on environmental factors affecting historical subjects." This meant that theological education at Chicago would "adopt social psychology and sociology as indispensable tools for research into the realities of theological doctrine."[11] That outlook, especially the application of a rigorous sociohistorical approach to the study of the Bible, had staggering implications for the Disciples, whose traditional hermeneutics had sharply delineated between "divine revelation" and the "traditions of human beings." The wide influence of "the Chicago School" among Disciples, particularly through the work of biblical scholar Herbert Willett, historian Winfred E. Garrison, philosopher of religion Edward Scribner Ames, and editor Charles Clayton Morrison, has been viewed as critically important in the liberal reformulation of the Disciples tradition that took place in first half of the twentieth century.[12]

The pattern for Disciples theological education at the University of Chicago was largely set by the Divinity House, established in 1894, which combined housing, administration of denominational financial aid, and the provision of instruction in the particular denominational tradition of the residents. A dean provided leadership for the House. Willett, Garrison, and Ames each served in this capacity in the early years of the operation. The Disciples Divinity House embodied several elements of change for the denomination's approach to ministerial education. It was an institution devoted to graduate theological education, was integrally related to a non-Disciples university, and created an intellectual center for Disciples in the Midwest. When the efforts began to formalize and facilitate the presence of Disciples theological students at Vanderbilt, the model that seemed most immediately pertinent was that of the Disciples House of the University of Chicago.[13]

The models for ministerial preparation among the Disciples that appeared in the nineteenth century involved attention to three major concerns: (1) the proper context for ministerial formation—should it be congregation, collegial mentors, liberal arts college, or theological school? (2) the content for ministerial education—should it be liberal arts, Bible (with a particular Disciples hermeneutic), practical skills for ministry, or scientific and historical studies of religion and its social and cultural sources? (3) the regional geographic factor—does it matter where theological education takes place?

The Disciples Foundation at Vanderbilt

Questions of institutional context, curricular content, and geographic location underlay the beginnings of the Disciples' efforts at Vanderbilt. The early promotional literature for the Disciples Vanderbilt Foundation defined its institutional context as that of "the most strategic educational center of the South and in some ways the most unique educational center in America." Along with the School of Religion, the other local collegiate institutions made up an intellectual and cultural center. Further, Nashville itself was described as "the religious center of the South." Because there were "located in Nashville more schools, colleges, administrative boards, publication headquarters, and printing plants, which are operated by the various churches, than may be found in any other city south of the Ohio River," the claim was made that "the young minister who trains [in Nashville] will keenly feel the best intellectual currents of America and of the South."[14]

Beyond the affirmation that the Disciples theological student in Nashville would encounter "the best intellectual currents," three particular curricular emphases were identified as part of the program of the Disciples Foundation. First, the prospective student was promised that "at least one course of study will be given in the history of the Restoration [Stone-Campbell] movement." Second, what it termed contextual or field education, "the ideal of having every student preparing for the ministry, actually serving in some church," was highlighted. Third, and closely related to field education, the Rural Church School conducted at Vanderbilt was lauded as "the greatest rural church school ever gathered in the South." The "ecumenical setting" for the teaching of the history of the Disciples and the opportunity to conduct this class for students in all three major branches of the Stone-Campbell movement were early dimensions of the Disciples' curricular vision for its connection to Vanderbilt.[15]

The importance of geography figured prominently in the arguments for supporting the Disciples Foundation. In 1930 Edward T. Small, an early student of the Foundation, noted that the "most promising students were attracted to the northern universities for the pursuit of graduate studies." Because such students "found most attractive work in the section where they had been trained, few of them ever returned to the South." Small emphasized Nashville's identity as "the Athens of the South" and, in addition to the aforementioned institutions of the "center," mentioned the presence in that city of Fisk University, a "school for Negroes" whose "highly trained faculty" and capacity to support graduate study offered "one of the finest opportunities in America for the study of race relations."[16] At least a decade later, the geographic issue was still important in the self-understanding of the Vanderbilt Disciples. A post-1941 brochure quoted survey data indicating that "95 per cent of our ministers trained here in the South locate in this area." This was contrasted to the fact that "ministers going East and North for their training seldom return to the South for their work. In many instances we lose them to other communions."[17]

"Ministers going East and North for their training" had been a growing trend among the Disciples during the first four decades of the twentieth century. The preeminent example of such a school in the East was Yale. In the North it was Chicago. After granting only nineteen degrees to Disciples ministers in the years prior to 1900, Yale granted thirty in the first decade of the twentieth century and an average of ninety-six in each of the next three decades. Similarly, the University of Chicago had granted eight degrees to Disciples ministers prior to 1900. However, in the first decade of the new century it awarded thirty-eight and an average of fifty-five during each of next three decades.[18] Although the University of Chicago did lie in a region of some numeric strength for the Disciples, the same could not be said of Yale.

A second dimension of the geographic argument, closely related to the lament about losing promising students to other regions, was that of the need of the southern churches for quality leadership. Vacant pulpits or inadequately pastored churches in northern Alabama, middle Tennessee, and southern Kentucky were identified as immediate opportunities for Vanderbilt Disciples. Further, because the northern and eastern educational centers largely lay outside of the regions of Disciples of Christ numeric strength, Vanderbilt promoters could speak of the need for "an educational center in Disciple territory."[19]

Prior to the beginnings of the Disciples Foundation, the relationship between the Disciples and Vanderbilt seems to have centered in the ministry of Carey Morgan, who had served as president of both the Kentucky Christian Missionary Society and the American Christian Missionary Society and had held pastorates in Richmond, Virginia, and Paris, Kentucky. During his pastorate at the Vine Street Christian Church, Nashville, Morgan was active in local civic organizations and became well known in the city. Appointed as an adjunct member of Vanderbilt's faculty in homiletics in 1916, Morgan is credited with doing "much to encourage [Disciples] ministers to study there." He "wrote letters to young men preparing for the ministry, inviting them to come to Vanderbilt for advanced study," and is identified as being the "first to see and grasp [the] opportunity" for the Disciples to conduct theological education in Nashville. Morgan's efforts helped to bring seventy-five Disciples students and ministers to the School of Religion between 1913 and 1927.[20]

The presence of Disciples at Vanderbilt became more formally institutionalized with the creation of the Disciples Vanderbilt Foundation in July 1927 and the organization of a board by the following December.[21] The purpose of the Foundation was to facilitate the graduate theological education of Disciples of Christ ministerial candidates at the School of Religion "and its correlated institutions." Initially this was pursued through recruiting, providing a professorship in the school, participating in the placement of students in pastorates, and assisting students in seeking scholarship aid from the school. One way the Foundation provided aid was to supplement student pastorates in churches that could not otherwise afford to pay an acceptable salary. It stressed that "our work is an integral part of the Vanderbilt University School of Religion." Recruitment was limited to those who held undergraduate degrees, with the exception of those enrolling in the Rural Church Department.[22]

The first director of the Foundation was George N. Mayhew, who was also appointed to Vanderbilt's faculty in church administration; he later taught in the area of history of religions. The initial appointment for five years called for him to be freed from teaching in the winter quarter so that he could visit colleges and universities and recruit students for the school. Mayhew would receive a salary of $3,500 per year and an expense account of $1,500 (for travel and administrative expenses). A pledge of $2,500 per year for five years had been offered to the school, and Mayhew assumed the obligation to raise a matching amount through the denomination, which meant that the arrangement came at no cost to the school.[23] Described as "a young man of great energy and executive ability, a tireless worker, and endowed with splendid physical powers," Mayhew's recruiting work reflected the Foundation's regional strategy. That is, Mayhew went "all over the southern states, visiting the schools and the churches for the purpose of selecting and placing students."[24] Mayhew's identity as a member of the Vanderbilt faculty and a graduate of Yale and Chicago expressed the Foundation's aspiration to be an academically credible, integrally related part of a quality university that could plausibly compete for the Disciples' best students. At the same time, Dean O. E. Brown clearly indicated how important the coming of the Disciples was to the School of Religion. Writing to Mayhew as the program was beginning, he declared, "We have a very real concern for the increasing of our student body, and we felt that possibly you would want to make some field contacts not only with students, but with financial prospects."[25]

Disciples' participation in the programs and conferences of Vanderbilt's Rural Church School is a prominent subtheme in the story of the Disciples at Vanderbilt. Riley B. Montgomery called Vanderbilt's program "the largest and most effective" of the rural church schools. Disciples' attendance there was reported as part of the ministry of the Foundation and the number of those in attendance was sometimes added to that of the regularly enrolled students to compose the "total of Disciples students . . . for the year." (By 1930, that number was sixty, equally divided between regularly enrolled and Rural Church School students.) The Foundation's relationship to the Rural Church School signals another dimension of Vanderbilt's ethos as understood by Disciples. That is, in contrast to Yale and Chicago, Vanderbilt was perceived as both southern in character and rural in sensibility. The Foundation elected to dedicate its Wesley Hall office during the Rural Church School in April 1928.[26]

The Disciples Divinity House at Vanderbilt

In the late 1930s events in the Disciples region of Tennessee began to set the stage for a transformation of the Foundation. W. P. Harmon was elected state secretary of the Tennessee Christian Missionary Society (TCMS, precursor of the current Disciples "region") in 1938. Continuing as director of religious education for the region and assuming the editorial duties of the *Tennessee Christian*, Harmon became dissatisfied with conducting the regional ministry of the Disciples from his Nashville home. His aspiration to house the regional work in an office coincided with the desire of the Disciples Foundation to open a residential facility for its students. In March 1941 the Board of the TCMS voted to purchase the apartment building at 2005 Grand Avenue to house the offices of the state secretary, provide housing for Disciples theological students, and headquarter campus ministry for Disciples undergraduates in Nashville.[27]

The opening of the Disciples Divinity House in February 1942 signaled a significant change from the earlier work and institutional relationships of the Foundation. The new Disciples House was under the sponsorship of the TCMS. Not only did the facility house the TCMS offices, but its opening occasioned the end of George N. Mayhew's service as director of the Foundation, as Harmon assumed responsibility for House operations. In other words, the administration of the Foundation had been by a member of the Vanderbilt faculty; the administration of the House was by a denominational executive. The other change, the expansion of the Foundation's work into the direct provision of housing for Vanderbilt theological students has endured as a feature of Disciples life at Vanderbilt. It was a change that was enormously appreciated by the twenty-one new residents who occupied the House in the winter of 1942.[28]

During Harmon's administration, which coincided with the years of World War II, the operation of the Disciples House as a program of the TCMS seems to have been satisfactory. One lingering issue was the indebtedness on the remodeling of the building ($22,500 of $40,000 expended), an obligation that was to be shared by the TCMS and the Foundation. In 1945 the Disciples House at Vanderbilt was recognized as a "member of the Board of Higher Education" of the Disciples, thus beginning a formal relationship that continues today. Six years later the board recognized Vanderbilt as a "related theological institution," and in 1953 the Foundation became part of the denomination's fund-raising program.[29]

Harmon resigned his position as state secretary of the TCMS in 1945 to return to the pastorate and was replaced the following year by George D. West, a Vanderbilt graduate whose study had been facilitated by the Foundation. During West's tenure the relationship between the House as an academic residential facility and as a program of the TCMS deteriorated. Programmatic emphasis and the financial support of TCMS seemed to favor causes such as the Tennessee camp facility at Bethany Hills over the Disciples House. In 1950 the decision was made to separate the House from the TCMS program and establish it as an independent institution rechartered as the Disciples Foundation, Inc. That action also ended West's role as director of the House and led to an acrimonious division between him and William Hardy, the president of the new board.[30] This decision was the occasion for returning the directorship, or deanship, of the House back to an academic with ties to Vanderbilt's faculty. The new director (as of January 1951), shortly thereafter named dean, was Herman A. Norton.

For the next thirty-five years, the central character in the story was Herman Norton. He was a native Virginian, a graduate of (the Disciples') Lynchburg College, and an Army veteran of World War II who continued to be active in the Army Reserves. Having been recruited by both Mayhew and Harmon, Norton came to study at Vanderbilt's School of Religion in 1947. He became a student of church history professor J. Minton Batten and completed B.D., M.A., and Ph.D. degrees in 1949, 1951, and 1956, respectively. He was appointed instructor in church history in 1951 and promoted to associate professor in 1954 and to professor in 1960. At the beginning of his tenure as dean of the Disciples House, the Disciples student community consisted of twenty-three residents in the House. By the end of the decade the number had reached forty-five (twenty-four of whom were studying for the ministry). During the next decade and a half Disciples enrollment at Vanderbilt and related institutions hovered in the fifties, with normally over thirty students preparing for the ministry. Two significant building projects were undertaken during the Norton era. In 1957 the property at 2005 Grand Avenue was sold and construction begun on two lots at 1917 and 1919 Adelicia Avenue. Designed by Nashville architect Terrill Hall, a $200,000 residential building with eight apartments, four rooms for single students, a lounge, chapel, conference room, and kitchen was completed and dedicated in April 1959.[31] In 1966–67 a third story was added to the new House to provide additional apartments and rooms.

A third building project that was to redound to the benefit of the Disciples community at Vanderbilt was the location of the Disciples of Christ Historical

Society in Nashville and the construction of its Phillips Memorial Library and archive facility on Nineteenth Avenue, a short distance from the House. Norton was a member of the planning committee that facilitated the Society's move to Nashville. The presence of the best single historical collection of materials related to the Stone-Campbell traditions in such close proximity to Vanderbilt would provide many students with opportunities for graduate research in topics related to this movement.

Norton's style as a teacher, mentor, and administrator was positive, plain-spoken, honest, responsible, and generous. He admired these qualities in others, and when he encountered them in students rewarded them with extravagantly high regard. On the other hand, he had little patience for cant, foppery, or irresponsibility, and when he encountered these qualities in students he could be extremely blunt. The laypeople of Vanderbilt's hinterland loved Norton for this. His positive outlook received a major challenge in 1960 and in the years follow-ing with the controversy surrounding James Lawson. Norton noted that other theological institutions were exploiting the Lawson affair (see Chapter 6) to Vanderbilt's detriment and their benefit in their efforts to recruit prospective students. Nevertheless, by 1963 Norton's positive tone had returned as he re-ported "our best year to date."[32]

The era of the Vietnam conflict brought some irony to the texture of Norton's ministry at Vanderbilt. He continued to serve in the Army Reserves Chaplain Corps and was promoted to colonel in 1970 and to brigadier general in 1975. Many in the Divinity School community were deeply opposed to the United States' involvement in Vietnam and actively protested against it. Norton steadily supported the ministry of military chaplaincy, guided interested stu-dents through its credentialing process, and continued his own scholarly work on its history. His focus was on the religious needs of the soldiers. He had little to say about global geopolitical policy.[33]

Norton sounded an uncharacteristically pessimistic note on recruitment in his 1973 report to the board of the House. High tuition charges at Vanderbilt and the limited receipts for the House from churches and individuals caused him to anticipate a period of decreasing Disciples enrollment at Vanderbilt through the middle 1970s. Nevertheless, in 1976 the Disciples was the second largest denominational group in the student community (after United Methodists). By the early 1980s, however, the pattern of having many Disciples student pastors in Tennessee, northern Alabama, and western Kentucky had begun to erode sig-nificantly. This represented an "off the books" loss of a significant source of financial support for Disciples students at Vanderbilt.[34]

Upon Norton's retirement in 1986, Richard L. Harrison, Jr., was called to become dean of the Disciples Divinity House. Like his predecessor, Har-

rison was a southerner, a Ph.D. graduate of Vanderbilt, and a church historian—
a student of the sixteenth-century Reformation as well as of the Disciples'
"nineteenth-century Reformation."[35] During his tenure as dean, Vanderbilt's
steady tuition inflation necessitated placing great emphasis on fund-raising for
both short- and long-term goals. In spite of these efforts, financial pressures
contributed to a slow decline in Disciples enrollment from the low fifties to the
low forties. Residential patterns were further complicated by a necessary major
renovation of the House in the early 1990s.

Perhaps Harrison's greatest gift to the Disciples Divinity House at Vanderbilt was his ministry of encouragement. A person of warm and affable spirit, he
ministered sensitively to many bright Disciples who had chosen a university-
related divinity school over a denominational seminary because of ambivalent
feelings toward the church and traditional forms of ministry. Harrison held
before such students the challenge to consider ministry as a real option and the
congregation as one locus for this ministry. He also offered support for women
and ethnic-minority divinity and graduate students in religion.

In 1993 Harrison became president of Lexington Theological Seminary. A
two-year search for his successor and the attendant interim arrangements created significant difficulties in both fund-raising and recruitment of students.[36]
The Disciples of Christ community at Vanderbilt, however, was strengthened
by a number of developments in succeeding years. In 1995 Mark Miller-
McLemore, a graduate of the Divinity School of the University of Chicago,
became dean of the Disciples Divinity House and assistant professor of the
Practice of Ministry at the Divinity School. His coming to Vanderbilt coincided
with the appointment of his spouse, Bonnie Miller-McLemore, to the faculty in
pastoral theology and counseling. Further, the Disciples faculty ranks have enlarged with the appointments of L. Susan Bond in homiletics and Viki Matson
in field education. These appointments should bode well for the future health of
Vanderbilt's Disciples community.

Influence and Impact

Disciples of Christ faculty in the Divinity School have manifested a number
of different patterns during the twentieth century. One of the earliest patterns
was for a local Disciples pastor to teach preaching or the practice of ministry as
an adjunct faculty member, as Carey Morgan had done in homiletics. A generation after Morgan, Vine Street pastors Roger Nooe and G. Curtis Jones repli-
cated this. Disciples pastors of other Tennessee congregations also served as
adjunct faculty, including Frank Drowota of the Woodmont Christian Church
in Nashville and William G. West of First Christian Church in Chattanooga,

and were a significant part of the growing relationship between the Disciples and Vanderbilt. Nooe, West, and Drowota served on the first board of the second Disciples Divinity House.[37]

Alongside these pastoral adjuncts were a number of regular faculty affiliated with Disciples congregations during their Vanderbilt years. Among those whose affiliation was well known and enduring were the biblical scholars J. Philip Hyatt, Walter Harrelson, and Leander Keck. Hyatt came to the faculty in 1941 to teach Old Testament. He had been brought up a Southern Baptist and educated at Baylor University, Brown University, and Yale University. When Hyatt came to Nashville "he found himself in tension with the fundamentalism of Baptist churches" there and "sought a churchly context akin to the free church tradition of the Baptists, but more open to the kind of critical approach to biblical studies Hyatt had cultivated" in his graduate studies and teaching. Therefore, he united with the Woodmont Christian Church, "adopted, and was adopted by, the Disciples as his spiritual home," was ordained in 1946, and was an active member of his denomination until he died in 1972.[38]

Walter Harrelson was another scholar who "gravitated to the Disciples from [another] denomination." He was educated at the University of North Carolina and Union Theological Seminary in New York. He taught Old Testament at Union, Andover Newton Theological Seminary, and the University of Chicago (where he was also dean of the Divinity School) before coming to Vanderbilt in 1960; he had been ordained to the ministry in the American Baptist Convention in 1951. While in Nashville the Harrelsons held membership at First Baptist Church, Capitol Hill, but later joined Vine Street Christian Church as well. The Christian Church (Disciples of Christ) granted him ministerial standing in 1970.[39]

Leander Keck received his education at Linfield College, Andover Newton Theological Seminary, and Yale. He spent the 1960s on the Vanderbilt faculty, during which time he transferred his membership and ministerial standing from the North American Baptist Convention to the Disciples of Christ. Keck became active in Disciples life, preaching, lecturing to pastors' conferences and Disciples laypeople, and writing for lay as well as scholarly audiences. Wayne Bell, former pastor of Vine Street Christian Church, recalls that Keck was a very active member, teacher, and elder in that congregation; particularly, he developed a curriculum on the Bible and race relations that was taught in the ideologically divided congregation in the 1960s.[40]

A number of other Vanderbilt faculty had Disciples of Christ connections that were less public or shorter in duration than the ones just mentioned. The gravitation of such persons toward the Disciples of Christ may best be explained as the interplay of denominational, sectional, and congregational factors. For

the most part, the formerly non-Disciples faculty who affiliated with or participated in Nashville Disciples congregations during their Vanderbilt years were
from Baptist backgrounds. The worship style, hymnody (particularly in the
1950s and 1960s), baptismal practice, and polity of the Disciples did not, in many
respects, represent great changes from their former denomination. However, in
Nashville (as in the South generally) the ethos of the Disciples was more liberal
than that of the Baptists. In part this was the case because the division between
the Disciples of Christ and the Churches of Christ had taken the most conservative elements of the Stone-Campbell traditions into the latter communion and
left the more progressive elements in the Disciples of Christ. Thus, the Disciples
were, denominationally, a "Baptist" option and, in terms of ethos within the
section of the country, a "liberal" one. It should also be noted that the Vine
Street Christian Church and the Woodmont Christian Church were local congregations whose vitality, leadership, and programs made them attractive to
Vanderbilt faculty and their families.

A few of the Disciples faculty members at Vanderbilt should be noted
because of their impact on the development of the denomination and its self-
understanding. Alva W. Taylor, credited with having "initiated and promoted
for seventeen years the social welfare work of the Disciples of Christ," was
professor of social ethics from 1928 to 1936. He had served on the Commission
on Social Service and the committees on Inter-Racial Relations and International Good Will of the Federal Council of Churches. He had also been on
the staff of the *Christian Century*, editor of the journal *Social Trends*, and one of
the very few Disciples who became leaders in the Social Gospel movement. He
helped to create for the denomination the Board of Temperance and Social
Service (of the American Christian Missionary Society) and served as its "un-
salaried secretary."[41] Taylor was thus a bridge figure who helped keep alive an
interest in public issues and social ministry during a time when they were
receiving relatively little attention.

J. Philip Hyatt has been identified as a scholar who saw his "biblical scholarship as informed and complemented by [his] religious commitment" and understood his "scholarship to be interior to and in the service of Disciples tradition." Christ as the "normative center of the canon," a concern for Christian
unity, and the quest for a biblical understanding of Christian baptism were
themes of Hyatt's scholarship that identify it with Disciples' traditional affirmations and concerns. Yet Hyatt's treatment of these themes and others kept "Disciples tradition and biblical theology in dialogue with each other."[42]

Herman Norton's impact on Disciples of Christ scholarship was particularly in the field of the history of the Stone-Campbell traditions. He discouraged
the romanticism and narrow focus on the Campbells that had characterized

much of the historiography of the movement, while encouraging students to broaden the chronological focus of their studies to include Disciples' "prehistory" as well as twentieth-century developments. A committed Disciple, Norton nonetheless cultivated a community of student/scholars across the spectrum of the divided Stone-Campbell traditions and mentored members of the Churches of Christ and "independent" Christian churches as well as Disciples. He was interested in "sect-like" religious movements and encouraged students to engage plain and populist streams of Christian history with empathy. In a similar vein, he modeled in his activity and scholarship an interest in regional, local, and congregational concerns in the life of the church.[43]

H. Jackson Forstman has been an active ecumenist, with service on the Disciples' Council on Christian Unity's Commission on Theology as well as involvement with the Faith and Order Commission on the World Council of Churches, and an active local leader at Vine Street Christian Church. His voice in Disciples of Christ theological circles was heard not only in the Vanderbilt classroom but also through his participation in the Association of Disciples for Theological Discussion and his wide public speaking. A teacher of historical theology, Forstman's method has been to "probe changing understandings of the gospel at crucial junctures in the tradition." He has encouraged his students "to learn from the history of Christian thought without recourse to traditionalism by means of critical, self-critical, and constructive thinking." For students of the Stone-Campbell traditions, Forstman's impact was especially significant in encouraging their studies toward greater engagement with the relationships among those traditions and "European Christianity, the Reformed tradition, the ecumenical movement, and 'modernity' along with its cultured despisers."[44]

The impact of Vanderbilt on scholarship among the Disciples may be further illustrated by turning to recent publications. Twenty-four of the sixty-seven books listed in biblical and historical studies by the *Disciples Theological Digest* (vols. 1–8, 1986–93) were written by persons who received all or part of their graduate theological education at Vanderbilt.[45] The school has also been an important training ground for administrative leadership in Disciples of Christ theological education. Brite Divinity School of Texas Christian University, Lexington Theological Seminary, Christian Theological Seminary, Phillips Graduate Seminary, and the Disciples Divinity House at Vanderbilt all have had either presidents or deans during the 1980s or 1990s or both who were educated at Vanderbilt.

Part of the vision of those who formed the Disciples Foundation was to provide Disciples of Christ ministerial candidates a seminary option in a university context in the South. As noted earlier, an explicit and oft-stated concern was to retain for the region talented ministers and church leaders and to do so (implicitly) by offering an attractive alternative to Chicago and Yale. Vanderbilt's continuation as an alternative for Disciples students is one form of the institutionalization of this founding vision. That it provided part of the leadership for Brite Divinity School of Texas Christian University, another Disciples university option in the South, represents another expression of this vision.

Those who began the Foundation also hoped that a critical mass of Disciples with a perception of their group identity would be drawn to Vanderbilt. This writer's experience was that, although Vanderbilt is not denominationally affiliated, the presence of the Disciples Divinity House, the Disciples of Christ Historical Society, and the regional office of the Christian Church (Disciples of Christ) in Tennessee, together with strong Disciples congregations in Nashville and the proximity of congregations in contiguous regions (such as in southwestern Kentucky) with strong ties to Vanderbilt, made theological education there feel strongly Disciples oriented within an ecumenical context.

The primary legacy of the Disciples Foundation and the Disciples Divinity House at Vanderbilt has been the scores of women and men who have been trained for congregational ministry, chaplaincy, and other forms of Christian service. Many of these persons have, indeed, remained in the South, equipping Disciples of that region for their ministries. Just as the antiparochial context of the Divinity School was a challenge to the Disciples community, Vanderbilt's own southern context forced critical reflection. Indeed, the Divinity School has not often explicitly celebrated its region in its recent history because there was so much about which to be suspicious. Yet the Divinity School and the Disciples community within it have recognized that the South is a reality attended by all of the ambiguity that particular contexts always contain and remains a context in which faithful ministry is much needed.

PART V
Perspective

The final chapter is a singular endeavor at a perspective that offers a reflection on theology as it has been taught and written over the history of the school. In the process of mapping individual positions and generational shifts of emphasis, exploring several strands in the history of American theology, James O. Duke probes even more subtle questions to illumine institutional character and ethos as well as the impact and influence upon students. Although it is only one strand in the entire educational process, focusing on what was thought and taught in the field of theology probably brings one as close as possible to seeing how successive generations were shaped by their studies at Vanderbilt. With his long view, Duke is also able to chart continuities and changes in the transition from a denominational to an interdenominational school with a liberal Protestant orientation, connecting the work of its faculty to wider American and European currents in religious thought.

A Century and a Quarter of Theology:
A Review

James O. Duke

From its founding, the Divinity School has appointed to its faculty teacher-scholars entrusted with distinct responsibilities for teaching theology. I make here a very modest attempt to survey their handling of that trust.

My title, then, specifies the historical reportage that follows. It is also a shameless play on words, alerting anyone familiar with theology of the sort taught at Vanderbilt University to why I call this account an attempt, and very modest. Its namesake is "Half a Century of Theology: A Review," a 1908 article by Ernst Troeltsch, then professor of systematic theology at Heidelberg University.[1] Troeltsch's study is less than perfect. It is, for instance, exceptionally parochial, ignoring nearly all else in the world except the scholarship of a few grand Teutons and Scotsman Thomas Carlyle. Yet Troeltsch managed to shoulder burdens of theology's long and wide history, cast light on hidden dynamics and unacknowledged sore spots of theological reflection, and pinpoint challenges so formidable that theology struggles even now to overcome, or circumvent, them. This descriptive overview of theology at Vanderbilt compares with Troeltsch's article in that its title is as chronologically imprecise as his: my "century and a quarter" is, like his "half century," a rough approximation.

Reference to Troeltsch, however, signals a point other than prefatory play or posturing. Vanderbilt's theologians, save its first, have known of Troeltsch. His works have had an impact on the thinking of the vast majority of them, though none has sought or rightly deserves billing as exponents of "Troeltsch-ianism." More important to them than any of Troeltsch's answers to the difficult questions of theology have been his capacity to identify the most difficult questions and his resolve to address them head-on rather than pretend that Christian theology need not bother itself with such vexing and discomforting concerns. During the last half-century in particular, the theology taught at Vanderbilt has typically advised that serious theological studies involve thinking more (not less!) broadly, deeply, and carefully yet more boldly than even Troeltsch ever had, bound as his thought was by his social location in the bygone days of Imperial and Weimar Germany.

Explanations or disclaimers are in order with regard to several conventions (some sheerly ad hoc) that I have followed in this account. By the phrase "en-trusted with distinct responsibilities for teaching theology," I mean faculty ap-pointed to a disciplinary or field-specific post that, already at the school's found-ing, distinguished its theologians of the line from colleagues in other areas of theological study. Systematic theology is the most common designation for the post, its field, and its task(s); but other terms such as doctrinal, philosophical, historical, and constructive theology at times come into play, usually as subtle distinctions without much difference. This focus for my mandate is so familiar, so long established in theological education, and so practicable that it might pass without comment. Even so, a full history of school theology would have had to add to the cast of characters appearing here the scholars in biblical studies, church history, ethics, and practical theology who contributed as much to the-ology at Vanderbilt and at large as the school's line theologians.

Publications by and about the Vanderbilt theologians are my primary data-base. I have not inspected all the literature: I salute but do not envy anyone who has. My phrase "theology taught at Vanderbilt" refers therefore to what I gather from such writings that these professors professed. On occasion I offer an esti-mate of student responses, even though theologies that Vanderbilt students actually learned and perhaps preached and practiced await separate study in their own right.

The Mainlining of Methodist Theology: Three Generations

The Biblical Department in 1875 included a faculty post in systematic theology. This post, along with the others, betokened its founders' embrace of the four-fold division of theological study widespread in Protestantism at the time. Equally widespread, and built into the design, ethos, and operations of the school was the "clerical paradigm," which envisioned these several theologi-cal studies as converging to supply the church with ordained ministers equipped to carry out their duties of office. In the school's early history, the church meant first and foremost the Methodist Episcopal Church, South (MECS). After 1914, the University "allowed" the Department to scratch for its survival as a university-related nondenominational School of Religion. This jump—or push—from the confines and securities of its past was to have far-reaching consequences. But at the time and long afterward the theology taught there remained by and large as it had been from the start—definitively church theology, Protestant theology, Methodist theology.

For financial reasons if none other, the school maintained until 1950 only one position in systematics and relied on its occupant (supplemented by occasional or cross-over course instructors or both) to tend the field.[2] The order of succession ran: Thomas O. Summers, Wilbur Fisk Tillett, and Edward T. Ramsdell. Each represented, for Methodism and for Vanderbilt, a generation of change in theology.[3]

Thomas O. Summers (1812–82)

The appointment of Summers as Vanderbilt's first systematic theologian and dean capped his long career as pastor, editor, author, and general conference secretary of the MECS. Liturgics (worship, sacraments, and above all hymnology) was his area of competency and special love. In theology he neither sought nor discovered anything distinctly "new." His claim to fame was vast erudition and unfailing orthodoxy. He was one of his church's leading intellectuals: an omnivorous reader, a perfectionist in English composition, guardian of the Wesleyan Arminian heritage in general, and a staunch defender of southern Methodism in particular.

It is tempting to understate the case by tagging Summers and his theology as conservative and moving on. But that tag conceals more than it reveals about him or the history of theology at Vanderbilt. His school service had as much to do with preparation for ministry through what theological educators today call "formation" and "role modeling" as anything else. He embodied the theology he taught. He "got religion" in Methodism, and the religion he got was that of the ongoing evangelical Methodist revival: an "amazing grace," yet also a matter of a responsible decision of a free will and a lifelong commitment to spiritual discipline and moral rectitude. In his view, the study of theology was a means to the higher goal of directing individuals and society along the path of devout, righteous living, and divine blessing.

Understanding why Summers represented a generational mainlining of Methodist theology requires a measure of historical distance and contextualization. Summers was one of the nineteenth century's "gentlemen theologians."[4]

The rock-ribbed conservatism of his Vanderbilt years, 1875 to 1882, had not always or universally been identified as altogether rock-ribbed or conservative. The South's antebellum gentleman theologians, like countless Christians in the North, aimed at a broad, presumptively centrist, coalition of evangelical Protestants who would be capable of advancing Christianity and "civilized" culture as conjoint causes in America and beyond. Their theologies were at root variations of a rational orthodoxy, an *entente cordiale* between the claims of a Protestant biblical-historic faith and a moderate Enlightenment acceptance of "modern" scientific method, Newtonian cosmology, and the empiricism of Baconian, Lockean, and then Scottish Common Sense epistemologies.

The result of such thinking was a rational supernaturalist ontotheology. At its base was a dualist metaphysics of nature and the supernatural (divine). Its method was typically a two-step model of reasoning. Its starting point was a display of presumptively rational, and hence universally credible, evidences for the divine origin of Christianity's revealed truths. The task thereafter was to exposit those truths as a complex yet coherent description of the order and telos of the cosmos, in terms that were sometimes above but never contrary to experience and reflection. When various "reasons of the heart" were included as "internal" evidences of divinity, John Wesley and other well-schooled pietists readily adapted and adopted this "rationalist" model for use on behalf of evangelical revivalism.

Transplanted to America by the end of the eighteenth century, the model moved westward across the frontier with Protestant settlers engaged in Christianizing and civilizing the wilderness. The model's flexibility added to its appeal. Useful to Protestants generally in combat with deism, skepticism, and indifference, papal authoritarianism, or sectarian fanaticism, it could also be retooled to serve nearly any denominational or interdenominational need. And so it was, by Unitarian and Trinitarian, Calvinist and Arminian, high church and low church, and many others. Sociologically speaking, the rational supernaturalist model of reasoning—in league with text criticism and grammatico-historical hermeneutics—reached its peak of American popularity during the middle of the nineteenth century. Its terms were at that time the lingua franca of evangelical Protestantism's unstable but potent unity-in-diversity.

That time was the middle of Summers's career as well. During his tenure as Vanderbilt's theologian and dean, he was conserving gains hard-won just yesterday, determined as always to bring and keep Methodist ministry within evangelical Protestantism's main line. His goal was not ecumenical unity. It was rather to defend the legitimacy of the Methodist way, and thereby contribute to its growth and secure its position in the competitive religious marketplace. The goal required above all showing that this way was neither fanatical nor sectarian but estimable, warranted by scripture and tradition, doctrinally sound, and churchly. The success of Methodism on the one hand and the accumulated mass of Wesley scholarship on the other make it hard today to grasp why such a demonstration was "required," although the spawn of rival Wesleyan-heritage churches is a tip-off that the movement was highly fissiparous.

In context, the traditionalism of Summers was that of Methodist progressivism, one of the means by which American Methodism aspired to gain mainline status. In antebellum times, an Arminian plea was ipso facto theologically "liberal." Masses of evangelical Protestants considered Methodism's "evangelical Arminianism" an oxymoron and its resort to "new measures" revivalism an ecclesiological menace. By the end of Summers's career, the situation had changed. So many evangelicals were Arminian in practice if not always in doctrinal theory, so institutionalized were revivalist conversions, and so altered was the intellectual and cultural climate that those like Summers had (been) shifted from the progressive to the conservative camp simply by never changing at all.

Summers, however, belonged to the party that pressed Methodists to be as well informed as they were passionate. He held that the Wesleyan movement was in fact and by rights a theological as well as a revivalistic tradition. It was and should be an Arminianism that was also a truly biblical, catholic, and reformed evangelicalism. It should foster a rational orthodoxy in tune with both historic church doctrine and modern thought. Its worship should be grounded in the church's historic liturgical heritage. Its standards of spiritual and moral discipline should reflect principled rather than fanatic or arbitrary judgments. Ministers should manifest broad learning and genteel culture as well as pious feelings.

Although Summers edited more works than he authored, his total collection is vast and diverse. The list ranges from biographies of eminent Anglo-Saxons, Methodist itinerants, Newton, popes, and of course Wesley, to studies of Greek Orthodox churches, proper uses of money, the moral duties of Christian slave owners, plants and trees of scripture, preaching, and then on to yellow fever and other medical topics. The potpourri reflects, among other things, his church's attempt to provide its itinerant pastors and lay ministers access to the "liberal arts and sciences" and worldly wisdom. The works of theology per se on the list were the once and in some cases the lasting classics of Methodist rational orthodoxy and moral philosophy. They were either required by the church's Course of Study program or supplementary to it. Summers's own scholarly publications included commentaries on the Gospels and Acts as well as expositions of his understanding of Methodist doctrine regarding baptism and holiness.[5]

The lecture course on systematic theology Summers offered at Vanderbilt was edited and published posthumously by his student, John J. Tigert, whose hand in the writing of the book's introduction and extensive documentary notes forbids making confident claims about Summers's own command of theological method and theological literature.[6] Several general characteristics are easily identified. Theology is construed as setting forth truths of revelation in scientific form. These truths are doctrinal, meaning "propounded by God for humans to believe." Dogmata follow, from the nature of God to moral theology. The guiding principle is that theological truth has been exposited in three forms— God's biblical revelation, Wesley's Twenty-five Articles, and systematically clear and coherent concepts. More effort is spent explaining Methodism's views of universal grace, free will, and moral accountability versus predestinarian Calvinism than on rational orthodoxy's trademark handling of the claims of revealed and natural religion. Even so, the great Arminian-Calvinist debate does not predominate. Summers sets it within the larger framework of historic church doctrine and related church-theological concerns. At the critical junctures, and for much of the journey along the way, Summers follows the course taken long ago in Richard Watson's *Theological Institutes.*

Watson's course had, in its own way and in its original context, set Methodist theology within the unity-in-diversity of evangelical Protestantism at large and along the early nineteenth-century main line of Anglo-American religious and scientific thought. Having devoted a lifetime to the defense of this tradition of post-Enlightenment Methodism against enemies both foreign and domestic, Summers upheld it still in his theology lectures at Vanderbilt. That main line, however, was in fact dividing even while he was lecturing. With the advances of developmental-oriented thinking in philosophy, history, science, and the emergent social sciences, rational orthodoxy was no longer representative of enlightened, progressive, or even rational thought at all. Methodists, like many other Protestants, were later if not sooner constrained to take sides for various kinds of liberalism or modernism on the one hand or for forms of conservatism or fundamentalism on the other.

Summers was no fence sitter. Had he lived on, his theology unchanged, he might have tried to build the school into an Arminian "Princeton of the South," a financially and educationally ambitious goal, but perhaps not an utter impossibility. In that event, his school may have passed like Princeton Theological Seminary into a fundamentalist era. But when Summers died in 1882, polarization was yet not so clear or clearly inevitable to anyone committed to Protestantism's main line, least of all to a mainline Methodist in the South. The moment of an either-or decision for Vanderbilt came just a few years afterward.

Wilbur Fisk Tillett (1854–1936)

It would be hard to overstate the importance of Summers's successor, Wilbur Tillett, for theological studies at Vanderbilt.[7] During his long service as theologian, dean, and then dean emeritus, the school entered on the course it would follow throughout the twentieth century. Too many forces were at play to credit or blame Tillett alone for the change. Even so, he was its living embodiment, its pioneer guide, and long its most mighty champion. The redirection might be reduced to a deceptively simple formula: if Summers was conservative, Tillett was liberal.

Tillett did not start out that way. Indeed, the line of succession was marked by multiple similarities and continuities. Both theologians were southern Methodist loyalists. Summers had become a gentleman theologian; Tillett was the son of one. They (and their church, as a general rule) agreed that a theologian's tasks included active involvement in decision-making about church doctrine and discipline and in the rough-and-tumble of church politics. Even Tillett's church-delegated and unofficial or freelance efforts on behalf of pan-Methodist and wider church unity belong in that latter category, though such "ecumenism" had become a notably liberal cause by the time Tillett represented his denomination in the Federal Council of Churches.

In any case there was good reason to expect, at the outset of his career, that Tillett would teach very much the same theology as Summers, only very much better. He was well schooled in rational orthodoxy. All that Princeton taught except Calvinist confessionalism, which Tillett was somehow able to skirt with impunity, prepared him to advance the cause of Arminian rational supernaturalism. His first publications fulfilled this expectation—or might be read to do so in light of their modulated style and tone. Instead of merely citing precedents and evidentiary testimony from authoritative sources, he scrutinized, compared and contrasted, and weighed them. He dealt with issues of higher criticism, for example, on a case-by-case basis before concluding that, on balance, the "new" historical-critical views failed the burden of proof.

By 1900 Tillett's opinion of higher criticism had changed, and in this and other respects his career as a liberal was already underway.[8] The transition, it seems, was gradual. A datable "experience," if there were one, would have given rise to some conversion narrative of great interest to his friends and foes alike. My own judgment is that none was involved, because the character of Tillett's liberalism is better described as an extension and modification of rational supernaturalism rather than a break with it.

The first, most familiar and heavily traveled, of the break-away routes leading by the end of the nineteenth century to more or less the same "liberal" destination was what might be called the German cut. It departed with Kant from the rational supernaturalist schools of Leibniz-Wolff and Locke and immediately plunged one into the thickets, delights, and dangers of a post-Kantian world: Romanticism of many hues; Germany's diverse philosophical and theological options; the awakening of historical consciousness, along with its methods and results; and the embrace of a science attentive to development as well as new developmental sciences. During the nineteenth century Protestant rational orthodoxy in America, busy forming and reforming alliances between church doctrine and Common Sense Realism, had added to its long list of major tasks those of dissuading anyone from participation in Kant's Copernican revolution and guarding them against its harmful effects. The American theologians who defied this continental embargo appear in most history books as the precursors and pioneers of liberalism and the scholarly study of theology.

Tillett's liberalism did not involve crossing over to the German route. He himself never made Kant's turn to the subject. Philosophically, he remained a Common Sense theistic realist, following the lines set out by his Princeton teacher James McCosh. In articulating his own views, Tillett drew primarily on the British-American tradition of theological apologetics and moral philosophy. Yet he was a "historically conscious" thinker, accepting the newer currents of developmental science and social scientific thought, the notion of progressive revelation, and historical-critical method, regularly offering assurances that such advances in learning were no danger to faith and yet without endorsing any specific finding or hypothesis as "assured."

Theologically, the position he arrived at was classical or evangelical liberalism, as distinct from "modernism." Strict classification, however, is rather complicated. His own idiom betokens British broad church liberalism; evangelical liberals were his homeland associates and allies; the modernists and their thought received friendly attention in his writings and at the school. The spirit and terminology of evangelical liberalism predominated in his accounts of Methodism's doctrinal standards. Explicit commitment to its characteristic themes and causes was evident in other writings, as in his work as dean and church leader. His forte, it is surely safe and fair to say, was in popularizing the "new theology" by minimizing the shock of leaving "the old" (Tillett favored the term "traditional"). His three most important monographs were *Personal Salvation* (1902), *The Paths that Lead to God* (1924), and *Providence, Prayer and Power* (1926). All were written, as he stated in the preface to the second book, "not for the learned, but for learners." The materials had been developed in and for the classroom, pulpit, and lecture hall and were meant to be inspirational as well as intellectually solid.[9]

As the titles suggest, Tillett's chief concerns were not just academic. The point of theology was to clarify the Christian way of life and direct and strengthen the faithful to pursue it. Shifting from traditional to new theology was possible, desirable, and indeed necessary because failing to do so meant failing to identify and undertake the divine calling of service to the world as revealed in Jesus Christ. Primarily an apologist, Tillett urged theology to face up to doubt and uncertainty and seek to address them. His apologetics, however, were in actuality directed less to unbelievers than to believers who, by clinging to outmoded ideas, miss the delights of vital faith and shirk their spiritual and moral duties as Christians. God's "fatherly" love, he avowed, is one such delight; forgiveness of sins through Jesus Christ is another; personal experience of the power of the Holy Spirit's working within and with the faithful is still another; and assurance of eternal life with God is the greatest of all.

The list could go on. And it does in *Personal Salvation*, Tillett's review of the cardinal themes of evangelical Arminianism. No break with Wesleyan tradition was made, but the elements of the "order of salvation" (*ordo salutis*) were reformulated. Sanctification, for example, was "the cultivation of every virtue, both active and passive, and the performance of every Christian duty"; perfection was "complete love of God and continuous service to the neighbor." By virtue and duty, Tillett meant no less than Summers's devotionalism and moral rectitude, but all that and more. Humanitarian commitments and social gospel concerns were integral to Tillett's view of faith's meaning. He took an active interest in movements for social reform, including advocacy of world peace through international courts of arbitration during the 1920s.

The Paths that Lead to God emerged from his course lectures on philosophy of religion. Its starting point is anthropological and its apologetical strategy is an updating of the literature on evidences of Christianity. The paths noted in the title were in effect evidentiary proceedings leading to the conclusion that (the) one God exists, as a personal being transcendent of and yet immanent in nature and history. It is the range of evidence that distinguishes Tillett's newer, liberalized rational supernaturalism from traditional apologetics. In his view, God is reached by reflecting on nature, science, human nature, philosophy, reason, the Bible, Christ, the church and its creeds, human doubt (!), human religious experience (including study of comparative religions), and suffering and death.

His other book-length writings dealt with his long-held, deep-rooted convictions about divine providence and human affairs. *Providence, Prayer, and Power* focuses on the immanence, the attainment, and the divine and human use of spiritual power capable of meeting the needs of individuals and the world. Here one finds, corresponding to progressive revelation, testimony to the progressive realization of God's purposes in human history. *The Hand of God in American History* made the same point with specific reference to America's role in world affairs. Citing with approval Hegel's "pronounced and outspoken" affirmation of God's guiding hand in the course of human events, Tillett recounted God's wonder-working providences and lessons in the history of America, extending from Columbus "the Christ Bearer" to the "ethical and altruistic motives of the American people" in the Spanish-American War and then on to the nation's opportunity for "Messianic service" by practicing "with generous altruism the golden rule and the law of love" in the aftermath of World War I.[10]

Edward T. Ramsdell (1902–57)

Tillett's successor in theology was Edward Ramsdell, who taught from 1938 to 1953. His appointment signaled no sea change of theological orientation. On the contrary, the continuity was near maximal, considering that Tillett had labored to put the school in mainline Protestantism's orbit and was in some ways irreplaceable. Like Tillett, Ramsdell was a Methodist, offspring of a minister's family (but a northerner, from Michigan), and an evangelical liberal. His academic credentials from the University of Michigan and Boston University were all in order. Religious and moral philosophy were of considerable concern to him, as to Tillett. He also taught historical surveys of Christian theology, and his dealings with that subject matter signal a turn in the theology taught at Vanderbilt.

His list of courses indicates that offerings in theology had taken on a standardized academic format easily recognized by students, colleagues, and outsiders from then to now. There is coverage of classics and classical backgrounds of philosophy and theology, recent developments, and major figures. Conspicuous by their absence are courses in any way resembling Tillett's "Doctrines of Christianity Pertaining to Personal Salvation" or "Theology of the Poets."

One change occasions pause: by the study of major figures Ramsdell had in view working through the issues raised not only by Luther, Calvin, and Wesley but Kant, Schleiermacher, Hegel, Kierkegaard, Ritschl, Nietzsche, Troeltsch, and Barth as well. Given his wide reading and far-flung contacts, Tillett would have easily identified all these names. At times he mentioned some of them and quoted quotable quotes. Yet except for Wesley and Calvin(ism), none was formative of the theology he taught, much less decisive. His intellectual funding came from other sources. Changes were underway in Tillett's successor with respect to approach, coverage, and substance of the teaching of theology.

The changes were actually neither as abrupt nor as bold as one might think, given what has been said so far. Ramsdell was by no means hell-bent on Germanizing Vanderbilt theology. On the contrary, it is difficult to imagine how a theologian could have been more attuned to the school's Tillett legacy. Ramsdell was thoroughly trained in and devoted to the liberal thought of Boston personalism. Beginning with its founder, Borden P. Bowne, the personalist school was an eclectic, multifaceted movement, one of Methodism's earliest and most popular routes to theological liberalism, and arguably that church's most distinctive and influential contribution to philosophical theology during the twentieth century. Tillett had taken Bowne's position very seriously, praising it as the most worthy of the idealist theisms to date, yet without declaring himself a disciple.[11]

Ramsdell was a second-generation personalist, a student of Bowne's students Edgar S. Brightman and Albert C. Knudson. His early articles assured him a career as a personalist scholastic and gave some hints that he might vie, in time, for office as the school leader.[12] The continental drift of his list of courses was by no means antipersonalist. Even so, Ramsdell's new interests showed he understood theological study to demand not only keeping up with current trends but also self-critical reflection: the overall thrust of the diverse contemporary trends under study challenged basic premises of liberalism, including his own.

The no-compromise assault on "liberalism" came from Karl Barth and Barthians. But between the times of the Weimar Republic, worldwide depression, the rise of Hitler and his Confessing Church opponents, and the coming of World War II, liberalism's capacity to serve either God or the world well was scrutinized from every angle and found wanting in part if not in whole. The new generation of scholars and ecumenical theologians made up a mixed, and often discordant, chorus that called in loud voice for a theocentric, realistic turn in theology and the church.

Ramsdell took that call very seriously and read along with his students the literature of significance to the making of the "theological renaissance" of the day. His personalist liberalism emerged chastened, perhaps as much by world events and beneficial results of the theological revival as by the strength of theological argument per se. His popularized description of theology's "new phase," written for church readers in 1943–44, touched on all these bases: once again the Bible and its gospel were being preached and widely read; great insights of historic faith were being rediscovered; the world was seeking and theologians were providing Christian resources for timely responses to the crises of western civilization; and appreciation for many traditional thinkers and concepts that liberals considered outdated was increasing. In several scholarly articles he compared and assessed the relative merits of liberal and neo-orthodox-realistic views of faith, sin, and other disputed matters.[13] The substance of his own, mediating, position was set forth in *The Christian Perspective* (1950), his only book. He left Vanderbilt for Garrett Biblical Institute in 1954 and died three years later, at the age of fifty-five.

Personalist elements survived in his thought to the end. Chief among them were personalistic theism; stress on the objective goodness of God; an insistence that the use of reason, with due regard for its limits, is wholesome and that faith is not irrational; and a denial that the fall, though radical, obliterates the "telic" character of human beings, that is, their God-created and hence natural orientation toward purposive living. But these elements appear within a framework and web of meaning that can no longer be aptly labeled "liberal." Grateful to Brightman and Knudson, Ramsdell nonetheless drew heavily on the thought of Gustav Aulén, Emil Brunner, and Reinhold Niebuhr, and embraced the necessity of Kierkegaardian paradoxes.

From H. Richard Niebuhr he took the phrase, "faith brings 'the discovery of rational pattern.' " His own creative proposal was a follow-up to that point: by revealing what is ultimately significant, the Word of God offers a faith perspective that views, situates, and judges all other perspectives and patterns. His starting point and bottom line, then, was this: "The unifying insight, or intuition, which comes to the Christian in faith is that of the Truth revealed in the life, death and resurrection of Jesus Christ. Christian faith is the faith that the Word of God Incarnate, climactically expressed on the Cross as the power of the divine Agapé, is the most significant fact in our total experience." Incarnation and the cross provide the categories for interpreting the church's doctrinal tradition, and tradition provides the means by which to "plumb the depths of human experience" as a whole.[14]

Ramsdell was the last in Vanderbilt's succession of distinctly Methodist theologians. He was as loyal to his church heritage as were Summers and Tillett. Yet all three had sought to set their church's tradition into its wider Christian framework, and with each generation that wider context had become ever more significant for doing theology. The Methodist traditionalism of Summers had yielded to the Methodist ecumenism of Tillett. With Ramsdell the practice of relying on denominational standards as the basis of one's theological judgment had ceased altogether. These developments at Vanderbilt were in line with those in the Methodist and other churches formative of "mainline Protestantism."

Precisely for this reason, Vanderbilt students during each of these three generations of change faced decisions that were very much their own, but in sum and substance were much the same as their theological teachers. "Gentleman theologian" Summers prepared his students to serve as polished, cultured leaders of the church and the community in the South. For many of those he taught, such a leadership role would have been beyond reach except by virtue of upward social mobility through a Vanderbilt education. Those who responded positively to his role modeling would likely commit to a combination of "piety and learning" in their lives and their ministries.

The decision to align themselves and their church(es) with emergent "fundamentalism," "modernism," or "middle-of-the-roadism" would fall on their shoulders alone. A Summers-trained minister might justify any of these stances. Those who adored his flinty orthodoxy were primed to lead the resistance movement against the rising "new" philosophy, science, and theology. Those who fixed on his concern for an intellectually credible account of Christian faith's meaning, or his great passion for learning, would have good cause to thank him for leading them to value sound reasoning and proceed on their own to read literature and adopt views that he himself never countenanced. Some "gentleman ministers," of course, might depart his classes for ministries devoted to diplomatic peace-making in their church(es).

The MECS was theologically conflicted at the time of the transition from Summers to Tillett, who faced, quite early on, the troubles that befall the leader of a house divided. In light of his comments on Lincoln's divinely providential role in American history (written in the 1920s amid the resurgence of the Ku Klux Klan), a history in the "Romantic" style might easily depict him as a Lincolnesque figure. His students faced exactly the same decision he did: that of coping with—that is, accepting—the reality of historical change. Another way to put the point is to say that "historical consciousness" came to Vanderbilt during Tillett's era and that he had much to do with its arrival.

Students of that era were also exposed in his classes to what were, viewed in retrospect, several of the most noble and most objectionable features of classical liberalism. No class in the area of "philosophical theology" in the South during these times was even a near competitor to Tillett's with regard to its breadth of critical studies or commitment to ecumenism and social concern. Vanderbilt's reputation for academic and social "progressivism" was first set during the Tillett years, and that reputation was due in considerable measure to Tillett's "spirit" as well as, or perhaps more than, his scholarship. His finest students, one surmises, were prepared for advanced studies at any Anglo-American university and encouraged their home church(es) to eschew dogmatism and privatism in favor of open-minded inquiry and works of compassion.

Yet precisely because of that heritage of deep commitment to academic and social progressivism, the liberalism of Tillett and students who embraced his theology seems in so many respects dated, limited, and even misguided. Inasmuch as he taught that Christian doctrines were to be interpreted and evaluated in terms of their ethical grounds and consequences, it was quite possible for his students to reduce theology to ethics. Although the ethics being taught were avowedly idealistic, humanitarian, and altruistic, they were also tainted by spots of noblesse oblige, cultural condescension, Christian triumphalism, and nationalistic jingoism. The fact remains, however, that Tillett's students fostered in churches of the times the social principles of Methodism, ecumenical concern, and openness to the wider world of thought and Christian service.

The effects of Ramsdell's years of teaching on students are somewhat more difficult to estimate. There is every reason to assume that his finest students were taught "who was who" and "what was what as well as up-to-date" in the-

ology. They also knew that Christian ministry was a learned and socially engaged profession, that church doctrine was very important, and that a minister's
role as teacher of the church was a calling demanding lifelong theological study.
His finest students were certainly equipped to take part in the "theological
renaissance."

What is not clear (to me) is how many under his care would or could have
been as self-searching as he was. By the time Ramsdell came to Nashville,
Vanderbilt students were a rather self-selective lot. Well-known as a center of
"liberalism" in the South, the school's most promising students would have been
those who self-consciously sought theological education in that setting. To such
as these, introduction to the line of thought from Kant and Schleiermacher to
Ritschl and Troeltsch and *also* to dialectical theology's criticisms of that line was
not merely an academic but a personal challenge. The finest of his students
presumably picked up on his critical and self-critical responsiveness to challenging ideas, the warmth and enthusiasm of his concern for "pastoral teaching," or,
optimally, a rich mixture of both traits.

Vanderbilt's 1950s Faculty: The Great Leap Forward, Overcome by History

"Great leaping, forward" is age-old rhetorical phraseology for striking
changes someone, somewhere, greets with approval. It serves here to capture the
sense of élan at Vanderbilt itself in the years after World War II, when the school
took steps to gain distinction as a major seat of learning at the forefront of
mainline Protestant theological studies. Strong Ph.D. programs were a component of the advance. So too was a faculty the equal in size and talent of theology's
premier schools.

Vanderbilt made numerous strides in this direction. The breakout in theology per se came in 1950 with the appointment of a second, and senior, scholar
in the field, Nels Ferré of Andover Newton Theological Seminary. Vanderbilt's commitment to multiple posts in theology held firm thereafter. Although
Ramsdell left in 1953 and Ferré returned to Andover Newton in 1957, the
theology area expanded. Vanderbilt's success in attracting younger and midlevel
scholars of accomplishment is clear: the 1950s faculty included Langdon Gilkey,
Roger L. Shinn, J. Robert Nelson, and Gordon Kaufman.[15] All of them were
working at theology's cutting edges and already underway on career paths leading to widespread recognition. None was from the South. Nelson, an ecumenical theologian hired as the school's dean, was the only Methodist. Denominational and regional considerations were no longer of decisive importance for
theology taught at Vanderbilt.

By luring Ferré to Nashville, Vanderbilt had caught its first star theologian, one still rising at the time. His first book, *Swedish Contributions to Theology* (1939), quickly became America's standard introduction to the thought of Gustav Aulén, Anders Nygrén, and associates of the Lund(ensian) school. Scholarly and popularized publications streamed forth each year thereafter. His sermons and public lectures won him special acclaim. Shortly before his move to Vanderbilt, the *Christian Century* featured him in its prestigious series "How My Mind Has Changed." Shortly thereafter, he appeared alongside Tillich and the brothers Niebuhr in David M. Soper's profiles of the "major voices in American Theology."[16]

Vanderbilt had also hired its first theologian with a distinctive scholarly agenda that had as its aim reshaping the course of theological discussion at large. While Ramsdell very patiently examined each point in dispute between liberalism and neo-orthodox-realist theologies, Ferré had already declared himself passing into territory "beyond" those two movements. Divine *agape*, the leitmotif of Lund's non-normative motif studies, was actually, so Ferré argued, the normative core of biblical Christian faith and historic Christianity, as well as the solution to the problems that beset theology, the church, and the world. Its reality was alpha and omega, ultimacy itself, cosmic truth. Jesus Christ was divine *agape* incarnate; and by the agency of God's Holy Spirit, *agape* love was a mighty transformative power that overcame the sins of the world and led the human family to perfect fellowship with God and one another. Agapéism became the shorthand term for Ferré's theology as the Word of God was for Barth's, divine imperative for Brunner's, kergyma for Bultmann's, and ultimate concern or the New Being for Tillich's.

Two other terms used to specify Ferré's program vis-à-vis theology's major options are also illuminating—postcritical and the extreme center. The former was, and is, perhaps best explained in terms of a parallelism or linkage between theology's recent history and Ferré's own autobiographical testimony to three conversion experiences. Raised in a Swedish Baptist household, Ferré had uncritically accepted its literalist, "traditional" theology of an uncompromisingly righteous God whose demands were total, whose wrath was fearsome, and whose mercy was unpredictable. Emigration to America at age thirteen and education there led Ferré to a liberal, critical stance, correct in its affirmation of human dignity and intellectual integrity but in the final analysis too human-centered and shallow to grasp faith's full meaning or address humanity's problems. Neo-orthodoxy rightly exposed the failings of liberalism, including Ferré's own. But in his view its criticisms were far too over-reactive, negative, and pessimistic, and its correctives too timid (lacking trust in the Spirit's transformative power) and uncreative to guide Christians in the ways of faithfulness. The postcritical step beyond liberal criticism, then, was not a truly neo-orthodox but a truly *agape* theology.

This step was a move to "the extreme center," as Ferré explained it at some length. By the term he referred to at least three merits of his *agape* theology. First, it places the sovereign *agape* of God at and as the center of faith, the church, and the world. Second, it stands midway on the spectrum that extends from fundamentalism and neo-orthodoxy to its right and liberalism and naturalism (and its humanism) to the left. Third, it accepts all that is true and valuable about the other options while discarding everything false, partial, misleading, and counterproductive in them.[17]

Vanderbilt did not become a school of *agape* theology during the 1950s. Certainly *agape* love counted among the important themes of contemporary theology. Yet Ferré's program itself proved to be an episode in theology's history rather than a tradition at Vanderbilt and elsewhere. "Why?" is a question in its own right. It suffices here to suggest that Ferré combined elements and moves from pietist fundamentalism to liberalism and to brushes with neo-orthodoxy in a fashion so personal and personalized that his step "beyond" them all was in effect inimitable. Emphasis on constant responsivity to the Holy Spirit's synergistic promptings was the Ariadne's thread of his own journey through precritical, critical, and postcritical faith commitments, but that thread could not be mass-produced and distributed for common use, much less "scholasticized."

In some respects, however, Vanderbilt's other theologians of the 1950s were much like Ferré. They focused on similar concerns and worked in their own ways to bring similar resources to bear on similar issues. Pressed to state these in summary terms, it may be helpful to resort to the phrase "faith and history." It serves the purpose at hand, not because the rubric is so broad and abstract that anything goes but because it distinguishes Vanderbilt theology at mid-century from earlier and later twentieth-century developments.

Faith and history were for these theologians a problematic, using the term now not merely for some theological problem or problems (as it has been throughout theology's history) but in the sense of a way of fixing on Christian theology's substance and rationale, as well as its varied tasks and root issues. This was not of the Vanderbilt school's own making. It was a legacy from their teachers, the theologians of the theocentric turn who between the times of two world wars had challenged their own teachers, liberalism's magisterium, and had emerged as dominant figures in scholarly, ecumenical, and (some) churchly theology. The rhetoric of "crisis theology" seemed as apt in the aftermath of World War II as in the days of the Weimar Republic. Authentic Christian faith in the present crisis situation entailed heeding and committing at each moment to the self-disclosure of the one and only God—the God to whom the scriptures witness as nothing else can or does, the God made known in Jesus Christ as nowhere else, the God who is the ultimate reality encompassing and yet transcending every other reality.

This formulation, though ad hoc, clumsy, and compressed, conveys perhaps something of the tenor of Vanderbilt theology during the 1950s, as well as its thrust—its "existentialist posture," as Shinn put it.[18] Word substitutions were commonplace, for example, for God's self-disclosure, insert God's revelation, self-revelation, or Word; for witness of scripture, insert biblical authority; for encompassing, insert grounding; and so on. Such variations were often harmless stylistic color, but equally often tokens of serious disagreements about how to understand and articulate the paradoxical relations of God, faith, and history.

The shared faith and history problem can now be somewhat better specified. It arises (only, as it were) when faith means faith in the one Creator God of history who remains always transcendent of and in some sense other than everything created and historical. The problem emerged for first-generation neo-orthodox-realist theologians when liberal faith failed and good news from God was found to enter into history from "beyond." This finding gave rise to a generically theocentric movement, which, much like the Roosevelt coalition, was a big tent gathering of many diverse, and at points irreconcilably divided, elements. At Vanderbilt, Ramsdell and Ferré were liberals undergoing metamorphosis in response to changing circumstances. The others, all younger, were schooled as neo-orthodox realists and beneficiaries of the coalition's ongoing vitality. As a group, they approached the problem from faith's side, seeking mainly to sweep away confusions, adjudicate and if at all possible resolve competing coalition claims, and address any challenges history happened to present. Shinn, for example, in his dissertation revised for publication, wrote that "the problem of history is the problem of the sovereignty of God, from which the meaning of history derives." God, God's sovereignty, and history's God-derived meaning are already assumed as givens in the very formulation of "the problem" itself. It is not surprising, then, that what was implicit before long became explicit: "In the final analysis the problem of history *for faith* is the problem of the sovereignty of God. If God rules the world, then provisional chaos and meaninglessness finally contribute to His purpose, and history is not in vain. If God does not rule, then whatever achievements may be wrought, the final words pronounced upon history are doom and despair." Shinn's framing of the issues was characteristic of generic neo–orthodox-realist theology. So too was his vivid language—chaos, meaninglessness, vanity, doom, and despair versus faith in the sovereignty of God.[19]

The burden of the argument was to clarify faith's claim that because God rules the world, history's chaos and meaninglessness are only provisional, somehow contributory to the purpose(s) of God, and no occasion for hopelessness or inaction. Clarifying the "distinctive" claims of biblical, historic faith was the chief task that all Vanderbilt's 1950s theologians undertook. Their modus operandi was reconstructive, in the sense of rescuing these ancient categories from misleading, obsolete, foreign, or false entanglements and highlighting their unique contributions to a proper understanding of God's will for people in modern times. Biblical historical criticism, studies of the history of Christian doctrine and philosophy, as well as attention to scientific, social scientific, and contemporary thought generally were means to these ends.

Shinn's second formulation of the problem of history as the problem of the sovereignty of God acknowledged that this two-in-one problem was a problem for faith. Ferré's topical schema in *The Christian Understanding of God*, arguably his most substantive work, tells why: chapter-length analyses of the nature of God, God and the world, and time and eternity lead to the faith claim of God's transcendent sovereignty in and over all things. The transcendence of that sovereignty necessitates explaining how God can be said to "work" in creation, providence, revelation, incarnation, the church, and last things.[20] The other Vanderbilt theologians were well aware of this necessity. Shinn addressed it at the level of Christian theology in relation to secular philosophies of history. Kaufman's dissertation focused on epistemological issues relating to convictions of faith on the one hand and historical methodology and historical-cultural relativism on the other.[21]

Maker of Heaven and Earth, Gilkey's revised dissertation, offered an account of biblical faith's affirmation of *creatio ex nihilo* by way of its comparison and contrast to ancient cosmology and modern historical, scientific, and philosophical views. At the time of its publication, the book was especially intriguing because neo-orthodox thematics were led into conversation with process thought and late-breaking scientific theory. Read in retrospect, the book's other features are more striking: in this work Gilkey had already taken pains to identify the peculiar character and force of "God-talk" and specify the meaning of the term "divine transcendence" more clearly than neo-orthodox-realist theologians usually did. Robert Nelson's reflections on God's will for and work in the church began before his Vanderbilt appointment with a study of the doctrine of the church as "the realm of redemption" and continued throughout his time as dean.[22]

In short, the theology taught at Vanderbilt passed from rational supernaturalism to classic liberalism to generic neo-orthodox realism. The neo-orthodox traits, however, were broader than they were deep. The 1950s theologians leaned toward the realist, apologetical, and correlationalist wings of the coalition rather than Barthian loyalism or churchly neoconfessionalism. They were somewhat less pure in their neo-orthodoxy than even their mentors had been at the time they associated with that "cause." Ferré was slightly "left" of the Lund theologians; Shinn of Reinhold Niebuhr and John Bennett; Gilkey of Reinhold Niebuhr and Tillich; Nelson of Emil Brunner; and Kaufman of H. Richard Niebuhr. Common to thinkers along these bands of the theological spectrum, despite their differences, was a commitment to running dialogue with "culture." Indeed for Tillich, as for Rudolf Bultmann, the label neo-orthodox realist was by the 1950s no longer accurate, if it ever had been. To judge by their later careers, unfolding over the years after their Nashville sojourn, the same would have to be said of Vanderbilt's theologians of the 1950s.

Another common characteristic was a resolve to embrace nearly all of liberalism's agenda while discarding its theological rationale, absolutist moralism, and optimism regarding the basic goodness of human nature or the inevitability of historical progress. In one sense everything had changed since Tillett's day. In another sense, nothing had. Biblical criticism; the identification of so many cherished biblical "truths of history" as myth, legend, fable, or fancy; commitments to ecumenical, social, and social gospel causes, including political action; and freedom of inquiry—the list could go on and on—were more prominent than ever before.

The ethical imperatives bound up with God's sovereign claim on life were integral to the work of these theologians. By 1959 Kaufman had sketched the theological foundations and norms for Christian ethics in terms of contextual decision, sorting out and interrelating the "metaphysical context" (relationship with God made known in Jesus Christ), the sociological context (issues of church and world), and the personal-biographical context ("the Christian understanding of the free and creative individual").[23] Shinn, who in 1958–59 shifted posts from line theologian to (theological) ethicist, had constantly addressed Christian moral concerns and social-political issues. Nelson pressed churches to undertake "life and work" services as well as "faith and order" studies.

How many, and how well, Vanderbilt students grasped the terms, names, and positions under study and the sophisticated, typically dialectical, arguments of their teachers must remain here an open question. The transition, or weekly commute, that many of them made from the church field to the school was surely a shock to the system unlike that experienced by those who had enrolled in Summers's defense of Arminian divinity, Tillett's advocacy of liberal ideals, or even the classes of Ramsdell. Yet all but the most dim-witted and cold-hearted were likely to pick up on something of the nontheoretical meaning of existential commitment amid crisis, aware as they were that Ferré had daily endured excruciating arthritic pain, that during World War II Shinn had been a decorated war veteran, that Gilkey had been imprisoned in China by the Japanese invaders in the Shantung Compound while still a young social service worker,[24] and that Kaufman had been inducted into alternative service in a stateside hospital as a Mennonite conscientious objector.

The context of the times and place was also in some ways advantageous to the study of theology at Vanderbilt. Although the theological renaissance seems now to have had less impact on grassroots church life than its devotees believed, the great resurgence of religious interest that went along with postwar family life, social patterns, and the baby boom was itself a welcome development. Protestant mainline churches prospered, and Vanderbilt did as well. Decades later, longings remain in many quarters for those bygone days, when liberal churches were thriving "as they should." Known as a bastion of liberalism in the nation's Bible belt, the school was a favorite target of the old religious right. Yet in the main such attacks only confirmed the importance and relevance of the theology taught there. The Vanderbilt theologians had not only an audience but also a method and a rhetoric for conveying their messages. They were capable of laying claim to fidelity to the biblical, historic faith of the church as neither liberal-modernism nor evangelical-fundamentalism could. At the same time they understood faith and faithfulness in terms such that people of intelligence and conscience in the emerging "new South," as elsewhere, might find the Christian message credible, timely, and enlivening.

There were problems, however. A neo-orthodox-realist faith was difficult, ill-suited for cultural comfort and even less for cultural dominance. Ironically, the more neo-orthodox side of the movement, shading off into true-blue biblicism or traditionalism, was frequently more easily accommodated to its cultural settings than were realistic, apologetical, and correlational forms. None of Vanderbilt's theologians was *that* neo-orthodox. Their theological insistence that God alone was faith's object of ultimate concern was, surely, a welcome alternative to its contraries, fanaticism and despair. Less welcome was the insistence that the biblical God could never be fully identified with or contained by anything in creation or history. Iconoclasm—the breaking of idols and idolatry in all its forms—was an essential component of the message.

This message, although rhetorically appealing to devoted and would-be Christians alike, had certain troubling practical implications. It meant acknowledging the relativity of all "worldly" things, even scripture, tradition, Jesus and the apostles, church, and the American way of life. How Gilkey, for example, could relativize not only secular science but also the "literalism" of the creation "story" and yet refuse to denounce Darwinian evolution was a riddle that not every member of his audiences could explain. Even more inassimilable, perhaps, was Vanderbilt's running theological critique of the idolatries of careerism, commercialism, and consumerism, capitalism as well as communism, feel-good as well as hellfire-and-brimstone religion, the superficiality of so much of work-a-day popular culture, and above all complacency. Neither Summers the "conservative" nor Tillett the "liberal" had argued that Christians, their church(es), and their society and their nation were as perfect as God wanted them to be. Both exhorted everyone to be and do better. But a dialectical (and sometimes simply blunt) critique of all that "good Christians" considered good and Christian was another matter: in effect, Vanderbilt's 1950s theologians at times bit the hands of those who fed them.

Unbeknownst to all, mainline Protestantism was, sociologically speaking, fast approaching its twentieth-century apogee. No one really knew, when Kaufman and Nelson came to the faculty, that within a decade theology and the church along with virtually everything else in the world would enter into a new era. At the time, Vanderbilt's neo-orthodox-realist theology relished its victories—partial, momentary, and historically relative as they were. Gilkey told of one in *How the Church Can Minister to the World without Losing Itself* (1964). It grew out of his ecclesiology course and bull sessions with Vanderbilt students. "A seminary student at Vanderbilt," he wrote, "once asked how he could most easily remove an elder who used alcohol as manifestly too 'worldly' for an official position in the church. He became conscious for the first time of the depth of the problem of the church in culture when he was asked whether this church, which desired no 'worldly' elders, was also segregated—as the world is."[25]

The *full* depth of American racism was, of course, by no means plumbed at this or any other moment in the teaching of theology at Vanderbilt during the 1950s. The later writings of Gilkey and his Vanderbilt colleagues, Ferré included, admit as much, either explicitly or by changes they make in their theological method and their message. But "later writings" refer to works they wrote after leaving Vanderbilt. Ferré's departure in the mid-1950s had been just another career move, as was (it seems) Ramsdell's before. This was not precisely or fully so for the others, each of whom faced an issue of existential faith-commitment when James Lawson was expelled for participation in the non-violent civil rights struggle. With "the Lawson affair" (see Chapter 6), the school's "great leap forward" came to an abrupt end.

Vanderbilt's theologians were by no means unaware of relativities of history at play in their teaching of theology and its reception. They knew well of Troeltsch and the problem(s) of history and historicism, and also of crisis theology's biblical-theological critiques of liberalism's responses to those problem(s) as a naive, lame *Kulturprotestantismus*. This knowledge was not book learning alone: it interpreted their own experience of the twentieth century, and did it so well that no other interpretation seemed either as Christian or viable. Even so, how situationally contextualized and hence how limited and temporary the neo-orthodox-realist message was in theology's history could hardly have been recognized at the time. It was virtually unimaginable that the 1950s decade was only a few steps short of the end of an era in American history, the history of theology and the church, and so too the theology they taught at Vanderbilt.

The Vanderbilt Quintet

It took the Divinity School some time after its protest of the University's handling of the Lawson case to regain full strength and stability. When Kaufman accepted a call from Harvard Divinity School in 1963, the last of Vanderbilt's theologians of the 1950s had bid the school farewell. Visiting Professor Walter Sikes and faculty in related fields covered theology courses, and H. Jackson Forstman and Ray Hart were appointed as the first two of the new, permanent faculty in theology. Other appointments followed: in 1965 Peter C. Hodgson and in 1969 Eugene TeSelle, a specialist in historical theology who was first appointed in church history and in 1975 designated professor of church history and theology. Also in 1969 Edward Farley was chosen to succeed Hart, who had left for a religious studies post at the University of Montana. Sallie McFague joined the faculty in 1972. Hence 1975 is an apt date to mark the transitional era's end. Fully assembled was a new cadre of scholars who, together, gave Vanderbilt theology its primary identity to the end of the century. The rebuilding process had privileged the field of theology.

The qualifier "primary" or some equivalent is necessary for at least two reasons. One is that although Vanderbilt was no more immune from the effects of disciplinary overspecialization and fragmentation than other theological schools, it sought throughout this period to foster awareness of the theological character of the dispersed theological fields. Not every member of the school's faculty could be called "theologian" or wanted to be. Even so, an above-average number of them belonged to theologically oriented wings of their disciplines and augmented the teaching of the school's line theologians. Thus despite the risk of omitting or misjudging someone, it is proper to mention for the record that many colleagues shaped theology at Vanderbilt, as did distinguished scholars such as Sikes, Wilhelm Pauck, James Barr, and Marjorie Suchocki (on two visiting professorships).

Another reason for speaking in terms of primary rather than total identity is concern for the theological field's "diversity and unity," and at two levels at the same time. At the level of national-international reputation, Vanderbilt theology was at least as unified as any of its competitor "schools of thought" that gained wide brand name recognition, for example, the Yale school of narrativism or neoliberalism, the revisionism or public theology of the (third) Chicago school, or process thought at Claremont. There is no such well-known label to pin on the Vanderbilt whole. Time will tell if one will emerge ex post facto. At the intramural level, the faculty was diverse, each member very independent-minded and distinct(ive). No one familiar with their writings could possibly confuse one for another. They represent, I think, a quintet, in the sense of an improvisational jazz combo rather than a score-bound chamber ensemble.

Continuities with the 1950s faculty were striking. The school had recommitted to multiple lines in the field and open, national searches—at the time still strictly within the mainline Protestant network of Ph.D. programs and feeder schools. The result was again an interdenominational mix. McFague was Methodist (as was Hart); she later became Episcopalian. Farley, Hodgson, and TeSelle are Presbyterians. Forstman belongs to the Disciples of Christ. None, however, is a denominational theologian, much less an advocate of a church confessionalism or traditionalism.

The graduate school training, credentials, and general theological orientation of the new faculty made it uncannily similar to the one Vanderbilt had lost. It is as though the school, in self-conscious defiance of that loss, resolved to pick up almost exactly where it had left off circa 1960, advancing as well by the addition of its first woman theologian. The quintet's members had been schooled in neo-orthodox-realist thought, and that faith and history problem was as much their focus as it was that of Ferré, Gilkey, Shinn, Nelson, and Kaufman. Also, like the 1950s faculty, the new group attended to correlationalist issues and themes rather than dismissed "modern" and the "latest" modes of critical analysis as though they were foreign, irrelevant, or faithless. Precisely this orientation put them, like their predecessors who had left Vanderbilt, in an arena that during the 1960s was still considered "the center" of genuinely serious theological (scholarly, churchly, and ecumenical) inquiries. The task common to the old and the new-formed faculties was to move *this* center onward, "forward."

Finally, unique as they were as individuals, members of the quintet were of the same era. All of them were born in the five-year period 1929 to 1934 and were products of two graduate schools: New York's Union Theological Seminary (Farley and Forstman) and Yale (Hodgson, McFague, and TeSelle). At Union, correlationist neo-orthodox realism prevailed. The ethos at Yale was, by comparison, more distinctly neo-orthodox, although there H. Richard Niebuhr's prowess in handling both sociocultural analyses of theology and theologically neo-orthodox analyses of sociocultural history set a virtuoso standard for colleagues and students alike.

Similarities between the old and new Vanderbilt theologians could be pursued, perhaps with some benefit, beyond these few notations and suggestions. This momentary stress on the continuities, however, is mainly a device for ferreting out some other points. One is that things might well have turned out differently. There was no certainty the school would survive its conflict with University authorities, even less that it would rebuild by recommitting to and privileging Christian theological studies, and less still that its new faculty would make Vanderbilt once again a force at the center of theology at large. A "what if" question is not, strictly speaking, a proper topic of historical research. Yet merely to raise it is a reminder that at the time the school faced important decisions regarding the *sort* of theology, if any, it would teach and that its decision was to *continue* teaching theology of the sort taught by its faculty of the 1950s. That the sort of theology "happened" to be generic neo-orthodox-realist thought with correlationist, apologetic, and culturally responsive leanings was surely because of many factors, among them the continued sociocultural sway of such thinking as the field-dominant, and vital, front of scholarly, churchly, and ecumenical discussion.

But between 1960 and 1980 (the critical turn is now perhaps most plausibly put between 1965 and 1975), theology itself changed. It disintegrated perhaps into chaos, as some claim; expanded its core and reach, in the view of others; regrouped with multiple centers, according to still others; or at last attained center-free existence, in the opinion of others. Exactly how, when, and why this change came about are open, much-disputed questions. Its effects are still unfolding. This is no place to try to resolve the historiographical puzzle, but a few well-known features of the change deserve brief mention.

One feature was a function of internal, half-life decay of the generic neo-orthodox-realist coalition itself, given its avowed commitment to critical and self-critical thinking. The brightest and the best of the movement's younger scholars were already at mid-century aware that the key categories they had inherited were far less clear than they appeared to be. They were also aware that reconstructive theology—in the sense of merely re-sounding and reapplying certain putatively unique, God-given themes of biblical faith and "faithful" interpreters in ever-changing contexts—was methodologically suspect. This suspicion accounts in part for the fact that on the American scene especially, the correlationist leaders of the postwar coalition, like Bultmann and Tillich, became more rather than less prominent as years went by.

It also partly accounts for a growing restiveness among their students with regard to the adequacy of the movement's leitmotifs. Historical research along the lines that Bultmann commended, for example, found kergymata rather than "the" kerygma. His insistence that the cross was an "act of God" never fit comfortably into a phenomenological ontology of the mode of existence called

Dasein. Tillich's earlier and widely popularized version of the method of correlation as Christianity's answers to the existential questions raised by human life, culture, and philosophy proved too facile. (It is foolish to think this critique came as news to Tillich; always more restive than any of his critics, he had long since moved on.) The list of illustrations could go on. The Vanderbilt theologians of the 1950s on occasion indicated they shared this suspicion and were restive coalitionists. So too did the careers of the Vanderbilt quintet—in the cases of Farley and Forstman, the process began before moving to Nashville.

Another feature of the massive change emerged during the transitional period from 1960 to 1975. The neo-orthodox-realist coalition as well as the mainline churches entered a time of travail and decline during the presidency of Lyndon Johnson. It cracked much as the old Roosevelt coalition did, and so far as sociocultural and political factors were concerned, for surely many of the same reasons. Along with the country itself, Vanderbilt underwent "the sixties revolution." Some of its issues, such as war and peace and race relations, were serious indeed. Yet in retrospect this initial wave of antiestablishment fervor seems far less daring than it did at the time. It was a harbinger of greater sociocultural changes yet to come.

The school's newer and incoming theologians had no wish to hold a self-defensive line against "protesters." They too were concerned and frustrated with the state of the nation. And they agreed that theology was to be "relevant" and "meaningful," not irrelevant and meaningless or, surely worse, reactionary. But how to make it so was far from self-evident. The breach in the postwar coalition gave a new right to life to countless theologies of concern—for secular and religionless religion, the "death of God," hope, the future, story, and "play," to name only a few. An annual, if not monthly, proliferation of "new theologies" transformed the standard introductory courses on current trends in theology into roller coaster rides, at once exhilarating and exasperating.

The most substantive of the distinctly new developments to emerge as the 1960s rolled on to the 1970s and beyond were praxis-oriented theologies of liberation (African American "black theology," feminist, third world, and others) and varieties of "postmodern" thought. Both movements challenged historic as well as prevailing features of theology's establishment, at points in radical fashion. The Vanderbilt quintet were not pioneering advocates of either movement, but they took both seriously. They were responsive to critical edges of both movements and sympathetic to protests against using theology to legitimate the status quo. In the case of liberation theologies particularly, they appreciated the commitment to transformationist goals of equality, social justice, and freedom from oppression.

Their common educational background and long tenure make Vanderbilt's quintet a case study of generational passage in theological education that most other Protestant seminaries and seminary-based graduate programs tried to negotiate by capitalizing on faculty turnover. Vanderbilt did not take that path, although all its theologians were eminently marketable. The passage there took place in very individual ways, and (without pretending it was smooth) its theologians managed to maintain a certain group coherence in the sense of rough-fit complementarity.

Describing that group coherence is by no means easy, in part because it is still going on. Several of the quintet's members have retired, but all are still engaged in ongoing research and publication that demonstrates their thinking remains in progress. Hence a historian is in no position to plead any sense of historical distance at all. An account of the theology taught at Vanderbilt, then, shifts by necessity from historical to journalistic analysis, if not mere punditry or guesswork.

One stab at characterizing the whole over some thirty years would be to say that the Vanderbilt quintet have been mediating theologians in an era when mediation has been under high pressure attack, as likely branded "hegemonic" as "feckless." With neither a constituency nor a conceptuality for middling or centrist appeals ready at hand, their mediating efforts are perforce more dialectical than "dialectical theology" in its heyday, and exploratory and suggestive rather than constrictive. The poles to be mediated are no longer two fixed positions but multiple, moving targets—an acknowledgment born of due regard for the diversity, particularity, interconnectedness, and historicality of all things, including mediators, their mediations, and their antimediatorial critics. Hence, the mediating theologies taught at Vanderbilt in the late twentieth century are of another sort and order than was Ramsdell's concern to reconcile classical liberalism and neo-orthodox-realist thought or the quest of reconciling "Christianity and culture." The common task has been to argue on the one hand that reflection on Christian faith can yield certain valuable insights into human existence in the world *coram deo* that cannot be accessed either as readily or as well otherwise, and on the other hand that these insights emerge only if and when reflection on Christian faith refuses to idolize Christianity's particular (re)sources and authorities.

Another stab at a general characterization of the quintet's approach to theology might be made by way of the introductory texts composed by the Workgroup in Constructive Theology, a Vanderbilt initiative of the mid-1970s—one a historical theological survey of doctrinal loci and the other a companion book of readings.[26] A collaborative undertaking with multiple authors at liberty to express their own views in light of (rather than total conformity with) the drift of group discussion, the two-volume set is neither altogether harmonious nor a transcript of Vanderbilt teaching. Even so, the entire quintet contributed to the shaping and the content of the materials, and three of them—Farley, McFague, and especially Hodgson—were prominent coauthors.

The features of the books most characteristic of the quintet's approach to the teaching of theology include (1) a focus on faith's persistent themes, identified as the "symbolic tradition" in the sense not of creedal authority but of discursive imagery at once disclosing and concealing faith's objects and objectives; (2) the historical and quasi-dramatized passage of that symbolic tradition over time as a process involving continuity, conflict, and change; and (3) the division of the story line into three acts or phases: classic formation, an Enlightenment and post-Enlightenment turn to critical and historical-critical thinking, and challenges and paradigm shifts emerging in recent times and demanding reappraisals and revisions of the symbol set itself. By means of this picturing, Vanderbilt's theologians, as well as their attentive students, understand themselves to continue to participate in an ongoing dialogue about Christian faith from which some greater good than that attained so far may result.

One comes, I wager, one step closer to the quintet's teaching *en ensemble* by reading the two-volume set with a wary eye. None of them is a devotee of the classic theological format. Moreover, they are likely more pleased with the set's airing of the issues raised by modern and postmodern critical reflection on classic formulations than with the constructive suggestions for discounting or resolving them that various contributors offer. The critique of "authoritative"—hence de facto authoritarian—appeals to theology's "authorities," including the so-called scripture principle, in these textbooks is a Vanderbilt leitmotif. The school's handling of the doctrinal tradition, then, is most compatible with those who refuse to blunt or bypass the force of this critique.

The effort to show and tell why acceptance of such examination of Christianity's symbolic tradition is a constitutive element of Christian faith itself and necessary in order to foster "postcritical" faithfulness is, it seems to me, the hallmark of Vanderbilt's school of theology in the late twentieth century. This mark is not unique; indeed, precisely because the effort entails engaging so much of tradition from multiple angles of criticism, the Vanderbilt theologians draw upon resources and find allies in varied, even unexpected, quarters. That said, however, the school's theological orientation is more or less "peculiar." It puts more emphasis on studies of Christian theology's history than many thoroughgoing liberationist and avowedly post-Christian theologians are inclined to consider necessary or desirable. At the same time, they subject the history of Christian doctrine to greater criticism and propose reformulations of it more "radical" than postmodernity's neotraditionalists are willing to consider apt.

Although Farley, back in 1960, had been speaking of liberals before "the coming of the 'realistic' temper" (and before his coming to Nashville), one phrase he wrote then volunteers for intertextual use here, with reference to the quintet as a whole. They are "willing to regard neither tradition and sources in tradition nor contemporary movements as wholly normative in relation to each other."[27] By this standard, the Vanderbilt theologians are heirs of theological "liberalism." Their focus has been on historically informed constructive theologies that permit neither traditionalism nor contemporaneity to function as wholly normative in relation to each other. Yet this "school" of theology differs from older liberalisms (and from those movements' despisers, too) by incorporating into its thinking the thrust of neo-orthodox-realist critiques of liberalism's cultural accommodationism *and* the thrust of ongoing, contemporary critiques of neo-orthodox-realist traditionalism. Having been taught to think theologically "between the times," Vanderbilt's theologians now teach students to think theologically "between the norms." By this (admittedly odd) phrase I mean that students are taught, first, to construct and evaluate theologies in light of multiple, and concatenating, criteria of judgment and, second, to make explicit their warrants for the multiple norms they employ.

Each of the quintet's members has pursued the task in a quite individual way. The remarks that follow are intended merely to illustrate the point. It must suffice to register a few points without lapsing into caricature. Because no ordering of the materials is "really" more natural or logical than another, the one I have chosen is ad hoc and only two small steps short of random innocence. Three members of the quintet (Farley, Hodgson, and McFague) have worked on what they identify as a theological series or program—Farley on two programs. These I place after the others, who appear here in the order they did at Vanderbilt.

Forstman and TeSelle have primarily engaged in investigating significant figures and episodes in theology's history in order to clarify still-current theological issues and draw from those resources cautionary and constructive implications for theology today. Forstman's first monograph, on Calvin, grew out of his dissertation at Union. It was at once a contribution to a late-breaking wave of fresh "neoreformation" research as well as a critique of the scripture principle of one of "the reformers" beloved by neo-orthodox-realist theologians. Calvin's dealings with the Bible were found to be mixed, at times sensitive and profound and at times inconsistent and uncritically "biblicist." The chronically tensive interlacing in Christianity of faith-commitment and critical, and indeed self-critical, thinking was of concern in this study. In later studies this concern emerged as Forstman's signature theme.[28]

From study of Luther, for example, one should learn, if nothing else, the theology of the cross, which is, as Paul preached and sometimes practiced, the end of human boasting. From Schleiermacher, compared and contrasted to theologians of his day and their cultured despisers (who were his best friends), Forstman reflected on theology as transcendental jest. Constrained by the gospel to speak of God and things of God that transcend the full grasp of humanity, Christian theologians cannot in honesty do other than view their own theological claims with a certain ironic, seriocomic bemusement. For more than two decades, including his years as dean, Forstman focused on Christian faith in the "dark times" of Hitler's rise to power, asking why the brightest and best of Germany's Christian theologians responded as they did and, beyond that, whether the faith assists in spotting the power of monstrous evil before that power casts off its disguises and strides forth as the monster it is. The case study's results are sobering. There were some of the Jewish faith as well as some professing no religious faith at all with eyes to see early on the signs of the times. Some Christian theologians were more perceptive than others. Yet the resources of faith in this regard were never easily (or, as events proved, very effectively) tapped, for to do so required removing layers of illusions about faith and culture and their relationship.[29]

Eugene TeSelle carried primary responsibility at Vanderbilt for instruction in Catholic thought. Although his colleagues regularly surveyed "the symbolic tradition" as a whole and on occasion gave Catholic thought special attention, for example, Farley on Anselm, Forstman on the twelfth-century renaissance, Hodgson on Rahner, and McFague on woman mystics and activists, TeSelle has served as the resident expert on patristics, medieval and Tridentine scholasticism, Modernism, and later Vatican II developments. His writings have gained him widespread recognition as a leading figure in Augustine scholarship.[30] The clarity, care, and circumspection that typify his historical theological work may lead an unwary reader to underestimate its relationship to contemporary theological reflection. In and through close readings of traditional texts, TeSelle is meticulously sorting out issues and options that remain at present disputed, divisive, and all too often a jumble of confusion. This aim is joined to his long-term commitment to community activism and his analyses of sociopolitical and church-political affairs.

In light of the neo-Augustinianism of generic neo-orthodox-realist theologies, TeSelle's studies of Augustine and the Catholic tradition are in effect revisionist history. The complexities, subtleties, and inadequacies of what has passed for "Augustinianism" over the course of theology's history come into view. Revisionism is also the hallmark of TeSelle's most explicitly constructive work, *Christ in Context*. Its aim was not to develop yet another account of the doctrine of Christ's person, but by "treating theological topics as though they were still worthy of consideration," to dispel the "nonsense" and the "vague and inflated thinking" that accompanied the contemporary cry for Christocentrism and to identify the set of relations that form the context within which an adequate Christology might emerge. TeSelle's "opponents" were theologians he admired (for example, Blondel, Teilhard, Barth, and Rahner). But he contested their common advocacy of "the 'Scotist' view that the incarnation is the center and aim of all creation and of all God's activity in the world." His response moved at once behind the fifth-century Christological disputes and forward to evolutionary, process thought, in hopes of clearing the way for a reformulated Christology that stresses the humanity of Jesus, that respects human consciousness and its development, and that affirms Christocentrism with respect only to the outworking of Jesus' influence in the world rather than to God's purposes from the beginning.[31]

The thought of Hodgson and McFague developed during their Vanderbilt careers into theological programs, quite distinct but certainly consonant. Oriented at Yale to "Word of God" theology, Hodgson's early work focused on the impact of historical consciousness for understanding the development of Christian doctrine, McFague's on convergences and divergences of theology and literature. Both were significantly affected, personally and professionally, by the cultural ferment of the 1960s and its aftermath, which called into radical question the foundations as well as the ways and results of their theological schooling. Both of them, in beats of rhythm their own, took steps to appropriate for themselves the challenges and opportunities associated with liberation, praxis-oriented, and then postmodern concerns.

In each case the initial results were transitional. Both sought for a time (but not exactly at the same moment) to find in "new hermeneutic" initiatives a theological bridge broad, wide, and stable enough to span the gap between answers to theology's prior situation and questions arising in its "new" one. Hodgson's first fully constructive work, *Jesus: Word and Presence,* was of this sort—a rethinking of the meaning and validity of appeals to God's Word in light of ontology after the later Heidegger and their "practical" consequences. The effect of self-searching engagement with the history and emerging literature of liberation theology, as well as teaching on theology of freedom and "theology and the black experience" (with James Lawson and ethics colleague Thomas Ogletree), led to *Children of Freedom: Black Liberation in Christian Perspective* (1974) and *New Birth of Freedom: A Theology of Bondage and Liberation* (1976).[32]

McFague's interests shifted in these times from standard academic theology-and-literature topics to explorations of varieties of forms of faith life. She focused on experience-based and life-transformative theologies of women and men, and their articulation in modes of discourse other than conceptual formulas, such as images, parables, stories, novels, poems, and autobiographies.

From the new hermeneutic literature came insights into the potency of metaphor and extended metaphors (the parabolic discourse of Jesus, for example) to illumine and transform the human lifeworld of meaning. The path from *Speaking in Parables: A Study in Metaphor and Theology* (1975) to *Metaphorical Theology: Models of God in Religious Language* (1982), which included many articles along the way, capitalized on these initial investments. Liberationist, feminist, and ethical concerns appear in these writings, but the "Barthianism" of the program then in the making was captured well by the title of her 1975 *Christian Century* article, "An Intermediary Theology: In Service of the Hearing of God's Word." Intermediary, or metaphorical, theology was defined as "a style of theological reflection which stays close to characteristics of the parables but also, as a discursive mode, is coherent, consistent and precise—characteristics of a systematic theology." The rationale for this undertaking was made plain: " 'Bible stories' on the one hand and abstract, conceptual theology on the other hand will not, I think, address the hearing of the word."[33]

The work of these two scholars from the 1980s on reflected very significant midcourse changes. The process involved in both cases and among other things deconstructing the "Word of God" motif. Commitments to causes of political, social, and cultural transformation widened and deepened, and perceptions of the necessity of revisioning Christian theology gained focus. For Hodgson, the breakthrough leading to a distinctive, constructive message came by (inter)relating emancipatory, ecological, and dialogical concerns and a fresh, close reading of the thought of Hegel, which yielded resources for a theology at once ontologically radical and socially transformative. Hegel studies, a revisionary ecclesiology, reflection on God in relation to "shapes of freedom" in human history, and a long list of shorter publications mark this turn. The payoff for theology is most amply set forth in *Winds of the Spirit* (1994).[34] The book, growing out of his introductory courses in systematic theology, advances a theology of "trinitarian holism" in which the central themes of theology are reconstructed in light of "God in the world as Spirit."

For her part, McFague has written of her self-conscious turn to "an earthly theological agenda":

My constructive phase began upon reading Gordon Kaufman's 1983 Presidential Address to the American Academy of Religion. Kaufman called for a paradigm shift, given the exigencies of our time—the possibility of nuclear war. He called theologians to deconstruct and reconstruct the basic symbols of the Jewish and Christian traditions—God, Christ and Torah—so as to be on the side of life rather than against it, as was the central symbol of God with its traditional patriarchal, hierarchical, militaristic imagery. I answered this call, and my subsequent work has been concerned with contributing to that task.

The result, to date, has been many articles and a trilogy of major monographs: *Models of God: Theology for an Ecological, Nuclear Age* (1987); *The Body of God: An Ecological Theology* (1993); and *Super, Natural Christians: How We Should Love Nature* (1997). All are in their own ways wide-ranging works of theologicoethical advocacy: explicitly contextual, feminist, and action-oriented rationales for a transvaluation of the Christian symbolic tradition, uplifting the symbols contributing to justice, world peace, and "the liberation of the oppressed, including the earth and all its creatures."[35]

These books remain examples of intermediary theology, in that they deftly negotiate between the concrete language of human life experiences and the "conceptualities" of historiographical, scientific, social scientific, and philosophical inquiry. No longer, however, is intermediary theology bound to—or bound by—a Christian-specific term like "Word of God" as *norma normans sed non normata*. In *Models of God*, for example, the case for imaging God as mother, lover, and friend (as opposed to, say, father, monarch, and judge) turns on taking into account factors and norms other than biblical precedent alone. In basic accord with regard to contemporary theology's setting and tasks, and devoted to many of the same values and goals, McFague and Hodgson have sought to respond as well as contribute to the emergence of "new" paradigms of Christian theological reflection suitable for a life of faith that "participates in the redemptive love of God as it moves toward the transformation of the world."[36]

During his Vanderbilt career Farley developed not one but two programs, interrelated but distinct. The point of departure for both was concern to press behind and beyond the teachings of the church, as well as confessional or sociology of knowledge accounts of them, to the matrix within which the founding realities constitutive of Christianity as a particular faith can be discerned. Earlier, pre-Vanderbilt works provide a few clues to explain, at least in part, incentives for this criticoconstructive undertaking. In *The Transcendence of God* (1960), then-current accounts of divine transcendence proved under rigorous scrutiny unsatisfactory on multiple grounds. *Requiem for a Lost Piety* (1966) detailed the passing of the sociocultural and theological force of patterns of religiosity and of theological reflection long dominant in theology and the church.[37] As theologians questioned if it were even possible to do theology and disputed the meaningfulness of any "God-talk," Farley turned to the tasks of uncovering faith's peculiar objects and objectives (*teloi*) and appraising their reality status—in a fashion aimed at avoiding the pitfalls of confessionalist parochialism and correlationist (over)generalization.

His first Vanderbilt courses and a book on theological method set forth a "social phenomenology of faith and reality" by employing Husserlian and post-Husserlian thought to disclose the elements, shape, and dynamics of ecclesia or ecclesial existence. By those terms is meant a historically determinate faith, in the sense of a mode of human being-in-the-world-with-others-*coram-deo*. This faith emerged in history amid the founding events of Christian origins as an intersubjective awareness and acknowledgment of a God-given gift *and* goal of a "redemptive" life for all; it endures as an "interpretation of the human condition" in Christianity's church(es)—if and when and only to the extent those church(es) convey by their "faith and order, life and work" rather than forget, ignore, or distort its meaning.[38]

The primary trunk arising from Farley's dealings with the ecclesial roots of theology has been made up of investigations of key components of ecclesia's faith. *Ecclesial Reflection* focused on theology's method, sources, authorities, and tasks; *Good and Evil*, on the multidimensional, complex, and subtle interpretation of the human condition bound up with faith's symbols of sin and redemption; *Divine Empathy*, on "the way God redemptively comes forth as God and the way a symbolics of God attends this coming forth."[39] Each study is at once an exposé of Christian theological misunderstandings and distortions of ecclesial faith and a set of correctives and proposals for doing better now and in the future.

Alongside this programmatic series of works arose another, dealing with concerns and issues related to theological education quite specifically. *Theologia* (1983) and *The Fragility of Knowledge* (1988) belong to this line, as do a cloud of articles on selected short subjects.[40] Of all that might be said of these studies, only two points of contact and overlap between the programs will be noted here. First, theologia refers to a wisdom, an existential understanding, that arises when faith's awareness of grace and divine self-disclosure opens itself to reflective inquiry. Hence theologia is to theology as ecclesia is to the Christian church(es). The Latinate terms signal an arrhythmia: at the heart of theology and the church is a living wisdom of ecclesial faith regarding God, humanity, and the world that theology and the church have conveyed over their long, still ongoing histories only spasmodically, always only partially, and often not at all. Second, theology and the church themselves are to blame for some of the most difficult obstacles facing anyone who seeks to nurture ecclesial wisdom. The "house" and way(s) of authority they have created mistakenly *equate* their own biblical canon, ecclesiological traditions, institutional arrangements, values, and goals with God and things of God, and in so doing suppress not only truly critical and self-critical reflection on faith but ecclesial faith and its wisdom as well.

For their part, Christian efforts in modern and postmodern times to resist "traditionalism," and with it authoritarianism, parochialism, and status quo complacency, have too often reduced ecclesial faith's reflective openness to keeping up with contemporary sociocultural megatrends. So, for example, it has come to pass that churches that disavow reducing faith to obedience to authority are likely to reduce it instead to a form of therapy promotive of healthy, happy living. And theological schools, having long ago adopted a clerical paradigm that confused the task of cultivating ecclesial wisdom with that of providing for the church(es) clergy with a modicum of expertise in scholarly disciplines and professional skills, are now concerned to add "spirituality" into the mix. Farley's critique of theological study today and his proposals for its reform go hand-in-hand with his critique of theology's history and his proposals for reinterpreting ecclesial faith's symbolic tradition.

In Lieu of a Conclusion

Vanderbilt at 125 years is this history's end, as well as its point overlook. In fact, and of course, theology there is in transition: the line theologians replacing members of the Vanderbilt quintet as they retire from active school service will not only create the school's future (for better or worse) but in so doing re-create the story or stories of its past, too.

According to this telling of the history, the teaching of theology at Vanderbilt has tracked major developments sweeping across (Protestant) Christianity and American culture—evangelical revivalism, rational supernaturalist orthodoxies, liberalisms, neo-orthodox-realist thought, and—in the making still—fin-de-siècle reappraisals of Christian theology's tradition in light of times today and in anticipation of the future. The term "track" seems especially apt in this context because it is multivalent. "Tracking" means to follow or pursue, to run along with or keep abreast of, and also to scout out or point ahead to some course of motion. Over time, Vanderbilt's theologians have "tracked"—in all three senses of the word—the course of and for theology and the church.

Appendix A

Deans of the Divinity School

Thomas O. Summers	1875–82
A. M. Shipp	1882–85
Wilbur Fisk Tillett	1886–1919
Oswald Eugene Brown	1919–31
George B. Winton	1931–36
Umphrey Lee	1936–39
John Keith Benton	1939–56
J. Robert Nelson	1957–60
William C. Finch	1961–64
James E. Sellers	1965–67
Walter Harrelson	1967–75
Sallie McFague	1975–79
H. Jackson Forstman	1979–89
Joseph C. Hough, Jr.	1990–99
James D. Hudnut-Beumler	2000–

Chairs of the Graduate Department of Religion

John Keith Benton	1942–44
J. Philip Hyatt	1944–60
Lou H. Silberman (acting)	1960–61
Walter Harrelson	1961–62
J. Philip Hyatt	1962–64
Walter Harrelson	1964–67
Robert W. Funk	1967–69
H. Jackson Forstman	1969–72
Howard L. Harrod	1972–75
Peter C. Hodgson	1975–80
Thomas W. Ogletree	1980–81
Eugene TeSelle	1981–90
Peter C. Hodgson	1990–92
Eugene TeSelle (acting)	1992–93
Peter C. Hodgson	1993–96
Eugene TeSelle	1996–99
Douglas A. Knight	1999–

Appendix B

Divinity School Faculty Roster
This list does not include lecturers or temporary and adjunct faculty.

Thomas O. Summers	1875–82	Theology
John C. Granbery	1875–83	Practical Theology and Moral Philosophy
A. M. Shipp	1875–85	Bible
T. J. Dodd	1877–85	Hebrew and Ecclesiastical History
John J. Tigert	1882–85	Bible and Moral Philosophy
Wilbur F. Tillett	1882–1936	Theology
Gross Alexander	1885–1902	New Testament
Elijah Embree Hoss	1886–90	Church History
William Wallace Martin	1886–93	Hebrew and Old Testament
Austin H. Merrill	1886–1900	Preaching and Speech
A. Coke Smith	1890–92	Practical Theology
Oswald Eugene Brown	1892–1937	Church History
James H. Stevenson	1893–1919	Old Testament
J. J. Rapp	1899–1900	Old Testament
John A. Kern	1899–1914	Practical Theology
Gustavus W. Dyer	1899–1925	Sociology and Applied Christianity
Jesse Lee Cuninggim	1902–14	Christian Education
Albert M. Harris	1902–42	Public Speaking and Debate
Henry Beach Carré	1903–28	Bible
Thomas Carter	1903–34	New Testament, Practical Theology, and Homiletics
W. W. Alexander	1915–21	Rural Church Work
William Knox Tate	1916–17	Community Activities of the Country Church
Albert Henry Newman	1917–18	Church History and Missions
Charles Anderson Scott	1918–20	Church History
John L. Kesler	1919–36	Religious Education and Librarian
Douglas Hilary Corley	1923–25	Bible and Comparative Religion
George B. Winton	1927–36	Bible, History of Religion, and Christian Missions

George N. Mayhew	1927–63	Church Administration, Comparative Religion and Missions, and Bible
Henry M. Edmonds	1928–31	Practical Theology
Charles Carroll Haun	1928–31	Rural Life and Religion
Mims T. Workman	1928–31	Biblical Literature
Alva W. Taylor	1928–36	Social Ethics
Robert Martyr Hawkins	1928–55	New Testament
G. Floyd Zimmerman	1929–33	Religious Education
William James Campbell	1929–48	Church History and Practical Theology
Guy W. Sarvis	1931–35	Comparative Religion and Missions
George W. Burroughs	1931–45	Practical Theology
Samuel Bernard Thompson	1931–37	Church History
F. Fagan Thompson	1932–37	Practical Theology and Church Music
William Allen Harper	1932–42	Religious Education
Umphrey Lee	1936–39	Church History and Philosophy of Religion
Edward Thomas Ramsdell	1937–53	Theology and Philosophy of Religion
John Keith Benton	1939–56	Psychology and Philosophy of Religion
Roy Wesley Battenhouse	1940–46	Church History
J. Philip Hyatt	1941–72	Old Testament
Wilfred P. Harmon	1942–45	Practical Theology; Director of Disciples Divinity House
Joseph Minton Batten	1946–54	Church History
W. Kendrick Grobel	1947–65	New Testament and Biblical Theology
Samuel E. Stumpf	1948–52	Theology and Ethics
Samuel Sandmel	1949–52	Jewish Literature and Thought
Nels F. S. Ferré	1950–57	Theology
C. Everett Tilson	1951–60	Old Testament
Herman A. Norton	1951–86	Church History; Dean of Disciples Divinity House
Lou H. Silberman	1952–80	Jewish Literature and Thought
Roger L. Shinn	1954–59	Theology
Langdon B. Gilkey	1954–63	Theology
D. Bard Thompson	1955–61	Church History
Frank P. Grisham	1956–65	Librarian and Religious Literature
James D. Glasse	1956–69	Practical Theology and Field Work
J. Robert Nelson	1957–60	Theology

Ronald Sleeth	1957–64	Preaching
James E. Sellers	1957–71	Theology and Ethics
Paul S. Sanders	1958–60	Church History
Gordon D. Kaufman	1958–63	Theology
Arthur L. Foster	1959–62	Pastoral Theology and Counseling
Leander E. Keck	1959–72	New Testament
Walter J. Harrelson	1960–90	Old Testament
William C. Finch	1961–64	Religion in Higher Education
Gregory T. Armstrong	1962–68	Church History
Ben M. Barrus	1962–68	Church History
Liston O. Mills	1962–98	Pastoral Theology and Counseling
Kenneth R. Mitchell	1963–65	Pastoral Theology and Counseling
Egon Gerdes	1963–67	Church History
Ray L. Hart	1963–69	Theology
John C. Irwin	1964–68	Practical Theology and Methodist History
Winston L. King	1964–73	History of Religions
John R. Killinger, Jr.	1964–81	Homiletics
H. Jackson Forstman	1964–96	Theology and Historical Theology
Peter C. Hodgson	1965–	Theology
J. William Lee	1966–67	Theology
Richard C. Mapes	1966–67	Practical Theology
Robert W. Funk	1966–69	New Testament
David W. Jewell	1966–69	Christian Education
James T. Laney	1966–69	Ethics
Herbert G. May	1966–70	Old Testament
Harold W. Fildey	1966–72	Practical Theology
Richard C. Wolf	1966–78	Church History
Frank Gulley, Jr.	1966–98	Church History
Wilhelm Pauck	1967–72	Church History
Richard G. Bruehl	1967–74	Pastoral Theology and Counseling
Kelly Miller Smith	1968–84	Church and Ministries
Donald F. Beisswenger	1968–96	Field Education; Church, Ministry, and Community
Howard L. Harrod	1968–	Ethics
Edward Farley	1969–97	Theology
Eugene A. TeSelle, Jr.	1969–99	Church History and Theology
Dale A. Johnson	1969–	Church History
A. Neil Housewright	1970–75	Church and Ministries
Chris M. Meadows	1970–76	Pastoral Theology and Counseling

Paul W. Meyer	1970–78	New Testament
Thomas W. Ogletree	1970–81	Ethics
James L. Crenshaw	1970–87	Old Testament
Peter J. Paris	1972–85	Ethics
Sallie McFague	1972–2000	Theology
Frank W. Robert	1973–77	Theological Bibliography and Divinity Librarian
John R. Donahue, S.J.	1973–81	New Testament
Douglas A. Knight	1973–	Hebrew Bible
Daniel M. Patte	1975–	New Testament and Early Christianity
Peggy A. B. Way	1977–87	Pastoral Theology and Counseling
James K. Zink	1978–79	Theological Bibliography and Director of Divinity Library
Gerd Luedemann	1979–83	New Testament
Dorothy Ruth Parks	1979–87	Theological Bibliography and Director of Divinity Library
Mary Ann Tolbert	1981–94	New Testament and Early Christianity
David G. Buttrick	1982–2000	Homiletics and Liturgics
M. Jean Porter	1983–90	Ethics
Fernando F. Segovia	1984–	New Testament and Early Christianity
Richard M. Zaner	1984–	Medical Ethics
David M. Greenhaw	1986–90	Homiletics and Liturgics
Richard L. Harrison, Jr.	1986–93	Church History; Dean of Disciples Divinity House
John R. Fitzmier	1986–99	Church History
Walter E. Fluker	1987–91	Ethics
Wallace Charles Smith	1987–91	Practice of Ministry and Homiletics
William J. Hook	1987–	Theological Bibliography and Director of Divinity Library
Renita J. Weems	1987–	Hebrew Bible
Joretta L. Marshall	1989–93	Pastoral Theology and Counseling
James Barr	1989–98	Hebrew Bible
Joseph C. Hough, Jr.	1990–99	Ethics
Forrest E. Harris, Sr.	1991–	African American Studies and Practice of Ministry
Eugene T. Sutton	1992–95	Homiletics and Liturgics
Victor Anderson	1992–	Ethics
Amy-Jill Levine	1994–	New Testament Studies
L. Susan Bond	1995–	Homiletics
Bonnie Miller-McLemore	1995–	Pastoral Theology and Counseling

Mark Miller-McLemore	1995–	Practice of Ministry; Dean of Disciples Divinity House
Lloyd R. Lewis	1996–	Practice of Ministry and Field Education
Viki B. Matson	1996–	Field Education and Practice of Ministry
Paul J. DeHart	1997–	Theology and Historical Theology
M. Douglas Meeks	1998–	Wesleyan Studies and Theology
J. Patout Burns	1999–	Catholic Studies and Church History
Leonard M. Hummel	1999–	Pastoral Theology and Counseling
Jack M. Sasson	1999–	Jewish Studies and Hebrew Bible
Kathleen Flake	2000–	American Religious History
James D. Hudnut-Beumler	2000–	American Religious History
Mary McClintock Fulkerson	2002–	Theology

Appendix C

Cole Lecturers

1894	Alpheus Waters Wilson	1928	Edwin Hughes
1896	Charles Betts Galloway	1929	Charles Abram Ellwood
1898	Alexander Sutherland	1930	Harris Kirk
1900	John C. Granbery	1931	John R. Mott
1903	Eugene Hendrix	1932	Kenyon Butterfield
1904	James Chapman	1933	Henry Sloane Coffin
1905	Charles Hall	1934	Shailer Mathews
1906	Francis H. Smith	1935	Paul Kern
1907	John Watson (Ian Mac-	1936	Rufus M. Jones
	laren)★	1937	Frederick B. Fisher
1908	George Jackson	1938	Gaius Glenn Atkins
1909	Charles McTyeire Bishop	1939	Albert W. Beaven
1910	William McDowell	1940	Edwin Aubrey
1911	Robert Speer	1941	George Buttrick
1912	William H. P. Faunce	1942	Edgar Brightman
1913	George A. J. Ross	1943	Frederick C. Grant
1914	Francis J. McConnell	1944	Edwin Mims, Robert L.
1915	Walter Russell Lambuth		Calhoun
1916	Herbert Workman	1945	Paul Scherer
1917	James Macdonald	1946	Umphrey Lee
1918	Charles E. Jefferson	1947	Wyatt Smart
1919	Lynn H. Hough	1948	Luther Allan Weigle
1920	Henry Churchill King	1949	Nels Ferré
1921	John Kelman	1950	Pitirim Sorokin
1922	Harry Emerson Fosdick	1951	Rudolf Karl Bultmann
1923	Charles D. Williams	1952–53	(No Cole Lectures)
1924	Samuel Parkes Cadman	1954	Nathaniel Micklem
1925	Edwin Mouzon	1955	Albert Victor Murray
1926	Cornelius Woelfkin, Shailer	1956	Shaun Herron
	Mathews★★	1957	Wilhelm Pauck
1927	Charles Whitney Gilkey	1958	Albert C. Outler

★ Watson was pastor of Sefton Park Presbyterian Church, Liverpool. He died before the lecture, so his manuscript was read by someone else.

★★ Woelfkin died before the Cole Lectures. Mathews lectured on a different topic but Woelfkin's prepared address was published as the Cole Lecture for 1926.

1959	Paul Tillich	1977	Langdon Gilkey, Robert
1960	Harold DeWolf, Wayne		Handy, Paul Pruyser
	Oates, Roland Bainton,	1978	Elizabeth Sewell, Stephen D.
	Walter Harrelson		Crites, Erich Heller
1961	H. Richard Niebuhr	1979	Burgess Carr
1962	Ernest Colwell	1980	Raymond Brown
1963	Gunther Bornkamm	1981	Fred Craddock
1964	Seward Hiltner	1982	Paul Ricoeur
1965	Roger Shinn	1983	Walter Brueggemann
1966	Sidney Mead	1983	Elisabeth Schüssler Fiorenza
1967	Joseph Fletcher, Gabriel	1984	Lou H. Silberman
	Vahanian, Colin Williams	1985	(No Cole Lecture)
1968	Nathan A. Scott, Jr.	1986	Albert Raboteau
1969	Langdon Gilkey	1987	Leander Keck
1970	Martin Marty	1988	James Barr
1971	Krister Stendahl	1989	Margaret Miles
1972	Robert Bellah	1990	Gustavo Gutiérrez
1973	Jaroslav Pelikan	1991	Wendy Doniger
1974	James M. Gustafson	1992	Enrique Dussel
1975	Ernest Campbell, John Kil-	1993	E. Brooks Holifield
	linger, Michael Novak,	1994	Rebecca Chopp
	Aquin O'Neill, Walter Har-	1995	Sheila Greeve Davaney
	relson, Donald Shriver, Sallie	1996	James H. Cone
	TeSelle, William Stringfel-	1997	Donald Beisswenger, Ed-
	low, David Napier, Charles		ward Farley
	Wellborn, James Crenshaw,	1998	Eugene TeSelle
	Martin Marty, Julian Hartt,	1999	David G. Buttrick
	David Tracy	2000	Marcus Borg
1976	Robert Coles	2001	Parker Palmer

Appendix D

Antoinette Brown Lecturers

1974   Beverly Harrison
1975   Phyllis Trible
1976   Eleanor McLaughlin
1977   Rosemary Radford Ruether
1978   Claire Randall
1979   Elisabeth Schüssler Fiorenza
1980   Carter Heyward
1981   Ada Maria Isasi-Diaz
1982   Yvonne V. Delk
1983   Sallie McFague
1985   Carol P. Christ
1986   Joan Chittister
1987   Toinette M. Eugene
1988   Bernice Johnson Reagon
1989   Eleanor Scott Meyers
1990   Sheila Briggs
1991   Katie Cannon
1992   Rita Nakashima Brock
1993   Sharon Welch
1994   Mary Ann Tolbert
1995   Elizabeth A. Johnson
1996   Elizabeth A. Clark
1997   Jacquelyn Grant
1998   Letty Russell
1999   Diana Eck
2000   Renita J. Weems
2001   Kwok Pui-lan
2002   Susan Thistlethwaite

Appendix E

Coordinators of the Office of Women's Concerns
The names given are those at the time of office holding.
Some names have changed subsequent to holding office.

1975–76	Ann Day
1976–77	Jo Clare Wilson
1977–78	Nancy Brink-Spleth
1978–79	Susan Cox
1979–80	Peg Leonard-Martin
1980–81	Tracey Harris DeVol
1981–82	Ann Millin
1982–83	Laura Lee (Dolly) Swisher, Tara Seeley
1983–84	Tammy Estep
1984–85	Helen Alexandra (Alix) Evans
1985–86	Ellen Armour
1986–87	Penny Campbell
1987–88	Shirley Majors-Jones
1988–89	Shirley Majors-Jones
1989–90	Cynthia Chapman, Mona Bagasao-Crane, Holly Toensing
1990–91	Deborah Creamer
1991–92	Amy Carr, Vicki Phillips
1992–93	Melissa Donahue, Jeanine Dorfman
1993–94	Joanne Robertson, Margaret (Margo) Richardson
1994–95	Adrianne Hopper, Jule Nyhuis
1995–96	Jule Nyhuis
1996–97	Michele Bruer, Jennifer Koosed
1997–98	Sarah Parsons, Kathy Williams
1998–99	Leslie Linder
1999–2000	Shannon Sellers Harty, Emily Viverette
2000–2001	Janetta Cravens, Krista Hughes
2001–2002	Erika Callaway, Heather Godsey

Appendix F

The Divinity School Commitments

The Divinity School is committed to the faith that brought the church into being, and it believes that one comes more authentically to grasp that faith by a critical and open examination of the Hebraic and Christian traditions. It understands this faith to have import for the common life of men and women in the world. Thus the school is committed to assisting its community in achieving a critical and reflective understanding of Christian faith and in discerning the implications of that faith for the church, society, and the lives of individuals. Concretely, this commitment entails the education of women and men who will be forceful representatives of the faith and effective agents in working for a more just and humane society, for the development of new and better modes of ministry, and for leadership in church and society that will help to alleviate the ills besetting individuals and groups. It entails as well the education of men and women who have, or are helped to develop, strong resources of personal faith, without which their leadership in church and community would be jeopardized.

The school affirms its commitment to do all in its power to combat the idolatry of racism and ethnocentrism that remains widespread in our society. Positively, this includes a commitment to take full account of the contributions of African Americans, Hispanic Americans, Asian Americans, and Native Americans. It requires the appointment of faculty members and the recruitment of students from these groups and adequate provision for their support. The school recognizes a special connection with the contributions of the black church to church and society and a commitment to further these contributions.

The school is committed to opposing the sexism that has characterized much of the history of the church and western culture and is still present in our society. This commitment entails the conviction that women have a larger place in the ministry and in teaching than they now enjoy. It requires appointment of women to the faculty, enrollment of a larger number of women students in all programs, and concerted effort to eliminate all forms of discrimination in attitudes, practices, and language. The school regards the use of inclusive language as an expression of its opposition to gender-based prejudice.

The school is committed to confronting the homophobia that prevails throughout much of the church and society. We recognize the rights of lesbians and gay men within the religious community and the need for the eradication of civil discrimination based on sexual orientation. This commitment involves the exploration in the curriculum of lesbian and gay concerns as well as affirmation and support of gay and lesbian people within our community.

The school is committed to a program of theological education that is open to and takes account of the religious pluralism in our world. It seeks to familiarize students with interreligious dialogue and the diverse manifestations of Christianity throughout the world, recognizing that to know one's own tradition one must know and participate in others as well. This commitment entails the appointment to the faculty of scholars in other religious traditions and from diverse branches of Christianity, as well as the provision of resources for students to study in global contexts.

The school acknowleges the close and special relationship between Judaism and Christianity, and it wants to ensure an appropriate and sympathetic understanding of the Jewish tradition. It abhors the anti-Semitism that has pervaded much of Christian history and seeks to promote productive and healing dialogue among Christians and Jews.

The school is committed to active participation in the struggles of individuals and groups for a healthier, more just, more humane, and more ecologically wholesome world. It has special concern for the oppressed, for prisoners, for the poor, for victims of warfare and militarism, for the effects of environmental destruction, and for the securing of equal opportunity for all individuals, peoples, and creatures to enjoy God's gifts.

In seeking to act upon such commitments, the school seeks to bear in mind that its fundamental task is educational. The commitment to education is primary. Even so, if such education is to be significant, the school may often be required to identify issues confronting church, society, and individuals that summon various groups within the school, or the school itself, to appropriate action.

The school is committed to conducting its work in an atmosphere conducive to free expression of opinion and judgment and in such a way as actively to enlist the insights and judgments of the church, alumni/ae, students, faculty, staff, the University community, and the larger community.

Notes

PREFACE

1. The only previous history of the school is a twenty-three-page pamphlet by Bard Thompson, "Vanderbilt Divinity School: A History" (Nashville: Vanderbilt University, 1958). Paul K. Conkin's *Gone with the Ivy: A Biography of Vanderbilt University* (Knoxville: University of Tennessee Press, 1985) discusses a number of events in the school's history.

CHAPTER 1

1. James Waits, *Theology in the University: A Study of University-Related Divinity Schools* (Report of the University Divinity School Project, sponsored by the Lilly Endowment, Inc., 1995), 2. Waits was shortly to become executive director of the Association of Theological Schools in the United States and Canada.

2. Ibid., 19.

3. Portions of this chapter are taken from my essay, "The Marginalization of Theology in the University," in Joseph Mitsuo Kitagawa, ed., *Religious Studies, Theological Studies and the University Divinity School* (Atlanta: Scholars Press, 1992), 37–68. The essay also appeared in modified form as an occasional paper, "The Theological Work of the University Scholar," published as a commissioned paper for the University Divinity Schools Project (Pittsburgh: ATS, 1995).

4. George H. Williams, *Wilderness and Paradise in Christian Thought* (New York: Harper and Brothers, 1962), 190–91.

5. Friedrich Paulsen, *The German Universities and University Study* (New York: Scribner's, 1906), 29–47.

6. Ibid., 42–48.

7. See Johann Gottlieb Fichte, *Deduzierter Plan einer zu Berlin zu errichtenden hohern Lehranstalt*, in Ernst Anrich, ed., *Die Idee der Deutschen Universität: Die fünf Grundschriften aus der Zeit ihrer Neubegrundung durch klassischen Idealismus und romantischen Realismus* (1817; reprint, Darmstadt: Hermann Gentner Verlag, 1956), 125ff. Fichte's argument is discussed briefly in Wolfhart Pannenberg, *Theology and the Philosophy of Science*, trans. Francis McDonagh (Philadelphia: Westminster, 1976), 373n.

8. Friedrich Schleiermacher, *Brief Outline of the Study of Theology*, trans. William Farrer (Edinburgh, 1850; reprint, Lexington, KY: ATLA, 1963); it was published by Schleiermacher in 1808. For Schleiermacher's views on the university, see *Occasional Thoughts on Universities in the German Sense*, trans. and annotated by Terrence N. Tice with Edwina Lawler (San Francisco: EM Text, 1991).

9. Pannenberg notes that Schleiermacher wrote much of his work before Fichte's essay appeared; the latter, although written in 1807, was not published until 1817. Pannenberg, *Theology and the Philosophy of Science*, 373n.

10. For a contemporary expression of the same argument, see David H. Kelsey, *To Understand*

God Truly: What's Theological about a Theological School (Louisville, KY: Westminster/John Knox, 1992).

11. There was strong opposition to the teaching of theology in the university in Germany throughout the nineteenth century. For a history of the debate about the "science" of theology, see Pannenberg, *Theology and the Philosophy of Science*, 228–76.

12. See Edward Farley, *Theologia: The Fragmentation and Unity of Theological Education* (Philadelphia: Fortress, 1983), chap. 4.

13. Sydney E. Ahlstrom, "The Middle Period (1840–80)," in George H. Williams, ed., *The Harvard Divinity School: Its Place in Harvard University and in American Culture* (Boston: Beacon, 1954), 135–39.

14. Ibid., 146; and Levering Reynolds, Jr., "The Later Years (1880–1953)," in Williams, ed., *The Harvard Divinity School*, 170–72.

15. Williams, Introduction to *The Harvard Divinity School*, 5. See also Conrad Wright, "The Early Period (1811–40)," in Williams, ed., *The Harvard Divinity School*, 23; and William Adams Brown, *The Case for Theology in the University* (Chicago: University of Chicago Press, 1938), 33–38.

16. Roland H. Bainton, *Yale and the Ministry* (New York: Harper and Brothers, 1957), 79.

17. Robert M. Healey, *Jefferson on Religion in Public Education* (New Haven: Yale University Press, 1962), 210–26.

18. Henry P. Tappan, *University Education* (1851), reprinted in Richard Hofstadter and Wilson Smith, eds., *American Higher Education: A Documentary History* (Chicago: University of Chicago Press, 1961), 2:506.

19. Ibid., 507.

20. Henry Tappan, "The University: Its Constitution and Its Relations, Political and Religious," in ibid., 538.

21. For a detailed study of Harper, see James P. Wind, *The Bible and the University: The Messianic Vision of William Rainey Harper* (Atlanta: Scholars Press, 1987).

22. From Conrad Cherry, "The Study of Religion and the Rise of the American University" (unpublished essay).

23. Abraham Flexner, *Universities, American, English, and German* (New York: Oxford University Press, 1930), 29.

24. Robert Maynard Hutchins, *The Higher Learning in America* (New Haven: Yale University Press, 1936), 96–97, 102.

25. Reynolds, "The Later Years (1880–1953)," in Williams, ed., *Harvard Divinity School*, 212–13.

26. Brown, *The Case for Theology*, 51, 76–77, 83–84.

27. Williams, ed., *Harvard Divinity School*, 5–6 and 247.

28. George Lindbeck with Karl Deutsch and Nathan Glazer, *University Divinity Schools: A Report on Ecclesiastically Independent Theological Education* (New York: Rockefeller Foundation, 1976), vi (emphasis mine).

29. Edward Farley, "Reform of Theological Education as a Theological Task," *Theological Education* 17:2 (1981): 93–117.

30. I refer to the growing number of publications that focus on the nature of theological education as such. For a partial listing of the major works, see Clark Gilpin, "Basic Issues in Theological Education: A Selected Bibliography, 1980–1988," *Theological Education* 25:2 (1989):

115–21. See also David Kelsey, *Between Athens and Berlin: The Theological Education Debate* (Grand Rapids, MI: Eerdmans, 1993), for a discussion of the major proposals for reform generated by the discussions. Kelsey's *To Understand God Truly* is one of the more interesting proposals offered to the national conversation.

31. For a discussion of the responsibility of the university for the common good, including the distinction between the external and internal common good of the university, see my essay, "The University and the Common Good," in David R. Griffin and Joseph C. Hough, Jr., eds., *Theology and the University* (Albany: State University of New York Press, 1991), 97–124.

32. Gordon D. Kaufman, "Critical Theology as a University Discipline," in Griffin and Hough, eds., *Theology and the University*, 35–50.

33. Schubert M. Ogden, "Theology in the University: The Question of Integrity," in Griffin and Hough, eds., *Theology and the University*, 67–80.

34. H. Richard Niebuhr, "Theology in the University," in *Radical Monotheism and Western Culture* (New York: Harper and Brothers, 1960), 93–99.

35. For the term "Christian mythos," Farley cites Bernard Meland's definition, "the pattern of meaning which arises from the structured experience of a people and having to do with the ultimate nature and destiny of human being." Edward Farley, *The Fragility of Knowledge: Theological Education in the Church and the University* (Philadelphia: Fortress, 1988), 22.

36. Ibid., chap. 2.

37. David Griffin has mounted a very convincing argument that even under the provisions of separation of church and state in the United States, there is neither a legal nor a conceptual reason why the study of theology should not be part of the life of public universities, either as part of a department of religious studies or as a separate offering. For example, under Griffin's argument, an entire department of theology, conceived in the way Gordon Kaufman has suggested, would not only be possible but desirable. See David Griffin, "Professing Theology in the State University," in Griffin and Hough, eds., *Theology and the University*, 3–34.

38. Ironically, while both theology as a discipline and the divinity schools themselves were under attack in the universities, support for the teaching of religion, even in state universities, was becoming very strong. In 1927, Herbert L. Searles of the University of Iowa argued that any university that aspires to interpret and understand the highest and best of culture in the past and present must make a place for the study of religion in its curriculum. Herbert L. Searles, *The Study of Religion in State Universities*, University of Iowa Studies in Character 1:3 (Iowa City: University of Iowa, October 1927), 10. His view was fairly typical among the leaders of state universities through the 1940s; see Merrimon Cuninggim, *The College Seeks Religion* (New Haven: Yale University Press, 1947), 79–95.

Since 1945 there has been a significant increase in the number of religious studies programs in both state and private universities. It is important to note that almost all of the faculties of religion in state universities and a majority of those in private universities are careful to distinguish what they do from theological studies. Even graduate programs in religious studies at private universities are increasingly being organized as the study of the history of religions, in contrast to the traditional graduate Christian theological studies programs that have long existed at the major university divinity schools. Within the last few decades, developments at Yale, Harvard, and Chicago indicate that the line between the faculty of the divinity school and the graduate faculty in religion is being drawn more sharply, even though those faculty members in historical and biblical studies usually cross the line rather easily. These faculty members would probably remain in the university even if the divinity school did not. Faculty members whose subject matter is more directly related to the faith and practice of the churches are at home in the university *only* so long as the divinity school remains a vital professional school in the university.

CHAPTER 2

1. Minority Report, The Committee on Education (1870).

2. Some of the strongest critics of Methodist theological schools were men like Pierce or, before him, Peter Cartwright, who were active supporters of colleges and served on more than one college board.

3. I have found the concept of a culture of professionalism in Burton Bledstein's *The Culture of Professionalism: The Middle Class and the Development of Higher Education in America* (New York: Norton, 1976) analytically useful. For him, the culture of professionalism was a set of assumptions about the social and economic order that, though largely invisible, functioned as a mazeway through the routines of ordinary life. In other words, professionalism became part of the patterns, conscious and unconscious, that Americans used to organize their lives.

4. See Thomas A. Langford, *Practical Divinity*, 2d ed. (Nashville: Abingdon, 1999).

5. Robert L. Kelly, *Theological Education in America* (New York: George H. Doran, 1924), 98. This was the first systematic survey of the subject.

6. This is one of the reasons that Abraham Flexner, in his famous report on medical education, argued that the only reputable medical schools were those that were located in a university context. See Abraham Flexner, *Medical Education in the United States and Canada: A Report to the Carnegie Foundation for the Advancement of Teaching* (New York: Carnegie Foundation, 1910).

7. For a detailed examination of the Winchell case, see Frederick Mills, "Alexander Winchell," in George Shriver, ed., *Dictionary of Heresy Trials in American Christianity* (Westport, CT: Greenwood, 1997), 457–65, and Robert E. Chiles, *Theological Transition in American Methodism: 1790–1935* (Nashville: Abingdon, 1965).

8. At about the same time, James Woodrow, who was a professor at both Columbia Seminary and the University of South Carolina, found himself under attack for overstepping the theological bounds of his professorship. He was removed from his seminary chair, but later became president of the University of South Carolina. Like Winchell, Woodrow was passionate about the possibilities of science.

9. See Ben Primer, *Protestants and American Business Methods* (Ann Arbor, MI: UMI Research Press, 1979).

10. Of course, power never apologized. Mitchell was still without a job.

11. Dorothy C. Bass, "The Independent Sector and the Educational Strategies of Mainstream Protestantism, 1900–1980," in Conrad Cherry and Rowland A. Sherrill, eds., *Religion, the Independent Sector, and American Culture* (Atlanta: Scholars Press, 1992), 55.

12. For a discussion of the Briggs case, see Robert T. Handy, *A History of Union Theological Seminary in New York* (New York: Columbia University Press, 1987), chap. 4.

13. In *New Faith for Old: An Autobiography* (New York: Macmillan, 1936), Shailer Mathews listed five schools that served southern progressivism in the 1920s: Duke, the University of North Carolina at Chapel Hill, the University of Richmond, Vanderbilt, and Emory (80). He could have added Wake Forest to this list.

14. *Register* (1915–16), 108. The title for what is commonly called the school's "catalogue" varies over the institution's history; it is variously named *Register*, *Catalogue*, and *Bulletin* (the latter

being the present title). For a few years, there is no title beyond the name of the school and the academic year.

15. Jerry Dean Weber, "To Strengthen and Develop Protestant Theological Education: John D. Rockefeller, Jr. and the Sealantic Fund" (Ph.D. diss., University of Chicago, 1997), 150.

16. Dorothy Ruth Parks, "The Cole Lectures: A History of Distinction," *The Spire* 15:2 (Winter 1993): 14. Programs like the Cole Lectures were increasingly caught in a rising cost spiral.

17. George A. Coe, *The Religion of a Mature Mind* (Chicago: Fleming H. Revell, 1902). The phrase is the title of chap. 10; Coe used the phrase repeatedly, almost as a trademark.

18. Cited in Leonard I. Sweet, "The University of Chicago Revisited: The Modernization of Theology, 1890–1940," *Foundations* 22 (1979): 335.

19. Shailer Mathews, "Vocational Efficiency and the Theological Curriculum," *American Journal of Theology* 16:2 (April 1913): 165.

20. *Register* (1945–46), 206.

21. Edward Farley, *Theologia: The Fragmentation and Unity of Theological Education* (Philadelphia: Fortress, 1983).

22. "Social Aspects of Theological Seminary Training," *Bulletin of the Conference of Theological Seminaries* 6 (1928): 48.

23. One of the classic studies was Edmund de S. Brunner and J. H. Kolb, *Rural Social Trends* (New York: McGraw-Hill, 1933).

24. See James H. Madison, "Reformers and the Rural Church, 1900–1950," *Journal of American History* 73:3 (December 1986): 645–68.

25. *Catalogue* (1970–71), 39–41.

26. Woodrow A. Geier, "Sit-ins Prod a Community," *Christian Century* 77 (March 30, 1960): 380.

CHAPTER 3

1. This body, composed of clerical delegates from the several regional bodies called annual conferences, met every four years.

2. The Tennessee Conference in 1866 was not coterminous with the boundaries of the State of Tennessee. The eastern part of the state was included in the Holston Conference, while a part of Alabama was included in the Tennessee Conference.

3. For an extended treatment of this period, see Paul K. Conkin, *Gone with the Ivy: A Biography of Vanderbilt University* (Knoxville: University of Tennessee Press, 1985), part I.

4. *Wesley Hall Missionary* 1:1 (June 1891): 1.

5. *Register* (1876–77), 23.

6. *Register* (1875–76), 62.

7. "Class meetings" were a Methodist institution going back to the days of John Wesley and the beginnings of English Methodism. Small groups would gather for an hour or so of singing, prayer, and sharing of personal religious experiences.

8. In time Vanderbilt's name would be well known among Christians in the Far East, especially China. One of the first international students to study in the Biblical Department was Charlie Soong (1882–1885), later founder of the wealthy and politically powerful Soong Dynasty in China. He was the financial backer of Sun Yat-sen, married to Soong's middle daughter, Ching-ling. His youngest daughter married Chiang Kai-Shek. See "Saga of the Soongs," *Vanderbilt Magazine* (Winter 1997): 17–19.

9. At the meeting of the Board of Trust, May 24, 1881, McTyeire received approval to appoint a committee of the faculty to make monthly inspection of student rooms "to see how [they] are kept and to report monthly any defacement of the building or furniture, or any cause of disorder."

10. The Methodist Articles of Religion prepared by John Wesley are an abbreviated and revised edition of the Anglican Thirty-nine Articles of Religion. In 1784 Wesley sent twenty-four Articles to the American Methodists as that group was forming the Methodist Episcopal Church. To these the American Methodists added one, making a total of twenty-five Articles of Religion, the closest thing they had to a confession of faith.

11. Philip Schaff, *History of the Apostolic Church*, trans. E. D. Yeomans (New York: Scribner's, 1867). Schaff was the most prominent American historian of Christianity at that time. McTyeire's own work, *A History of Methodism* (Nashville: Publishing House of the Methodist Episcopal Church, South, 1884), quickly established itself as the definitive study of the subject among southern Methodists. As late as 1924 it was still being reprinted.

12. The English Curriculum covered all those subject areas required for ordination in the MECS. The program remained in effect until 1907.

13. The S.T.B. degree was first awarded in the spring of 1882.

14. Giving Summers and his successors the title "dean" should not be interpreted as making the Biblical Department a clearly distinguished entity from the Academic Department, the title used for what later was called the College of Arts and Science. Records suggest that in the earliest years the faculty of the Biblical Department participated as full colleagues in the decision-making of the Academic Department and taught courses in that department as needed. On the other hand, they met as a faculty separate from the Academic Department, maintaining their own record of decisions reached. Deans of the Biblical Department through the administration of Tillett also carried the largely honorific title of vice chancellor of the University.

15. Quoted to the author by Bishop Nolan B. Harmon of the United Methodist Church. Harmon reported having heard this from his father, who knew Bishop McTyeire.

16. Also appointed to the original faculty were A. M. Shipp, professor of exegetical theology, J. C. Granbery, professor of practical theology (later elected to the episcopacy), and R. M. McIntosh, adjunct professor of vocal music. Ecclesiastical history was not offered until academic year 1877–78, when T. J. Dodd came to the faculty. From the catalogues one gets the impression that these faculty were all full-time. Board of Trust minutes reveal this was not always the case: Summers was half-time, with his other time given to the editorial work of the Methodist Publishing House. Some gave half-time instruction to students in the Academic Department.

17. From 1876 to 1887 Vanderbilt was forced to provide the equivalent of subcollegiate education for the many students seeking admission who could not qualify for admission to the University proper, a practice not uncommon among colleges and universities across the country. McTyeire and Garland had hoped that such a step would not be necessary, but the reality of the situation dictated otherwise. As McTyeire stated, "we must have students," another way of saying that budgetary considerations required that the University have a minimum income from student tuition and fees.

18. Vanderbilt University Board of Trust, June 19, 1876. This judgment applied to all levels of the University, including the Medical School, whose students received especially harsh criticism.

19. The situation was so desperate that many students took a large number of the courses in the Academic Department of the University, although enrolled in the Biblical Department.

Indeed, "not a few won their baccalaureate degrees in the Academic Department some two or three years after having been graduated from the Biblical" (*Wesley Hall Missionary* 1:1 [June 1891]: 1).

20. The Board of Trust Minutes of May 26, 1882, show the precise cost to have been $145,404.77.

21. The building was constructed on what is currently called "Library Lawn," the space located immediately behind the Jean and Alexander Heard Library.

22. Exactly how this system operated is not clear. The *Register* for 1885–86 describes it as follows: "This system is a kind of club under the management of officers chosen by the club . . . and all expenses are shared equally by the members" (13). The arrangement may also have involved housekeeping, but this is not certain.

23. In the early years the University regularly provided housing for its entire faculty, in some instances constructing individual houses on the campus to accommodate them. Tillett lived in Wesley Hall for many years, as did other members of the Biblical Department faculty.

24. Report of Dean Wilbur F. Tillett to the Vanderbilt Board of Trust (Board of Trust, June 17, 1901).

25. *Nashville Daily American*, January 17, 1885.

26. Tillett received his B.A. at Randolph Macon College in 1875 and his M.A. at Princeton University in 1879; while completing the M.A., he also completed requirements for a certificate in ministerial education at Princeton Theological Seminary. The certificate was awarded in 1880. At that time Princeton Seminary did not award degrees in theology. From 1880 to 1882, he served as minister of the Lynn Street Methodist Church, Danville, Virginia.

27. Board of Trust, May 25, 1885.

28. Reports on admission indicate that for many years five to ten students in the Biblical Department had not completed the sophomore level of a B.A. program. With no accrediting organizations to provide standards, each institution had to struggle to assess the academic quality of an applicant's previous education and the level of his or her accomplishments.

29. Board of Trust, August 24, 1883.

30. "Some Currents of Contemporaneous Theological Thought," *Methodist Review*, 3d ser., 27 (1901): 483–95.

31. Wilbur F. Tillett, *The Paths That Lead to God: A New Survey of the Grounds of Theistic and Christian Belief* (New York: George H. Doran, 1924), viii.

32. Board of Trust, June 13, 1904.

33. *Register* (1899–1900), 85–86.

34. Chancellor Garland retired from office in 1892 and was succeeded by James H. Kirkland, a member of the faculty, in 1893.

35. Shortly after the establishment of the Correspondence School, its director undertook a survey of the 1,155 persons enrolled and found that 36 percent had some college education, less than 17 percent were college graduates, and less than 3.5 percent were graduates of a theological school.

36. *Vanderbilt University Quarterly* 11 (1911): 214.

37. Board of Trust, June 14, 1904.

38. That action was a ploy designed to attract money from the church. The numerous efforts to squeeze money from the MECS had been futile. It was hoped that placing all the bishops on the Board might lead them to appreciate the University's financial need and become its advocates among the Methodist constituency.

39. The most detailed account of these matters is to be found in Conkin, *Gone with the Ivy*, 147–84.

40. The new universities that resulted were Emory in Atlanta and Southern Methodist in Dallas.

41. From Tillett's "Concluding Word" in his annual report to the Vanderbilt Board of Trust, June 1914.

42. Edwin Mims, *History of Vanderbilt University* (Nashville: Vanderbilt University Press, 1946), 339. Persons like Tillett who were ordained Methodist clergy teaching in an academic institution had two appointments, one from the institution itself and one from the church. The one from the institution was not dependent upon appointment from the church; on the other hand, appointments from the church presupposed a valid appointment from the institution. Prior to 1914, Tillett had both. After the split between the church and Vanderbilt, Tillett of course continued to have a valid appointment from the University. On the other hand, the church, through its bishop in Tennessee, no longer recognized Vanderbilt as an appropriate place to assign a minister. But the bishop did appoint Tillett to the West End congregation, recognizing all the while that he would not serve there but would continue his service at Vanderbilt.

CHAPTER 4

1. Conrad Cherry, *Hurrying toward Zion: Universities, Divinity Schools, and American Protestantism* (Bloomington: Indiana University Press, 1995), ix.

2. Ibid., 60–61.

3. W. Clark Gilpin, *A Preface to Theology* (Chicago: University of Chicago Press, 1996), 111, 90.

4. *Alumnus* 1:6 (April 1916): 5–6. Conrad Cherry refers to Chicago, Harvard, Yale, and Union as the "Big Four" schools that served "throughout the twentieth century as the paradigms for Protestant education in divinity" (*Hurrying toward Zion*, 14).

5. Board of Trust, June 15, 1914.

6. Board of Trust, June 16, 1914.

7. Board of Trust, June 14, 1915.

8. Ibid.

9. Board of Trust, June 12, 1916.

10. Ibid.

11. George M. Marsden, *The Soul of the American University: From Protestant Establishment to Established Nonbelief* (New York: Oxford University Press, 1994), 279.

12. Board of Trust, June 12, 1916.

13. Ibid.

14. Board of Trust, June 13, 1916.

15. Paul K. Conkin, *Gone with the Ivy: A Biography of Vanderbilt University* (Knoxville: University of Tennessee Press, 1985), 264.

16. Board of Trust, June 9, 1919; Conkin, *Gone with the Ivy*, 264.

17. Conkin, *Gone with the Ivy*, 264.

18. Board of Trust, June 11, 1923.

19. *Alumnus* 9:4 (February 1924): 101.

20. "Vanderbilt University School of Religion: A Statement of Its Place in the Field of Theological Education, as Well as of the Reasons Why It Should Be Adequately Endowed and

Equipped" (1924), 30—32. A copy of this brochure is in the Vanderbilt University Special Collections (VUSC), Divinity School, RG 530, Box 835, file 53.

21. Ibid., 108.

22. *Alumnus* 13:3 (January—February 1928): 97.

23. "Vanderbilt University School of Religion," 108.

24. Ibid., 85.

25. Ibid., 5—11, 64—65, 74, 77. Carré envisioned the need for at least one chair and perhaps a department to address the race problem.

26. Board of Trust, June 7, 1927.

27. Conkin, *Gone with the Ivy,* 265.

28. *Alumnus* 12:4 (February 1927): 117; *Alumnus* 12:5 (March 1927): 152; *Alumnus* 13:4 (March—April 1928): 136; *Register* (1928—29): 140—42; *Register* 31:5 (April 1931): 12; Conkin, *Gone with the Ivy,* 265.

29. *Chattanooga Times*, April 21, 1929; *Tulsa Tribune*, March 22, 1929; Board of Trust, June 11, 1928; Conkin, *Gone with the Ivy,* 265.

30. Board of Trust, June 11, 1928; Conkin, *Gone with the Ivy,* 266.

31. George M. Marsden, "Scopes Trial," in Daniel G. Reid, ed., *Dictionary of Christianity in America* (Downers Grove, IL: InterVarsity Press, 1990), 1058—59. Defiance of this law was a misdemeanor, carrying a fine of up to $500. See *Alumnus* 10:5 (April 1925): 136—37.

32. Cherry, *Hurrying toward Zion,* 168. See also George M. Marsden, *Fundamentalism and American Culture: The Shaping of Twentieth Century Evangelicalism, 1870—1925* (New York: Oxford University Press, 1980), 184—95.

33. *Alumnus* 10:5 (April 1925): 136—37.

34. *Alumnus* 12:3 (January 1927): 97.

35. Oswald Eugene Brown, James Hampton Kirkland, and Edwin Mims, *God and the New Knowledge* (Nashville: Cole Lecture Foundation, 1926), iii—iv, 26.

36. Kirkland to Rockefeller, March 17, 1930 (Chancellor's Office, RG 300, box 217, ff. 34, "Sealantic Fund, 1952—62," VUSC); Board of Trust, February 11, 1931, and February 5, 1934.

37. Board of Trust, June 8, 1931. Winton was appointed dean in 1932.

38. Board of Trust, February 1, 1932.

39. *Alumnus* 17:4 (February 1932): 101—2.

40. Kirkland had secured a pledge of $150,000 from Frederick W. Vanderbilt to rebuild Wesley Hall after the fire. However, when the University acquired the YMCA building due to indebtedness, Vanderbilt agreed that this building could serve as the new Wesley Hall. Conkin, *Gone with the Ivy,* 367—68, 388—89; *Alumnus* 22:1 (October 1936): 7.

41. Conkin, *Gone with the Ivy,* 367—68.

42. *Bulletin of Vanderbilt University* 32:9 (January 15, 1933): 4. Similar points are listed in *The Vanderbilt School of Religion: Its Present Needs and Its Prospects* (1933) (Divinity School, RG 530, box 835, ff. 27, "School of Religion—Planning," VUSC).

43. Quoted in Anthony P. Dunbar, *Against the Grain: Southern Radicals and Prophets, 1929—1959* (Charlottesville: University Press of Virginia, 1981), 29; Robert T. Handy, *A Christian America: Protestant Hopes and Historical Realities,* 2d ed. (New York: Oxford University Press, 1984), 135. See also Cherry, *Hurrying toward Zion,* 194—95.

44. *Bulletin / Register* 31:5 (April 1931): 29; Conkin, *Gone with the Ivy,* 370. See also Stanley Lincoln Harbison, "The Social Gospel Career of Alva Wilmot Taylor" (Ph.D. diss., Vanderbilt University, 1975), 273.

45. Alumni petitions to Chancellor Kirkland (n.d.); "Taylor, Alva W.," VUSC.

46. Granberry to Frank Rand, president of the Board of Trust; Chancellor Carmichael; and Dean Umphrey Lee, June 17, 1938 (AWT Papers, box 3, Disciples of Christ Historical Society).

47. Board of Trust, June 8, 1936, and June 25, 1936.

48. Kirkland to Granberry, June 20, 1938; Chancellor's Office, RG 300, box 97, ff. 14, "Taylor, Alva W.," VUSC.

49. Harbison, "Alva Wilmot Taylor," 257–58.

50. Conkin, *Gone with the Ivy*, 373–74.

51. Harbison, "Alva Wilmot Taylor," 264–65.

52. *School of Religion Notes* 1:1 (October 15, 1936): 7–10; *Alumnus* 22:3 (December 1936): 2–3; *Bulletin* 37:8 (July 1937): 18.

53. *School of Religion Notes* 3:3 (August 15, 1939); Conkin, *Gone with the Ivy*, 389; Board of Trust, June 12, 1939.

54. Board of Trust, June 10, 1941, and June 7, 1946; Conkin, *Gone with the Ivy*, 389. The school's accreditation may have been due, in part, to the unification of the Methodist Church in 1939. This merger may have ameliorated some of the remaining bitterness between the school and the MECS. For an examination of the merger, see Frederick E. Maser, "The Story of Unification, 1874–1939," in Emory Stevens Bucke, ed., *The History of American Methodism* (Nashville: Abingdon, 1964), 3:407–78.

55. Board of Trust, August 2, 1946.

56. Board of Trust, June 4, 1947, and June 6, 1947.

57. Board of Trust, February 3, 1947, and June 4, 1948.

58. "Report of the Chancellor," *Bulletin of Vanderbilt University* 51:1 (June 1951): 28–30; Conkin, *Gone with the Ivy*, 501.

59. Conkin, *Gone with the Ivy*, 445–47, 502–3; Board of Trust, February 6, 1950.

60. Conkin, *Gone with the Ivy*, 447; *Alumnus* 34:4 (March 1949): 7.

61. *Alumnus* 34:4 (March 1949): 7.

62. Conkin, *Gone with the Ivy*, 503–5; Board of Trust, February 6, 1950, and May 1, 1953.

63. Conkin, *Gone with the Ivy*, 506–7; Benton to Branscomb, September 14, 1953 (Divinity School, RG 530, box 833, ff. 25, "Branscomb, Harvie," VUSC).

64. Branscomb to Werlein, September 22, 1953 (Chancellor's Office, RG 300, box 166, ff. 20, "Ferré, Nels F. S.—Controversy," VUSC).

65. Ferré, *The Christian Understanding of God* (New York: Harper, 1951), 191; Conkin, *Gone with the Ivy*, 507.

66. *The Sword of the Lord* 16:8 (February 19, 1954); Chancellor's Office, RG 300, box 166, ff. 20, "Ferré, Nels F. S.—Controversy," VUSC.

67. Alexander to Branscomb, January 21 and March 22, 1954; Chancellor's Office, RG 300, box 166, ff. 20, "Ferré, Nels F. S.—Controversy," VUSC.

68. Conkin, *Gone with the Ivy*, 508.

69. Branscomb to Alexander, September 12, 1955; Chancellor's Office, RG 300, box 166, ff. 20, "Ferré, Nels F. S.—Controversy," VUSC.

70. Branscomb to Mrs. Frank Thurmond, December 15, 1954; Chancellor's Office, RG 300, box 166, ff. 20, "Ferré, Nels F. S.—Controversy," VUSC.

71. Benton to Branscomb, August 5, 1955; "Branscomb, Harvie," VUSC.

72. "Methodists Cancel Ferré Lectures," *Christian Century* 72 (August 24, 1955): 963–64.

73. Conkin, *Gone with the Ivy*, 508–9.

74. "Report of the Chancellor," *Register* 51:1 (July 1951): 30.

75. Bard Thompson, *Vanderbilt Divinity School: A History* (Nashville: n.p., 1960), 21; Rockefeller to Branscomb, August 13, 1952; "Sealantic Fund," VUSC.

76. Memorandum to the Sealantic Foundation Concerning the School of Religion, April 12, 1955, 2–3, 16.

77. Branscomb to Creel, October 10, 1955; "Sealantic Fund," VUSC.

78. Creel to Branscomb, December 14, 1955; "Sealantic Fund," VUSC.

79. Minutes of the Faculty of the School of Religion, January 5, 1956 (Divinity School, RG 530, box 833, ff. 3, VUSC); Press Release, Sealantic Fund, Inc., December 19, 1955 ("Sealantic Fund," VUSC). The press release stated that regionalism was a major factor in the decision-making process.

80. Conkin, *Gone with the Ivy,* 501.

81. Cherry, *Hurrying toward Zion*, 206. Cherry makes this claim for the divinity schools at both Vanderbilt and Duke.

82. Benton to Branscomb, September 24, 1952 ("Branscomb, Harvie," VUSC)—the faculty adopted the resolution on September 27, 1952; Branscomb to Rockefeller, October 27, 1952, and Rockefeller to Branscomb, October 31, 1952 ("Sealantic Fund," VUSC); Memorandum, 5.

83. "Branscomb, Harvie," VUSC; *Alumnus* 38:4 (March–April, 1953): 7.

84. *Alumnus* 38:6 (July–August, 1953): 7.

85. Sarratt to Benton, June 16, 1953; "Branscomb, Harvie," VUSC.

86. Benton to Harwell, July 24, 1954 (Divinity School, RG 530, box 835, ff. 7, "Negroes, Admission of," VUSC); Minutes of the Faculty of the School of Religion, May 19, 1955 (VUSC).

87. "Will of Kate Schoolfield Tillett Smith," June 3, 1954 (Divinity School, RG 530, box 835, ff. 34, "Smith, Kate Tillett," VUSC); Minutes of the Faculty of the School of Religion, May 29, 1957 (VUSC).

88. "Report of the Chancellor," *Bulletin* (1954–55): 21–22.

89. Conkin, *Gone with the Ivy,* 501; "Report of the Chancellor," *Bulletin* (1955–56): 24, and *Bulletin* (1954–55).

90. Branscomb to Benton, May 9, 1956; Divinity School, RG 530, box 833, ff. 26, "Branscomb–Benton Correspondence, 1956," VUSC.

91. *Nashville Banner*, August 21, 1956; "John Keith Benton: Two Tributes," November 28, 1956 (Divinity School, RG 530, box 833, ff. 24, "Benton, John Keith," VUSC).

92. *VU View* (January–February, 1957): 5.

93. Board of Trust, October 19–20, 1956.

94. James Sellers, "Recruitment Proposals for the B.D. Program," February, 1958; Divinity School, RG 530, box 840, ff. 91, "Minutes—Admissions and Scholarships, 1956–1961," VUSC.

95. For the announcement of intentions to launch the conference, see Minutes of the Faculty of the Divinity School, November 22, 1957. For the actual proposal submitted, see Minutes, January 14, 1958.

CHAPTER 5

Acknowledgment: I wish to acknowledge the assistance of Joshua E. Perry, a joint Law-Divinity student, who read early drafts of this chapter and provided useful comments.

1. *Nashville Christian Advocate* 29 (February 20, 1869): 1.

2. *Nashville Christian Advocate* 29 (February 27, 1869): 2.

3. *Nashville Christian Advocate* 29 (September 4, 1869): 1.

4. By focusing on these individuals, I do not claim that everyone engaged in theological education at Vanderbilt fit neatly into the respective "prophetic" typologies listed. Nor do I argue that these prophetic visions were limited to particular times and generations. Although the cultural context must influence any institutional vision and sense of purpose, variants of these three prophetic visions (and others) are found running throughout the school's history. The rationale behind this chapter's arrangement is to focus on three of the more notable types in the history of theological education at Vanderbilt as a way of engaging the larger dilemma of the New South.

5. J. C. C. Newton, *The New South and the Methodist Episcopal Church, South* (Baltimore: King Brothers, 1887), vi.

6. C. Vann Woodward, *Tom Watson: Agrarian Rebel* (New York: Macmillan, 1938), 89.

7. W. J. Cash, *The Mind of the South* (New York: Knopf, 1941), 183–89.

8. Paul M. Gaston, *The New South Creed: A Study in Southern Mythmaking* (New York: Alfred A. Knopf, 1970), 190, 9.

9. Newton, *The New South*, vii.

10. "1866 Bishops' Charge to Committee on Education," *Nashville Christian Advocate* 32 (March 9, 1872): 10.

11. *Nashville Christian Advocate* 29 (October 9, 1869): 1. According to Garland, McTyeire and Summers recruited him "to write a series of essays for the *Advocate* upon the necessity of a higher culture of the ministry" ("The Founding of Vanderbilt University," *Nashville Christian Advocate* 50 [May 24, 1890]: 10). The fact that Garland's essays ran on the front page of the *Advocate* suggests Summers's interest in and support of the concept. One may also infer that McTyeire may have appointed Summers as the first dean of the Vanderbilt theological school as reward for providing McTyeire and Garland a forum to market their ideas of theological education to the MECS.

12. *Nashville Christian Advocate* 29 (November 6, 1869): 1; and (November 13, 1869): 1. In addition to "manufacturing preachers," other disdainful epithets for theological education included "man-made ministers" and "aping other denominations." See Summers's editorial, *Nashville Christian Advocate* 32 (January 13, 1872): 8.

13. *Nashville Christian Advocate* 29 (November 13, 1869): 1.

14. Ibid. At this point Summers offered tepid public support for Garland's agenda. "We [the *Advocate*] are on all sides of this question, except that of the laissez-faire party. We are eminently conservative, but we are progressive too." What Summers ultimately hoped to avoid, however, was MECS ministerial candidates "going off to any one of the three Northern Methodist theological seminaries. We want our young Apolloses to go to our Aquilas and Priscillas to learn 'the way of God more perfectly' " (ibid., 2).

15. *Nashville Christian Advocate* 29 (November 27, 1869): 1.

16. *Nashville Christian Advocate* 29 (December 25, 1869): 1.

17. *Nashville Christian Advocate* 30 (January 29, 1870): 1.

18. *Nashville Christian Advocate* 30 (February 19, 1870): 1.

19. *Nashville Christian Advocate* 30 (April 16, 1870): 1.

20. *Nashville Christian Advocate* 30 (April 23, 1870): 1.

21. *Nashville Christian Advocate* 30 (February 26, 1870): 1; and (March 5, 1870): 1.

22. Robert H. Wiebe, *The Search for Order, 1877–1920* (New York: Hill and Wang, 1967), xiii–xiv, 111–32.

23. *Nashville Christian Advocate* 32 (April 27, 1872): 14. See John J. Tigert, *Bishop Holland Nimmons McTyeire* (Nashville: Vanderbilt University Press, 1955), 177.

24. *Nashville Christian Advocate* 32 (February 10, 1872): 14; (February 3, 1872): 14; and (March 23, 1872): 14. Boland also noted that the financial burdens would have a ripple effect. Not only would the theological institution burden the MECS with its obvious institutional costs, but the church would also need to maintain theological graduates at a higher level of subsistence than their less educated counterparts.

25. *Nashville Christian Advocate* 32 (May 18, 1872): 14; (March 23, 1872): 12; (April 27, 1872): 14; (May 18, 1872): 5; and (March 23, 1872): 12.

26. *Nashville Christian Advocate* 32 (March 23, 1872): 12; and (April 27, 1872): 14.

27. *Nashville Christian Advocate* 32 (April 27, 1872): 14.

28. *Nashville Christian Advocate* 32 (March 2, 1872): 14; "Letter to Editor," ibid., 15.

29. *Nashville Christian Advocate* 32 (March 2, 1872): 14; (April 27, 1872): 14; (May 18, 1872): 5; and (March 2, 1872): 14.

30. *Nashville Christian Advocate* 32 (May 18, 1872): 14; (February 17, 1872): 15; and (March 2, 1872): 10.

31. *Nashville Christian Advocate* 32 (May 4, 1872): 4. McTyeire used Pierce as an example of how slavish adherence to the old plan could be threatening. He noted that in 1870, Pierce had admitted forty preachers on trial, and then immediately sent twenty-nine of them as pastors of large, demanding congregations or circuits (e.g., 400 members). In 1871, Pierce admitted forty-four young, untrained men into the ministry, and immediately put forty of them in charge of churches.

32. *Nashville Christian Advocate* 32 (April 6, 1872): 4. The debate between Pierce and McTyeire continued in the April 27 and May 4 issues of the *Advocate*.

33. *Nashville Christian Advocate* 32 (May 18, 1872): 5. The debate over theological education for Methodist ministers did not abate once Vanderbilt University emerged. Another notable round took place a decade later between F. C. Woodward, representing the progressives, and W. T. Bolling, speaking for the populists ("Methodism and Ministerial Education," *Southern Methodist Review* 1 [September 1886]: 208–17; and 2 [March 1887]: 54–60).

34. *Nashville Christian Advocate* 32 (June 15, 1872): 14; and (May 4, 1872): 10.

35. As the successful editor of the *Nashville Christian Advocate*, Summers not only had name recognition within the denomination, his personal story served as a case study of the intellectual and cultural progress McTyeire desired for MECS clergy. Born in 1812 in England, he was orphaned as a young child and reared by his Calvinist aunt. In his adolescent years, he became a devout reader of John Wesley and eventually converted to the Methodist Church—but only after his aunt died. Four years after emigrating to the Chesapeake Bay region of the United States in 1830, he preached his first sermon. The next year the Baltimore Conference licensed Summers and sent him out alone on a circuit. He left the Mid-Atlantic region in 1840 to serve as a missionary and help found the Texas Conference of the Methodist Church in the new Lone Star Republic. Although he had little formal education, Ruter College conferred the Doctor of Divinity degree on him while he was in Texas. By the mid-1840s he had returned east and was working in the Alabama Conference; in 1845 he served as both a delegate and the secretary of the convention forming the MECS when it divided over slavery. The next year he moved to Charleston, South Carolina, to assist the editor of the MECS's new connectional paper, *The Southern Christian Advocate*. During the Civil War, however, publishing became so expensive and mail delivery so irregular that religious journalism in the South ceased. Summers resumed his journalistic career after the war, this time as the editor of the *Nashville Christian Advocate*—a position he would hold 1868–78.

36. O. P. Fitzgerald, *Dr. Summers: A Life Study* (Nashville: Southern Methodist Publishing House, 1885), 152, 187, 191, 207, 330–31.

37. L. Edward Philips, "Thomas Osmond Summers, Methodist Liturgist of the Nineteenth Century," *Methodist History* 27 (July 1989): 241–53. In 1873, Summers published his *Commentary on the Ritual of the Methodist Episcopal Church, South* (Nashville: A. H. Redford for the M. E. Church, South).

38. Josephus Anderson, *Our Church: A Manual for Members and Probationers of the Methodist Episcopal Church, South*, ed. Thomas O. Summers (Nashville: Southern Methodist Publishing House, 1860), 251–52.

39. Newton, *The New South*, 70, 76–77.

40. Wilbur Fisk Tillett, "Seed Corn for the World" (n.d.); Wilbur Fisk Tillett (WFT) Papers, box 2, ff. 38, Vanderbilt University Special Collections (VUSC).

41. "Bishop Haygood's Address to Vanderbilt University," *Nashville Christian Advocate* 51 (June 28, 1890): 2–3.

42. Wilbur Fisk Tillett, "The White Man of the New South," *Century Magazine* 33 (March 1887): 769–76. For the same thesis more than a generation later, see Wilbur Fisk Tillett, *The Hand of God in American History: A Study of Divine Providence as Seen in the Life and Mission of a Nation* (Nashville: Cokesbury, 1923), 23–25.

43. Tillett, *Hand of God*, 51, 41. Military force, of course, was not desired, but it served as an effective means to providential ends.

44. Henry F. May, *Protestant Churches and Industrial America* (New York: Harper and Brothers, 1949), 91; Henry Steele Commager, *The American Mind* (New Haven: Yale University Press, 1950), 184.

45. Robert T. Handy, *A Christian America: Protestant Hopes and Historical Realities*, 2d ed. (New York: Oxford University Press, 1984).

46. Tillett, *Hand of God*, 27, 12, 48.

47. Wilbur Fisk Tillett, *The Paths That Lead to God: A New Survey of the Grounds of Theistic and Christian Belief* (New York: George H. Doran, 1924), 35.

48. Tillett, *Paths*, 65–66. In fact, writing one year after the Scopes trial in Dayton, Tennessee, Tillett threw his support behind the "evolutionists" because "the principle of evolution, as something expressive of progress upward from that which is lower to that which is higher in physical nature and spiritual life, is all but universally recognized as describing what we may call the providential method of Divine activity" (*Providence, Prayer and Power: Studies in the Philosophy, Psychology and Dynamics of the Christian Religion* [Nashville: Cokesbury, 1926], 155). He illustrated how theologically progressive ideas could undergird a socially conservative agenda. Thus, while Vanderbilt's "school of the prophets" may have had a theologically progressive reputation, it also had a socially conservative ethos.

49. Tillett, *Providence, Prayer and Power*, 168–69.

50. Wilbur Fisk Tillett, *Theological Seminaries and Teacher Training* (Nashville: Smith and Lamar, 1910); WFT Papers, box 2, ff. 39, VUSC. See also various clippings from Tillett's articles, box 3, ff. 49, VUSC.

51. Clipping of a Tillett article from the April 19, 1900, *Nashville Christian Advocate*, in the WFT Papers, box 3, ff. 50, VUSC. Tillett also called attention to the fact that while only one-tenth of MECS ministers had theological education, nine-tenths of the MECS bishops had such training—thus underscoring the ability of education to make the minister more successful.

52. Newspaper clipping from the time Tillett lived in Danville, Virginia, in the early 1880s; WFT Papers, box 3, ff. 49, VUSC.

53. From Tillett's "The Prepared Man" speech, published in the *Blue Ridge Voice*; WFT Papers, box 3, ff. 49, VUSC; see also Tillett's "The Value of Theological Education," a clipping in the WFT Papers, box 3, ff. 48, VUSC.

54. A clipping of Jones's bombast is found in the WFT Papers, box 3, ff. 56, VUSC.

55. Tillett, *Paths*, 436–38.

56. *North Carolina Christian Advocate*, March 7, 1890; WFT Papers, box 3, ff. 50, VUSC.

57. Information from an autobiographical sketch in the Alva Wilmot Taylor (AWT) Papers, box 1, Disciples of Christ Historical Society (DCHS), Nashville, Tennessee. See also Stanley Lincoln Harbison, "The Social Gospel Career of Alva Wilmot Taylor" (Ph.D. diss., Vanderbilt University, 1975), and Lois Anna Ely, *Concerned! Brief Sketches of a Few Disciples Involved in the Record of Progress of Human Rights* (Indianapolis: Missionary Education Department of the United Christian Missionary Society, 1952).

58. Alva W. Taylor, "The Function of the Board of Temperance and Social Welfare of the Disciples of Christ" (n.d.), Divinity School, RG 530, box 854, ff. 17, "Rural Church School," VUSC.

59. Alva W. Taylor, "Democracy and the Labor Movement" (n.d.); "'A Little Chapter in Labor's Progress': A Labor Day Sermon," (n.d.) (AWT Papers, pamphlet file, DCHS).

60. Taylor, *Procedures for Socializing Adult Christian Thinking* (Indianapolis: Department of Religious Education of the United Christian Missionary Society, 1931), 5, 12, 41, 14.

61. Taylor to Guy [Sarvis], May 4, 1936 (AWT Papers, box 2, ff. 16, DCHS), emphasis in original; Taylor to James H. Kirkland, November 11, 1931 (Chancellor's Office, RG 300, box 97, ff. 14, "Taylor, Alva W.," VUSC).

62. Compiled from letters to W. H. Hoover, December 17, 1929; Jerome Davis, August 5, 1933; Griggs, March 12, 1934; Chancellor J. H. Kirkland, March 31, 1934; and Sherwood Eddy, November 28, 1935; December 14, 1935; March 5, 1936; and May 16, 1936 (AWT Papers, box 2, DCHS).

63. Taylor to Jerome Davis, August 5, 1933, and Taylor to Sherwood Eddy, May 16, 1936 (AWT Papers, box 2, DCHS); Taylor "to friends," January 7, 1939 (AWT Papers, biographical file, DCHS).

64. Alva W. Taylor, "An Armistice Day Sermon," (n.d.) (AWT Papers, pamphlet file, DCHS.)

65. Taylor, *Procedures for Socializing Adult Christian Thinking*, 29–32. In 1932, Taylor helped coordinate an interracial ministers' meeting in Nashville. He was disappointed, however, with the poor turnout of white ministers.

66. Other popular themes in Taylor's "Correspondence from the New South" were the rights of women and children laborers, experiments in communal living like the Llano Cooperative in Leesville, Louisiana, and Sherwood Eddy and Howard Kester's Arkansas sharecropper commune. He also plugged educational initiatives like Don West and Miles Horton's Highlander School in Monteagle, Tennessee. Kester and West had been Taylor's students at Vanderbilt.

67. James Myers et al., *Social Progress and Christian Ideals* (Nashville: Cokesbury, 1931); and Alva W. Taylor, *Christianity and Industry in America* (New York: Friendship Press, 1933).

68. Harbison, "The Social Gospel Career of Alva Wilmot Taylor," 252–53.

69. Taylor to "Jim 'n Bill," May 18, 1933 (AWT Papers, box 2, ff. 8, DCHS); Taylor to

"Nevin," December 26, 1932 (AWT Papers, box 2, ff. 7, DCHS); letter, no designee (AWT Papers, box 2, ff. 5, DCHS); Taylor to John L. Lewis, President of the United Mine Workers, May 6, 1933 (AWT Papers, box 2, ff. 8, DCHS).

70. Taylor to Griggs, March 12, 1934 (AWT Papers, box 2, ff. 11, DCHS).

71. In the November 9, 1932, issue of the *Christian Century*, for example, Taylor wrote of Rev. Claude Williams's work in Paris, Arkansas. A recent graduate of the Vanderbilt School of Religion, Williams had helped unionize miners and farmers and had built an interracial church in the community. Taylor then praised Chancellor Kirkland for his four decades of service to the cause of training southern ministers. Although Taylor made no direct connection between Kirkland and the work of Williams, Kirkland may not have appreciated the company Taylor was arranging for him in print.

72. Taylor to Jerome Davis, March 3, 1934 (AWT Papers, box 2, ff. 11, DCHS).

73. Taylor to Gifford Gordon, May 29, 1934 (AWT Papers, box 2, ff. 12, DCHS); Taylor to "Frank," May 29, 1934 (ibid.); Taylor to "Paul," September 13, 1934 (ibid.).

74. Taylor to Dean Lhamon, May 3, 1935; Taylor to Guy Sarvis, July 16, 1935; and Taylor to C. C. Haun, April 19, 1934 (AWT Papers, box 2, ff. 11, 13, and 14, DCHS).

75. Taylor, "Autobiography of Select Events," 1952 (AWT Papers, biographical file, DCHS).

76. Taylor to "Dick," April 24, 1937; Taylor to Jerome Davis, May 8, 1937; Taylor to O. H. King, April 28, 1937; Taylor to "Milo," January 3, 1937 (AWT Papers, box 2, ff. 18, DCHS).

CHAPTER 6

1. Lawson was imprisoned from April 1951, to May 1952, for resisting the draft. He was a missionary in India from 1953 to 1956. See David Halberstam, *The Children* (New York: Random House, 1998), pp. 39–49.—*Ed.*

2. When Paul Conkin's book was published, Jacque Voegeli, dean of the College of Arts and Science, realized that much was missing from what Conkin called "the most critical week in Vanderbilt's history." He asked me to prepare a report for the archives on my meeting with Chancellor Branscomb and Harold Vanderbilt on June 8, 1960. My report of this meeting and the other events of that week was shown to Chancellor Branscomb, Rob Roy Purdy, and Robert McGaw in 1985. They made minor suggestions, and all agreed that my report was in substantial agreement with their own memories of those events. It has been placed in the Vanderbilt Special Collections under seal for fifty years. It was made for the benefit of a future historian who may want to look back at the events of 1960.—*Charles Roos*

CHAPTER 7

1. I first heard about Vanderbilt Divinity School in 1960 when stories about "the Lawson affair" circulated among the students and faculty at Duke Divinity School, where I was a student. Very few, if any, of the students or faculty (with the possible exception of H. Shelton Smith) fully grasped the meaning of the forces that were sweeping across the South. Then in the spring of 1960 the sit-in movement came to Durham, and I was one of several Duke University students arrested and jailed as a consequence of a sit-in demonstration at the S. H. Kress store. That experience changed me fundamentally, shaping my attitudes and actions in ways that influence the interpretations that appear in this chapter.

2. In this chapter I focus particularly on two periods in the life of the school: from 1960 to the

end of the Vietnam War and the late 1980s. While the entire history covered in this chapter cannot be exhausted by analysis of these two time periods, they do illustrate the dynamics of social change and transformation that are central to my interest.

3. I would like to thank the following former students for providing reflections on their experiences during the late 1960s and early 1970s: Mara Donaldson, Riggins Earl, Harley (Rye) Johnson, David Kidd, Joe Monti, Robert Olive, Don Welch, and Harmon Wray. One important book that helped me recall the power of the civil rights movement and the charismatic quality of King's leadership is Taylor Branch's *Pillar of Fire: America in the King Years 1963–65* (New York: Simon and Schuster, 1998). Another is Todd Gitlin's *The Sixties: Years of Hope, Days of Rage* (New York: Bantam Books, 1987). Other sources include issues of *The Movement*, a publication affiliated with the Student Nonviolent Coordinating Committee and Students for a Democratic Society.

4. My perspective here as elsewhere in this essay is informed by Karl Mannheim's frequently neglected essay, "The Problem of Generations," in *Essays in the Sociology of Knowledge* (London: Routledge and Kegan Paul, 1968).

5. I refer here to what might be called the "Yale group," represented during the 1960s by Peter Hodgson, Sallie McFague, Eugene TeSelle, Don Beisswenger, Ray Hart, and myself. Paul Meyer and Leander Keck represented the "Yale tradition" for a time when they were on the faculty. This ethos was expressed in working relationships with individuals in the philosophy department such as John Compton and Charles Scott, who were also Yale graduates. For most of the 1990s, Joe Hough, a Yale graduate and a classmate of the "Yale group" listed above, embodied a classical liberalism in various aspects of his deanship. Prior to 1968 the Divinity School experienced a number of changes in the composition of its faculty, with the departure of several persons in the aftermath of the Lawson affair and the arrival of faculty members as a result of the merger with Oberlin Graduate School of Theology. As faculty members came and went, new appointments were made. During the three decades between 1966 and 1996, the faculty achieved a remarkable degree of stability. Even though there were departures, new hires, and deaths during this period, a core group of faculty remained, providing institutional stability and coherence in terms of programs. Beginning in 1996, however, a new process of institutional change began: those faculty members who had been together for thirty years or more began to retire; by 2002 that process will be virtually complete.

6. Since the 1960s, students who represented greater diversity in terms of gender and race began to appear. Even though the actual number of African American students has never been large, their influence has often been great. Since 1960 the number of women has grown steadily; in 1998, women accounted for 53 percent of the students enrolled in the Divinity School. In addition, student members of formerly invisible groups, such as gays and lesbians, have increasingly made their presence felt. These developments have been fully institutionalized—some graduates from the 1960s might say "co-opted"—into offices for Women's Concerns, Black Seminarians, and Gay, Lesbian, and Bisexual Concerns (the latter going by the acronym GABLE). Such a set of organizations is, of course, not unique to the Divinity School.

7. Some seventy students entered the Divinity School each year in 1969 and 1970; that number had been cut in half by 1973, in the later stages of the war.

8. Chapter 10 takes up more specifically and in greater detail some of the matters I introduce here, but my analysis is done from a slightly different perspective and for different purposes. It is intended, however, to complement that chapter.

9. The model I am proposing has been influenced by Peter Berger, *The Sacred Canopy* (New York: Doubleday, 1966), and Peter Berger and Thomas Luckmann, *Social Construction of Reality*

(New York: Doubleday, 1967). In my treatment, as in theirs, the sociology of knowledge as articulated by Karl Mannheim and, more particularly, Alfred Schutz forms the background for analysis.

10. For details concerning the curriculum committee's recommendations as well as the responses and modifications made by the faculty at the Paris Landing retreat, see "Report of the Curriculum Committee to the Vanderbilt Divinity School Faculty," April 27, 1967, and Vanderbilt Divinity School Faculty Minutes, April 27–29, 1967.

11. See Thomas Kuhn, *The Structure of Scientific Revolutions* (Chicago: University of Chicago Press, 1962).

12. A novel that greatly stimulated specific memories of the Vietnam War era is John M. Del Vecchio, *The 13th Valley* (New York: Bantam Books, 1982). The events mentioned in this paragraph are included in his very helpful chronology, pp. 599–607.

13. That the tensions and creative instabilities as well as the hopes and fears so prominent during this time had an effect on faculty deliberations is asserted by at least two who were there, Liston Mills (correspondence) and Ray Hart (conversation). In addition to the sense of instability and tension in the society, the faculty also experienced an internal set of tensions connected with the arrival, in 1966, of faculty members and students from the Oberlin Graduate School of Theology, through its merger with the Divinity School.

14. One consequence of this decision was that Professors Sellers and Laney sought to constitute ethics as a separate discipline. Prior to this point, ethics had been taught as a part of the theology offerings.

15. In 1968 the faculty members responsible for teaching this course were Tom Boyd, David Jewell, and myself. This group was convened by the director of field education, Don Beisswenger. It was somewhat serendipitous that Beisswenger and I were appointed in the first year that this course was taught, as both of us were interested in social ethics and the sociology of religion. These interests complemented those of Boyd and Jewell and, ironically, brought into the planning of the course some of the elements that the curriculum committee had in mind when it proposed the formation of the new field called "Studies in Religion and Culture."

16. Most of these Listening Posts were in institutional settings focused on the problems of African Americans, the elderly, the poor, the emotionally disturbed (both adults and children), alcoholics, and prisoners.

17. From a hand-out, "Introduction to Theological Education: The Listening Post."

18. Ibid.

19. A number of proposals for the content of Introduction to Theological Education had been circulating; one by Leander Keck and Walter Harrelson entitled "Proposal for Required First-Year Course: Foundations of Critical Theology" argued that the fundamental aim of the course should be "to open up the morphology of critical theology at the outset of one's study; the student needs to get his bearings at the beginning, not merely at the end." It went on to state that "it is not the aim of the proposed course to move the faculty into the student's horizons. Rather, its aim is to make clear . . . why certain issues elicit discussion today and why others do not, to indicate the reasons behind the present-day stance of theology." This proposal assigned more importance to understanding the dynamics of change within the historical disciplines constituting theological education than the course that was actually planned and taught.

20. I was the author of that 1969 internal document.

21. These judgments were expressed in a "Student Power Poll" conducted in the fall of 1968. Another questionnaire that assessed the Plunge in the same year came to a different conclusion.

Forty-five out of the fifty-six students who engaged in it responded to the questionnaire, and 86 percent of them thought that the experience should be made a permanent part of Introduction to Theological Education.

22. See Paulo Freire, *Pedagogy of the Oppressed* (New York: Penguin, 1972). Other ideas were closely associated with this notion, such as the authority of present experience as compared with the past, suspicion of the authority of the teacher and his or her ability to evaluate student work, and a growing critique of hierarchy that seemed to characterize the relationship between professors and students.

23. These ruminations were written in 1968 in a staff evaluation of the course.

24. While meeting with a small number of United Methodist students, he was alleged to have made offensive comments about the possibilities for education in South Africa. In response to a question concerning the reasons for continuing to separate blacks and whites in the educational process, he was reported as saying that "white schooling and black schooling are separate and that is only for educational reasons; there's no way you could possibly throw this lot together unless you wanted to go down several decades in standards. . . . I'm not therefore defending segregation except on pedagogical grounds" (quoted from a memo to all students, faculty, and staff from the Women's Office and the Black Seminarians, November 5, 1986).

25. It is ironic that these offices were originally formed with the support of the same faculty who were now being charged with racism.

26. The Davis Cup protest involved highly visible activities on the part of the Divinity School student body and faculty. Both students and faculty were involved in "old time" civil rights marches on campus. They carried placards, chanted slogans, and sang civil rights songs. On one occasion, the Divinity School faculty marched in full academic regalia to the steps of Kirkland Hall to present its demand to the University that the Davis Cup event be canceled.

27. The decision to strive toward equality in its appointment of women was driven in large part by faculty members such as Sallie McFague and Mary Ann Tolbert. Discussions of this issue resulted in a formal faculty vote adopting this goal in 1990. Pressure to hire African Americans and other minorities was also kept on the faculty by Kelly Miller Smith, Wallace Charles Smith, Forrest Harris, Walter Fluker, Renita Weems, and, most recently, by Victor Anderson. Since his appointment in 1984, Fernando Segovia has added a strong Hispanic voice to faculty discourse. The point here is that the faculty who represented the white male majority in the institution have maintained internal pressures toward inclusion of minorities by institutionalizing this goal in terms of faculty hiring practices.

28. Student leaders who were particularly vocal and effective included, among others, Gary Martin, Flora Wilson Bridges, Penny Campbell, Shirley Majors-Jones, Janet Wolf, Moses Dillard, Dorothy Gager, Ellen Armour, and Jon Carlock.

29. Wallace Charles Smith was at this time part-time professor of homiletics as well as the successor to Kelly Miller Smith as pastor of First Baptist Church, Capitol Hill, in Nashville. The document produced by the seminar was entitled "A Document on Racism at Vanderbilt Divinity School and the Graduate Department of Religion."

30. Some of these attitudes, particularly about the workshop, were expressed to Dean Jack Forstman by Walter Harrelson in a memo of March 22, 1988.

31. "A Letter from the Faculty," March 25, 1988 (my emphasis).

32. Memorandum from the Black Seminarians to the VDS/GDR Faculty, undated. This memo was signed by twenty black students and two black faculty members, indicating the importance of a critical mass of African American students in the school.

33. I was the first and only teacher of this course. Because of my training in the sociology of religion, this course was defined in terms of the sociology of American religion. Although I tried to attend to the issues of race, class, gender, and sexual orientation, these issues were treated analytically rather than ideologically. This was not entirely satisfying to the students who desired a more advocacy-oriented approach to these materials.

CHAPTER 8

1. This and succeeding citations from Sallie McFague are from a personal interview, November 12, 1998.

2. Paul K. Conkin, *Gone with the Ivy: A Biography of Vanderbilt University* (Knoxville: University of Tennessee Press, 1985), 81–82, 276–77.

3. Dorothy Bass Fraser, "Women with a Past: A New Look at the History of Theological Education," *Theological Education* 8:4 (Summer 1972): 217, 220; Martha Lund Smalley, research services librarian and curator of the Day Missions Collection at the Yale Divinity School Library; Richard Rosengarten, Dean of Students, University of Chicago Divinity School.

4. *Prospectus* 1:17 (February 14, 1958): n.p.; *Prospectus* 2:19 (February 27, 1959): n.p.

5. Divinity School Faculty Minutes, May 14, 1965.

6. *Prospectus* 11:1 (1968): 4.

7. "Role of the Woman in Seminary," *Prospectus* 7:2 (October 11, 1963): n.p.

8. *Spire* 7:3 (Fall/Winter 1983): 12.

9. In 1976 alumni/ae of the Oberlin Graduate School of Theology initiated a scholarship in honor of Jacob.

10. *Prospectus* (March 20, 1953): n.p.

11. *The Christian*, August 5, 1973.

12. *Prospectus* 25:7 (March–April, 1981): 3.

13. "Female Theologs at VDS," *Prospectus* 12:10 (1970?): n.p.

14. *Divinity School Catalogue* (1971–72).

15. Divinity School Faculty Minutes, April 15, 1971.

16. *Prospectus* 16 (October 13, 1972): 1–3; *Prospectus* 17:5 (December 11, 1973): 11–12.

17. Divinity School Faculty Minutes, February 26, 1971.

18. Personnel and Policy Committee Minutes, May 10, 1974.

19. *Prospectus* (September 1977): 5; *Spire* 2:4 (Fall 1977).

20. This and other citations from Peggy Way are from a telephone interview, May 22, 1999.

21. Divinity School Faculty Minutes, November 1977 and February 1978.

22. This and other citations from Peg Leonard-Martin are from a telephone interview, June 8, 1999.

23. *Prospectus* 25:7 (1981): 4–5.

24. Interview with Doris Hall, November 19, 1998; *Spire* (Summer 1998): 15.

25. Conkin, *Gone with the Ivy*, 719–21.

26. *Spire* 8:1 (Spring 1983): 12. Wiltshire came to Vanderbilt in 1971. In her analysis, the women students rather than faculty members possessed the gift of organizing around the issues relating to the advancement of women. She remembered that when approached by students in 1972 about offering classes in women's studies, she responded that new course approval took at least two years in the College of Arts and Science. But students continued to work toward the goal, resulting in approval of a "special topics" course in the Department of Philosophy within an

academic year. Students precipitated change through example. Wiltshire's first time to be served communion by a woman was in Benton Chapel, where Gay Welch was presiding. "This had an incredible impact on my faith and my life," she stated (interview, August 26, 1999).

27. *Spire* 2:1 (Fall 1976).

28. "A Ministry Begun," *Prospectus* 19:4 (November 10, 1975): 5–6; "Reflections on Being a Woman Minister," *Prospectus* 17 (March 26, 1973): 15–17.

29. Joseph P. O'Neill and Richard T. Murphy, "Changing Age and Gender Profiles Among Entering Seminary Students: 1975–1989," in Joseph P. O'Neill, ed., *Ministry Research Notes*, an ETS occasional report (Spring 1991).

30. *Prospectus* 28:3 (n.d.): 4–5.

31. Kim Maphis Early, *Report on Tier I Research for the Lilly Endowment, Inc.*, Vanderbilt Divinity School, September, 1989, 8.

32. ATS Self-Study, 5.

33. Renita Weems, written responses to questions, June 15, 1999.

34. Divinity School Faculty Minutes, May 10, 1985.

35. Wiltshire recalled one of her first solicitation calls on behalf of the organization. She approached Annette MacBean, assistant to the dean of the Divinity School. MacBean proceeded to empty the entire contents of her wallet on behalf of the group, stating, "I've been waiting twenty years for this" (interview, August 26, 1999).

36. Conkin, *Gone with the Ivy*, 719–21.

37. Barbara Brown Zikmund, Adair T. Lummis, and Patricia Mei Yin Chang, *Clergy Women: An Uphill Calling* (Louisville: Westminster John Knox Press, 1998), 71.

38. *Monday Morning*, December 21, 1992, 14 (Research Services, Presbyterian Church USA).

39. *Fact Book on Theological Education for the Academic Year 1997–98* (Pittsburgh: ATS in U.S. and Canada, 1998), 67.

40. "Following Mothers, Women Heed Call in Nation's Pulpits," *New York Times*, April 25, 1999, 26.

41. Remarks at celebration of the Carpenter Program in Religion, Gender, and Sexuality, August, 1995.

42. A.-J. Levine, written responses to questions, July 22, 1999.

43. Citations from Mary Aquin O'Neill, RSM, are from a telephone interview, June 28, 1999.

44. *Prospectus* 17 (n.d.): 3–4.

45. Personnel and Policy Committee Minutes, April 24, 1972.

46. *Spire* (Spring 1975): 4–5.

47. Divinity School Faculty Minutes, September 10, 1978. Susan Ford Wiltshire counts the Davis Cup controversy and the resulting political fallout as the organizational training ground for the women who later founded Women's Equity at Vanderbilt (WEAV).

48. Remarks on the inauguration of the Carpenter Chair, spring 1989.

49. *Spire* 8:1 (Spring 1983): 1, 8.

50. Remarks on the twenty-fifth anniversary of the Antoinette Brown Lectures, March 18, 1999.

51. "Language at VDS: 'It's Not a Man's World Anymore,'" *Prospectus* 22:3 (November 12, 1978): 11–16.

52. *Confessions of a Beginning Theologian* (Downers Grove, IL: InterVarsity Press, 1998), 70.

53. These and other citations from Nadia Lahutsky are from a personal interview, November 20, 1998.

54. *Divinity School Bulletin* (1979–80), 16.

CHAPTER 9

1. Conrad Cherry, *Hurrying toward Zion: Universities, Divinity Schools, and American Protestantism* (Bloomington: Indiana University Press, 1995), 168.

2. Ibid., 193.

3. Benton to Branscomb, September 22, 1952; Divinity School, RG 530, box 835, ff. 7, "Negroes, Admission of," Vanderbilt University Special Collections (VUSC).

4. Benton to Branscomb, September 24, 1952; "Negroes, Admission of," VUSC.

5. Statement released for publication February 13, 1953, by Chancellor Branscomb; Divinity School, RG 530, box 833, ff. 25, "Branscomb, Harvie," VUSC.

6. Copy of resolution adopted by the Board of Trust, May 1, 1953, and recorded in Minute Book, Vol. 36, 195; "Negroes, Admission of," VUSC.

7. Benton to Dr. Macolm P. Calhoun, September 23, 1953; "Negroes, Admission of," VUSC. Calhoun was conducting a study of colleges, universities, and schools of theology on behalf of the Presbyterian Church U.S., and he specifically requested Benton's opinion "about the special problems which you have discovered" (Calhoun to Benton, September 17, 1953, ibid.).

8. David Halberstam, *The Children* (New York: Random House, 1998), 124.

9. Johnson (1914–79) became a bishop in the Christian Methodist Episcopal Church (CME) in 1966, after teaching at Fisk University and the Interdenominational Theological Center (ITC) in Atlanta. He served the Fourth Episcopal District, covering Louisiana and Mississippi. Johnson was a member of the Faith and Order Commission of the World Council of Churches. He led worship and preached at the Cole Lectures at the Divinity School in 1973 and was a member of the Vanderbilt University Board of Trust from 1973 until his death. The Memorial Resolution adopted by the Board of Trust, November 2, 1979, honored him for "his gifted eloquence, his tenacious energy, his uncompromised ethical values, his undented religious convictions, and his abiding loyalty to Vanderbilt." His publications included *The Soul of the Black Preacher* (1970) and *Proclamation Theology* (1977).

10. From the Introductory Statement of an unpublished text, "Addresses Delivered during a Conference on Black Religious Leadership and the Needs of the Black Community," edited and compiled by Kelly Miller Smith, 1.

11. Kelly Miller Smith to Dean Sallie TeSelle, March 15, 1976; Kelly Miller Smith Papers, VUSC.

12. Dorothy Parks, Divinity School librarian, asked this writer to intercede with Alice Smith in an effort to persuade her of the wisdom of contributing her late husband's letters and papers to the establishment of a special collection. After she agreed to do so, the papers were collated by Marcia Riggs, an African American Ph.D. student at Vanderbilt; see *The Kelly Miller Smith Papers*, Arranged and Described by Marcia Riggs (Nashville: Vanderbilt University, 1988).

13. The list of honorary sponsors, beyond Vanderbilt administrators, included Carole Hoover, president of Concessions International of Cleveland; Frederick Humphries, president of Tennessee State University in Nashville; Coretta Scott King, president of the Martin Luther King, Jr. Center for Non-violent Social Change; Joseph Lowery, president of the Southern Christian

Leadership Conference; Henry Ponder, president of Fisk University; David Satcher, president of Meharry Medical College; John Siegenthaler, president and publisher of *The Tennessean*; and Andrew Young, mayor of Atlanta.

14. Minutes of the Divinity School Faculty Meeting, January 28, 1978.

15. McFague to "Friends of the Divinity School," March 16, 1978.

16. "Background on Current Student/Faculty Issues," *Communicator* (March 30, 1988): 1.

17. Martin to the Dean, Administration, Faculty, and the Student Body of VDS/GDR, February 18, 1988.

18. Ray Waddle, "Meeting Eases VU Divinity School Tension," *Tennessean*, April 7, 1988, 4B.

19. These lectures were published later in *The Journal of Religious Thought* 48:1 (Summer–Fall 1991): 5–19.

20. Forrest E. Harris, Sr., James T. Roberson, and Larry George, eds., *What Does It Mean to Be Black and Christian? Pulpit, Pew and Academy in Dialogue* (Nashville: Townsend Press, 1995); and Forrest E. Harris, Sr., ed., *What Does It Mean to Be Black and Christian? The Meaning of the African American Church* (Nashville: Townsend Press, 1997).

CHAPTER 10

1. In the course of its history, the school has traveled under three names: the Biblical Department (1875–1914), the School of Religion (1915–56), and the Divinity School (1956 to the present). In most instances throughout this chapter, I refer to the institution as the Divinity School.

2. This strain of competing values is one of the major themes of Conrad Cherry's study of university divinity schools. In fact, his inquiry is organized into areas of intrinsic tensions that arise with commitments to scholarship, church, social reform, practice of ministry, ecumenism, and social pluralism. See Cherry, *Hurrying toward Zion: Universities, Divinity Schools, and American Protestantism* (Bloomington: Indiana University Press, 1995).

3. Thomas Carter, Jr., *John Wesley as a Philanthropist and the Social Mission of Methodists* (Nashville: Missionary Training School, 1905); Lester H. Colloms, *Wilbur Fisk Tillett, Christian Educator* (Louisville: Cloister Press, 1949), 30.

4. Henry B. Carré, *Paul's Doctrine of Redemption* (New York: Macmillan, 1914); W. F. Tillett, *The Paths That Lead to God: A New Survey of the Grounds for Theistic Belief* (New York: George H. Doran, 1924); Umphrey Lee, *The Historical Church and Modern Pacifism* (New York: Abingdon-Cokesbury, 1943); Robert M. Hawkins, *The Recovery of the Historical Paul* (Nashville: Vanderbilt University Press, 1943); O. E. Brown, "Some Changes in Church History during My Years at Vanderbilt," *School of Religion Notes, 1936–1945* (Nashville: School of Religion of Vanderbilt University, n.d.).

5. For the distinction between modernism and liberalism, see Jerald Brauer, "A History of the Divinity School: Creatively out of Step," *Criterion* 29–30 (August 1990). In this essay Brauer is discussing the University of Chicago Divinity School.

6. The academy–denomination conflict did not disappear with the break with the Methodists. As a pan-Protestant divinity school, Vanderbilt developed special relations with certain Protestant denominations: a Disciples Foundation (1927) that led to an established residence program (1941); an affiliation with a Congregational seminary in Atlanta (1929); the use of local pastors as

adjunct professors and lecturers in practical theology; a merger with the Oberlin Graduate School of Theology in 1966; polity course arrangements with several denominations, including Presbyterian, Methodist, Disciples of Christ, and Baptist; and Methodist, Catholic, and Jewish endowed chairs on the faculty.

7. According to Cherry (*Hurrying toward Zion*, chap. 3), the study of religions in the divinity schools was not separated from the area of missions until after World War II. At the Divinity School after 1914, the study of world religions remained connected to missions until the 1940s, at which time it was taught in the area of historical studies. Only in 1953–54 did the area become independent.

8. George Lindbeck, "Theological Education in North America Today," *CSR Bulletin* 8 (October 1977).

9. Ray L. Hart, "Religious and Theological Studies in American Higher Education: A Pilot Study," *Journal of the American Academy of Religion* 59:4 (Winter 1991): 733–34.

10. W. Clark Gilpin, *A Preface to Theology* (Chicago: University of Chicago Press, 1996), chap. 1.

11. David H. Kelsey, *Between Athens and Berlin: The Theological Education Debate* (Grand Rapids, MI: Eerdmans, 1993), 6–12.

12. For a brief history of practical theology, see Edward Farley, "Practical Theology, Protestant," in Rodney J. Hunter, ed., *Dictionary of Pastoral Care and Counseling* (Nashville: Abingdon, 1990), 934–36. For an account of this tension between practical theology and the scholarly ideal in university-related divinity schools, see Cherry, *Hurrying toward Zion*, chap. 4.

13. The exception is a growing literature on feminist issues in theological education. Two early collections of essays were the Cornwall Collective, *Your Daughters Shall Prophesy: Feminist Alternatives in Theological Education* (New York: Pilgrim Press, 1980), and Katie G. Cannon et al. (the Mudflower Collective), *God's Fierce Whimsy: Christian Feminism and Theological Education* (New York: Pilgrim, 1985). See also Rebecca S. Chopp, *Saving Work: Feminist Theories in Theological Education* (Louisville: Westminster John Knox, 1995).

14. See Arthur M. Schlesinger, Sr., "A Critical Period in American Religion, 1875–1900," *Massachusetts Historical Society Proceedings* 64 (1930–32): 523–46. For the background and rise of social issues in the university-related divinity schools, see Cherry, *Hurrying toward Zion*, chap. 6. For an account of the opening of seminaries to women, see Dorothy Bass Fraser, "Women with a Past: A New Look at the History of Theological Education," *Theological Education* 8 (Summer 1972): 213–24.

15. H. Richard Niebuhr, Daniel Day Williams, and James M. Gustafson, *The Advancement of Theological Education* (New York: Harper and Brothers, 1957), 101.

16. Examples of organizing or "encyclopedia" concepts and decisions are the distinction between the liberal arts and the sciences, the trivium and quadrivium of the Middle Ages, the gathering of various fields into an overall concept such as "social sciences," the attachment of comparative or world religions to the area of missions or to religious history, the assignment of the study of ancient Israel to ecclesiastical history (as the School of Religion once did) or to an independent field based on a canon of texts, and the creation of new areas of study such as "church and culture," women's studies, or "the black church."

17. In this early period, Israel and the text of the Hebrew Bible appear to have more historical than canonical and authoritative status. The reason is that this era was linked to and taught as the initial period of Christian history.

18. *Register* (1915–16), 109.

19. Fifteen years later two more areas of study were added: "Rural Life and Religion" (1929–30) and "Church Music" (1930–31). Accordingly, the period from 1914 to the mid-1930s was marked by a proliferation of fields, so that by the mid-1930s twelve fields or areas of study were part of the course of study.

20. In 1948, 84 of 126 course hours were required, distributed over the four fields. In 1957–58, 90 of 119 hours were required for graduation, plus distributive requirements in the three "theory" fields. In this respect the school was part of a national trend toward a heavily required curriculum, a phenomenon that the Niebuhr-Williams-Gustafson study criticized (*Advancement of Theological Education*, 81).

21. "Memorandum to the Sealantic Foundation Concerning the School of Religion at Vanderbilt University," Chancellor's Office, RG 300, box 217, ff. 34, Vanderbilt University Special Collections.

22. In 1953–54, seven lecturers, most of them local ministers, taught in the area of practical theology.

23. Field education came late to Vanderbilt in comparison to other schools. It was present in some form at both Garrett and the Boston School of Religion before 1924; see Robert L. Kelly, *Theological Education in America* (New York: George H. Doran, 1924), 145–51. The Divinity School's several experiments with other schools began in the 1970s. Cooperation with Scarritt Graduate School for degrees in Christian education (1983) and church music (1985–86) ended with the demise of Scarritt as a degree-granting institution (1987–88). The joint Divinity and Law degree program (from 1975) and joint degree work with the Medical School continue to this day. The joint Divinity and Social Work degree program ran 1985–92.

24. Niebuhr, Williams, and. Gustafson, *The Advancement of Theological Education*.

25. Perkins at Southern Methodist University began discussing a new curriculum in 1951–52 and introduced it in 1953; see Merrimon Cuninggim, "The New Curriculum at Perkins," *Christian Century* 71 (April 28, 1954), and "Changing Emphases in the Seminary Curriculum," *Journal of Bible and Religion* 23 (April 1965). The peak of the heavily required curriculum at Union Seminary in New York was 1958; see Robert T. Handy, *A History of Union Theological Seminary* (New York: Columbia University Press, 1987), 228.

26. On this period and its effects on the divinity schools, see Cherry, *Hurrying toward Zion*, chap. 7.

27. Highlights of the proposal were as follows: a Doctor of Divinity degree, new introductory courses (18 hours) required in the first year, 8 required hours of field education and Clinical Pastoral Education plus a Senior Seminar, 30 hours of distributional requirements (6 hours in each of the five fields), a new area called "Studies in Religion and Culture," courses with multiple instructors, and a distributed list of religious classics.

28. Faculty Minutes, April 27–29, 1967. The response of some schools to the ethos of the 1960s preceded Vanderbilt by as much as ten years. Perkins abandoned its 1952 curriculum revision in 1961, substituting comprehensive exams and syllabi-based study for required courses. In 1965 even the comprehensive examinations were discontinued.

29. See *Divinity School Catalogue* (1970–71). Required were 6 hours of a basic course ("Introduction to Theological Education"), 13 hours of field education and internship, and 3 hours of Senior Seminar and Essay. There were no distribution requirements, but a concentration of 15–18 hours was required in one of the eight areas.

30. On the rise of professionalization in theological schools, see Cherry, *Hurrying toward Zion*, chap. 4. See also the "Theological Education for the 1970's" issue of *Theological Education* 4:3 (Spring 1968), containing a proposal by the Curriculum Task Force of the Association of Theological Schools; and Olga Craven, Alden L. Todd, and Jesse H. Ziegler, eds., *Theological Education as Professional Education* (Dayton, OH: AATS, 1969).

31. Wednesday student forums began in 1977–78, discussing written materials (but not as yet a curriculum proposal) provided by the CTE. A "Bible and Ethics" faculty seminar met during the Spring of 1978, and a "Theology and Ministry" faculty seminar met throughout the year of 1979–80. Faculty retreats were held in January 1978, August 1978, and September 1979. Until 1979 the faculty entertained no proposals about curriculum, but, by way of papers and responses to papers, sometimes by visiting scholars such as Robert W. Lynn, worked to expose what was fundamentally wrong about certain basic concepts that dominated theological education and searched for how to move in another direction. Finally, the faculty, with student participation, constructed a new course of study in two important meetings of September 14–16, 1979 and January 1980.

32. Some of the more important documents that describe the new course of study and its basic concepts are the following: the catalogue of 1980–81; a brochure, "Questioning an Axiom: the New Program for the Education of Ministers at Vanderbilt Divinity School"; Thomas Ogletree (CTE Committee), "Rethinking Our Work in Theological Education," *Prospectus* 21 (October 1977): 5–11; and Edward Farley, "The Minister as Theologian," faculty retreat paper.

33. This third feature, the reorganization of fields, did not survive long. In 1983–84 the sixfold organization of electives was replaced with specialty fields that more or less coincided with the areas of the Graduate Department of Religion (Bible, History of Christianity, Theology, Ethics, History of Religions), plus three practical theology areas (Church, Ministry, and Community; Pastoral Theology and Counseling; and Preaching and Worship) and Denominational Histories and Polities.

34. See Cherry, *Hurrying toward Zion*, chap. 13, for an account of pluralism and social issues in the divinity schools.

35. Committee Report, "The Future of the Divinity School," October, 1960.

CHAPTER 11

1. Paul K. Conkin, *Gone with the Ivy: A Biography of Vanderbilt University* (Knoxville: University of Tennessee Press, 1985), 3–9. Conkin goes well beyond the earlier discussion by Edwin Mims, *History of Vanderbilt University* (Nashville: Vanderbilt University Press, 1946), 27–35. The debates leading up to the founding of Vanderbilt are thoroughly traced by Hunter Dickinson Farish, *The Circuit Rider Dismounts: A Social History of Southern Methodism, 1865–1900* (Richmond, VA: Dietz Press, 1938), 262–78.

2. Letter from Cornelius Vanderbilt to Bishop Holland N. McTyeire, December 2, 1875, in Mims, *History of Vanderbilt University*, 40.

3. *Nation* (August 6, 1885): 14.

4. See, for example, *Report of the Commissioner of Education for the Year 1889–90* (Washington, DC: Government Printing Office, 1893), II: 788–89. This is noted by Mims, 146, quoting the report of Chancellor Garland to the Board of Trust, June 16, 1890.

5. Conkin, *Gone with the Ivy,* 117–20, 125–27, 149–84; Edwin Mims, *Chancellor Kirkland of*

Vanderbilt (Nashville: Vanderbilt University Press, 1940), 160–96; Mims, *History of Vanderbilt*, 291–318. There continue to be those, however, who bemoan the trend away from religious control of higher education. For a negative evaluation of Kirkland's strategy, see James Tunstead Burtchaell, C.S.C., "The Alienation of Christian Higher Education in America: Diagnosis and Prognosis," in Stanley Hauerwas and John H. Westerhoff, eds., *Schooling Christians: "Holy Experiments" in American Education* (Grand Rapids, MI: Eerdmans, 1992), 129–83.

6. *The Future of Graduate Education at Vanderbilt University: Promise, Need, Rationale* (Report of a Faculty Committee, November 1975), 10.

7. Mims, *History of Vanderbilt*, 160, 239–40; Conkin, *Gone with the Ivy*, 160, 172, 290; *In Memoriam: Herbert Cushing Tolman* (Nashville: Alpha of Tennessee, 1926).

8. Conkin, *Gone with the Ivy*, 290–94.

9. Minutes of the Graduate Faculty, October 20, 1942; Minutes of the Faculty of the School of Religion, October 7, 1946.

10. Minutes of the Graduate Faculty, April 16, 1946. The first Ph.D. degrees in Religion were awarded in 1952.

11. Minutes of the Graduate Faculty, June 2, 1950. An undated proposal was made in the early 1950s for a program in Historical Studies with the cooperation of the History Department, with a specialization in the American field alone. The proposal did not come to fruition, and the appearance of Bard Thompson in the European field may be what changed the situation.

12. Address by Chancellor James H. Kirkland, October 15, 1925, *Vanderbilt Alumnus* (October, 1925): 19; Mims, *Chancellor Kirkland*, ix, 268.

13. See Ernest W. Saunders, *Searching the Scriptures: A History of the Society of Biblical Literature, 1880–1980* (Chico, CA: Scholars Press, 1982).

14. See especially Henry T. Fowler, "The Place of the Bible in the College Curriculum," *Journal of the National Association of Biblical Instructors* 1:2 (1933): 25–28, and the recollections at the twenty-fifth anniversary dinner by Florence M. Fitch, Eliza H. Kendrick, and others, in the *Journal* 3:1 (1935): 36–44.

15. *Two Decades: The Story of the National Council on Religion in Higher Education (Founded by Charles Foster Kent), 1922–1941* (New York: National Council on Religion in Higher Education, 1941), 21; Patrick M. Malin, "The National Council on Religion in Higher Education," in Amos N. Wilder, ed., *Liberal Learning and Religion* (New York: Harper and Brothers, 1951), 324–34, and the entire volume, all of whose contributors were members of the Council. See also the discussion of the background and wider framework of Kent's activities in Bradley J. Longfield, " 'For God, for Country, and for Yale': Yale, Religion, and Higher Education between the World Wars," in George M. Marsden and Bradley J. Longfield, eds., *The Secularization of the Academy* (New York: Oxford University Press, 1992), 146–69, esp. 148–50.

16. The Committee on the History of Religions made plans "to conduct, during 1947, a small conference on graduate instruction in the scholarly aspects of the study of religions" (American Council of Learned Societies, Bulletin No. 40 [March 1947]: 76). This meeting was held May 16–17, 1947, at Columbia University. See report by H. Shelton Smith, Director of Graduate Studies in Religion, to Paul Gross, Dean of the Graduate School, Duke University, 1947, 6.

17. Letters from Harvie Branscomb, Chairman, January 19, 1950, and April 20, 1950, to representatives of the institutional members of the Council (Brown, Chicago, Columbia, Duke, Harvard, Johns Hopkins, Michigan, Pennsylvania, Vanderbilt, and Yale).

18. J. P. Hyatt to Chancellor Branscomb, April 8, 1957; Divinity School, RG 530, box 833, ff. 25, "Branscomb, Harvie," Vanderbilt University Special Collections (VUSC).

19. Conkin, *Gone with the Ivy,* 562–63, 567, 570–74.

20. Minutes of the Divinity School Faculty, March 8, 1963.

21. These organizational matters are traced in two volumes, Milton D. McLean and Harry H. Kimber, eds., *Teaching of Religion in State Universities: Descriptions of Programs in Twenty-Five Institutions* (Ann Arbor: Office of Religious Affairs, University of Michigan, 1960) and Milton D. McLean, ed., *Religious Studies in Public Universities* (Carbondale: Southern Illinois University, 1967). More "philosophical" reflections are to be found in Erich A. Walter, ed., *Religion and the State University* (Ann Arbor: University of Michigan Press, 1958); Clyde A. Holbrook, *Religion, A Humanistic Field* (Englewood Cliffs, NJ: Prentice-Hall, 1963); *A Report on an Invitational Conference on the Study of Religion in the State University* (New Haven: Society for Religion in Higher Education, 1965); and Paul Ramsey and John F. Wilson, eds., *The Study of Religion in Colleges and Universities* (Princeton, NJ: Princeton University Press, 1970).

22. See Kathryn O. Alexander, "Religious Studies in American Higher Education Since *Schempp*: A Bibliographic Essay," *Soundings* 71 (1988): 389–412.

23. See Horace M. Kallen and Prentiss L. Pemberton, eds., "An Introductory Word," *Journal for the Scientific Study of Religion* 1 (1961–62): 3–4.

24. See the Report of the NABI Self-Study Committee, 200–201, and Clyde A. Holbrook, "Why an Academy of Religion?" *Journal of Bible and Religion* 32:2 (1964), 97–105. The name of the publication was changed to *Journal of the American Academy of Religion* with volume 35 (1967). Saunders, *Searching the Scriptures,* 24, points out that members of the SBL had often regarded the Association as a "trade union" rather than a "research-oriented assembly of scholars."

25. Four members of the Vanderbilt faculty played a major role in the SBL during the 1960s and 1970s: J. Philip Hyatt, Kendrick Grobel, Walter Harrelson, and Robert W. Funk.

26. Claude Welch, *Graduate Education in Religion: A Critical Appraisal* (Missoula: University of Montana Press, 1971), 41–42. For the tensions created by the development at Yale, see Conrad Cherry, *Hurrying toward Zion: Universities, Divinity Schools, and American Protestantism* (Bloomington: Indiana University Press, 1995), 121 and the documentation cited 323, n. 103.

27. See the discussion of "Ph.D. Versus Th.D./S.T.D./D.H.L.," Welch, *Graduate Education in Religion,* 34–38.

28. Conversations with Professor Alexander Marchant (a self-proclaimed "Voltairean"), Winter 1970.

29. Letters from Professor Winston L. King, November 4, 1996, and July 29, 1998; Minutes of the College of Arts and Science Faculty Council, January 9 and April 2, 1968; Minutes of the Faculty, College of Arts and Science, April 19, 1968.

30. Minutes of the Graduate Department of Religion, October 27, 1969.

31. Report on the Ph.D. program in the Graduate Department of Religion, 1976, 3. The Minutes of the Graduate Department of Religion, October 28, 1966, already indicate that, despite the growth of studies in world religions, it was unlikely that the College would commit itself to a faculty appointment in Islamic studies to supplement what Winston King was doing in Buddhist studies. That stance has continued.

32. In this section, mention will be made of three studies: Welch, *Graduate Education in Religion: A Critical Appraisal;* the *Report on the Ph.D. Program in the Graduate Department of Religion,* 1976; and George Lindbeck (in consultation with Karl Deutsch and Nathan Glazer), *University*

Divinity Schools: A Report on Ecclesiastically Independent Theological Education, Rockefeller Foundation Working Papers, March 1976. Note should also be taken of Lindbeck's summary of the latter report, "Theological Education in North America Today," *Bulletin of the Council on the Study of Religion* 8:4 (October 1977): 85–89.

33. This was anticipated, on the basis of statistical projections and actual figures, in the Welch study, 97–104.

34. Two GDR students, Deanna Thompson and Inese Radzins, served in leadership positions in the AAR Graduate Student Caucus during this decade.

35. See, for example, two issues of the *Bulletin of the Council on the Study of Religion* 9:3 (June 1978) and 10:5 (December 1979), devoted entirely to the "employment crisis," its explanations, "finding the first job," and alternative careers such as teaching in public schools, librarianship, and religious journalism.

36. Introduction by Mary Daly to *Women and Religion, 1972*, Proceedings of the Working Group on Women and Religion, Mary Daly, Chairperson; edited by Judith Plaskow Goldenberg (Waterloo, Ontario: American Academy of Religion, 1973), 1. See also the narrative in Rita M. Gross, *Feminism and Religion: An Introduction* (Boston: Beacon Press, 1996), 46–56, and the retrospective comments by Judith Plaskow in her 1998 Presidential Address, "The Academy as Real Life: New Participants and Paradigms in the Study of Religion," *Journal of the American Academy of Religion* 67 (1999): 521–38.

37. *Guide to the Perplexing: A Survival Manual for Women in Religious Studies* (Atlanta: Scholars Press, 1992).

38. Welch, *Graduate Education in Religion*, passim.

39. Lindbeck, *University Divinity Schools*, v–vi, 7, 14.

40. Ibid., 16–17, 19, and 58. The "post-modern" shift was summarized in an essay by Langdon Gilkey, "The New Watershed in Theology," *Soundings* 64 (1981): 118–31. The "post-liberal" mood was presented by George Lindbeck, *The Nature of Doctrine: Religion and Theology in a Post-Liberal Age* (Philadelphia: Westminster, 1984).

41. See the comprehensive survey by Arnold J. Band, "Jewish Studies in American Liberal-Arts Colleges and Universities," *American Jewish Yearbook* 66 (1967): 3–30. Twenty-two universities, including Vanderbilt, are listed as offering programs in some phase of Judaic studies leading to the Ph.D. degree (ibid., 14). Jacob Neusner engages in significant reflection on the varieties of approach ("Judaism," "Jewish History," "Study of Torah," "Judaism within the History of Religions") in "Modes of Jewish Studies in the University" in Ramsey and Wilson, *The Study of Religion in Colleges and Universities*, 159–89.

42. In an essay, "The University and Jewish Studies," Lou Silberman, after tracing the refusal of German universities to appoint professors of Jewish studies (in contrast to British and then American universities), advocates strongly for programs of Jewish studies. These, he says, are far preferable to their being fragmented among religious studies, ancient Near Eastern languages and history, and Germanic studies; and he comments that the advocates of black studies recognize exactly this danger (Leon A. Jick, ed., *The Teaching of Judaica* [Waltham, MA: Association for Jewish Studies, 1970], 7–16).

43. Report of the External Review Committee, March 27, 1997, 5.

44. Self-Study of the Graduate Department of Religion, November 1996, 7, 17, and Appendices 2 and 10; Minutes of the Graduate Department of Religion, January 26, 1996.

45. Minutes of the Graduate Department of Religion, February 25, 1977.

46. "The Doctoral Education of Theological Faculties," Auburn Center for the Study of Theological Education, 1996, 4–5, 8–12.

47. Self-Study, 1996, 17–18.

CHAPTER 12

1. Paul Ritterband and Harold Wechsler, *Jewish Learning in American Universities* (Bloomington: Indiana University Press, 1994), 127.

2. Ibid., 127–28.

3. Ibid., 23–30, 45ff.

4. George Foot Moore, *Judaism in the First Centuries of the Christian Era,* 3 vols. (Cambridge: Harvard University Press, 1927–30).

5. Paul K. Conkin, *Gone with the Ivy: A Biography of Vanderbilt University* (Knoxville: University of Tennessee Press, 1985), 740–41, 489.

6. Letter to Mrs. Elbogen, December 6, 1944, cited in David Hopkins, *A Concise History of the Judaica Library* (Nashville: Vanderbilt University Divinity Library, 1987).

7. Ritterband and Wechsler, *Jewish Learning,* 233.

8. Franz Rosenzweig, *The Star of Redemption,* 2d ed. (1930), originally published as *Der Stern der Erlösung* (Frankfurt am Main: J. Kauffmann, 1921).

CHAPTER 13

Acknowledgment: I am grateful to William O. Paulsell for suggestions offered in a reading of an early draft of this chapter.

1. These include the Christian Church (Disciples of Christ), Churches of Christ, and "independent" Christian Churches and Churches of Christ; for a standard history of the Disciples, see William E. Tucker and Lester G. McAllister, *Journey in Faith: A History of the Christian Church (Disciples of Christ)* (St. Louis: Bethany Press, 1975).

2. Alexander Campbell, *The Christian System* (Bethany, [West] Virginia: By the Author, 1839; reprint, Nashville: Gospel Advocate Company, 1964), 61.

3. Alexander Campbell, "Reply to a Letter," *Christian Baptist* 1 (1823): 217, cited by D. Ray Lindley, *Apostle of Freedom* (St. Louis: Bethany Press, 1957), 185.

4. Occasional meetings for practice preaching had been held in Ohio under the leadership of Adamson Bentley beginning in 1819 or 1820. Scott and Alexander Campbell reinstituted this model in the middle 1830s. This approach to ministerial education seems to have passed with the decade of the 1830s and the attention of the movement's leaders to the beginnings of Bethany College; see Lester G. McAllister, "Models of Ministerial Preparation in the Stone-Campbell Movement," *Discipliana* 54:2 (Summer 1994): 35–36.

5. Lester McAllister has argued that the "antitheological" article was included in the charter to ensure its passage by the Virginia legislature and had not been "favored" by either Campbell or the Bethany trustees; see *Bethany: The First 150 Years* (Bethany, WV: Bethany College Press, 1991), 12, 92–93.

6. Ibid., 8.

7. William J. Richardson, "Models of Ministerial Preparation among Christian Churches/Churches of Christ and Churches of Christ," *Discipliana* 54:2 (Summer 1994): 49.

8. McAllister, *Bethany,* 92–93, and "Models of Ministerial Preparation," 37.

9. Dwight E. Stevenson, *Lexington Theological Seminary, 1865–1965: The College of the Bible Century* (St. Louis: Bethany Press, 1964), 409–15.

10. Ibid., 11–21.

11. William Jennison, "The University of Chicago and the Disciples of Christ: The Development of Biblical Criticism," *Discipliana* 38:3 (Fall 1978): 43–44.

12. Ronald E. Osborn, "Theology among the Disciples," in George G. Beazley, Jr., ed., *The Christian Church (Disciples of Christ): An Interpretative Examination in the Cultural Context* (St Louis: Bethany Press, 1973), 101.

13. An early expression of the recognition that the effort at Vanderbilt was "of the same type" as the approach at the University of Chicago is in Riley B. Montgomery, *The Education of Ministers of Disciples of Christ* (St. Louis: Bethany Press, 1931), 51.

14. George N. Mayhew, "For a Better Trained Ministry: The Disciples of Christ Create a Foundation at Vanderbilt University," *World Call* 9 (June 1928): 30.

15. Ibid., 29–30; "Disciples Foundation Launched at Vanderbilt University," *Tennessee Christian* 22:8 (December 1927): 10–11.

16. Edward T. Small, "The Disciples' Vanderbilt Foundation," *The Front Rank*, October 5, 1930, 6.

17. *The Disciples House* (pamphlet for the House, not the Foundation; n.d., but indicates post-1941 publication).

18. Edwin L. Becker, *Yale Divinity School and the Disciples of Christ: 1872–1989* (Nashville: Disciples of Christ Historical Society, 1990), 5.

19. *The Story of a Great Opportunity* (pamphlet, c. 1930).

20. Herman A. Norton, *Tennessee Christians* (Nashville: Reed and Co., 1971), 240–42; Mayhew, "For a Better Trained Ministry," 29; *Story of a Great Opportunity*; "Disciples Foundation Launched," 10.

21. Editorial, *Tennessee Christian* 22:8 (December 1927): 10. The Foundation's board was composed of Dr. W. A. Bryan (president), Bailie Gross (secretary), Herbert Fox (treasurer), along with Judge John R. Aust, A. S. Caldwell, and W. J. McGill (members). In an unpublished paper, "A History of the Disciples Divinity House at Vanderbilt University," Rachel Leigh Nance identifies R. H. Crossfield and Roger T. Nooe as having been involved in the earliest organization of the Foundation (2). The following several paragraphs detailing the formal organizational life of the Disciples at Vanderbilt are informed by Nance's work and undergirded by research that she graciously shared with the writer.

22. *Disciples Vanderbilt Foundation* (pamphlet, n.d. [c. 1929]).

23. Dean Brown to Chancellor Kirkland, January 21, 1927, RG 530, Box 852, ff. 27, Vanderbilt University Special Collections (VUSC).

24. Small, "Disciples' Vanderbilt Foundation," 6.

25. Brown to Mayhew, August 30, 1927, RG 530, Box 852, ff. 27, VUSC. The original financial arrangement clearly did not work. In 1931, Chancellor Kirkland closed Mayhew's expense account, saying that whatever promotional work Mayhew did should be between him and the denomination; to Dean Winton he declared, "the salary we pay Mayhew should be based on the amount of work he does for us, and the Disciples Vanderbilt Foundation should pay to Vanderbilt University one-half of his total salary." With a sense of disappointment, Kirkland added, "He has never accomplished anything of material benefit to us in raising money for scholarships, even for his own students" (June 25, 1931, RG 530, Box 852, ff. 27, VUSC).

26. R. B. Montgomery, "The 70 Per Cent Calls for 100 Per Cent Leadership: Training a

Ministry for Rural Work," *World Call* 13:5 (May 1931): 14; "Disciples Vanderbilt Foundation," *Tennessee Christian* 24:3 (February 1930): 3; "Facing the Rural Church Problem," *Christian-Evangelist* 65:19 (May 10, 1928): 19 [607].

27. Nance, "A History of the Disciples Divinity House," 6.

28. Ibid., 7; Norton, *Tennessee Christians*, 264.

29. Richard L. Harrison, Jr., "That Teaching, Preaching General: A View of the Life of Herman Albert Norton," in Anthony L. Dunnavant and Richard L. Harrison, Jr., eds., *Explorations in the Stone-Campbell Traditions: Essays in Honor of Herman A. Norton* (Nashville: Disciples of Christ Historical Society, 1995), 176; Nance, "A History of the Disciples Divinity House," 8, 16 (timeline).

30. Correspondence documenting this conflict is in the William Hardy biographical file, Disciples of Christ Historical Society, Nashville, TN (henceforth, DCHS).

31. "New Disciples Divinity House," *Disciples Divinity House: Vanderbilt University Bulletin* 5:2 (June 1957): 1; Nance, "A History of the Disciples Divinity House," 16.

32. Herman A. Norton, "Annual Report of the Dean to the Board of Directors of the Disciples Divinity House" (May 1961); Papers of William Moore Hardy and Nina Palmer Hardy, Series 4, ff. 22, "Disciples Foundation (Disciples Divinity House)," 1958–61, DCHS; "Annual Report . . . " (May 9, 1964), DCHS; Nance, "A History of the Disciples Divinity House," 16.

33. Harrison, "That Teaching, Preaching General," 181–83.

34. Herman A. Norton, "Annual Report . . . ," May 10, 1973; typescript, Disciples Divinity House: Vanderbilt University File, DCHS, 1; interview with Richard L. Harrison, Jr., November 28, 1999.

35. "Biographical Sketches of Disciples Scholars: Richard L. Harrison, Jr.," *Disciples Theological Digest* 7:2 (1992): 69.

36. Nance, "A History of the Disciples Divinity House," 16.

37. Norton, *Tennessee Christians*, 240–42, 265, 271.

38. M. Eugene Boring, *Disciples and the Bible: A History of Disciples Biblical Interpretation in North America* (St. Louis: Chalice Press, 1997), 326–27.

39. Ibid., 312; "Biographical Sketches of Distinguished Disciples Scholars: Walter Harrelson," *Disciples Theological Digest* 5 (1990): 41.

40. "Biographical Sketches of Distinguished Disciples Scholars: Leander E. Keck," *Disciples Theological Digest* 2:1 (1987): 81; interview with Wayne H. Bell, November 27, 1999.

41. *Disciples Vanderbilt Foundation*; Tucker and McAllister, *Journey in Faith*, 287, 293.

42. M. Eugene Boring, "The Disciples and Higher Criticism: The Crucial Third Generation," in D. Newell Williams, ed., *A Case Study of Mainstream Protestantism: The Disciples' Relation to American Culture, 1880–1989* (Grand Rapids, MI: Eerdmans, 1991), 31; *Disciples and the Bible*, 331–35. Students of Hyatt (some in his Old Testament specialty, others in the biblical field) who continued that "dialogue" in publication or teaching or both include Roger Carstensen, Leo G. Perdue, Ambrose Edens, James L. Crenshaw, Gary Phillips, O. Gerald Harris, and M. Eugene Boring (interviews with Leo G. Perdue, December 2, 1999, and M. Eugene Boring, December 2, 1999). The renowned Disciples preacher Fred B. Craddock was also a Vanderbilt Ph.D. student in Bible during the Hyatt era.

43. Anthony L. Dunnavant and Richard L. Harrison, Jr., "Introduction," in *Explorations in the Stone-Campbell Traditions*, 1–4. A number of these themes have been reflected in the graduate school research and/or subsequent writings of Norton Disciples students D. James Atwood, Hap

Lyda, J. Brooks Major, William O. Paulsell, Richard Harrison, D. Newell Williams, and Anthony Dunnavant.

44. "Biographical Sketches of Disciples Scholars: H. Jackson Forstman," *Disciples Theological Digest* 8:1 (1993): 37–38; James O. Duke and Anthony L. Dunnavant, "Editors' Introduction," in *Christian Faith Seeking Historical Understanding: Essays in Honor of H. Jack Forstman* (Macon, GA: Mercer University Press, 1997), 1, 5. This engagement is manifest in the research and writing of such Disciples students as James O. Duke, Richard Harrison, D. Newell Williams, Nadia Lahutsky, and Paul Jones (their respective essays in this collection illustrate this point). In the case of placing Disciples self-understanding into clearer relationship with the heritage of the Reformation, and particularly the Reformed tradition, the writings of Duke, Williams, and Harrison now constitute a significant body of work.

45. This publication of the Disciples of Christ's Division of Higher Education contained annotated bibliographies of works by Disciples authors.

CHAPTER 14

1. Ernst Troeltsch, "Half a Century of Theology: A Review," in Robert Morgan and Michael Pye, trans. and ed., *Ernst Troeltsch: Writings on Theology and Religion* (Atlanta: John Knox, 1977), 53–81; the essay first appeared in *Zeitschrift für wissenschaftliche Theologie* 61 (1908).

2. As the school's dean (1936–39), the Wesley scholar Umphrey Lee was upon arrival listed in the catalogue as theologian, and thereafter as church historian.

3. Standard Methodist accounts of their theological history typically refer to Summers, Tillett, and/or Ramsdell. See, for example, Emory Stevens Bucke, ed., *The History of American Methodism*, 3 vols. (Nashville: Abingdon, 1964); Robert E. Chiles, *Theological Transition in American Methodism, 1790–1935* (New York: Abingdon, 1965); and Thomas A. Langford, *Practical Divinity: Theology in the Wesleyan Tradition* (Nashville: Abingdon, 1983). In *Wesleyan Theology: A Sourcebook* (Durham, NC: Labyrinth Press, 1984), Langford includes a Ramsdell selection.

4. E. Brooks Holifield, *The Gentlemen Theologians: American Theology in Southern Culture, 1795–1860* (Durham, NC: Duke University Press, 1978). See also Theodore Dwight Bozeman, *Protestantism in an Age of Science: The Baconian Ideal and Antebellum Religious Thought* (Chapel Hill: University of North Carolina Press, 1977).

5. Only one volume Summers edited was resurrected for critical study a century later: William A. Smith, *Lectures on the Philosophy and Practice of Slavery, as Exhibited in the Institution of Domestic Slavery in the United States; with the Duties of Masters to Slaves* (1856; reprint, New York: Negro Universities Press, 1969).

6. Thomas O. Summers, *Systematic Theology: A Complete Body of Wesleyan Arminian Divinity*, 2 vols. (Nashville: Methodist Episcopal Church, South, 1888).

7. Lester Hubert Colloms, *Wilbur Fisk Tillett, Christian Educator* (Louisville: Cloister Press, 1949), includes a bibliography of Tillett's writings.

8. His evangelical liberal reading of historic Methodist doctrine is evident in Wilbur F. Tillett and James Atkins, *The Doctrines and Polity of the Methodist Episcopal Church, South* (Nashville: Methodist Episcopal Church, South, 1903) and in *A Statement of the Faith of the World-wide Methodism* (Nashville: Methodist Episcopal Church, South, 1906). Shortly after 1900, anti-liberal Methodists had added him to their target list of opponents; see, for example, George W. Wilson, *Methodist Theology vs. Methodist Theologians* (Cincinnati: Jennings and Pye, 1904).

9. Wilbur Fisk Tillett, *Personal Salvation: Studies in Christian Doctrine pertaining to the Spiritual Life* (Nashville: Methodist Episcopal Church, South, 1902); *The Paths that Lead to God: A New Survey of the Grounds of Theistic and Christian Belief* (New York: George H. Doran, 1924), xii; *Providence, Prayer and Power: Studies in the Philosophy, Psychology, and Dynamics of the Christian Religion* (Nashville: Cokesbury, 1926).

10. Wilbur Fisk Tillett, *The Hand of God in American History: A Study of Divine Providence as Seen in the Life and Mission of a Nation* (Nashville: Cokesbury, 1923), 4, 34, 49.

11. Tillett, *Paths*, 208, 222–30, 350–51, 551.

12. "The Religious Pragmatism of Borden Parker Bowne (1847–1910)," *The Personalist* 15 (1934): 305–14; "Pragmatism and Rationalism in the Philosophy of Borden Parker Bowne," *The Personalist* 15 (1935): 23–35; "The Sources of Bowne's Pragmatism," *The Personalist* 15 (1935): 132–41; and "The Perfectionism of Personalistic Ethics," *The Personalist* 23 (1942): 44–52.

13. In "Religion and the Issue of Ethical Relativism," *Religion in Life* 12 (1942): 212–22, Ramsdell took close but critical note of neo-orthodox-realist trends. The clearest sign of his own transition occurs in "The Resurgence of Christian Theology," a series of six articles in *Pastor* 8 (1944–45).

14. Edward T. Ramsdell, *The Christian Perspective* (New York: Abingdon-Cokesbury, 1950), 41, citing H. Richard Niebuhr, *The Meaning of Revelation* (New York: Macmillan, 1941), 94.

15. For Gilkey's bibliography, see D. W. Musser and J. L. Price, eds., *The Whirlwind in Culture: Frontiers in Theology, in Honor of Langdon Gilkey* (Bloomington, IN: Meyer Stone Books, 1989), and Brian J. Walsh, *Langdon Gilkey: Theologian for a Culture in Decline* (Lanham, MD: University Press of America, 1991); for that of Kaufman, see Alain Epp Weaver, ed., *Mennonite Theology in Face of Modernity: Essays in Honor of Gordon D. Kaufman* (North Newton, KS: Bethel College, 1996); for that of Shinn, see Beverly W. Harrison, Robert L. Stivers, and Ronald H. Stone, eds., *The Public Vocation of Christian Ethics* (New York: Pilgrim, 1986).

16. Nels F. S. Ferré, *Swedish Contributions to Modern Theology* (New York: Harper & Brothers, 1939); "Beyond Liberalism and Neo-Orthodoxy," *Christian Century* 66 (1949): 362–64: David Wesley Soper, "The Sufficiency of God: The Postcritical Theology of Nels F. S. Ferré," in *Major Voices in American Theology: Six Contemporary Leaders* (Philadelphia: Westminster, 1953), 71–106.

17. See Theodore Has, "The 'Extreme Middle' in Christian Theology: An Interpretation of Nels Ferré," *Theology and Life* 6 (1963): 144–53; Nels F. S. Ferré, *The Extreme Center* (Waco, TX: Word, 1973). Faith V. Ferré and Frederick Ferré offer a broad, personalized retrospective of their father's thought in "The Theology of Nels F. S. Ferré: Living toward the Age of Unimunity," *Theology Today* 53 (1996): 320–30.

18. Roger L. Shinn, *The Existentialist Posture: A Christian Look at Its Meaning, Impact, Values, Dangers* (New York: Association Press, 1959; rev. ed., 1970).

19. Roger L. Shinn, *Christianity and the Problem of History* (New York: Charles Scribner's Sons, 1953), 45, 24 (italics added).

20. Nels F. S. Ferré, *The Christian Understanding of God* (New York: Harper and Brothers, 1951).

21. Gordon D. Kaufman, *Relativism, Knowledge and Faith* (Chicago: University of Chicago Press, 1960).

22. Langdon Gilkey, *Maker of Heaven and Earth: The Christian Doctrine of Creation in the Light of Modern Knowledge* (Garden City, NY: Doubleday, 1959); J. Robert Nelson, *The Realm of Redemption: Studies in the Doctrine of the Nature of the Church in Contemporary Protestant Theology* (Chicago: Wilcox and Follett, 1951); Emil Brunner wrote the book's foreword.

23. Gordon D. Kaufman, *The Context of Decision: A Theological Analysis* (New York: Abingdon, 1961).

24. Gilkey later turned his reflections on the experience into a widely read monograph, *Shantung Compound: The Story of Men and Women under Pressure* (New York: Harper and Row, 1966).

25. Langdon Gilkey, *How the Church Can Minister to the World without Losing Itself* (New York: Harper and Row, 1964), 3.

26. The two works, coedited by Peter C. Hodgson and Robert H. King, are *Christian Theology: An Introduction to Its Traditions and Tasks* (Philadelphia: Fortress, 1982; 2d ed., rev. and enlarged, 1985; 3d ed., 1994), and *Readings in Christian Theology* (Philadelphia: Fortress, 1985, 1994).

27. Edward Farley, *The Transcendence of God: A Study in Contemporary Philosophical Theology* (Philadelphia: Westminster, 1960), 21.

28. H. Jackson Forstman, *Word and Spirit: Calvin's Doctrine of Biblical Authority* (Palo Alto, CA: Stanford University Press, 1962). See also "Coherence and Incoherence in the Theology of John Calvin," in Mary Potter Engel and Walter E. Wyman, Jr., eds., *Revisioning the Past: Prospects in Historical Theology* (Minneapolis: Fortress, 1992), 113–30.

29. On Luther, see "A Beggar's Faith," *Interpretation* 30 (1976): 262–70. On Schleiermacher, see "Theology as Transcendental Jest? Schlegel's Concept of Irony and the Theology of Schleiermacher," in Robert W. Funk, ed., *Schleiermacher as Contemporary: The Journal for Theology and the Church* 7 (New York: Herder and Herder, 1970), 96–124; and *A Romantic Triangle: Schleiermacher and Early German Romanticism* (Missoula, MT: Scholars Press, 1977). Forstman's research on theology from Bismarck to Hitler led, in addition to various articles, to *Christian Faith in Dark Times: Theological Conflicts in the Shadow of Hitler* (Louisville, KY: Westminster/John Knox, 1992). For a bibliography of Forstman's scholarly writings, see James O. Duke and Anthony L. Dunnavant, eds., *Christian Faith Seeking Historical Understanding: Essays in Honor of H. Jack Forstman* (Macon, GA: Mercer University Press, 1997).

30. In addition to numerous articles in patristics, TeSelle has written two major monographs on Augustine: *Augustine the Theologian* (New York, Herder and Herder, 1970), and *Augustine's Strategy as an Apologist* (Villanova, PA: Villanova University Press, 1974).

31. Eugene TeSelle, *Christ in Context: Divine Purpose and Human Possibility* (Philadelphia: Fortress, 1975), xi and passim.

32. Peter C. Hodgson, *Jesus—Word and Presence: An Essay in Christology* (Philadelphia: Fortress, 1971); *Children of Freedom: Black Liberation in Christian Perspective* (Philadelphia: Fortress, 1974); *New Birth of Freedom: A Theology of Bondage and Liberation* (Philadelphia: Fortress, 1976).

33. Sallie McFague TeSelle, *Literature and the Christian Life* (New Haven, CT: Yale University Press, 1966); *Speaking in Parables: A Study in Metaphor and Theology* (Philadelphia: Fortress, 1975); *Metaphorical Theology: Models of God in Religious Language* (Philadelphia: Fortress, 1982). Cited here is Sallie McFague, "An Intermediary Theology: In Service of the Hearing of God's Word," *Christian Century* 92 (1975): 625–29.

34. Peter C. Hodgson, *Revisioning the Church: Ecclesial Freedom in the New Paradigm* (Philadelphia: Fortress, 1988); *God in History: Shapes of Freedom* (Nashville: Abingdon, 1989); and *Winds of the Spirit: A Constructive Christian Theology* (Louisville, KY: Westminster John Knox, 1994), xii. Substantive findings of his Hegel scholarship are summarized in Peter C. Hodgson, ed., *G. W. F. Hegel: Theologian of the Spirit* (Minneapolis: Fortress, 1997).

35. "An Earthly Theological Agenda," *Christian Century* 108 (1991): 13, 14; this essay is

reprinted in James M. Wall and David Heim, eds., *How My Mind Has Changed* (Grand Rapids, MI: Eerdmans, 1991), 135–43. For further development of this interest, see Sallie McFague, *Models of God: Theology for an Ecological, Nuclear Age* (Philadelphia: Fortress, 1987); *The Body of God: An Ecological Theology* (Minneapolis: Fortress, 1993); and *Super, Natural Christians: How We Should Love Nature* (Minneapolis: Fortress, 1997).

36. Sallie McFague, "The Christian Paradigm," in *Christian Theology: An Introduction to Its Traditions and Tasks* (Philadelphia: Fortress, 1982; 2d ed., rev. and enlarged, 1985; 3d ed., 1994), especially 389–90 in the 2d edition. On paradigms old and new, see also Hodgson, *Revisioning the Church*, as well as *Winds of the Spirit*, especially chap. 5.

37. Edward Farley, *Requiem for a Lost Piety: The Contemporary Search for the Christian Life* (Philadelphia: Westminster, 1966).

38. Edward Farley, *Ecclesial Man: A Social Phenomenology of Faith and Reality* (Philadelphia: Fortress, 1975).

39. *Ecclesial Reflection: An Anatomy of Theological Method* (Philadelphia: Fortress, 1982); *Good and Evil: Interpreting a Human Condition* (Minneapolis: Fortress, 1990); and *Divine Empathy: A Theology of God* (Minneapolis: Fortress, 1996), xii. In addition to many articles, another book, *Deep Symbols: Their Postmodern Effacement and Reclamation* (Valley Forge, PA: Trinity Press International, 1996) relates to this program's thematics.

40. Edward Farley, *Theologia: The Fragmentation and Unity of Theological Education* (Philadelphia: Fortress, 1983); *The Fragility of Knowledge: Theological Education in the Church and the University* (Philadelphia: Fortress, 1988).

About the Contributors

JAMES P. BYRD, JR., is lecturer in American religious history at Vanderbilt Divinity School. He received his Ph.D. in Religion from Vanderbilt in 1999, and his doctoral dissertation on Roger Williams's use of Scripture will be published by Mercer University Press.

JAMES O. DUKE is professor of history of Christianity and history of Christian thought at Brite Divinity School, Texas Christian University. He holds three degrees, including a Ph.D., from Vanderbilt University. He co-edited (with Mark G. Toulouse) the companion volumes *Makers of Christian Theology in America* (1997) and *Sources of Christian Theology in America* (1999).

ANTHONY L. DUNNAVANT was dean and professor of church history at Lexington Theological Seminary. He held three degrees, including a Ph.D., from Vanderbilt University. He co-edited (with Richard L. Harrison, Jr.) *Explorations in the Stone-Campbell Traditions: Essays in Honor of Herman A. Norton* (1995). He died on February 7, 2001.

EDWARD FARLEY is Drucilla Moore Buffington Professor of Theology, Emeritus, Vanderbilt Divinity School. Among his works on the subject of theological education are *Theologia: The Fragmentation and Unity of Theological Education* (1983) and *The Fragility of Knowledge: Theological Education in Church and the University* (1988).

RICHARD C. GOODE is associate professor of history at Lipscomb University, Nashville, Tennessee; he earned a Ph.D. in Religion at Vanderbilt University, with a concentration in church history, and wrote his dissertation on the topic of Puritan missions to Native Americans. His current research focuses on more recent cultural interactions, specifically the Social Gospel, populism, and southern culture in the late nineteenth century.

FRANK GULLEY, JR., is Professor of Church History, Emeritus, Vanderbilt Divinity School. His research interests include the history and theology of Methodism. He has served as Divinity School librarian (1966–69), associate dean (1969–85), and associate dean for United Methodist Studies (1985–98).

PETER J. HAAS is Abba Hillel Silver Professor of Jewish Studies and the director of the Samuel Rosenthal Center for Judaic Studies at Case Western Reserve University. He was a faculty member in Vanderbilt's Department of Religious Studies 1980–99. His studies of the Jewish tradition include *Responsa: Literary History of a Rabbinic Genre* (1996).

HOWARD L. HARROD is Oberlin Alumni Professor of Social Ethics and Sociology of Religion, Vanderbilt Divinity School. His studies of Native American religions include *Becoming and Remaining a People: Native American Religions on the Northern Plains* (1995).

JOSEPH C. HOUGH, JR., is president and William C. Dodge Professor of Social Ethics at Union Theological Seminary, New York. He was dean of Vanderbilt Divinity School 1990–99. His works on theological education include *Christian Identity and Theological Education* (1985), co-written with John B. Cobb, Jr.

DALE A. JOHNSON is professor of church history at Vanderbilt Divinity School. His teaching and research interests cover modern European and American religious history. He is the author of *The Changing Shape of English Nonconformity, 1825–1925* (1999).

KIM MAPHIS EARLY received her M.Div. degree from Vanderbilt Divinity School and served as its director of admissions and student services 1990–99. She is a minister in the Presbyterian Church (USA) and a freelance writer and consultant.

GLENN T. MILLER is Waldo Professor of Ecclesiastical History, Bangor Theological Seminary. He has written extensively on the history of theological education, including *Piety and Learning: A History of Ante-Bellum Theological Education in America* (1990).

PETER J. PARIS is Elmer G. Homrighausen Professor of Christian Social Ethics at Princeton Theological Seminary and Senior Fellow, Mathey College, Princeton University. He taught at Vanderbilt Divinity School 1972–85. His works on religion and the black churches include *The Spirituality of African Peoples: The Search for a Common Moral Discourse* (1995).

EUGENE TESELLE is Oberlin Alumni Professor of Church History and Theology, Emeritus, Vanderbilt Divinity School. His multiple interests in Augustine and contemporary issues in theology and ethics are reflected in *Living in Two Cities: Augustinian Trajectories in Political Thought* (1998). At Vanderbilt he has been the chair of the Faculty Senate, president of the AAUP chapter, and chair of the Graduate Department of Religion.

Index